RUNNING WILD

Essays, Fictions and Memoirs Presented to Michael Wilding

RUNNING WILD

Essays, Fictions and Memoirs Presented to Michael Wilding

edited by

DAVID BROOKS
AND
BRIAN KIERNAN

Sydney Association for Studies in Society and Culture

MANOHAR
2004

Running Wild:
Essays, Fictions and Memoirs Presented to Michael Wilding

First published 2004

Sydney Studies in Society and Culture 22

ISSN 0812-6402

Published for the
Sydney Association for Studies in Society and Culture
School of English, University of Sydney, NSW 2006
by
Manohar Publishers & Distributors
4753/23 Ansari Road, Daryaganj
New Delhi 110002

Includes bibliography

SASSC: ISBN 1 86487 523 2
Manohar: ISBN 81-7304-550-X

1. Politics and literature. 2. Literature - History and criticism. 3. Short stories, Australian. I. Wilding, Michael, 1942-. II. Kiernan, Brian (Brian Francis), 1937-. III. David Brooks, 1947-. IV. Sydney Association for Studies in Society and Culture. (Series: Sydney studies in society and culture; 22)

809.93358

Typeset by Vulgar Press, Melbourne

Printed in India by
Lordson Publishers Pvt. Ltd.
Delhi 110007

Contents

Fiction and Memoirs

Editors' Preface

When Michael Wilding retired from his Personal Chair in English and Australian Literature at the University of Sydney in 2000, the Sydney Association for Studies in Society and Culture decided to honour one of its founders and most distinguished members with a Festschrift. As editors, we invited his former colleagues and students to contribute on whatever among their own interests they felt coincided with his. Fittingly, the result is wide-ranging.

Most responded to Michael's achievements as a scholar and critic in various fields, and many among them to his attendant interest in the politics of writing and criticism. Their essays on English and Australian literatures (including essays on Michael's own novels and short stories), some on European literature, and one on its interaction with Asian literature we have grouped together in a broadly chronological sequence according to topic.

Others invited to contribute responded, with equal appropriateness, to Michael's parallel career as a creative writer, contributing fictions and a variety of memoirs; these we have also grouped together.

DAVID BROOKS
BRAIN KIERNAN

Introduction

S.N. Mukherjee

I first met Michael Wilding sometime in 1972, in the Staff Club of the University of Sydney. Peter King of the Department of Government, introduced me to this young man, ruggedly handsome, sun-tanned, long blond hair, and beads round his neck. He said something about Queensland. I took it for granted that he was from Queensland. In fact he was talking about the University of Queensland Press. Michael was then the general editor of a series that UQP had started publishing on writers from the Asia-Pacific region. He wanted me to write an introduction to Manik Bandopadhya's novel *Padma River Boatman,* a short bibliography and a glossary, and to check the translation. It so happened that I knew this left-wing author from Bengal and I was happy to write about him. Our little venture with Manik Bandopadhya's novel is now forgotten, but that was the beginning of my friendship with Michael.

Since 1972 we have been involved in many academic ventures, teaching, writing and publishing. Some of our ventures were successful, others were not so successful, while some failed miserably, like our attempt to mount an inter-departmental course in the 1970s, or when Michael tried to get me elected Dean of the Faculty of Arts. Our most successful academic venture was SASSC (Sydney Association for Studies in Society and Culture). We organized seminars, workshops, international conferences and lectures. We got some important academics of international fame involved in our activities, men and women like Manning Clark, Sir Edmund Leach, Eric Hobsbawm, Christopher and Brigid Hill, Franco Venturi and Julia Kristeva. Some of them came to Sydney and took part in our seminars and conferences. We started in 1979 and by 2001 we had published twenty volumes in SASSC's Sydney Studies series. Volume 21 is now in press, this Festschrift will be volume 22, and yet another one on feudalism is being prepared.

Most of our publications were collections of papers, those submitted at our workshops or conferences. They were interdisciplinary and fostered alternative views of society and culture. Our aim was, as we said in our manifesto, 'to bring together concerned scholars from Australia and overseas to discuss and publish on themes which transcend the usual academic disciplines and establish links between subject areas'. We hoped that we would provide 'a forum for those who feel strongly about academic freedom, peace and intellectual achievement'. Although in our SASSC circle Michael was not much visible before 1993 (the year we started our monograph series, which was mostly due to Michael), he was involved with our Association from the beginning. Not only did he contribute to our first volume, but he also got Jack Lindsay's article on Tagore for our *Words and Worlds*, and helped us with his expert knowledge of 'desk top' publication; the word was not yet then invented.

The decade 1970–80 was a time of great ferment in the campus; the problems in South Africa, the Vietnam War, and the staff and student demand for participatory democracy in the University were the main causes of this ferment. Many students and young academics got involved in this upheaval. Some of us spoke out to the media or addressed meetings in and outside the Faculty Board. This was particularly so during the upheaval in the Philosophy Department. Michael was not one for slogans and marches, but he was an important supporter of our movements. Although he did not come with us when we saw the Vice Chancellor to demand funds for SASSC, he supported us in very practical ways, with funds and technical know-how.

I have been closely involved in all his SASSC publications: his two monographs, *Social Visions* and *Studies in Classic Australian Fiction*, his chapter on William Lane in our first volume, and his chapters on Milton in volumes 5 and 11. I was also instructed and informed by his *Milton's Paradise Lost* and *Political Fictions*. I am no expert on English literature, but English literature was the core of our 'liberal' education in colonial India; Michael's works illuminated my 'areas of darkness' in my studies of English literature and more. I am sure that Michael's works are in that great tradition of radical English literary criticism of Christopher Caudwell and Arnold Kettle. They are original, often controversial, and political.

I must confess that I am not *au fait* with Michael's fiction. I am however, impressed by his researches for his historical novels *The Paraguyan Experiment* and *Raising Spirits, Making Gold and Swapping Wives*. In fact I was involved in the translation of *The Paraguyan Experiment* into Bengali. I am also struck by his sense of humour.

In these thirty odd years Michael Wilding has amused me, entertained me, and sometime irritated me, but Sydney, without Michael, would be a very dull place indeed. Above all he has inspired many writers, young and old, 'European' and 'Oriental'. This is an ongoing process and Michael Wilding will continue with his own literary projects and inspire many future writers.

How Red Was Robin Hood?

Stephen Knight

In the summer of 1990 Nottingham council chamber was invaded by poll-tax rioters wearing green felt hoods, both in homage to the local outlaw and also, according to someone who was there, as a highly practical way to conceal identity – several of the rioters worked for the council.

But while the spirit of Robin Hood was animating this anti-Thatcher resistance, in another part of Britain Kevin Reynolds was shooting *Robin Hood: Prince of Thieves* in which the outlaw tradition validates American capitalist institutions from imperialist militarism (the arrow-nose camera), through liberal multiculturalism (a genuinely good black Muslim), to familial dramas ('Ah have a brother !') and insipid love songs (the theme tune was number one for fifteen weeks in the UK) – not to mention representing Robin as an absentee aristocrat returning from foreigner-bashing to re-establish true lordship, and a true peasantry to match.

The politics of Robin Hood are confusing, or multiple. It seems they have always been so. The earliest quasi-historical reference to the hero is in a Scottish verse chronicle by Andrew of Wyntoun: in about 1420, writing under the year 1293, he speaks of Robin Hood and Little John as 'waythemen', forest outlaws, who are by many people 'commendit gud'.[1] The date and the response strongly suggests Wyntoun sees them as English parallels to William Wallace and implies the public approved their quasi-guerrilla stand against English royal law. But a little later another Scots chronicler, Walter Bower, writing in Latin in about 1440, tells how Robin insists on finishing mass before fighting off his enemies, like some conservatively Catholic Drake.

Over nearly six hundred years the myth of the good outlaw, typified by Robin Hood both in England itself and, thanks to imperial culture-transference in the nineteenth century, also around the world, can range across the political spectrum from distinctly disruptive on the left to just as vigorously validating the right. But this is not a free variation. The contexts, the means of production, the audiences available all participate in the political variety of the Robin Hood tradition, and to trace these movements and counter-movements is to see a constant political battle for the control of this potent symbol of morally motivated physical resistance to the power of the state.

Robin Hood texts – ballads and short plays – survive from the very end of the fifteenth century onwards, but the tradition was certainly known before that and there are some fragments, jotted-down scraps of song and speech, that suggest the early Robin Hood was a distinctly threatening character. A Lincoln cathedral manuscript has a marginal jotting from the early fifteenth century that speaks in heavily stressed verse of a heavily armed outlaw:

> Robin Hood in Scherewod stod
> Hodud and hathud, hosut and schod,
> Four and twunty arrowus he bar in his hondus.[2]

Heavily armed, ready for action, this Robin seems to be the figure that some farm labourers identified with on a road in East Anglia in 1441 when, threatening to kill Sir Geoffrey Harsyk, they chanted, 'We aren Robynhodesmen, War, War, War.'[3] In much the same spirit, in May 1497 a hundred men, led by Roger Marshall in the guise of Robin Hood, marched to release their friends from Walsall jail, according to the Star Chamber charges.[4] Over a century later, when town councils across Britain were cracking down on all kinds of earlier eccentricity and untidiness, from wise women to festive gatherings, in 1561 the people of Edinburgh, offended that their choice of Robin Hood had been arrested to stop their carnival, seized the Toll Both, the old town jail, took the prisoners out and put the magistrates in.

Events of this kind mesh with Eric Hobsbawm's concept of Robin Hood as having been in his original formation an archetype of the social bandit – a charismatic young man, driven to resist oppressive authorities, joined by others, performing brave deeds, admired in wish-fulfilment by the ordinary people, and finally betrayed to death.[5] Almost every culture has such a figure, from Salvatore Giuliano in Sicily to the Water Margin bandits in China, Jesse James in America and, far from least, Ned Kelly in Australia – and there are many less well known like Il Passatore in Emilia-Romagna, Foufillaz in Galicia. Such figures are not necessarily on the left: they can be nationalist bandits, like most of the anti-Austrian heroes that Hobsbawm knowledgeably discusses, and their interests can be hostile to those of the proletariat, like Billy the Kid. Indeed, while Hobsbawm feels that Robin Hood was a redistributor of wealth, in fact the early texts about the most violent and anti-state Robin say nothing about robbing the rich to give to the poor: reimbursing his own class fraction is as close as the social bandit Robin gets to fiscal revolution. Rodney Hilton, one of the distinguished British Marxist historians of the near past, felt that the early outlaw ballads spoke the values of the 1381 'Peasants Revolt', but the narratives and the references of the texts do not sustain this view. Robin was not one of the names used in mythical support of the peasants, and J.C. Holt has noted that 'Hob the Robber', one of those figures, is not a variant of the good outlaw's name.[6]

Robin Hood's violence is not revolutionary. The most aggressive of the early ballads is 'Robin Hood and the Monk' in which the hero is arrested by the sheriff when he goes to Nottingham to pray to Our Lady (a mildly unauthoritative form of religion).[7] Little John and Much meet a monk on his way to get the king to approve Robin's execution; they kill him and his serving-boy; Little John masquerades as messenger to the king; returns to the sheriff, gets him drunk at dinner, kills the jailer and sets Robin free. But this guerrilla-style action is never against the king, and he in fact rather ad mires the outlaws at the end. Nor does the sheriff suffer – though in later texts like *The Gest of Robin Hood* and 'Robin Hood and Guy of Gisborne' he will be killed for his attempts to impose law on the disorderly outlaw. Respecting king and, via Mary at least, religion, the early Robin Hood texts merely attack corrupt agents of an unchallenged system. The political radicality is local, not national. Richard Tardif has argued lucidly for these ballads as displaced images of liberty and self-management from tradesmen oppressed by newly developed urban structures.[8]

This hero who vigorously resists local legal agencies was certainly popular and survived well past the medieval period: as the outlaw tradition is reconstructed in a market context in the seventeenth-century printed broadside ballads, some are quite violent, like 'Robin Hood's Progress to Nottingham', apparently a prequel which explains how the hero is in the first instance outlawed. On his way to an archery tournament in Nottingham the young Robin meets fifteen foresters. They mock his capability with a bow and one bets him he cannot hit a stag at distance: he does; the man refuses to pay; Robin threatens him; he runs away; Robin kills him and his fourteen friends, then wounds the Nottingham citizens as they run to see what the alarm is about. The Ramboesque spirit of this ballad appealed greatly – it is one of the most widely recorded – but this bristling, local riot form of outlaw activity was by no means the only version of Robin Hoodery known in the period. There were two other early versions of the hero: they both overlap with the social bandit, but have a very different politics.

One was an obscure, because scantily recorded, version of the hero, which may well be his earliest formation. This is the 'play-game' Robin Hood, referred to widely in southern and western England in the fifteenth and sixteenth centuries. He is the focus for a village celebration in May (not May Day but late May, usually Whit Sunday), where natural imagery is dominant, games and sports are enjoyed, as well as dancing and celebration – these events are sometimes called a 'Robin Hood Ale'. Money is also collected for the community, apparently at times with some pressure, even menaces.[9] The play-game Robin, it seems, primarily represents the community and celebrates its continuance. The only clear sign of resistance is in two plays, or scenes, preserved from *c.* 1475 where Robin and his men are in action against the sheriff. It is now usually thought these plays, recorded among the Paston papers, are a condensed script for play-game entertainments. This is also true of two plays added to the *Gest* by William Copland in his edition of about 1560, but they do not involve Robin at all with the sheriff: they are robust encounters with the Potter and the Friar, and where the Potter ballad does involve, and humiliate, the sheriff, the play does not. So the evidence for an anti-authority Robin Hood in the play-game is thin indeed; although Alexandra Johnstone has recently identified a strong spirit of carnival, quite possibly including anti-authoritarian meanings, in the play games;[10] it is only in the ballads that Robin is clearly an outlaw and an enemy of the agents of the law.

In all this early material it seems that the essence of Robin Hood is that he is a natural figure – realised among the beauty of early summer, never associated with autumn or winter – and he also represents natural law, a version of ethics and equity which is evidently preferable to the present imposed structure, whether administered by sheriff, or abbot, or their deputies. From the village viewpoint in the play-games that is a coherent and communal position; from that of the urban tradesmen who, as Tardif argues, seem to have been the audience for the early ballads, there is a more organised and more violent tone of dissent involved. For Andrew of Wyntoun, Robin's resistance could involve the parallel to Scots nationalism; for Walter Bower, the church's rights against those of the state. It is a very flexible form of resistance, and it is rarely associated with any forms of socially organised revolt – though there is a trace of Robin Hood's name being used as an alias or rallying point in Jack Cade's rebellion of 1451.[11] Yet the resistance of town councils to Robin Hood festivities, and the widespread cultural containment of the tradition suggests that it was in fact, perhaps in unrecorded ways, associated with popular resistance. As England grew more aware of and more explicit about social conflict in the seventeenth century, Robin Hood was at times linked with serious resistance: Sir Robert Cecil called the Guy Fawkes conspirators 'Robin Hoods' and Christopher Hill has noted that the hero's name was used on the parliamentary side in an election.[12] The most striking testimony to a politically resistant Robin is the remarkable short play, *Robin Hood and His Crew of Souldiers*, played in Nottingham, on the day of Charles II's coronation, in which Robin and his men cave in to royal rhetoric – no fighting, no ambush, no sheriff-killing this time – they merely sing and dance in honour of the newly restored monarch.[13]

The need for the play seems to suggest there were political depths to the Robin Hood myth in the period that have not yet been traced textually – and maybe never had written form, like the instincts of the Nottingham poll-tax rioters. What we do, however, have in literary form, apart from the debatable and variable politics of the early ballads and play-games already discussed, is the last of the early variations of the hero and his meaning, a major form of cultural containment, the thoroughly conservative tradition of the gentrified outlaw.

Gentrification can be seen first stirring in the *Historia Majoris Britanniae* (1521) by John Major, a conservative of longer duration than the recent cricket-loving nobody who followed Thatcher, a bit too closely. Yet another Scottish chronicler, also known as John Mair, Major was the first to date Robin in the fateful 1190s, though he made nothing of the Prince John connection. He did however admire the hero, admitting he was a villain, but calling him 'princeps' of thieves. The name has resurfaced as an image: it was used by Dumas in a novel's title,[14] and by Hollywood for the 1991 film starring Kevin Costner. But chroniclers after Major apparently read it as a title, and Richard Grafton, the very influential and much copied English language chronicler in 1569 first suggested that Robin had been an Earl who had been displaced through enemies and his own rash generosity, and so had become a noble outlaw. From here, via Grafton's imitators, Munday took up the conservativising theme.

But the gentrifying move was not restricted to chroniclers: there are other instances of writers drawing Robin Hood's radical sting and using the myth against its own most dangerous possibilities. In *George a Greene* (perhaps by Robert Greene, and written by 1594), Robin is depicted as second in command to the bold Pindar of Wakefield, who resists a rebellion by the Earl of Kendall, clearly figured as Robin Hood attacking – in Kendall green of course – the town of Wakefield in a manner analogous to the well-known ballad 'Robin Hood and the Pindar of Wakefield'. In George Peele's *Edward I*, printed in 1593, Llewelyn, the last Welsh prince of Wales, is on the run from Edward I's imperial incursions, here presented as benignly as possible, and for no very clear reason Llewelyn and his friends enact a Robin Hood play in which Edward and his ally Mortimer play the official roles opposing the outlaw. The social bandit ballad has been forcefully reversed: the politics of Robin Hood were already gentrified and his social bandit like activities are being contained, before Anthony Munday relocated the whole character as an earl in his own right in his play *The Downfall of Robert, Earle of Huntington*, in 1598.

Gentrifying Robin Hood performed a dramatic ideological feat. By suddenly locating him in the 1190s and making him a displaced nobleman, resisting not the malign everyday agents of law itself but the malpractice of Prince John in seizing royal power, the process turned Robin right round from a populist resister of oppressive authority into a faithful supporter of true aristocratic authority and kingship, from social bandit to distressed gentleman. This ennobled Robin may enlist the people in his cause, and may reward them with charity, but both are fully hierarchical actions, and the end of the story is his restoration to full aristocratic power by direct donation of the king. This major change is neatly encapsulated in Munday's title. Not only is Robin now an earl: being in the forest is his downfall. The hero whose glory was to stand in the summer forest and threaten all comers now feels humiliated to have to haunt the forest with a band of common men. This move to full gentrification had great impact on the tradition. Most Robin Hood stories since then have either followed Munday's model or, with a deliberate and more or less radical posture, rejected it. The plays – there was also *The Death of Robert, Earle of Huntington*, a morbid melodrama mostly given over to King John's pursuit of Marian, Lady Fitzwater, whom he finally drives to suicide – had almost no dramatic impact: a recent rehearsed reading in Stratford may have been the first production for hundreds of years. But they had great impact on the tradition, generating a version where the hero was comfortably conservative, the kind of fellow that Elizabethan magnates could watch their companies perform, that Hollywood moguls could finance to caper across the worldwide screens. Munday, government spy as well as jobbing flatterer to the mercantile bourgeoisie, did his anti-radical work very well.

The lack of dramatic impact arises from a curious dialectic feature of the texts: in gentrifying Robin Hood, Munday and others (including Ben Jonson in his unfinished *The Sad Shepherd*, *c.* 1636) have to discard the energetic anti-authoritarian action of the ballads – which were still so popular in the very same period. Genteel Robin Hood kills no sheriffs, humiliates no monks, never plays hangman to rescue his men from the gallows. He lurks about the forest moaning, with his lady – she is an entirely new feature, as lords must have ladies along with the title, as well as the land, tomb and epitaph which are also elements of this new gentrified fetishisation.

Powerful though it is ideologically, and completely as Hollywood has subscribed to the idea, Lord Robin was not triumphant early on. The gentrified Robin was found only in feeble dramas – Jonson did not finish his inactive masque-like play and even feebler eighteenth-century ballad operas, which involved tenor Robin and soprano Marian with abductions and elderly suitors, a thousand theatrical miles from radical outlawry. Much more potent, though within unrevolutionary limits, was the hero of the broadside ballads, standing solidly in his galligaskins as a contemporary military outlaw – whatever that might mean in the mid-seventeenth century. His lively, frequently violent escapades were highly popular: it is true that his vigour was more oppressive now of the medieval Catholic church than the officers of royal law, and Martin Parker's 1632 ballad epic *The True Tale of Robin Hood* has a nervy conclusion noting that such troublesome activity is now a thing of the unregretted past, but overall the mid-seventeenth-century Robin Hood seems to be thoroughly dual, capable of the anti-conservative action of the street ballads as well as the revanchist gentrification coming down from Munday and Jonson.

Of the two figures, social bandit and distressed gentleman, the bold active hero – still respecting the king but now ignoring the Virgin Mary – is much the stronger, rollicking through Lives and the ballad collections known as garlands, as well as reprinted broadsides and by the later eighteenth century appearing in the new genre of anthologies. Thomas Percy judged seven of his eight Robin Hood ballads too damaged for appearance in his *Reliques* and perhaps also too violent – in 'Robin Hood and Guy of Gisborne', which was undamaged, he changed Little John's impact on the sheriff in the last line from 'Did cleave his heart in twinn' to 'Shot him into the back-syde'. Thomas Evans, one of the many Welsh scholars to illuminate London publishing in the period, produced a fine collection of *Old Ballads* in 1777 with twenty-seven of the broadside ballads in place, but the apotheosis of anthologisation came a little later.

In 1795 Joseph Ritson published his *Robin Hood: A Collection of All the Ancient Poems, Songs and Ballads Relative to the Celebrated English Outlaw*. It offered almost all the texts – he missed 'Robin Hood and the Monk', still mouldering in manuscript in Cambridge, but he added all the other early ballads to Evans's collection, which (unnoticed by any commentators) he left in exactly Evans's order. That transmitted the social bandit past, but Ritson had some surprises in his introductory matter. Ritson was a Jacobin who observed the revolutionary calendar, addressed his timid English colleagues as 'Comrade' and even went so far as to be vegetarian in the very heart of John Bullism. To him Robin Hood meant something like a medieval Tom Paine. The 'Life' that Ritson provided spoke vividly of the medieval period as a time of 'titled ruffians and sainted idiots', neatly embracing all the English kings from William I to Henry VI, and idolising Robin as a hero of 'the common people'.[15]

Fine radical stuff. Yet very strangely – or not, if you trace the history of the English Labour party – Ritson was also wedded to the love of a lord, and if his political account of Robin was thoroughly radical, the biography he offered was thoroughly conservative. He accepted in total the gentrified elements that had been gathered since Major, guesses, inventions, fantasies and lunacies, and trotted them out at the high tide of biographism. His Robin, this leader of the populace against their oppressors, was descended from one Robert FitzOoth who came over with the conqueror; a crazy genealogy linked him to the niece of William I, invented by William Stukely, the Stamford antiquarian who had also proved the existence of a university in, of course, Stamford in the eighth century BC. To the works, well gathered, crisply edited, scholarly annotated, Ritson added a fanciful, erratic and conservative Life which was to dominate thinking about the hero for – well, ever.

This was crucial. Ritson brought together for the first time the gentrified and the popular strands. The robust social bandit had all the good stories, but was increasingly marginal in a status-oriented culture; the displaced lord, an appealing enough topic, was bereft of any theatrical or narrative interest: the eighteenth-century ballad opera authors struggled to find interesting material – there is even a comic scene in the 1730 *Robin Hood: An Opera* lifted from the fifteenth century Wakefield *Second Shepherds' Play*.[16] Ritson, though, re-equipped the socially acceptable Earl with a set of adventures that were truly entertaining, memorable, even politically meaningful. He only juxtaposed the two: he never interwove them. But his crucial collocation of the disparate strands of the tradition was too tempting to be ignored, and before long the tradition took on new life as in the nineteenth century the formerly separate elements of the Robin Hood tradition interwove to create the complex, politically labile, usually conservative and possibly radical mix that we still have today.

Ritson's new position for the combined hero did not inspire any activity for a generation – perhaps his own radicalism was too forbidding until revolutionary France was beaten, and his hostility to the church created enemies – but when in a very active period around 1820 Robin Hood was reconstructed in a new role the figure gained three crucial features of what was for the most part to be a new conservatism. In *Ivanhoe* (published at the end of 1819) Sir Walter Scott gave the outlaw a clear national, indeed racial status: for the first time he was a Saxon hero resisting the Norman French, an appealing theme for the jingoistic times, and one rarely forgotten since. In *Ivanhoe* and in Thomas Love Peacock's *Maid Marian* (1822, though he started writing it in 1818 before reading *Ivanhoe*) he was also a distinctly masculine figure – Scott made him symbolically hyper-phallic in splitting his enemy's arrow for the first time, and Peacock made him the devil-may-care lover of the beautiful but ultimately subservient Marian. The third element of the modernising of Robin Hood was a refocusing on the forest: what for the medieval ballads had been a place of warrior security, an alternative world free of urban and royal power – as it was for many real outlaws in the period – became in the nineteenth century, and very forcefully in twentieth-century films, a place of retreat from unappealing modern civilisation: a pastoral outlaw was created, a theme partly glimpsed in the early gentrifiers, but never made dynamic.

Robin the rural English gentleman is a staple of the new tradition, as generated in the popular novel *Robin Hood and Little John, or The Merry Men of Sherwood Forest* by Pierce Egan the Younger (1840) and in Tennyson's much overlooked verse drama *The Foresters* (written by 1881 but not played until 1892 in America). The figure is inherently conservative, but it did not entirely dominate: the new Robin was created during a period of great political stress in England between the Napoleonic Wars and the first Reform Bill, and while there is hardly a trace of interest in the outlaw among the Chartists and the heroes of Thompson's *The Making of the English Working Class* (there are a few contacts between Robin and the midlands Luddites[17]), the figure is still available for some elements of contemporary resistance. In Keats's 1818 poem 'Robin Hood: To a Friend' he imagines, if briefly, a revived Robin and Marian lamenting the contemporary oppression of tenants and the encroachment of the cash-nexus.[18] In a more developed vein Leigh Hunt wrote a set of ballads which recreated the anti-authoritarian bandit in an occasionally theorised context, as when he imagines the return of tax money as a restitution of expropriated goods and labour value:

> Well, ploughman there's a sheaf of yours
> Turn'd to yellow gold:
> Amd, miller, there's your last year's rent,
> Twill wrap thee from the cold.[19]

Robin could also represent forms of civil democratic action, as in the novel *Royston Gower* (1838), where Thomas Miller, a basket-maker, later to work with G.M.W. Reynolds, Chartist, popular writer and founder of the long-lasting leftish *Reynolds' News*, made Robin, while Saxon, manly and definitely rural in the modern mode, seem more like an anti-aristocratic guerrilla, married as he was to a Saxon peasant girl, than the now usual liberal gentleman. G.P.R. James in *Forest Days* (1843) pursued a more upmarket line in making his Robin fight for Simon de Montfort, the alleged founder of the English parliament, a myth dear to liberals with a shaky grasp of history. But there is a sharper edge: at the end of the novel the king pardons the vile aristocrat who has been behind abduction and murder throughout, but Robin sends a black arrow through the villain's throat with the message: 'Whom Kings spare, the Commons send to judgement.'[20] A social use of the tradition somewhat more programmatic than these resistance fancies is implicit in the curious reprinting by the radical *The People's Journal* in 1846 of the whole of the early sixteenth-century *Gest of Robin Hood*, spread over two issues, clearly as a claim on the existence of an antique tradition of resistance to oppressive law, to validate present agitation.

These instances testify to the continuing possibility of reading Robin Hood as radical, to a greater or lesser degree, but the weight of the nineteenth-century tradition is towards the gentrification of the hero – though a distinctly bourgeois gentrification, for now for the first time Robin's enemies are vicious aristocrats, not merely local jacks in office. It should also be noted that Robin had a renewed – or is it continued? – existence as a popular comic hero in pantomime and comic play, where the long-standing tradition of performance and comedy, to be seen in early plays and implied in the existence of the late medieval play-games, flourishes in now recorded form, and the comedy can have satiric moments: in *Robin Hood and Richard Coeur de Lion* of 1846 the Sheriff is a property developer, blighting Sherwood with red-brick houses. The nineteenth century also saw the continued reprinting, usually from small provincial presses, of the chapbooks, Lives and garlands of the earlier period, representing usually a non-gentrified bandit hero, sometimes in distinctly comic and carnivalesque form. One chapbook Robin dresses as a woman: a young lord takes him aside into the forest with sexual malpractice in mind, but is rapidly surprised and robbed. Something of this vigorous and popular spirit is communicated in the very influential *Merry Adventures of Robin Hood* by the American illustrator Howard Pyle in 1883, a set of stories aimed at children, with very fine William Morris style pictures by the author. While the stories are sentimentally medievalised, it is not a gentrified text – Robin is not a lord and lacks Maid Marian and Pyle did transmit the vigour of the ballad stories and a sense of democratic egalitarianism both to children and into the American mainstream where the thrust of Robin Hood in film was to occur.

The strongest genre in the twentieth century was visual: film and television versions almost all celebrated Robin as a liberal gentleman, automatically taking over the leadership of the pre-existing outlaws, as by class right, and standing up for true aristocracy and kingship, validated by a sense of Saxon racial justice and a general aura of charity. There can be other political grace-notes: the 1922 film starring Douglas Fairbanks appears to validate American isolationism, as Robin returns from Crusade to rectify domestic wrongs; the 1938 film starring Errol Flynn clearly links Norman thugs with contemporary German social violence; the 1991 film starring Kevin Costner enacts international liberalism towards both American blacks and Arabs through the Little John-like new character Azeem. But the dominating ideology throughout all of these is liberal-conservative and that remains the pattern of recent feminised versions like Jennifer Roberson's *Lady of the Forest* (1993) or the 2001 Disney film *Princess of Thieves*, starring Keira Knightley as Robin's daughter. Though these in varying degrees radically empower the long-constrained female figures in the tradition, they do so in a context of aristocratic excitement, as ladies rather than women.

But the Hollywood continuation of the Romantic Robin Hood has not been the only one. The early twentieth century saw, in addition to the films, a rash of outlaw plays and poems mostly aimed at schools which were inherently Georgian, a mixture of homosociality, patriotism and occasional magic; while these can now be read as developing the inherently gay element of the Robin Hood tradition, they were not consciously radical. But clearly on the left was the ballad opera written by Michael Tippett for a benefit for the ironstone miners of North Yorkshire in 1933 – this has never appeared in print or in performance since because Tippett reused the musical themes. Similar is the unpublished play written by Jack Lindsay for Unity Theatre, performed in 1938. But Geoffrey Trease's firmly Marxist novel *Bows Against the Barons* (1934) does survive: his first children's book, it has a proletarian Robin addressing his men as 'comrade', involves the outlaws in revolutionary action parallel to that of the 1381 Peasants' Revolt, and has a fine illustration of a popular assault on Nottingham castle in which are foregrounded two peasants waving a hammer and, of course, a sickle.

A second edition of 1948 removed the 'comrade' references and provided less political illustrations, indicating the elusive nature of any really radical Robin Hood activity in the present period, but even film and television have been able at times to remember that Robin sometimes dressed in red rather than Lincoln green. The television series *The Adventures of Robin Hood*, shown in 1956–8 in Britain, starred Richard Greene as a returning soldier – for all the world like those ex-officers who won Labour seats in 1945 – clearly represents the Normans as an oppressive class, and each episode focuses on righting some anti-democratic wrong. As is well known the series was largely written, at first at least, by black-listed Americans including Ring Lardner, Jr and Ian McClellan Hunter, who had a clear idea of what modern sheriffs might be capable of. The series was enormously successful on both sides of the Atlantic – thirty million viewers were claimed in Britain and the US and it showed around the world, including in Australia, for many years. Its success seems to depend on its combination of a real sense of social grievance with the euphemising mediation of the respectable gentlemanly form of Squadron Leader Robin Hood.

However, the largely conservative trend of Robin Hoodery continued with unremarkable B pictures – three from Hammer films between 1957 and 1962 and the full-length cartoon from Disney in 1973, in which Robin and Marian are winsome foxes, the sheriff is an ugly wolf and his supporters are large and notably African animals, an insidious form of American racism. But world politics had brought new forms of realism back to the screen: there were two basically unsuccessful leftish Robin Hoods: *The Legend of Robin Hood* starring David Warbeck was made (again by Hammer) as a television pilot but it was not taken up as a series and had a cinema release in 1969 as *Wolfshead.* This was a warts-and-all version with naturalistic costuming, weather, accents and plotting. The shock of realism, let alone radical politics, seemed too much for audiences, as is most strongly indicated by the failure at the box-office of Richard Lester's 1976 *Robin and Marian*, starring Sean Connery and Audrey Hepburn. Robin is here an elderly, tough, grumpy peasant soldier, who parts company with King Richard on Crusade because of his brutality. There is a clear sixties-style radicalism running through the film, which may in part account for its failure in America, though most commentators feel this is caused by realism: age, winter, provincial English accents appear along with distaste for authority, and, for the only time in film – and very rarely in print either – Robin and Marian die at the end. Whatever its politics, youthfulness, summer, some form of gaiety, must be part of the outlaw myth.

That was certainly observed in a later very successful television series which did pay some attention to radical themes. *Robin of Sherwood*, shown by Harlech Television from 1984, starred Michael Praed as a student radical type of Robin Hood, all long dark hair, cutting edge profile and unfocused enthusiasm. The series started with a flashback to the Norman destruction of his village – a My Lai moment – because his father was leader of a rebellion against the Normans. But Robin's anti-authoritarian activities are never so organised as revolt, and Richard Carpenter, who has also written scripts for children's television and adventures like *Dick Turpin* and *The Scarlet Pimpernel*, adds romance – in part in the beautiful summer forest settings, but also in that Robin is selected as the resistant hero by Herne the Hunter, in his misty cave, with stag horns on. Through his powers, Robin's death (Praed wanted to leave the series) leads to a new Robin, the silver-haired Jason Connery.

Palliated as it was by magic and beauty, not to mention Clannad's Celtic electronic folk soundtrack, *Robin of Sherwood* did maintain a certain level of radicalism in the narrative: Robin remains a peasant; hostilities are clearly class-based; Will Scarlet, played powerfully by the young Ray Winstone, has a distinct football terrace tone and has killed Normans for the rape of his wife; there is also a consistent representation of the oppression of ordinary people that clearly relates to the growing brutalities of the Thatcher regime. Both in its success and its restrictions

Robin of Sherwood characterises the possibilities and the limitations of the mainstream Robin Hood tradition for radical representation. Points can be made, even in unlikely contexts – the other 1991 film, *Robin Hood*, starring Patrick Bergin and Uma Thurman, while basically combining carnival with melodrama, offers some dark comments about Thatcherism and has the first definably feminist Marian, no doubt because it was rewritten by the sadly late John McGrath. But coherently radical accounts of the outlaw's activities are rare and fugitive, in the present as much as the past.

This is curious, because I believe it is possible to argue that the tradition has periods of intense activity when government is widely recognised to be oppressive. The 1980s in Britain and America are a clear case; the 1820s in Britain also; probably the late seventeenth century after the Restoration, and also the period leading up to the Civil War. I suspect the late Elizabethan period is another instance. There may be others, including the period around 1500 when the texts are first recorded and, conceivably, the troubled later fourteenth century when many feel that the stories were first formed. However clear or vague their definition, these are all periods when there is a lot of activity not only in major production but also in the cultural undergrowth, periods when Robin Hood is unusually alive. But the impact of the texts in such periods is not primarily or systematically political if they have any political thrust it may merely be Utopian, a fantasy of freedom that locates itself more in an aura of liberty and alternative communality than in purposive planning for reform or revolution.

Utopian dreams, however, have a role to play in politics. What seems to come out of a consideration of Robin Hood's radical status is that it is, and has been, always there: from the start, and to the present, there is a sense that bad authority should be resisted, however euphemised or contained that message might be. There also seems to be a potential – sometimes deeply buried – for the tradition to take on a politically potent edge. There have been a whole series of manoeuvres which have made that less possible – in the world of publishing, drama production and most notably film-making, but also it would seem in the quest for major success with audiences. Too realistic a version, too radical an account of dealing with oppression, does not succeed on a large front. The systems of cultural production and reception can themselves operate like sheriffs.

But the social bandit is an elusive fellow, and the Robin Hood tradition takes many forms. The underlying myth that oppression can be resisted, that arrows can strike from nowhere, is one that accords ill with conservative ideology; there are no Robin Hood texts in the high canon of English Literature, itself a sign of rude political health. The present world response to armed outlawry indicates the power of the myth: Osama Bin Laden has at times been spoken of, with some nervousness, as an Arab Robin Hood. The power of the outlaw tradition to be politically resistant has long – perhaps always – been under consistent containment from gentrification and other forms of trivialisation, all deflecting, appropriating, concealing, ignoring, but never quite destroying, the radical potential of the myth of the good outlaw. Twenty-four arrows is a lot of fire power.

NOTES

1. The text of Andrew's comment, and those by other early chroniclers, can be found in *Robin Hood and Other Outlaw Tales*, ed. Stephen Knight and Thomas Ohlgren, 2nd. edn. (University of Western Michigan Press, Kalamazoo, 2000).
2. The lines are discussed in Douglas Gray's essay, 'The Robin Hood Poems' *Poetica* 18 (1984) 1–19, reprinted in *Robin Hood: Anthology of Scholarship and Criticism*, ed. S. Knight (Brewer, Cambridge, 1999), pp. 3–32, see pp. 13–14. There are some editing difficulties with this fragment: the text reads 'four and thunti': it is more likely that the original was 'twunti' not 'thurti': 'w' and 'h' can be confused in this script and in any case thirty-four would be a very odd number to cite.
3. This was first identified by the Australian historian Philippa Madden in her 1985 Oxford D.Phil. thesis; the first published reference is in Colin Richmond, 'An Outlaw and Some Peasants: The Possible Significance of the Robin Hood Tradition', *Nottingham Medieval Studies* 37 (1993), pp. 90–101; reprinted in *Robin Hood: Anthology of Scholarship and Criticism*, ed. Knight, pp. 363–76, see p. 376.
4. For details see J.C. Holt, *Robin Hood*, 2nd. edn. (Thames and Hudson, London, 1989), pp. 147–9.
5. See Eric Hobsbawm, *Bandits*, 2nd. edn. (Pelican, London, 1985).
6. See Holt, *Robin Hood*, p.157.
7. The fullest source for the Robin Hood ballads is F.J. Child's *English and Scottish Popular Ballads*, 10 vols. (Barker, Boston, 1869–92), reprinted in 5 vols. (Dover, New York, 1965): Child prints all the available ballads in variant texts. A selection of the most important ballads can be found in R.B. Dobson and J.Taylor, eds., *Rymes of Robyn Hood*, 2nd edn. (Sutton, Stroud, 1997) and in *Robin Hood and Other Outlaw Tales*, ed. Knight and Ohlgren.

8. Richard Tardif, 'The "Mistery" of Robin Hood: A New Social Context for the Texts', in *Words and Worlds: the Social Role of Verbal Culture*, ed. S. Knight and S. Mukherjee (Sydney Association for Studies in Society and Culture, Sydney, 1983), pp. 130–45.
9. These games are described and discussed in Stephen Knight, *Robin Hood: A Complete Study of the English Outlaw* (Blackwell, Oxford, 1994), pp. 99–115 and Jeffrey L. Singman, *Robin Hood: The Shaping of a Legend* (Greenwood, Westport, 1998).
10. Alexandra F. Johnstone, 'The Robin Hood of the Records', in *Playing Robin Hood: The Legend as Performance in Five Centuries*, ed. Lois J. Potter (University of Delaware Press, Newark, 1998), pp. 27–44.
11. See I.M.W. Harvey, *Jack Cade's Rebellion* (Clarendon, Oxford, 1991), p. 65.
12. Cecil's comment is noted by Holt, p. 170; Christopher Hill, 'Robin Hood' in *Liberty Against the Law* (Lane, London, 1996), pp.71–82; reprinted in *Robin Hood: Anthology of Scholarship and Criticism*, ed. Knight, pp. 285–95, see p. 290.
13. For the text of this play see *Rymes of Robyn Hood*, ed. R.B. Dobson and J. Taylor and *Robin Hood and Other Outlaw Tales*, ed. Knight and Ohlgren.
14. Alexandre Dumas, *Robin Hood, prince des voleurs* (Levy, Paris, 1872).
15. Joseph Ritson, ed., *Robin Hood: A Collection of All the Ancient Poems, Songs and Ballads Relative to the Celebrated English Outlaw*, 2 vols. (Egerton and Johnson, London, 1795), pp. xi–xii.
16. For a discussion see Knight, *Robin Hood*, pp. 148–9.
17. See Brian Bailey, *The Luddite Rebellion* (Sutton, Stroud, 1998), pp. 20, 31 and 69.
18. See the discussion in Nicholas Roe, *John Keats and the Culture of Dissent* (Clarendon, Oxford, 1997), pp. 146–55.
19. Hunt's poems were published in November 1820 in *The Indicator*, and then reprinted in *Stories in Verse* (Routledge, London, 1852); for a discussion see Knight, *Robin Hood*, pp. 167–70.
20. G.P.R. James, *Forest Days*, 3 vols. (Saunders and Otley, London, 1843), III, p. 302.

The Poetics of Sycophancy: Ben Jonson and the Caroline Court

Andrew McRae

In a cluster of poems published in his posthumous collection *The Underwood*, Jonson relentlessly exposes the mechanics of the early Stuart patronage structure. 'The humble Petition of poore Ben. To th'best of Monarchs, Masters, Men, King CHARLES', for instance, is typically forthright. It begs an increase in the 'free Poëtique Pension' of 'A large hundred Markes annuitie', granted to Jonson by King James, 'For done service, and to come' (ll. 10–11, 13).[1] The pension, he argues,

> Hath drawne on me, from the times,
> All the envie of the *Rymes*,
> And the ratling pit-pat-noyse,
> Of the lesse-*Poëtique* boyes;
> When their pot-guns aim to hit,
> With their pellets of small wit,
> Parts of me (they judg'd) decay'd,
> But we last out, still unlay'd. (ll. 17–24)

Thus besieged, Jonson claims that the extra income 'would all their envie burst: / And so warme the *Poëts* tongue / You'ld reade a Snake, in his next Song' (ll. 30–2). Yet, despite the unnerving articulation of humility shading into humiliation, the terms of his appeal in fact bespeak a subtle pragmatism. Patronage, he suggests, has its costs as well as its benefits, and the patronized poet requires at once insulation and ammunition. Moreover, the closing promise of a 'Snake' implies a poetic asperity that may serve poet and king alike, bound as they were in the early 1630s in struggles against 'envie': a word regularly deployed in the Jonsonian lexicon to moralize both personal antagonism and political deviance. While never so straightforward as to state that loyalty may literally have a price, Jonson nonetheless gestures towards a milieu of nascent political and cultural division, and subtly reminds his monarch of their mutual dependence. Charles evidently agreed, and granted the poet his suit.[2]

Such an approach to patronage poetry presents important challenges to readers. For one of his most careful critics, the *Underwood* poems addressed to Charles and members of his court 'represent the most embarrassing portion of Jonson's poetic output', and are valuable only as evidence of the poet's 'doggedness of ... spirit' in years of illness and adversity.[3] Yet others have attended profitably to the ways in which these poems, like the *Underwood* collection as a whole, illuminate Jonson's position as 'a beleaguered intellectual courageously rethinking his priorities ... in the uncongenial Caroline environment'.[4] For Annabel Patterson, forthright appeals for money and insistent allusions to a courtly context shaped by factional rivalry and ideological contestation, 'take their place in the ironic economy of *Underwood*', which unsettles the volume's overt statements of political allegiance.[5] Others have accepted the poems as part of a concerted effort by Jonson to 'reestablish his ties with the court', but have identified within this framework notes of artistic ambivalence and political disquiet.[6] In the words of Sara J. van den Berg, Jonson at once 'wants to affirm the past – both his world and his work – and to accept a diminished present'.[7] No previous critic, however, has considered the evident changes in Jonson's panegyric in relation to wider shifts in poetic practice and political discourse in the 1620s and 1630s: a time when a commitment to 'royalism' was taking shape as a divisive political position rather than an universal assumption.

In this essay, then, I want to resituate Jonson as a central artistic figure within a context of political division.[8] Jonson's earlier panegyrics, which I will consider briefly at the outset, are marked by the author's struggle to uphold orthodox assumptions of a nation united by common moral and political values. Within this context, praise may be defended as a statement of accepted fact, and thus distinguished from flattery, its shadowy other. Consequently, to ask what happens to Jonson's poetry of praise in the latter half of his career is to a considerable extent to ask what happens to panegyric itself when fragile assumptions of common values disintegrate. His response, in poems written from the early years of the 1620s but not widely disseminated until the publication of *Underwood*, accords with that of other contemporary writers, particularly those active within the period's lively manuscript culture. The poems do not categorically identify with a particular political position, in part because such positions had not yet been defined; instead, within these texts Jonson sceptically examines the very language through which division was being conceived. They serve to delineate, with a clarity borne out of world-weary despair and a ferocious spirit of self-criticism, the emergent contours of early Stuart royalism.

The poetry of praise, grounded as it is in traditions of epideictic rhetoric, depends heavily upon assumptions of common values. According to orthodox Renaissance theory, the poet's authority to apply those values, and thus make accurate discriminations between the praiseworthy and the blameworthy, distinguishes not only panegyric from flattery but also satire from libel. As one of the leading panegyrists of the era, Jonson struggled to maintain these distinctions; 'It cannot be Flatterie, in me ... and lesse then Love, and Truth it is not,' he argued, 'where it is done out of *Knowledge*' (7.232).[9] Yet the degree of obfuscation involved in his idealizing fusion of 'love', 'truth' and 'knowledge' betrays an unease which was becoming more pervasive in early Stuart culture. While Francis Bacon, for instance, might state boldly that 'Praise is the reflection of virtue', he was also well aware of the extent to which the position of the praiser will inform statements of panegyric.[10] Jonson, meanwhile, cagily displaces himself from a reflex of self-loathing in an early poem reflecting on the mechanics of patronage. 'To My Muse', published in *Epigrams*, accuses the poet's 'most abhord' muse of betraying him 'to a worthlesse lord', and thus leading him into 'most fierce idolatrie'. Although intended to suppress from his work anything 'smelling parasite', the poem on the contrary threatens to undermine the volume's very project of discrimination, as it highlights the extent to which a poet committed to patronage networks is enmeshed perforce in the factional and ideological confrontations that shaped the era (8.48).

The *Epigrams* is indeed a collection well-wrought – or, on occasion, overwrought – under the strain of welding abstract humanist codes of virtue to contemporary practices of court patronage. As Stanley Fish has argued, Jonson's typical response to these pressures is to resist the troublesome labours of representation, generating a community of virtuous 'author-readers', 'not by creating its members (who are what they are), but by providing a relay or network by means of which they can make contact with and identify one another'.[11] This strategy is exemplified in one of three epigrams written to Robert Cecil, James's secretary of state, probably around 1605. Cecil, Jonson commented to William Drummond, 'never cared for any man longer nor he could make use of him'; however, in the first decade of James's reign, a time when Jonson's own career at court oscillated between ostracism and endorse ment, his patronage was crucial.[12] Rather than openly praise his subject, Jonson dwells upon the function of the poet:

> What need hast thou of me? or of my *Muse*?
>   Whose actions so themselves doe celebrate;
> Which should thy countries love to speake refuse,
>   Her foes enough would fame thee, in their hate.
> 'Tofore, great men were glad of *Poets*: Now,
>   I, not the worst, am covetous of thee.
> Yet dare not, to my thought, lest hope allow
>   Of adding to thy fame; thine may to me,
> When, in my booke, men reade but CECILL's name,
>   And what I write thereof find farre, and free
> From servile flatterie (common *Poets* shame)
>   As thou stand'st cleere of the necessitie. (8.40–1)

There are some tensions here, borne out of the poet's struggle to reconcile himself to his subordinated position. While it is perhaps an overstatement to claim that the poem is 'full of suppressed violence', there is definitely a subtext of edgy constraint, evident especially in the isolated and 'covetous' Jonsonian 'I', a central note of self-assertion on which the piece hinges.[13] Jonson is aware that the lines of a patronage poet can never simply be 'free'; rather, in a careful qualification underscored by enjambment, they are 'free / From servile flatterie'. As much as it may draw attention to this context, however, the poem functions nonetheless as an artful statement of praise, established on the familiar conceit of the poet's inability to augment Cecil's 'fame'. Hence it ultimately rests on 'CECILL's name', thereby assuming 'a circle of admiration, sympathy, obligation, and common effort' which aligns the poet with his patron – lifting them both above the level of the 'servile' and the 'common' – even while ostensibly denying the efficacy of panegyric.[14] In a subsequent poem to Cecil, 'thy name' renders both poet and statesman passive; it alone 'labour'd in my thought', and it alone 'wonder … hath wrought' (8.47–8).

Yet the enclosed circle of virtue merely defers the nagging question of authorization; and Jonson appreciates that if the poet and his patron are to function in a public arena 'names' require legitimacy. Hence in numerous poems he appropriates the authorizing stamp of James: 'so wise a king', who lends to true 'worth' its requisite 'reward' (8.48). Critically, however, in his early poetry Jonson is by no means a dogmatic spokesman for royal absolutism, but seeks rather a more inclusive model of a 'country' happily united under the Stuarts.[15] In 'To Thomas Earle of Suffolke', for example, he begins with the abstract authority of 'truth', but ends with the legitimizing assent of the 'people':

Since men have left to doe praise-worthy things,
  Most thinke all praises flatteries. But truth brings
That sound, and that authoritie with her name,
  As, to be rais'd by her, is onely fame.
Stand high, then, HOWARD, high in eyes of men,
  High in thy bloud, thy place, but highest then,
When, in mens wishes, so thy vertues wrought,
  As all thy honors were by them first sought:
And thou design'd to be the same thou art,
  Before thou wert it, in each good mans heart.
Which, by no lesse confirm'd, then thy kings choice,
  Proves, that it is gods, which was the peoples voice. (8.49)

The poem curiously mystifies the relation between the constituent loci of authority in the state. The late conflation of king and god is hardly unconventional, and it seems appropriate that the 'designer' of Suffolk's greatness should remain syntactically ambiguous. Yet the focus, in the same sentence, on 'each good mans heart' invokes a model of political subjectivity that is apparently contained though theoretically autonomous; and this image reinforces a concern for the 'eyes' and 'wishes' of the nation's 'men', that interweaves the poem's exploration of 'authoritie'. The closing couplet, with its resonant rhyme on 'kings choice' and 'peoples voice', further suggests a delicate coalition of interests, syntactically and ideologically tenuous yet informed by a powerful myth of unity and cohesion.

Given this effort to efface tensions between 'people' and 'king', Jonson's problems become acute precisely when the 'good mans heart' is claimed as a site of radically independent judgement and political subjectivity. By the 1620s such assertions were presented with unprecedented urgency, as critics of the Church and court identified the heart with the unfettered conscience; Jonson's antagonist George Wither, for example, in a poem designed 'to draw the true Picture of mine own heart', contrasts the arts of 'The Parasite, and smooth tongu'd Flatterer' to his own 'bold truth-speaking *Lines*'.[16] At the same time, George Villiers, Duke of Buckingham, the court favourite invested with unprecedented powers by both James and Charles, provided a central focus for divergent notions of political identity. Partly as a function of his preeminent position in the state, and perhaps also partly as a result of a personal craving for affirmation, Buckingham's years of influence, from the late 1610s until his assassination in 1628, placed unsustainable strains on Jonson's informing myths of unity, and fractured the epideictic commitment to discrimination. Under such conditions, with contending forces demanding respectively 'freedom' and 'loyalty' of the subject's heart, the early Jonsonian vision of national cohesion was rendered virtually untenable. Indeed in these years the only effective form of panegyric was of necessity sycophantic, while poetry itself was inexorably enlisted into a politics of confrontation and division.

Jonson's shift within this context towards new forms of panegyric was not without parallel. Indeed, while the fact that Jonson wrote relatively little poetry in the 1620s makes the *Underwood* poems all the more arresting, other writers were artfully accommodating themselves to the changing cultural milieu. For example, the literary career of Richard Corbett, one of the most popular poets in the lively manuscript culture of the 1620s, whose rise in the Stuart Church was heavily dependent on the patronage of Buckingham, throws into relief the trajectory of Jonson's own career. For Corbett, the bonds of patronage demanded not a lofty Jonsonian discrimination, but rather a complete and unashamed commitment to one's patron. 'A New-Yeares Gift, To my Lorde Duke of Buckingham', presumably written to thank Buckingham for the poet's advancement in 1620 to the position of Dean of Christ Church, begins with an audacious effort to define the significance of the patronage relationship:[17]

> When I can pay my Parents, or my King,
> For life, or peace, or any dearer thing:
> Then, *Dearest Lord*, expect my due to you
> Shall be as truly paid, as it is due. (pp. 71–2; ll. 1–4)

'A New-Yeares Gift' does not resist its status as an inadequate token within a system more dependent upon financial interactions; instead the poem is replete with barely-veiled mercantile imagery and diction. Corbett asserts that his 'conscience bindes not to restore but owe', and offers 'Thankes *Sterling*' to a patron who knows 'a true *Diamond* from a *Bristow stone*' (ll. 10, 19, 22). In this frank exchange of gifts the poet offers not only praise but also protection, as he embraces a politicization of panegyric, and sets himself the task of confronting forces opposed to his patron. His controlling vision is that of a familial circle of royal patronage – in one image, with Charles sitting to the right of James and Buckingham to the left, and the king himself 'Safe in the mid'st, you both invironing' – hedged from criticism by the lines of a loyal poet.[18] Most notably, as the rancorous decade progressed, this task involved targeting the parliament, an institution in which the 'lower strive to gett the upper hand', and 'Prince and Peeres to Peysants must obey' (pp. 82–3).[19] In his combination of satire and sycophancy, Corbett thus typified a fresh willingness among courtly poets to seize upon panegyric as an instrument of division, and to contribute in the process to a pivotal refiguration of a fractured nation. 'Royalism', here, was defined against an increasingly distinct other.

Jonson was a friend of Corbett, and wrote a touching poem on the death of his father, describing him as a man so mild and 'pure' that he 'could not reprehend' (8.151–2); however, he remained sceptical, at least, about the influence of his friend's patron. He never addressed a poem to the favourite, while the singular balance between panegyric and satire in his masque *The Gypsies Metamorphosed*, presented by Buckingham and his wife in honour of James in 1621, remains a matter of critical dispute.[20] Later in the decade, Jonson was suspected, though cleared, of writing a poem in support of Buckingham's assassin, John Felton.[21] Significantly, however, Patterson's perception of *Underwood* as a volume staging 'a retrospective of Jonson's career' invites a re-assessment of poems clearly written in the 1620s. Several such poems were addressed to statesmen who subsequently fell from power, in some cases because of involvement in factional and ideological struggles. For instance, poems on Sir Edward Coke and Francis Bacon, separated in the volume by only a few pages, praise men who were in fact bitter rivals, so that the poems (as Patterson argues) 'interrogate each other'.[22] Consequently, as much as Jonson, in the Coke epigram, celebrates a career in which 'Integritie, / And skill in thee, now, grew Authoritie', the Jonsonian nexus between morality and power is in fact subtly disrupted. The self-consciously awkward conclusion, which repeats yet qualifies an earlier claim that Coke's career has been founded on 'Vertue' rather than 'Fortune', underscores the poet's anxiety; 'Or if Chance must,' he concludes 'to each man that doth rise, / Needs lend an aide, to thine she had her eyes'. And for a reader in the 1630s, the final switch back to the past tense – in which the poem begins, but which it shrugs off for the purposes of direct address – might well have served as a reminder of the costs of Coke's defence of the 'Lawes' (8.217). He was removed from his position of Lord Chief Justice in 1616 in part because of his efforts to restrict the royal prerogative, and by the time the poem was published he had played a leading role in some of the pivotal battles of the 1620s between the Crown and the parliament.[23]

Another epigram, almost certainly written to Bishop John Williams, Lord Keeper from 1621 to 1625, looks pointedly away from terrestrial sources of authority. The poem appears to relate to the addressee's removal from office, as it looks askance at a milieu within which the contention for reputation and office is reduced to the 'wretched rate' of a grotesque 'mercat' [market]. The poem begs forgiveness for the 'nation's sin', closing with the lines:

> He, that in such a flood, as we are in
> Of riot, and consumption, knowes the way
> To teach the people, how to fast, and pray,
> And doe their penance, to avert Gods rod:
> He is the Man, and Favorite of God. (8.234–5)

The missing term here – which becomes unmistakable if the poem is compared with the conclusion of the earlier Suffolk epigram – is 'king'. Consequently, Jonson's satiric glance at the dominant 'Favorite' within Charles' court simultaneously opens to question the role and function of the monarch himself, presiding over a court characterized by 'riot', 'consumption' and corruption. Although the poem lacks the vitriolic excess of a libel, and may have served in the 1620s as an entirely private epistle, it nonetheless bears the marks of a poet rethinking his preconceptions about power relations, and resituating himself in relation to the centres of authority.

In the subsequent decade, this nexus of anxieties concerning authority itself, and the divergent ideological interests becoming evident within the nation, informed Jonson's flurry of new poems addressed to the king and his court. Indeed, as much as these poems, which immediately follow the Williams epigram in *Underwood*, may commit themselves to the monarchy, they equally betray urgent concerns about the costs of Caroline royalism. In this respect they reflect upon – even as they conform to – the conventions of the newly sycophantic mode of royal panegyric which prevailed in these early years of personal rule. Much of this verse focused on the expanding royal family, stimulated especially by the succession of royal births that punctuated the 1630s.[24] The resultant volumes of panegyric, emanating especially from the universities, helped to consolidate a dominant Caroline iconography, structured around values of chaste love and sexual fertility.[25] Hence, in Jonson's 'Epigram to the Queene, then lying in', he emphasizes the distance between the royal family and the people, figuring the latter as united in wonder:

When was there seene
(Except the joy that the first *Mary* brought,
Whereby the safetie of Man-kind was wrought)
So generall a gladnesse to an Isle,
To make the hearts of a whole Nation smile,
As in this Prince? Let it be lawfull, so
To compare small with great, as still we owe
Glorie to God. Then, Haile to *Mary*! spring
Of so much safetie to the Realme, and King! (8.238)

The Christian parallels, though evasively playful enough, underline the poem's definitive commitment to a mood of compliant wonder, as 'the hearts of a whole Nation' are mysteriously 'ma[d]e' to 'smile'. Moreover, the parenthesized noun 'safetie' recurs significantly at the close, thereby setting politics more purposefully alongside religion. The safety that 'spring[s]' wondrously from wombs thus effaces the contingencies of business and contestation, signifying for the believers a magnificent and self-sufficient seclusion.

The poems directly addressed to Charles, by comparison, register the dissension which is effaced in the mysterious retreat into 'safety'. Here, Jonson is drawn almost unavoidably into political discourses of confrontation and division, as he perceives a political and cultural centre besieged by popular forces. In 'An Epigram. To K. Charles for a 100. pounds he sent me in my sicknesse', the poet himself speaks as one freshly cured by the king's largesse:

Great CHARLES, among the holy gifts of grace
Annexed to thy Person, and thy place,
'T is not enough (thy pietie is such)
To cure the call'd *Kings Evill* with thy touch;
But thou wilt yet a Kinglier mastrie trie,
To cure the *Poëts Evill*, Povertie:
And, in these Cures, do'st so thy selfe enlarge,
As thou dost cure our *Evill*, at thy charge.
Nay, and in this, thou show'st to value more
One *Poët*, then of other folke ten score.

O pietie! so to weigh the poores estates!
  O bountie! so to difference the rates!
What can the *Poët* wish his *King* may doe,
  But, that he cure the Peoples Evill too? (8.235)

The concept of the king's evil (scrofula), an illness purportedly cured by the monarch's touch, invites Jonson's mobilization of religious discourse for the articulation of royal power; the arts of 'Kinglier mastrie', therefore, are purposefully mystified as 'holy gifts of grace' invested in Charles' body. Yet the poem dilates in the eighth line, when the long opening sentence focusing on the individual poet admits an ambiguous, though not strictly incorrect, first-person plural pronoun. The potential of that 'our' is exploited in the latter half of the poem, which alludes to the national predicament in the first year of the personal rule. Hence the signification of 'evil' becomes unstable, as 'Peoples Evill' resonates troublingly against '*Kings Evill*', and consequently hovers between a condemnation of an evil populace and a concern for evil perpetrated against the people.[26] The prescribed 'cure' is therefore rendered uncertain (possibly a majestic touch of monarchical power, though possibly instead a concession for reform), while the potential irony might well have been compounded for some readers in the knowledge that Charles was in fact notoriously reluctant to engage himself in the traditional practice of 'curing' the king's evil.[27]

This strikingly unsettled representation of political discord is continued in 'An Epigram. To our great and good K. CHARLES On his Anniversary Day'. This poem begins with the exclamation, 'How happy were the Subject if he knew, / Most pious King, but his owne good in you!', and seeks imaginatively to fill an otherwise sullen land with festivity. 'Indeed,' he asks, 'when had great *Britaine* greater cause / Then now, to love the Soveraigne, and the Lawes?' As much as the relation between 'Soveraigne' and 'Lawes' might be seen as the central question of constitutional debate in the 1630s, Jonson seeks to suppress this latent tension by uniting the nation within the terms of the Caroline politics of 'love'.[28] In the final passage, though, the erosion of common values in the nation unmistakably forces itself upon the poet's attention, and the troubled marriage between king and country elicits a satirist's lament:[29]

How is she barren growne of love! or broke!
  That nothing can her gratitude provoke!

O Times! O Manners! Surfet bred of ease,
The truly Epidemicall disease!
'T is not alone the Merchant, but the Clowne,
Is Banke-rupt turn'd! the Cassock, Cloake, and Gowne,
Are lost upon accompt! And none will know
How much to heaven for thee, great CHARLES, they owe! (8.236–7)

While the 'barren' nature of the relationship contrasts that of the king's own family, the lines are more pointedly informed by anxiety about Charles' struggle to obtain supply after the closure of a hostile parliament. (Corbett was more explicit on this point, declaring that 'When kings get sonnes, they get withall supplies/And succours, farr beyond five Subsidies'.)[30] Yet in the self-consciously hectoring tone – underscored by the echo of Cicero's '*O tempora, o mores!*'– the rhetorical excess of Jonson's panegyric undoes itself, and the poem as a result registers a curious measure of disaffection and detachment.[31] The closing gesture to an unappreciated and implacable 'heaven' thus epitomizes this surly expression of praise, produced by a poet now resigned to the inevitability of dissension in political discourse. Within this context he accepts, albeit grudgingly, that panegyric may no longer serve as an instrument of unification, but must rather side with its subject in political struggles.

Jonson's direct appeals for material support, which can seem clumsily frank in comparison with his earlier poetic practice, concur with this new cultural situation of panegyric. One poem in *Underwood* reflects on the Cecils, and observes on the way in which, as a result of his labour in the cause of crown and country, William Cecil was elevated from his relatively humble origins, and 'saw his branches shoot, / And in the noblest Families tooke root / Of all the Land'. For the poet, whose carefully fashioned laureate identity bound him also to the interests of the monarch and his court, the observation elicits a closing note of envious pragmatism; 'Who now at such a Rate, / Of divine blessing,' he asks, 'would not serve a State?' (8.185).[32] As a man similarly seeking advancement on the basis of merit, Jonson accepted this logic and pursued reward and recognition from the crown throughout his career. As a poet trying fiercely to sustain simultaneously humanist ideals of virtue and integrity, however, he was well aware of the costs of doing so.

The strains underscore his poetry. In a remarkable commendatory poem written for the outspoken Michael Drayton, Jonson fleetingly entertains the fantasy of a paradoxically 'authoriz'd wickednesse', which might transform 'Rebells' actions' into 'valiant crimes' (8.397). By comparison, the poems written to Charles and members of his court are indubitably restrained, though shaped by understated concerns about the operation of chance and favouritism at court, and the king's seclusion from the concerns of his people. Consequently, while it would be wrong to identify Jonson as an 'oppositional' figure, he was definitely a poet painfully aware of the *construction* of opposition, within a realm previously held together by myths of common cultural and political values.[33] His poems betray a clear-sighted scepticism about the structures of courtly power, but also proclaim a commitment nonetheless to serve those structures to the end. As such, they contribute to the very definition of Caroline royalism: a cause which subsequent writers would clarify and consolidate, throughout years which increasingly replaced Jonsonian discrimination with the poetics of partisan polemic.

NOTES

1. All references to Jonson's poems are from *Ben Jonson*, ed. C.H. Herford, Percy and Evelyn Simpson (11 vols., Oxford, 1954–70), 8.259–60.
2. *Ben Jonson*, 1.245–8; cf. David Riggs, *Ben Jonson: A Life* (Cambridge, Mass., 1989), p. 317.
3. Michael McCanles, *Jonsonian Discriminations: The Humanist Poet and the Praise of True Nobility* (Toronto, 1992), p. 201.
4. Martin Butler, 'Late Jonson', in *The Politics of Tragicomedy: Shakespeare and After*, ed. Gordon McMullan and Jonathan Hope (London, 1992), p. 166.
5. *Censorship and Interpretation: The Conditions of Writing and Reading in Early Modern England* (Madison, 1984), pp. 126–44 (quote at p. 135).
6. Riggs, *Ben Jonson*, p. 317; cf. John Lemly, 'Masks and Self-Portraits in Jonson's Late Poetry', *ELH*, 44 (1977), 248–66; and Butler's 'Late Jonson' (a study concerned principally with drama).
7. *The Action of Ben Jonson's Poetry* (Newark, 1987), p. 171.
8. The essay is informed by my own wider research in this field, leading to the forthcoming *Satire and the Early Stuart State* (Cambridge, 2003). I began this project as a research fellow at the University of Sydney, where I benefited from the wisdom and wit of Michael Wilding.
9. See further Jean Le Drew Metcalfe, 'Subjecting the King: Ben Jonson's Praise of James I', *English Studies in Canada*, 17 (1991), 135; and, on Jonson as a patronage poet, Robert C. Evans, *Ben Jonson and the Poetics of Patronage* (Lewisburg, 1989).
10. 'Of Praise', *The Essays*, ed. John Pitcher (London, 1985), p. 215.
11. 'Author-Readers: Jonson's Community of the Same', *Representations*, 7 (1984), 40.

12. *Conversations with Drummond*, ll. 353–4 (*Ben Jonson*, 1.142); quoted in Robert Wiltenburg, '"What need hast thou of me? or of my *Muse*?": Jonson and Cecil, Politician and Poet', in "*The Muses Common-Weale*": *Poetry and Politics in the Seventeenth Century*, ed. Claude J. Summers and Ted-Larry Pebworth (Columbia, 1988), p. 37.
13. Cf. Wiltenburg, '"What need hast thou of me? or of my *Muse*?"', p. 42.
14. Wiltenburg, '"What need hast thou of me? or of my *Muse*?"', p. 40.
15. Cf. Jonathan Goldberg, *James I and the Politics of Literature: Jonson, Shakespeare, Donne, and Their Contemporaries* (Baltimore and London, 1983), pp. 219–30.
16. *Wither's Motto* (1622), sigs. A2v, C8v. See further Michelle O'Callaghan, *The 'shepheards nation': Jacobean Spenserians and Early Stuart Political Culture* (Oxford, 2000), esp. ch. 4; and McRae, *Satire and the Early Stuart State*, ch. 3.
17. The title was given to the poem in the first printed volume of Corbett's work, *Poetica Stromata* (1648). It has been retained by Corbett's modern editors, despite the fact that Buckingham was not elevated to a dukedom until 18 May 1623, probably over a year after the poem was written (*The Poems of Richard Corbett*, ed. J.A.W. Bennett and H.R. Trevor-Roper (Oxford, 1955), p. 143).
18. 'A Letter to the Duke of Buckingham', ll. 80–2.
19. 'Against the Opposing of the Duke in Parliament, 1628', pp. 82–3 (ll. 6–7).
20. A satiric interpretation of this masque is posited by B.J. Randall, *Jonson's Gypsies Unmasked* (Durham, N.C., 1975); for an adept critique of Randall, however, see Richard Helgerson, *Self-Crowned Laureates: Spenser, Jonson, Milton, and the Literary System* (Berkeley and Los Angeles, 1983), p. 178.
21. Riggs, *Ben Jonson*, pp. 300–1.
22. *Censorship and Interpretation*, p. 132.
23. See further Robert C. Evans, '"Games of Fortune, Plaid at Court": Politics and Poetic Freedom in Jonson's Epigrams', in *The Muses Common-Weale*, pp. 54–5.
24. Raymond A. Anselment, 'The Oxford University Poets and Caroline Panegyric', *John Donne Journal*, 3 (1984), 181.
25. Ann Baynes Coiro, '"A ball of strife": Caroline Poetry and Royal Marriage', in *The Royal Image: Representations of Charles I*, ed. Thomas N. Corns (Cambridge, 1999), pp. 26–46.
26. Cf. Patterson, *Censorship and Interpretation*, pp. 135–6.
27. Judith Richards, '"His nowe Majestie" and the English Monarchy: The Kingship of Charles I before 1640', *Past and Present*, 113 (1986), 88–93.
28. See esp. Kevin Sharpe, *Criticism and Compliment: The Politics of Literature in the England of Charles I* (Cambridge, 1987), ch. 6.
29. Cf. McCanles, *Jonsonian Discriminations*, p. 204.

30. 'On the Birth of the Young Prince Charles', *Poems*, p. 86.
31. Cicero, *In Catilinam*, I i 2.
32. On Jonson's laureate identity, see Richard Helgerson, *Self-Crowned Laureates: Spenser, Jonson, Milton and the Literary System* (Berkeley, 1983), ch. 3.
33. On arguments surrounding Jonson as 'a poet of opposition', see esp. Butler, 'Late Jonson', pp. 166–8.

The Genesis of Milton's Sentences

Barry Spurr

'Milton's impossible', commented Muriel Spark to John Mortimer. 'I can never get to the end of his sentences.' Mortimer agreed about their 'interminable quality'.[1] It was his poetic sentences – not the prose (where the sentences are also long enough) – that they were discussing. Their length is their most obvious feature and this is particularly apparent in Milton's imitation of the 'ancient liberty' of Homer and Virgil in *Paradise Lost* where he eschews 'the troublesome and modern bondage of rhyming'.[2] Rhyme gives the sense of regular sentence division even where a full stop is absent – notably in the rhyming couplet, with its end-stopped lines. Milton's disposal of rhyme for his epic in English ('our sage and serious' Spenser[3] had used it, of course, in the earlier, incomplete English epic poem, *The Faerie Queene*) was combined with his adaptation of the iambic pentameter to the longer six-beat dactylic hexameter of Homer and Virgil. It was further extended by prolific enjambment. The expansion of the poetic sentence in *Paradise Lost* may be seen as a carefully-structured metrical and syntactical expression of the ambiguous theological freedom Milton proposes in the poem's thesis and to which Adam, after bitter experience, submits:

> Henceforth I learn, that to obey is best,
> And love with fear the only God, to walk
> As in his presence, ever to observe
> His providence, and on him sole depend,
> Merciful over all his works, with good
> Still overcoming evil, and by small
> Accomplishing great things, by things deemed weak
> Subverting worldly strong, and worldly wise
> By simply meek; that suffering for truth's sake
> Is fortitude to highest victory,
> And to the faithful death the gate of life;

Taught this by his example whom I now
Acknowledge my redeemer ever blessed.[4]

Long such sentences may be, interminable they never are. This sentence, both abundant and disciplined, typifies the limited liberty it expresses.

We can trace the origins of this circumspect freedom in versification, with its thematic connotations, to Milton's earliest work. All but three of the thirty-seven stanzas in his first English poem, the Nativity Ode, are eight-line sentences. The most striking of the exceptions to this pattern, stanza nineteen, is about the silencing of pagan poetry and prophecy. The old order which it describes is presented in a verse lacking the 'ancient liberty' Milton appreciated in Homeric and Virgilian epic poetry. The stanza consists of short rhyming sentences:

The oracles are dumb,
No voice or hideous hum
Runs through the archèd roof in words deceiving.
Apollo from his shrine
Can no more divine,
With hollow shriek the steep of Delphos leaving.
No nightly trance, or breathèd spell,
Inspires the pale-eyed priest from the prophetic cell.

The bathetic introductory rhyme, with its satirical onomatopoeia; the subsequent sequence of halted utterances; the stanza's pointedly punctuated negativity ('no' repeated twice, present in each short poetic sentence) and its raucous oxymoronic onomatopoeia of expiring prophecy ('hollow shriek') combine to present the silencing of the Apollonian voice at the Incarnation.

We note that the dumbness is focused at Delphi, called 'Delphos'. Milton appropriates the medieval conflation of Delos (the distant island birthplace of Apollo) and Delphi, indulging this old fancy – being 'almost the last person' to do so[5] – to signal the pastness of that deceptive world. His appropriation lends support, also, to his idea of the Pythian priestess, her corrupt male subordinates and their sorceries as pagan types of the pre-Reformation *cultus* and error of Roman medievalism. This subversive typology is glimpsed again in the 'sable-stolèd sorcerers' of Osiris in stanza XXIV, vested like chantry priests at their requiems.[6] Milton here makes the general point first (about oracles at large), then provides an instance of it albeit the most famous, at the world's *omphalos* – contracting significance as he proceeds: more is less. Instead of the sense of accumulation to be resonantly capped in the Alexandrine (as in the first stanza, for example, where the specificity of the Nativity opens out to a vision of the 'perpetual peace' of the Father's works, or in Adam's sentence, above, with its development to sober exultation), there is, rather, the reversal of the process. The visual image of the 'pale-eyed priest' adds to the sense of exhaustion, with a suspicion of southern European debauchery. In that 'cell', also critically, but at another extremity, there is an allusion to monkish asceticism and its vanities. Seven more stanzas detail the departure of the pagan oracles, trooping 'to th' infernal jail'.

Constraint, debility and contrariety prevail as 'each fettered ghost slips to his several grave', unlike the evocation of the advent of the new dispensation which Milton forecasts earlier in the Ode, giving priority to blessed futurity. In the fifteenth stanza, for example, an extended elaborated sentence, introduced with a keynote of affirmation, recalls Virgil's evocation of the golden age in his fourth 'Messianic' eclogue (a true pagan prophecy, as it was supposed):

> Yea Truth, and Justice then
> Will down return to men,
> Orbed in a rainbow; and like glories wearing
> Mercy will sit between,
> Throned in celestial sheen,
> With radiant feet the tissued clouds down steering,
> And heaven as at some festival,
> Will open wide the gates of her high palace hall.

The expansive, elevated imagery of the concluding Alexandrine celebrates the liberation wrought by the moral trinity of truth, justice and mercy, with the political subtext of their availability to all as the palace gates are opened wide. Anticipating (to amplify) its generosity, is the sequence of conjunctions and enjambment of lines 2 and 3, as the syntax bears down on the participle, and of 3 and 4, as it focuses on the personified subject, proposing the accumulating certainty of this economy, with only a caesura (in the third line, as an awestruck taking-of-breath in momentary meditation on the beautiful symbol of the divine covenant), not a sentence break. The seamlessness of the process will not – as it cannot – be violated. The versified sentence is the mimesis of its inevitability.

The same cumulative effect in prophecy of the rainbow covenant, in coloured triplicity, with conjunctions and enjambment in celebration of the irresistible triumph of justice, resonantly closes the extensive verse-sentence at the end of the eleventh book of *Paradise Lost*, in the archangel Michael's address to Adam:

> but when he brings
> Over the earth a cloud, will therein set
> His triple-coloured bow, whereon to look
> And call to mind his covenant: day and night,
> Seed time and harvest, heat and hoary frost
> Shall hold their course, till fire purge all things new,
> Both heaven and earth, wherein the just shall dwell.

The sense of finality in futurity is captured as decisively by the cadence of the sentence's long-awaited closure as by the idea of the fulfilment of the vision at the end of time.

Milton's exploration of the extended sentence which blank verse further encouraged began with the masque known as 'Comus', written five years after the Nativity Ode. There are some rhyming lyrics ('the certain Doric delicacy' appreciated by Sir Henry Wotton[7]), but much of the poetry gives promise of the sentence and verse-paragraph structure which achieve their consummation in *Paradise Lost*. Milton had written in the masque tradition before, in miniature in *Arcades*, an imitation of Ben Jonson. But as Douglas Bush notes, *Comus* subverts the customary indulgence of spectacle, music and dancing, for their own sakes, strenuously developing moral and religious themes.[8] Based on the archetypal Homeric test of heroic virtue in the story of Odysseus and Circe, Milton's masque reverses the sexes with Comus as the son of Circe and the Lady in Odysseus' position. The Attendant Spirit signals the uniqueness of the enterprise in the opening speech, when he proclaims that

> I will tell ye now
> What never yet was heard in tale or song . . .

which is echoed in the opening paragraph of *Paradise Lost* where the author announces his intention to pursue 'things unattempted yet in prose or rhyme'. We notice from the beginning the concentration on literariness which recurs through the masque as it does in the later epic.

The Spirit celebrates 'the crown that Virtue gives',

> After this mortal change, to her true servants
> Amongst the enthroned gods on sainted seats.

In striking contrast, Comus, whose name is Greek for revelry, speaks of Bacchanalian abandon in prim rhyme:

> Meanwhile welcome joy and feast,
> Midnight shout and revelry,
> Tipsy dance and jollity . . .

This finely-ordered verse, with its pert alliteration, is strikingly ironic. First, because Comus is introduced in the stage direction, with his 'rout of monsters', 'making a riotous and unruly noise' when the precision of Wotton's Doric delicacy follows and, second, because of the commotion Comus proposes in the *netteté* of his rhyme, with his caricatures of restraint ('Strict Age, and sour Severity'). Milton fulfils the convention of the anarchic spirit of the anti-masque, but his moral point, registered as strongly in the style of the poetic sentences as in what they say, is that this licentious story is typically dressed up in seductive mellifluousness. In our own time, A.N. Wilson has succumbed to this 'pretty' passage and its 'supreme tastefulness'.[9] More perceptive, Michael Wilding sees that it is 'explosive with religious and political tensions'.[10] It is as tasteful as poison can be, as the Spirit later warns the brothers. The affectation of stylistic correctness indicates that Comus' domain, like Hell in *Paradise Lost*, is the embodiment of paradox, perversion and vapid casuistry:

> Come, let us our rites begin,
> 'Tis only daylight that makes sin,
> Which these dun shades will ne'er report.
> Hail, goddess of nocturnal sport . . .

In climax, he asserts that his rabble should

> . . . knit hands, and beat the ground,
> In a light fantastic round.

But, again ironically, what immediately ensues in the so-called 'Measure' is the subversion of metrical measurement as Comus breaks both the rhyme and metre when he senses the presence of the virtuous Lady. The modulation of the poetry marks the movement from licentiousness to chastity:

> Break off, break off, I feel the different pace
> Of some chaste footing near about this ground . . .

'pace' and 'footing' calling attention to this new versification as well as to the manner of the Lady's walking. The abruptness of these modulations is dramatically effective (in a work written, after all, to be staged), but it is also the antithesis of the serene ceremoniousness of edifying motions. This was a distinction Milton was to explore extensively in *Paradise Lost,* where Satan's moral and spiritual anarchy is realised in the extremity and abruptness of his characteristic movements (and in Hell itself, which he embodies).[11]

Comus, like Satan, is capable of introspection and discerns his evil-doing. His self-knowledge is articulated in his recognition of his mode of utterance:

> I, under fair pretense of friendly ends,
> And well-placed words of glozing courtesy
> Baited with reasons not unplausible,
> Wind me into the easy-hearted man,
> And hug him into snares.

The winding sentence envisages bondage to a suspect freedom. As surely as Comus' invitation to abandonment in the lyric, this is liberty *in maschera*. The liberated (but precisely measured) sentence structure, distinctively Miltonic, with its syntax suspended over a sequence of subordinate clauses, with enjambment impelling the accumulation of meaning and significance, nonetheless discloses a disabling profusion of negative substantives and epithets to indicate that its momentum is for evil rather than good. They are there plainly in 'pretense' and 'glozing courtesy' (deriving from the debased courtly world with its 'amours / Mixed dance, or wanton masque, or midnight ball'[12]); more subtly in 'reasons not unplausible' which will 'hug' the 'easy-hearted man' (as distinct from the keen-minded one) into 'snares'. It cannot be too strongly stressed that, always and everywhere in Milton, the medium is intrinsic to the message. The litotes here, for example, indicates the moral confusion adumbrated by this courteous-seeming advocate of chaos and old night.

Comus' sinuous sentence, proposing beguiling insinuation, was an apprenticeship for Milton in the serpentine quality of Satan's sophistry, exercised in the climactic ninth book of *Paradise Lost*, where 'glozed the tempter, and his proem tuned; / Into the heart of Eve':

> Fairest resemblance of thy maker fair,
> Thee all things living gaze on, all things thine

By gift, and thy celestial beauty adore
With ravishment beheld, there best beheld
Where universally admired; but here
In this enclosure wild, these beasts among,
Beholders rude, and shallow to discern
Half what in thee is fair, one man except,
Who sees thee? (and what is one?) who shouldst be seen
A goddess among gods, adored and served
By angels numberless, thy daily train.[13]

Like Eve removed from Adam, the Lady in *Comus*, although embodying Faith, Hope and Chastity, is endangered through separation from her brothers.

As literary qualities and quantities repeatedly provide a method of moral discrimination in the masque, the arousal of the Lady's suspicions about Comus is accordingly expressed (in her first verse-sentence) in her insight that his revelry will bewitch 'unlettered hinds'. Seduced by his sophisticated language, they will be led into moral confusion and spiritual error: 'in wanton dance' to offer praise to 'bounteous Pan / And thank the gods amiss'. Comus, contrariwise, hearing her song to Echo, differentiates it from the siren-voices of pagan temptresses, like his mother, and appreciates its 'divine enchanting ravishment'. It brings 'waking bliss' as opposed to Circe's drug-induced 'slumber', lulling the senses. Stupidly convinced, nonetheless, of the ultimate power of his own linguistic sorcery – revealing the limitations of his self-knowledge and his libidinous captivity – Comus makes this confident announcement: 'I'll speak to her, / And she shall be my queen', as if it were as simple as that. He does so, in an overblown oratorical address: 'Hail, foreign wonder' which proves comically ineffectual, as the Lady disdainfully replies:

Nay, gentle shepherd, ill is lost that praise
That is addressed to unattending ears.

The differentiation between the stylistic modes of these sentences, florid rhetoric and proverbial good sense as the Lady, although dismissive, also displays true courtesy in saluting the 'gentle' shepherd, establishes the discontinuity between the characters and their moral contexts, between excess and restraint.

Similarly, in the discussion between the brothers about the fate and rescue of their sister, Milton's characterisation in terms of the distinctiveness of their moral and theological responses is articulated not only in what they say but how their sentences are framed and constituted. The anxious younger brother uses extreme images of the perilous situation of 'that hapless virgin':

> Perhaps some cold bank is her bolster now,
> Or 'gainst the rugged bark of some broad elm
> Leans her unpillowed head fraught with sad fears.
> What if in wild amazement and affright,
> Or, while we speak, within the direful grasp
> Of savage hunger or of savage heat?

The Elder Brother's response, almost in the manner of the literary critic, rejects these over-heated scenarios with their febrile repetitions:

> Peace, brother, be not over-exquisite
> To cast the fashion of uncertain evils.

His rhetorical questions (of contrasting philosophical cast) decisively dispose of the younger brother's anxious queries, rooted in physicality, by transcending them:

> What need a man forestall his date of grief,
> And run to meet what he would most avoid?
> Or if they be but false alarms of fear,
> How bitter is such self-delusion?

Elsewhere, the restrained vocabulary of the brother's sententious response to the younger man's florid adjectivalism marks the prudence of his faith: 'I incline to hope rather than fear'. The persuasion of such wisdom finally triumphs and we note that the second brother confirms his understanding in analogies with artistic form and feasting in which restraint, again, is the keynote:

> How charming is divine philosophy!
> Not harsh and crabbed, as dull fools suppose,
> But musical as is Apollo's lute,
> And a perpetual feast of nectared sweets,
> Where no crude surfeit reigns.

He advocates embracing well-managed freedom, whereas Comus, at his Bacchanalia, sneers at any 'pet of temperance'.

Milton became increasingly impatient of compromise in ecclesiastical and political matters, but he was a champion of the genius of the *via media* in the moral life, of the well-tempered response to the apparently conflicting physical and spiritual demands of human existence. The caricature of the sour Puritan, 'harsh and crabbed', is challenged not only in passages such as this, where the poet explicitly addresses the allegation, but more tellingly when his humanity speaks to us in his praise of the created world and the 'human face divine'.[14] In the famous passage in *Paradise Lost*, celebrating pre-lapsarian sexuality, 'wedded love', there is a series of sentences with various characteristics of restrained abundance, as in the use of 'here' in these lines, a rhythmic punctuation as regular as it is sensuous:

Here Love his golden shafts employs, here lights
His constant lamp, and waves his purple wings,
Reigns here and revels . . . [15]

The third 'here', tantalisingly late, speaks linguistically of that 'sweet reluctant amorous delay'[16] which Milton had earlier celebrated in Eve's approach to Adam.

The Spirit, in warning the brothers of Comus' powers, not only emphasises his linguistic gifts, but imitates them, in 'many murmurs mixed', where the excessive alliteration foreshadows the 'overripeness' Professor Wilding has identified in Comus' discourse itself. Exposing the fraudulence of that mask of poetic rectitude (wittily, in a masque itself, as Milton distances himself from the form's usual playful register), the Spirit then refers to the 'barbarous dissonance' which is the other and true voice of the rabble. In contrast, as the golden mean between these extremes of artificiality and untutored nature, is the 'soft and solemn-breathing sound' of 'my most honored lady, your dear sister'. Comus himself recognises that the Lady's 'words' are 'set-off by some superior power', but acknowledging such qualities (like Satan, momentarily dumbstruck by beauty in Eden), he cannot be converted to them, and in the interest of his *amour propre*, must mock her 'mere moral babble'. Her expansive but measured sentences of praise of temperance, 'well-governed and wise appetite', are contradictory of this description of them, in form as well as substance. It is Comus who babbles. Again, Milton concentrates our attention on how subjects are articulated as well as the subjects themselves. The Lady's critique of Comus' lampoon of abstinence had focused on the way it was expressed:

this juggler
Would think to charm my judgment, as mine eyes,
Obtruding false rules pranked in reason's garb.
I hate when vice can bolt her arguments,
And virtue has no tongue to check her pride. . . .
Enjoy your dear wit and gay rhetoric
That hath so well been taught her dazzling fence;
Thou art not fit to hear thyself convinced.

Again, the emphasis is on masquerade and its power for delusion. His language, she says, is 'pranked', dressed and adorned as if it were reasonable. The vicious arguments are bolted, propped and padded, like the appurtenances of the theatre. The 'dear wit and gay rhetoric' bedazzle, producing an excess of light which is blinding rather than illuminating.

For all its distinction, the Lady's moral and intellectual insight is not sufficient to secure her freedom. She needs grace, in the person of Sabrina, summoned by the Spirit who recognises that 'the power of some adjuring verse' is required to secure her attendance. Once more, the poetry calls attention to its literary processes as a prayer to Sabrina, with the litany-like repetition of 'Listen and save', in a version of the sacramental *epiklesis*, brings the Goddess to the Lady's rescue in a ritual anointing:

Thus I sprinkle on thy breast
Drops that from my fountain pure
I have kept of precious cure,
Thrice upon thy finger's tip,
Thrice upon thy rubied lip.

This rhyming poetry of efficacious divinity complements the sorceries of Comus' earlier lyricism. It speaks of a high church Puritanism we also encounter in 'Il Penseroso' – 'in service high, and anthems clear'. We hear less of this, on earth, as Milton's life and career progress, although heavenly worship in *Paradise Lost* is richly ceremonial (as derived, of course, from the Book of Revelation). Throughout his works, Milton's rotundity of diction, reminiscent of Thomas Cranmer's in the Prayer Book, has its own quasi-liturgical richness.

In the extensive variety of Milton's poetic writing in his early poetry, the emergence of the extended sentence, particularly in blank verse, anticipates the grand style of his masterwork. It was the medium – instinct with amplitude, constrained within a nonetheless generous framework of syntactic rectitude – best suited not only to the epic voice, for which accumulating resonance was apt, but to express, linguistically, the abundance of creation and the freedom of thought and will, under God, which were at the heart of the great poet's Christian humanism.

NOTES

1. 'The Prime of Muriel Spark', *The Sydney Morning Herald*, 'Good Weekend' magazine, 1 May 1988, 50.
2. 'The Verse', introductory note to *Paradise Lost*. All references to and quotations from Milton's poetry are from Stephen Orgel and Jonathan Goldberg, eds, *John Milton* ('The Oxford Authors', Oxford University Press, Oxford, 1990).
3. Milton, 'The Tract for Liberty of Publication', in J. Max Patrick, ed., *The Prose of John Milton* (Anchor, New York, 1967), p. 288.
4. *Paradise Lost*, XII, 561–73.
5. Betty Radice, *Who's Who in the Ancient World* (Penguin, Harmondsworth, 1971), p. 101.
6. See my note, 'Sable-stolèd Sorcerers', *Milton Quarterly*, May 1992, 45–6.
7. Letter to Milton, April, 1638, in Douglas Bush, ed., *Milton: Poetical Works* (Oxford University Press, London, 1966), introduction to *Comus*, p. 110. Hereafter cited as 'Bush'.
8. Introduction to *Comus*, Bush, p. 142.
9. *The Life of John Milton* (Oxford University Press, Oxford, 1983), p. 51.
10. *Dragons Teeth* (Clarendon Press, Oxford, 1987), p. 40.
11. See my chapter, '"Marking time"? Milton's Recapitulation Revisited', in G.L. Little, ed., *Imperfect Apprehensions: Essays in English Literature in honour of G.A. Wilkes* (Challis Press, Sydney, 1996), pp. 101–3.
12. *Paradise Lost*, IV, 767–8.
13. *Paradise Lost*, IX, 549–50; 538–48.
14. *Paradise Lost*, III, 44.
15. *Paradise Lost*, IV, 763–5.
16. *Paradise Lost*, IV, 311.

Milton and Class

Thomas N. Corns

In 1984, in the period of dark despair for a broad spectrum of British socialism that followed the Falklands War, the popular acclaim for its victories, and Margaret Thatcher's election landslide, Christopher Hill returned to the study of Milton in the context of a wide-ranging and sometimes plangent consideration of how Civil War radicals coped with defeat. In his contemplation of *Samson Agonistes* he finds new signs of a resilient revolutionary optimism and a fresh direction in Milton's political ideology. Hill is discussing the report from the temple at the end of the verse drama, specifically the lines:

> those two massy pillars
> With horrible convulsion to and fro
> He tugged, he shook, till down they came and drew
> The whole roof after them, with burst of thunder
> Upon the heads of all who sat beneath,
> Lords, ladies, captains, counsellors, or priests,
> Their choice nobility and flower, not only
> Of this but each Philistian city round
> Met from all parts to solemnize this feast.
> Samson with these immixed, inevitably
> Pulled down the same destruction on himself;
> The vulgar only scaped who stood without.[1]

Hill, picking up a note in Gordon Campbell's edition,[2] fastens onto the fact that Milton's narrative differs from all available versions of Judges 16: 27 by excluding the common people from destruction; the biblical text is clear that lords are within the temple, and that 'the house fell upon the lords, and upon all the people that were therein' (AV; Judges 16: 30). However, there were 'about three thousand men and women' on the roof who 'beheld while Samson made sport' (16: 27); we are not specifically told what happens to them; we probably recognise it, from the everyday depictions of television news coverage, as the sort of disaster from which quite a few would escape with cuts and bruises, though that, of course, scarcely matches the idiom of the biblical account. The solemn assessment, 'So the dead which he slew at his death were more than they which he slew in his life' (16: 30), implies a general massacre.

Milton's life records give no indication when *Samson Agonistes* was composed, and it has variously been regarded as an early work revived and perhaps revised for later publication or else as approximately contemporary with *Paradise Regained* but somehow less authoritative than that brief epic, with which, of course, it was first published.[3] Hill, who unusually surmises a date of composition *after* its companion piece, comments:

> I can see no reason for these innovations of Milton's except to condemn the clergy and aristocracy whom he regarded as the principal enemies of God in restoration England: and perhaps to show that he now had more hope of 'the vulgar' responding to a purged and purified leadership than when he wrote *Paradise Regained*. What indeed could be achieved in England after 1660 without some participation of 'the people'?[4] (pp. 314–15)

There is an easy counter-argument to the last point: after all, the vulgar may be excused from the slaughter, but they are still *Philistine* vulgar, and his play is a celebration of the vengeance of the chosen people from which they are excluded. Milton's narrative does not suggest that they will link arms with their Hebrew comrades; that construction workers from the nearby Hebrew settlements will dig them from the rubble, like the Germans working to free trapped French miners at the end of G.W. Pabst's *Kameradschaft* (1931). Milton knows that the Philistine proletariat were of no world-historical significance; this is a history play; he knows, from his sacred source, that, if they survived, they did not matter, that they do not figure again in the historical process.

But Hill valuably and convincingly highlights the specificity of the groups that die. The obvious, perhaps the trivial point, is that, since the élite has been killed, the Hebrew victory is the greater; it accentuates Samson's achievement. But, as Hill observes, the groups are with precision socially marked. Besides the priests and the lords, who are identified by Hill, Milton also specifies councillors (probably a better choice of modern spelling than Carey's 'counsellors', though the words are not disambiguated in the seventeenth century) and captains, the political and military élite. Under the restored monarchy, the principal council is again the privy council; under the republic, the various councils of state. The senior officer corps plainly changes somewhat from the 1650s, with the death of Cromwell and the return of Prince Rupert; but there are some notable continuities in the role of George Monk (now Duke of Albemarle) and Edward Montagu (now Earl of Sandwich). (At the time of publication, the former had just died; the latter would shortly perish at the Battle of Southwold Bay.) The Son's scornful rejection in *Paradise Regained* of political and military distinction[5] finds endorsement in the explicit inclusion of cabinet ministers and top brass among the dead.

Milton had far easier options open in his depiction of the slaughter. An obvious analogue was with the Protestant interpretation placed on the Black Vespers or Blackfriars Assembly incident of 1623, in which a large group of Catholics, who had met clandestinely for a mass, perished when the floor collapsed. The catastrophe was represented as a providential punishment for the reprobate. In contemporary illustrations, the scene, with its crushed bodies and fallen classical columns, resembles the carnage that Samson causes.[6] Indeed, a poem by Milton's friend Alexander Gill compared the collapse of the chapel with Samson's destruction of the Temple, as Leo Miller has noted.[7] It would have been much simpler for Milton to have represented the events of Judges 16 as a similar general punishment, and to celebrate it as the sort of providential disaster that God metes out, from time to time, to reprobates. Instead, as we have seen, Milton ties the account to precisely differentiated socio-political groups.

The priests, politicians and soldiers are not primarily my concern (though I shall have something further to say about them), and to the vulgar I shall return later. I want first to analyse Milton's perspective on the aristocracy. Though I shall not argue that the English Civil War was a bourgeois revolution, I shall nevertheless argue that Milton was a bourgeois revolutionary, that is a bourgeois and a revolutionary. He develops with remarkable consistency across a surprising range of texts social and cultural values that match the interests and preoccupations of the metropolitan financier class, inscribed in a suspicion of and hostility towards the inherited power of the provincial aristocracy.

That ideological predisposition is evident in the terms in which he praises puritan grandees Vane, Fairfax, and Cromwell. The first was the son of a Kentish middling gentry office-holder and politician rich enough to settle lands worth £3000 per annum on him at his marriage.[8] Milton's sonnet 'To Sir Henry Vane the Younger' makes nothing of the status and respectability of his birth. Indeed, the filial role is troped into a concluding compliment on his proper understanding of the separation of church and state: 'on thy firm hand Religion leans / In peace, and reckons thee her eldest son'.[9] The venerable figure of his father, Sir Henry Vane the elder, the ancestor of what must have seemed a significant puritan dynasty, is displaced by an allegorised figure representing radical protestantism, though he was still politically active and prominent among the most senior statesmen associated with the parliamentarian cause. Praise of the young Vane conspicuously rests on his own merits, not his family's.

The sonnet 'On the Lord General Fairfax at the seige of Colchester' contrasts very starkly with Marvell's 'Upon Appleton House'. In the latter, a long section, stanzas XI–XXXV, which has exhausted the patience of generations of undergraduates, celebrates, not the current incumbent, but a significant ancestor of the family which had come to own a considerable part of Yorkshire. None of that figures in Milton's poem, which straightforwardly praises his military accomplishment before adding that frankly such glory is worthless without probity in public life: 'In vain doth valour bleed / While avarice, and rapine share the land.'[10]

Cromwell's social position is more compromised than Vane's or Fairfax's. As John Morrill puts it,

> His economic and social standing was far more brittle than [the term country squire] implies: his reference to himself as being 'by birth a gentleman, living in neither any considerable height, nor yet in obscurity' takes on a tenser, more anxious patina. . . . Economic circumstances for much of his early manhood beckoned him to the yoke of husbandry; and political miscalculation seems nearly to have completed the task.[11]

Milton's sonnet 'To the Lord General Cromwell May 1652' styles him simply but ambiguously 'our chief of men', both leader of our men and first among socially undifferentiated 'men', and his success is attributed to faith and fortitude;[12] unlike Marvell's Fairfax, he is not genetically predisposed to military accomplishment.

To this significant silence on Cromwell's social status may be added Milton's response to James Butler, the marquis of Ormonde and royalist plenipotentiary in Ireland, in *Observations upon the Articles of Peace* (1649). Printed among the documents that Milton's polemic engages with is the letter from Ormonde to Michael Jones, the parliamentarian governor of Dublin, urging him to swap sides because the regicide government is led by anarchists, who intend:

to change the Monarchy of *England* into Anarchy, unlesse their aime bee first to constitute an elective Kingdome, and *Crumwell* or some such *John* of *Leiden* being elected.[13]

The John of Leyden topos, which surfaced first in Elizabethan and Jacobean anti-puritan writing, had recurred frequently in conservative polemic since the very early 1640s; it carries, of course, a social slur: John of Leyden, a leader of the Münsterian anabaptist commune of 1535, had been a tailor. This is how Milton responds:

The *changing* forsooth *of Monarchy into Anarchy*, sounds so like the smattering of some raw Polititian, and the overworne objection of every triviall talker, that wee leave him in the number. But seeing in that which followes he containes not himself, but contrary to what a Gentleman should know of Civility, proceeds to the contemptuous naming of a person, whose valour and high merit many enemies more noble than himself have both honour'd and feard, to assert his good name and reputation, of whose service the Common-wealth receaves so ample satisfaction, tis answerd in his behalf, that *Cromwell* whom he couples with a name of scorne, hath done in few yeares more eminent and remarkable Deeds whereon to *found* Nobility in his house, though it were wanting, and perpetuall Renown to posterity, then *Ormond* and all his Auncestors put together can shew from any record of thir *Irish* exploits, the widest scene of thir glory.[14]

Of course, the passage is polemically complex. In part it works to animate English disdain for Irish achievements (in this case, the Butler family's achievements in suppressing the native Irish). Ormonde may be able to trace his aristocratic status back to *circa* 1200, but it's still only the *Irish* peerage we're talking about. Moreover, Milton knows a social defence of sorts could be made. Cromwell's grandfather had a knighthood, and Thomas Cromwell, Earl of Essex, was a remote progenitor. Hence his phrase 'though it were wanting'. But he leaves this approach significantly undeveloped, evidently preferring to develop a contrast between the limited achievements of those who inherit power and the glorious deeds of those who acquire it through faith and fortitude. Milton associates his defence of Cromwell with a recurrent interest in constructing a puritan ruling class on principles other than wealth or ancestry, an issue to which I shall turn shortly. But note that, even in the fulsome and unlikeable panegyric that concludes *The Second Defence* (1654), he still praises Cromwell in terms of his humble origins. Indeed, he is related to Thomas Cromwell (who significantly is described primarily as a civil servant: 'celebrated in former times for good administration under the monarchy'[15]). Of course, he really is too glorious merely to be a king. But his is the career of a new kind of statesman. His initial achievements are modest and his military rank low, 'in command of a squadron of horse',[16] and his later prominence reflects a recognition akin to a democratic process in which his accomplishments bring a 'concourse of good men . . . to his standards from all sides'.[17] His military advancement is carefully juxtaposed with his civilian status, which rests upon his election to parliament through the informed choice of 'his town's electorate'.[18] Interestingly and significantly, for Milton shows no enthusiasm for the social operations and structures of the countryside, it is on this account an urban, rather than rural, context from which Cromwell springs.

Who then should govern England? In *Of Education* (1644), his curious excursion into educational theory, Milton engages persistently with the question. In place of a provincial aristocracy and a gentry class accustomed to power, he offers instead a new social formation distinguished by its education and its godliness. Power, of course, remains with the propertied. But that group is both reconfigured to incorporate men of Milton's class, and purged and disciplined by godly exercise, both spiritual and physical. The notion will recur in his asseveration in *The First Defence* (1651) that 'the middle class . . . produces the greatest number of men of good sense and knowledge of affairs'.[19] Perez Zagorin, who would see in this new ascendancy a sort of redefined aristocracy of merit, observes, I think correctly, that 'Milton was probably echoing Aristotle's opinion in the *Politics* that men neither too rich nor too poor make the best citizens'.[20] But he is arguing, too, from his own class position as a financier's son and senior civil servant, and, in a sense, living exemplar of the Aristotelian argument.

What Milton offers in *Of Education* is explicitly a social programme to produce a new ruling élite more godly and effective than that produced by current educational practices – as he says in the opening paragraph, 'for the want whereof this nation perishes'.[21] He is clear about the failures of the professional clergy, of lawyers, of politicians, and of those who do not accept civic responsibilities, who 'retire themselves . . . to the enjoyments of ease and luxury, living out their daies in feast and jollity'.[22] He castigates the officer cadre, those 'empty & unrecrutible Colonells' fiddling their muster rolls 'to quaffe out, or convay into secret hoards, the wages of a delusive list' (p. 412). Milton is addressing the issues of godly leadership, weighing in the balance the likes of Denzil Holles and the Earl of Manchester and finding them wanting. The products of his academy are to make up a new élite, to whom in time of war 'fair and hopefull armies' may be trusted. The whole text, in a way, constitutes a radical critique of the dominant group within the Long Parliament, of the new presbyterian church leadership and of the failures of a parliamentary army in dire need of new modelling. His educational model is not cheap: a staff-student ratio of 6:5; and he is decidedly vague about funding. Presumably what is wasted on Oxford and Cambridge will suffice. Who would be admitted? He's vague again; but evidently these are the sons of gentlemen, who learn together the theory and practice of civic duty. It is to be an urban, even a metropolitan process of social transformation: 'as many edifices may be converted to this use, as shall be needfull in every City throughout this land, which would tend much to the encrease of learning and civility'.[23] Again, as in his response to Ormonde, behind that term 'civility' lurks, etymologically, 'the citizen' as surely as, on Milton's own account in *A Masque Presented at Ludlow Castle*, 'the court' lurks behind 'courtesy'.[24] Yet here there is nothing pretended; how citizens treat each other and how they accept the responsibilities of civic life inform his vision of the new men who will lead a godly England.

Of course, it may seem unsurprising that Milton advocates civic control by a grouping defined by their godliness and education. But, as surely as Cromwell's leadership is validated by his godliness and fortitude, these civic virtues, central to the traditional self-image of the class from which Milton comes, are revolutionary and challenging to an early modern England in which many aspects of secular and ecclesiastical governance are invested in those distinguished by inherited wealth, status and power. As late as the second edition of *The Readie and Easie Way* Milton is talking about the role of godly education in securing appropriate leadership: 'To make the people fittest to chuse, and the chosen fittest to govern, will be to mend our corrupt and faulty education, to teach the people . . . not to admire wealth or honour'.[25]

So far my class analysis has, perhaps a little pusillanimously, concentrated on Milton's redefinition of a godly ruling élite to displace the *Ancien Régime* of aristocracy and gentry; but what about the working classes? Again, a Marxist Miltonist may help to initiate the discussion. In a widely cited article which appeared first in *Prose Studies*, Michael Wilding analyses this passage from *Areopagitica*:

> Yet these are the men cry'd out against for schismaticks and sectaries; as if, while the Temple of the Lord was building, some cutting, some squaring the marble,

> others hewing the cedars, there should be a sort of irrationall men who could not consider there must be many schisms and many dissections made in the quarry and in the timber, ere the house of God can be built. And when every stone is laid artfully together, it cannot be united into a continuity, it can but be contiguous in this world; neither can every peece of the building be of one form; nay rather the perfection consists in this, that out of many moderat varieties and brotherly dissimilitudes that are not vastly disproportionall arises the goodly and the gracefull symmetry that commends the whole pile and structure.[26]

In an analysis of extraordinary lyrical power, Wilding comments:

> The class implications are unmistakable. . . . it is not aristocrats or bishops or business men who take things 'into their own hands': there is a powerful respect here for manual labourers. This is made quite explicit in the unambiguously mechanical trades that are specified in the building of temple; people are shown cutting, squaring, hewing. These are all manual activities; there is 'spiritual architecture' . . . but no architect, only 'builders'. . . The physical labours of the common people are here properly presented as dignified, noble, beautiful.
>
> The appropriateness of such analogies from physical labour, from working with one's hands, to defend the sects, composed in large part from the working classes, is yet another denial of that asserted Miltonic élitism. That the manual labour of the lower class sects is presented as beautiful makes clear Milton's sympathies. It is not only the radical ideas of the sects that he defends, but the social composition of the sects that he glorifies.[27]

Wilding's account, itself an eloquent celebration of a radical social vision, is locally very persuasive, but has seemed always open to powerful counter-arguments drawing on other, approximately contemporary parts of the prose oeuvre.

Most significantly, in the pamphlet Milton published less than six months later, the unlovely *Colasterion*, he incorporates into meeting an attack on his first divorce tract an extended class-sneer against his adversary, apparently – and 'none will guess him lower' – 'an actual Serving-man', though now turned lawyer.[28] When his adversary raises the perfectly reasonable point that divorces may leave a legacy of unborn children conceived before the separation, Milton observes 'good news for Chamber-maids, to hear a Serving-man grown so provident for great bellies'.[29] Miltonists, of course, have felt constrained to extenuate. Most recently, Barbara Lewalski in her new biography observes, that at issue 'is not class as such, but those qualities of mind that should accompany birth and station'.[30] But the implication of the tract is generalising, asserting that serving men may not debate the divorce issue with

Milton: 'this is not for an unbutton'd fellow to discuss in the Garret, at his tressle'.[31] The conclusion seems irresistible, that Milton, like Shakespeare's Coriolanus, is 'a very dog to the commonalty'.

And yet a number of points may be made which indicate that Wilding's judgement may be sounder than conclusions based on taking *Colasterion* at face value. Firstly, the builders of *Areopagitica* would have been artisans, tradesmen, among them no doubt petty masters at the lower end of what social historians now identify as 'the middling sort', not servants, who are seen as constituting an underclass of extreme dependency, even by Levellers. (And I should add that the term 'servant' remains a vexed one among political and social historians.) As *The Agreement of the Free People of England* (1649) puts it, the supreme authority of England should be determined by an electorate of 'all men of the age of one and twenty yeers and upwards (not being servants, or receiving alms, or having served the late King in Arms or voluntary Contributions'.[32] Dependency is disfranchising, and perhaps Milton in his own social assumptions anticipates this distinction. In the English class system, with its infinite gradations of social distinction, it is possible to be contemptuous of servants and yet a radical, to admire the man who mends one's roof while despising the man who empties one's chamber pot.

Secondly, there are obvious polemical advantages in the strategy assumed in *Colasterion*. It allows Milton to set up a social equation between himself and the reader, while excluding the adversary as an interloper. It asserts Milton's own respectability while devaluing the other by the dominant social standards of the day. The tactic is a common one, and indeed the Leveller Richard Overton plays the same card in 1649 against his arresting officer, Colonel Axtell: 'Surely the Lieutenant Collonel at that instant had forgot the Bugget from whence he dropt, I presume when he was pedler in Harford-shire he had not so lofty an esteem of himself.'[33]

Thirdly, the sheer gratuitousness of the *Areopagitica* celebration implies a sort of radical sincerity. In the imagery of political prose, we tend to trust the values expressed in the vehicles rather more than in the tenors.

Finally, it confirms a position Milton must, in the logic of his developing religious theory, feel constrained to hold. Radical Arminianism is premised on the assumption that salvation requires positive choice by each individual, an act of commitment that is necessary though not sufficient to ensure personal salvation. In this it is unlike ceremonial Arminianism on the Laudian pattern, which requires the individual to follow the guidance of church and state. And it differs from Calvinist soteriology, which presumes that the individual who is predestinately saved will choose to behave well, while the reprobate may do nothing to secure redemption. Everybody must be able to make a personal and individual choice that has nothing to do with levels of wealth, power, culture or education – or indeed, with gender. While individuals may well be incapable of disputing about divorce, justice would not be served if they are not capable of making those choices and commitments that lead to salvation.

Thus it is that, certainly as early as *The Reason of Church-Government* (1642), Milton acknowledges the rights and obligations of individuals to follow their consciences in matters of faith, even though that may produce sects which may be represented in opprobrious terms: 'Noise it till ye be hoarse; that a rabble of Sects will come in, it will be answer'd ye, no rabble sir Priest, but a unanimous multitude of good Protestants.'[34] In *Colasterion* he carefully repeats a point made in the closing pamphlets of his antiprelatical campaign, that working men may at an appropriate level exercise their faith according to their consciences and give expression to those beliefs. Indeed, he distinguishes the cultural over-reaching of his adversary from the example of plain, working men writing and speaking according to their inner light: 'Nor was the stile flat and rude, and the matter grave and solid, for then ther had bin pardon.'[35]

Though the ecstatic vision of *Areopagitica* is never recaptured, Milton's position emerges more clearly in his tracts of 1659, *Of Civil Power* and *Means to Remove Hirelings*. By then his anticlericalism had eroded any remaining respect for a learned ministry, and simple men, prompted by the spirit within, may make good preachers. Indeed, poverty confirms their true succession to the apostles and to Christ. He takes up a point made many times by radical sectaries, and extends it to a reflection on the history of the Reformation: 'They who after [Christ] first taught [the gospel], were . . . unlearned men: they who before *Hus* and *Luther* first reformd it, were for the meanenes of thir condition calld, *the poore men of Lions*',[36] and again, 'we may be well assur'd that he who disdaind not to be laid in a manger, disdains not to be preachd in a barn'.[37]

Milton's respect for the rights of conscience of the working classes reflects his beliefs in personal freedom and responsibility and his hatred of a professional clergy oppressing the operation and expression of inner illumination. (No wonder that 'priests' are specifically listed among the Philistine dead.) On some issues, such sympathy for the rights of all citizens places him on the extremer edges of Revolutionary Independency, the political grouping to which he belonged. Perhaps something other than indisposition caused him not to discharge the Council of State's first order to him, to refute a Leveller attack by John Lilburne.[38]

The late poems are replete with those same radical values. Samson, arguably, both embodies the godliness and fortitude of Milton's new men and a Spartacist defiance, for his action, after all, is a slave's revolt. More significant, however, are the perspectives developed in the two epics. In *Paradise Lost* Adam and Eve most surely dig, even if they don't spin, before the Fall. Or at least, they cultivate the garden purposefully to optimise its productivity. Indeed, Eve, still unfallen and acting like a constructive and innovative member of a workers' cooperative, anticipates the arguments for the division of labour in a speech that urges 'Let us divide our labours'.[39] What distinguishes labour after the fall from prelapsarian labour is its lack of optionality: who works may eat. But Adam responds to the curse placed on him with an assertion of the dignity of labour:

> with labour I must earn
> My bread; what harm? Idleness had been worse;
> My labour will sustain me . . .[40]

Sir Robert Filmer may suggest that Adam is the progenitor of kings; Milton demonstrates that a pair of agricultural labourers are the progenitors of us all.

In *Paradise Regained* a challenging social perspective emerges strongly. The values and priorities recapture those of Milton's tracts of 1659. Persistently, Satan reminds the Son of how wealth drives contemporary society:

> Get riches first, get wealth, and treasure heap,
> Not difficult, if thou hearken to me,
> Riches are mine, fortune is in my hand;
> They whom I favour thrive in wealth amain,
> While virtue, valour, wisdom sit in want.[41]

Recollections of the Restoration prosperity of the likes of Albemarle may cross the minds of old revolutionaries on reading those lines. In contrast, Satan reminds the Son of his poverty and obscurity:

> Great acts require great means of enterprise,
> Thou art unknown, unfriended, low of birth,
> A carpenter thy father known, thyself
> Bred up in poverty and straits at home;
> Lost in a desert here and hunger-bit . . .[42]

Throughout the poem, poverty is the badge of probity, and the Son's rejections of wealth, of military power, and of political distinction reiterate the radical critique of the old order implicit, for example, in *Of Education*. Milton, seeing in the Son a final paradigm of his new man, rejects a restored Stuart ascendancy that has learnt nothing and forgotten nothing. The poem ends with its hero's withdrawal to the house of his mother, but it looks forward, too, to the completion of his mission and beyond that to the apostolic age and the role of all godly wayfarers in a fallen world. Already, a cell is forming:

> Where winds with reeds, and osiers whisp'ring play
> Plain fishermen, no greater men them call,
> Close in a cottage low together got . . .[43]

Note the characteristic emphasis of that parenthesis, like a finger poked in the reader's ribs: 'no greater men them call'.

Milton offers no sustained analysis of the class system of his own age, nor does he engage directly with the politics of social transformation. Yet his writing is replete with class values and assumptions, which evolve but which are always challenging to the fiercely hierarchical society into which he was born. His advocacy of the formation through godliness, fortitude and education of a new élite to govern a newly reformed England constitutes a sustained critique of inherited power and status from a metropolitan and bourgeois perspective. But his soteriology allows that salvation stands open to all who choose to cooperate with a grace that is extended to all – without the agencies of church or state; necessarily that acknowledges the rights and freedoms of all classes, conceding, in the phrase of the Leveller Colonel Thomas Rainborough, that 'the poorest he that is in England hath a life to live'.[44] Milton's last heroes are the son of a carpenter's wife and the fishermen who follow him.

NOTES

1. John Milton, *Complete Shorter Poems*, 2nd edn. John Carey (Longman, London and New York, 1997) (hereafter *CSP*), p. 410, lines 1648–59.
2. Milton and ClassJohn Milton, *The Complete Poems*, ed. B.A. Wright, with notes and introduction by Gordon Campbell (Dent, and Dutton, London, Melbourne, Toronto and New York, 1980), p. 606.
3. For a review of the arguments, see *CSP*, pp. 349–50.
4. Christopher Hill, *The Experience of Defeat: Milton and Some Contemporaries* (Faber, London, 1984), pp. 314–15.
5. See, especially, *Paradise Regained*, II. 433–86, III. 43–108, 121–44, 386–440, *CSP*, pp. 461–3, 465–7, 468–9, 480–2.
6. See Alexandra Walsham, '"Fatal Vespers": Providentialism and Anti-Popery in Late Jacobean London', *Past and Present* CXLIV (1994), 36–87.
7. Leo Miller, 'On Some Verses by Alexander Gil which John Milton Read', *Milton Quarterly* XXIV(1990), 22–5.
8. *Dictionary of National Biography*, s.n. Sir Henry Vane.
9. Lines 13–14, *CSP*, p. 331.
10. Lines 13–14, *CSP*, p. 325.
11. John Morrill, *The Nature of the English Revolution* (Longman, London and New York, 1993), p. 123.
12. Lines 1. 3, *CSP*, p. 328.
13. *Complete Prose Works of John Milton*, ed. Don M. Wolfe et al. (Yale University Press, New Haven, 1953–82), III, 292 (hereafter *CPW*).
14. *CPW*, III, 312.
15. *CPW*, IV.i, 666.
16. *CPW*, IV.i, 667.
17. *CPW*, IV.i, 667.
18. *CPW*, IV.i, 667.
19. *CPW*, IV.i, 471; see, also, *CPW*, IV.i, 319.
20. Perez Zagorin, *Milton Aristocrat Rebel: The Poet and his Politics* (Brewer, Rochester, New York, and Woodbridge, Suffolk, 1992), p. 85.
21. *CPW*, II, 363.
22. *CPW*, II, 375–6.
23. *CPW*, II, 380–1.
24. Lines 321–5, *CSP*, p. 196.
25. *CPW*, VII, 443.
26. *CPW*, II, 555.
27. Michael Wilding, 'Milton's *Areopagitica*: Liberty for the Sects', *Prose Studies* IX, 2 (1986), 7–38 (pp. 16–17).
28. *CPW*, II, 726.
29. *CPW*, II, 734; on contemporary concerns about serving men debauching and impregnating women servants, see David Cressy, *Birth, Marriage, and Death: Ritual, Religion, and the Life-Cycle in Tudor and Stuart England* (1997; Oxford University Press, Oxford, 1999), p. 74.

30. Barbara K. Lewalski, *The Life of John Milton* (Blackwell, Oxford and Malden, 2000), p. 183.
31. *CPW*, II, 746.
32. John Lilburne, William Walwyn, Thomas Prince and Richard Overton, *An Agreement of the Free People of England*, in A.L. Morton, ed., *Freedom in Arms: A Selection of Leveller Writings* (Lawrence and Wishard, London, 1975), p. 268.
33. Richard Overton, *The Proceedings of the Councel of State against Richard Overton*, in Morton, *Freedom in Arms*, p. 204; interestingly, Morton cautions that Colonel Axtel 'was not of quite such humble origins as is here suggested' (p. 195).
34. *CPW*, I, 787–8.
35. *CPW*, II, 725.
36. *CPW*, VII, 302.
37. *CPW*, VII, 304–5.
38. See Lewalski, *Life*, p. 240, who shares this surmise.
39. John Milton, *Paradise Lost*, ed. Alastair Fowler, 2nd. edn. (Longman, London and New York, 1998), IX. 214, p. 481 (hereafter *PL*).
40. *PL*, X. 1054–6, pp. 595.
41. Lines 427–31, *CSP*, p. 460.
42. Lines 412–16, *CSP*, p. 460.
43. Lines 26–8, *CSP*, p. 445.
44. 'The Putney Debates', in *Puritanism and Liberty, Being the Army Debates (1647–49) from the Clarke Manuscripts*, ed. A.S.P. Woodhouse, 3rd edn. (Dent, London and Melbourne, 1986), p. 53.

Changeling Epithets

Robert Cummings

'Changeling' is Puttenham's word in the *Arte of Poesie* for the figure whose Greek name he thinks is *hypallage*, *submutatio* in Latin, in English the 'underchange'. 'Hypallage' is the figure in use, say the mid-seventeenth-century editions of *Riders Dictionarie* 'when the words are understood contrariwise'. It is neatly defined in Johnson's *Dictionary* as a figure 'by which words change their cases, tenses, or relations with each other'. Johnson gives no examples. Webster's *Dictionary* defines it much as Johnson does, but then gives the ludicrously opaque example: 'You are lost to joy' for 'Joy is lost to you'. It's based no doubt on a standard grammar book example (and the *OED*'s example), which comes from Servius, who explains Virgil's *dare classibus austros* ('to give the winds to the fleet') as a hypallage for *dare classes austris* ('to give the fleet to the winds'). In Latin this can be understood simply as an exchange of the dative and accusative case endings. But in English the rhetorical character of the exchange is less transparent, and it looks more like a mistake than a figure of speech – we can't in English justify words ending up in the wrong place as the result of something like a grammatical slip. The only place we're likely to recognise the confusion as figurative is the case of the so-called 'transferred epithet'. But the history of that term is surprisingly short (*OED* gives 1866 as the date of the first use), we can't confidently identify what we mean by it, and its use is problematic. Despite the incomprehension, there is evidently a pressure to make available in English this liberty of misplacing epithets, enjoyed in Latin and Greek.

I begin, however, with an outright rejection of the figure. When Cadmus sowed the dragon's teeth in *Metamorphoses* III, there emerged from his newly ploughed furrows a succession of spears, plumed helmets, shoulders, torsos, hands laden with weaponry – there grew, says Ovid, *seges clipeata virorum*. This is not a particularly easy expression in Latin, but in English 'shielded cornfield of heroes' is absurd. What in

Latin may be only a matter of exchanged inflexions – a prettiness – is necessarily in English a matter of exchanged properties. English translators accommodate the difficulty in different ways. Golding's 1565 version tries to mitigate the effect: 'Thus grew up men like corn in field in ranks of battle ray / With shields and weapons in their hands to fight the field that day.' That these soldiers are in any sense like corn is safely bracketed in a simile. Sandys's 1626 version decides to cancel the effect altogether: 'And target-bearing troops of men up-grew'. We get no corn at all. Addison's 1717 version gives us: 'O'er all the field the breathing harvest swarms, / A growing host, a crop of men and arms'. He relaxes the conceit. The harvest can breathe, the host can grow, to prepare for an almost embarrassed 'crop of men and arms'. The shields have vanished. In the notes to his translation Addison observes of the Ovidian phrasing that 'The beauty in these words would have been greater, had only *Messis* [for *seges*] *virorum* been expressed without *clypeata*.' The two different ideas of crops and men would have delighted us enough, the attempt to yoke those two with the notion of shields is excessive and distracting. We 'can scarce attend to such a complete image as is made out of all three' – the crop, the shields, the men.

Bentley, who presumably decodes the figure to get the intended seges *clipeatorum virorum*, affects surprise that Addison should have taken exception to a figure which had already been used in this very context by Euripides, 'a golden-helmed crop of Sown-men'. But the precedent would not have weighed much with Addison, who knew that whatever the Greeks did, Latin poets were full of it, 'especially the worst of them'. He knew well enough too that while it might be 'a great beauty in poetry' it was so only 'if there be sufficient ground for it in the nature of the thing that is described'. He wanted to be able to take literally the expression 'shielded corn', or at least he wanted the possibility of an imaginative association, not a merely grammatical one, between 'shields' and 'corn'. The fault for him was in the quirkiness of the association: 'When any thing we describe has accidentally in it some quality that seems repugnant to its nature, or is very extraordinary and uncommon in things of that species, such a compounded image as we are now speaking of is made, by turning this quality into an epithet of what we describe'. Virgil on the other hand, as with his *auri frondentis* – the 'leafy gold' – of Aeneas's Golden Bough, can happily graft novel circumstances on to alien stock. In Virgil, such things are surprising, but they are imaginatively ratifiable. The source of Addison's complaint is the sense of an imaginative dead-end in the mechanically witty deployment of improbable associations, of 'rhetoric' in the bad sense. Virgil, he says, 'loves to suggest a truth indirectly . . . to let us see just so much as will naturally lead the imagination into all the parts that lie concealed'. Ovid, he feels, is witty at the expense of imaginative integrity, and for something truly novel gives us a merely ludic substitute.

Addison's objection to Ovid's 'shielded cornfield of heroes' comes from his obtuseness to a rhetoric that might have made irrelevant the pictorial excess he complains about. But an imaginative misdirection suggested by the grammar may take readers where they are delighted to follow, and sometimes it may not be desirable to sort out an image by invoking a mere figure of speech. Latin poetry habitually makes a game of gesturing to alternative possibilities in the combinations of words, and sometimes the gestures go beyond game. Horace commends the *callida iunctura* – the 'artful positioning' – that re-energises ordinary words. So, in Macrobius's *Saturnali*, Servius is represented as commending Virgil's *tepidaque recentem / Caede locum* ('fresh with warm slaughter the ground') as exhibiting a special Virgilian grace. When he comes on the lines in his great commentary he concedes the existence of an emended form, *tepidumque recenti / Caede locum* ('warm with fresh slaughter the ground'). This more cautious placing gives the sense, and cancels the surprise. Servius prefers the riskier reading, which does of course leave the suggestion of the common sense reading, and the fragility of the daring is presumably part of the point. The words are the same and their order is the same. The surprise in Virgil's line is not in the order of words, which is conventional for poetry, but in their application, carried by the inflexions – with the force of *recens* shockingly jerked towards 'renewed' or some such expression. There's no accepted way of dealing with this in English. There is an impressive neatness to Joseph Trapp's solution: 'The recent slaughter and the reeking ground'. The hypallage is corrected (though 'reeking' nicely echoes '*recentem*') but the pretended pattern of subordination is abandoned, so preserving the uncertain relation of the components. This vagueness, which I'll come back to, conforms with English prejudices about what poetry should do at least as much as imaginative vividness.

It is a feature of Virgil's style in particular that adjectives operate in uncertain relation to their contexts: the grammar pulls them into one relation, but they have a habit of wanting to be elsewhere. So famously in *Aeneid* II the Greek ships approach Troy from Tenedos *tacitae per amica silentia lunae* – 'through the friendly silences of the noiseless moon'. Explanations are various for the 'noiseless moon'. But the mutual attraction of the noiselessness and the silence (as if it were *tacita silentia*) overwhelms the grammar. Or it may do. In any case, Virgil's sixteenth-century translator Thomas Phaer unravels the pattern in just this way and redistributes the epithets, 'full friendly shone the Moon / In silence great'. Phaer makes sense of the line by cancelling the 'artful positioning'. He misreads in order to make easy sense; but we may misread in order to maximise the possibilities of meaning. In *Aeneid* VI, as Aeneas watches the pageant of Roman history unfold in the underworld, Augustus's heir Marcellus appears, *Sed nox atra caput tristi circumvolat umbrâ* ('But black night with its sad shade hovers round his head'). Here the 'head' of the doomed Marcellus has been admitted to an otherwise only slightly rewritten line from Book II (*nox atra cavâ circumvolat umbrâ*), so that it appears surrounded by 'black' and 'sad', adjectives which do not grammatically qualify it, but which as John Hollander says, seem to qualify it metaphorically. Latin verse can produce 'phantom images', he says, by way of syntactically irrelevant juxtapositions. Phaer's version catches the 'phantom image' perhaps by accident, 'But cloud of louring night his head full heavy wraps about'. To approximate the grammatical sense of the Latin, 'full heavy' should be given adverbial status (how the cloud wraps the head), but it is certainly more natural to take it as adjectival, and suppose that the heaviness is the head's.

Translators who work in response to these phantoms are often castigated. Pound's translation of Propertius's *Coi sacra Philetae* ('rites of Coan Philetas') as 'Coan ghosts of Philetas' is a much visited case. It's easy to find other examples in the *Homage*: *fera Galatea sub Aetna* ('Galatea beneath harsh Etna') becomes 'harsh Galatea . . . under Aetna', *molli recubans Heliconis in umbrâ* ('lying in the soft shade of Helicon') becomes 'in the shade, recumbant on cushioned Helicon'. And this is not a novel crime. Phaer is commonly guilty of it in his version of the *Aeneid*. Gavin Douglas in his version transfers epithets to neighbouring nouns with great frequency, because the new combinations are readier rhythmically or because they are pictorially more compelling. So *atri ianua Ditis* is translated as 'the blak yettis of Pluto', or *magna Iovis coniunx* as 'the spous of gret Iuppiter'. A similar low-level opportunism motivates Milton to reassemble Virgil's *stridenti miserum stipula disperdere carmen* ('spoil a wretched song on a scrannel straw') as 'Grate on their scrannel pipes of wretched straw' – as if *miserum stipula* were a sense-unit. Some examples are less trivial. Virgil writes *nebulaque ingens specus aestuat atra*, and Douglas writes 'With huge sop of reyk and flambis myrk, / So that the caif did glevyn of the heyt'. He does so because he wants our attention on the bulk of the smoke rather than the scale of the cave. Virgil writes *campi ingentes ossibus albent* and Douglas writes 'of our huge banys quhite semys the plane' because he wants the bones of those whose blood made the Tiber hot to be heroically large. Some of Douglas's confusions are probably culpable. But sometimes the transfers seem to result from a reimagination of what Virgil wrote, using the material to hand but deploying the words to different effect.

Douglas's transfers are opportunistic, Pound's are systematic. They are sometimes defended on the grounds that they preserve the original word order. John Sullivan rejects this defence because, he says, the belief seems implicit in it 'that the close association by position of an adjective, say, with a noun not grammatically connected with it, infects that noun with certain associations of the adjective'. His rebuttal of it brings in Milton's version of Horace's Pyrrha ode – where Milton simulates 'as near as the Language will permit' Horace's artful arrangement of emphases – to demonstrate that adjectives 'do not affect the connotation of nearby words simply through juxtaposition'. Not 'simply' perhaps, but the argument is strange, for English normally works precisely though infection by juxtaposition, and Milton's English – as in 'Who now enjoys thee, credulous, all gold' is, by virtue of our reliance on mere juxtaposition, unintelligible without recourse to the Latin. And Milton's wilful dislocations or relocations of his epithets make up a large part of what we call 'Miltonic'. The motives are various, its consequence, along with a sense of deliberation, is a degree of ambiguity as to where epithets actually belong, or even whether or not they are epithets. The results are not always in all views happy.

Milton typically ignores the rules that govern the placing of English adjectives, separating them from the nouns they qualify. He liberates the epithet from its grammar. A like impulse, *mutatis mutandis*, drives what looks like opportunistic misreading of Latin. That is, it looks as if Milton allows grammatically irrelevant juxtapositions to yield a sense which can be entertained as an alternative to the one supplied by the grammar. Here and there in Milton, and elsewhere in seventeenth-century writing, 'phantom images' surface, derived from grammatical misconstructions of sequences of Latin nouns and adjectives. The rendering 'scrannel pipes of wretched straw' is one case, but it is euphony rather than any phantom image that has determined the order. On the other hand when in *Il Penseroso* Orpheus is daringly made to draw 'iron tears' down Pluto's cheek we may suppose that the transfer of the epithet (which we all recognise) is suggested by the ungrammatical juxtaposition of *duri lacrimas* in Lucan's *mala duri lacrimas motura Catonis* ('sorrows to draw tears from iron Cato'). That is, it may be that Milton has taken advantage of an accident in Lucan's line, and that his own line begins with a conceit of 'iron tears' imaginatively deeper than the mere transfer of epithets. Take another example. When Aeneas lands on the North African coast in *Aeneid* I, it is at a bay sheltered by shadowing rocks and woods – *tum silvis scaena coruscis*: there is a 'scene' a background such as were built in Roman theatres – with trembling woods. Phaer struggles with this ('greene wood like a garland growes'), but Dryden writes 'a silvan scene/ Appears, and groves for ever green' and Trapp follows him 'a trembling silvan scene'. They owe the solution to Milton, who had already re-imagined Satan's entry into Eden as on to a 'silvan scene, and as the ranks ascend / Shade above shade, a woody theatre'. It echoes the Virgilian line – at least it echoes *silvis scaena*, as the editors say – but in a dismantled or ungrammaticised form, and makes an ellipsis, its daring now lost, of 'wood' and 'scene' that Virgil did not risk.

Examples of this deforming echo can be multiplied – not readily, for they are not designed to be discovered at all, but without great strain. In *Paradise Lost* Milton writes that on the fifth day of creation 'the tepid caves, and fens and shores / Their brood as numerous hatch'. 'Tepid' suggests liquid, and so suggests womb-like moisture in these fertile caves or fens or shores. This is by no means an inapposite epithet for 'caves', but it would not have been a ready one had Virgil not already described in *Georgics* I the autumn rain flooding the irrigation ditches so that 'the hollow trenches sweat with warm moisture' – *unde cavae tepido sudant humore lacunae*. The hollowness, the warmth, and the sweat have come together in Milton's mind, and he has found in the grammatically nonsensical *cavae tepido* a formula for that conjunction, apt for his account of marine creation. One example from the Ludlow *Masque* is regularly noticed. The Spirit warns the Brothers that Comus and his monstrous rout can be heard howling like 'stabled wolves'. This is a hard notion. Milton, the editors say, is remembering or mis-remembering Virgil's *triste lupus stabulis* in *Eclogues* 3, ('The nightly wolf is baneful to the fold', in Dryden's version – 'nightly' is his addition). In *Aeneid* VI Virgil 'stables' beasts in the forest, and he 'stables' centaurs and scyllas at the gates of hell, just as Milton stables sea-monsters in drowned palaces in *Paradise Lost* XI. But Virgil does not 'stable' wolves where they do not belong: he juxtaposes the wolf and the fold, but in opposition. In Milton the juxtaposition is read, not simply as if the wolves had noisily and triumphantly intruded into the fold, but as if they were at home in the fold they had spoiled. There is another example later in the *Masque*. When tempting the Lady, Comus argues that an unexploited abundance of wild-fowl would make 'the winged air darked with plumes' – a phrase we could unpick, if we were inclined to, as 'the air dark with feathered wings'. But the 'winged air' already suggests itself in Ovid's description (in *Fasti* III) of how the sun *alatis aethera . . . carpit equis*. The sense is that the sun takes to the air with his 'winged steeds', but the Latin has juxtaposed the alliterating but otherwise unrelated words for 'winged' and 'air'.

Marvell's 'green thought in a green shade' (in *The Garden*) may or may not owe something to 'green pleasures of a meadow' in Euripides's *Bacchae*. Probably it owes nothing. But the 'green shade' itself – and his 'green night' in *Bermudas* – is generally reckoned to derive from Virgil. The 'misreading' is not Marvell's here, but a straight translation of Virgil's own. In *Eclogues* 9 one singing shepherd tells another that, had he died, there would be no one to strew the earth with flowering grasses or 'cover the springs with green shade' (*viridi fontes induceret umbrâ*). Coloured shadow is observable, but seems not to have been a feature of poetry before this. Virgil is abnormally interested in the interactions of shadow with what it falls on or what it falls from. The 'trembling woods' that supply the 'silvan scene' already visited make 'a dark grove with bristling shadow' (*horrentique atrum nemus . . . umbrâ*); but it is the grove that should bristle, it is the shadow that should be dark – but Virgil's *horrens umbra* is the ancestor of Milton's 'horrid shade', now a cliché. The *umbra viridis* in Eclogue 9 comes from Virgil's 'misreading' of his own line in Eclogue 7: a shepherd asks the mossy springs and the soft grass to sustain his flock in the noon heat, those 'and the green strawberry-tree that covers you with its scant shade' (*et quae vos rarâ viridis tegit arbutus umbrâ*). It is the tree that is green and the shade that is scant; but the ideas of scant and green, close together here and distinguished grammatically only by the vowel length of *rarâ*, easily float free of their grammatical moorings and reattach themselves to the alternative nouns. Marvell does not invent 'green shade'. But he invents 'gelid strawberries'. When in *Appleton House* (stanza 67) he writes how 'I careless on the bed / Of gelid strawberries do tread', we are no doubt meant to recognise the chill of the fruit, growing low in shade, but the designation remains extraordinary. The phrase is, as it were, a gift from Virgil's third Eclogue, *Qui legitis flores et humi nascentia fraga, / frigidus, O pueri, fugite hinc, latet anguis in herba* (in Abraham Fleming's version: 'O pretty boys which gather flowers and *strawberries* also, / Creeping or growing on the ground, hence get you fast away, / For in the grass doth lurk a snake whose poison is full cold'). Virgil's snake is chill, as snakes conventionally are, and his strawberries grow from the earth; but Marvell's strawberries are chill ('gelid' like spring-water) and the snakes have vanished altogether, only reappearing in the serpentine motion of the Wharfe, 'Among these meads the only snake' (stanza 79). The ungrammatical but alliterating juxtaposition *fraga / frigidus* suggests Marvell's combination. 'Green shade' and 'gelid strawberries' are lucky finds of a momentarily ungrammatical Latinity, one Virgil's and one Marvell's. I suspect that Time's iconographically surprising 'winged chariot' in *To his Coy Mistress* has a similar origin.

Faced with examples of mismatched noun and adjective, readers have a choice. They may disengage epithets from what they qualify grammatically – generally because they allow a stronger semantic attraction between themselves and neighbouring alternatives; or they may preserve the grammatical relation of substantive and epithet and rationalise what they feel is a semantic anomaly. What motivates one choice rather than another will vary. The complications can be illustrated from a famous case, again from Virgil – the case taken by John Minsheu in his 1617 *Guide to Tongues* to illustrate the figure 'hypallage'. In *Aeneid* VI Aeneas follows the Cumaean Sibyl, at speed, into a deep cave that leads to the underworld – and suddenly, says Virgil, *ibant obscuri sola sub nocte per umbram* ('they were going dark under the lone night through the shadow'). The line says three times that it is dark: *obscuri*, *nocte*, *umbram*. But quite what is dark is not clear. The dark and the loneliness are welded together by an interchange of attributes. The walkers are dark, Virgil says, and the night is alone – 'black night', he says as the simile continues, 'that withdraws colour from things'. We know already, and almost every commentary on the line tells us, that the night must be dark, and that it is the walkers who are alone.

So many translators give it, and they do so at least partly because they don't see the point of the figure as anything more than accidentally related to things in the world. They see it as a rhetorical trick, which it is either not possible or not desirable to reproduce. That explicitly paraphrasing versions like Dryden's, should do so is unsurprising. But it is striking that those with pretensions to literalism should. Joseph Trapp's version, despite being what Johnson calls 'the clandestine refuge of schoolboys', renders the line as 'Lonely they went, in night obscure, thro' shades'. It was published in 1718, the year after Addison's complaint about Cadmus's 'shielded cornfield of heroes', and Trapp may be avoiding what he thinks of as an objectionable conceit. Or he may be avoiding what he regards as irreproducible in English. He is commonly ready with such stuff as 'We *feel* that elegant expression in the Latin; but it is impossible to render it in English'. Another anomaly is Robert Andrews, whose strange and strangely neglected blank verse translation of 1766 – beautifully printed by Baskerville – advertises its intentions of translating line by line and lays about those translators who 'give only the word implied' and fail to attend precisely to what the original says. The 'word implied' is what is picked up from prose commentary, the decoded version of a figurative original. Yet Andrews's ostentatiously peculiar version refuses the figure.

At least as early as Joseph Davidson's 1743 prose version, translated 'as near the original as the different idioms of the Latin and English languages will allow', the different idioms of Latin and English were held to allow a version somewhat closer: 'Darkling they travelled under the solitary night through the shade'. Here, Aeneas and the Sibyl are obscure and the night is alone – or by the surreptitious glossing habit he adopts, 'solitary'. But 'darkling' is stylistically easier than *obscuri*. When Davidson writes 'darkling they travelled' the surprise is mitigated because we're not committed to supposing that 'darkling' qualifies the travellers. We can suppose instead that it's an adverb 'in the dark', with an only potential adjectival competence, rather as 'full heavy' operates ambiguously in the line from Phaer quoted earlier. The position of 'darkling' in Davidson's sentence suggests it's an adjective, but its sense is supplied by its adverbial function: they are travelling *in* the dark. This glossing habit is common more or less to all the translators, mainly or exclusively modern, who preserve the sense of the transferred form. Even in William Morris's relatively uncompromised 'All dim amid the lonely night on through the dusk they went', 'all dim' allows the adverbial 'all' to infect the adjective 'dim'.

This bargaining with the grammar damages the already imperfect symmetry of Virgil's original relation between the humans and the dark, between the night and loneliness. Sometimes and more radically, it is altogether disposed of. This is done mainly by suppressing one or more of the components. There is no night in Gavin Douglas, and no loneliness: 'Thai walking furth sa dyrk, oneth thai wyst / Quhidder thai went, amyd dym schaddowys thar'. Neither is there in Dryden: 'Obscure they went through dreary shades'; nor in Christopher Pitt: 'Now through the dismal gloom they pass'. Night is here supposed from its being dark (either the travellers cannot see their way, or they cannot be seen); the loneliness is translated into bewilderment or dreariness or dismalness. Sometimes the loneliness is only implicit. In John Vicars's 1632 version, it's suggested in a loss of materiality and motive: 'Then in dark night, black shades, they ramble round'. Sometimes the obscurity of the humans is only implicit. Phaer cancels the dark and supplies silence (its auditory analogue): 'They walking went in night alone, in silence through the shade'. Bridges' 'They wer' amid the shadows by night in loneliness obscure' keeps all the relevant components – the walkers, the dark, the night, the loneliness – but he shuffles their relations: so that now it is loneliness that is obscure, not the walkers, and not the night.

One might suppose that this free variation from a difficult original, the common procedure over a history of four centuries, would be in the interests of smoothing out. But it is manifestly not. Whereas the strangeness in those translators who observe Virgil's grammar is generally mitigated by playing down the symmetry – mainly by adverbialising the dark – some at least of those who abandon the symmetry altogether energise the oddity of their versions by a perverse kind of literalism. Douglas cancels the night, but writes 'They walking furth sae dark', clinging to Virgil's order, to his peculiar imperfect tense, and in what should in English be an adverbial position a firmly adjectival form. Dryden cancels the night, but writes 'Obscure they went', clinging to Virgil's word and forcing it into an adjectival position where it hangs uncomfortably, not sure where to go. None of the paraphrases I've quoted or could quote are unpeculiar. That is, they all signal an anomaly. However differently they deal with it, they all register a response to some mystery in the original.

It seems that the predispositions of English poets, and maybe the constitution of the English language, encourage resistance to the Virgilian formula, or at least distrust of it. And it seems the case that the available English equivalents of the Latin transferred epithet function in a different way: re-reordering words strikes us by and large not as artful but mysterious. In Latin it perhaps typically would not. When Servius prefers the reading of *tepidâque recentem / Caede locum* to *tepidumque recenti / Caede locum* – the reading which preserves the hypallage – he congratulates Virgil on a novelty of expression. But the opposite happens when he says of *ibant oscuri sola sub nocte* that 'it is either a hypallage to be decoded as "under the dark night alone they went," or "under the lonely night" could mean "when there was nothing else apart from night". In this latter case, when we understand a hypallage to be working, we actually mitigate the extraordinariness of the image, excusing it as 'only a figure of speech'. That is, the less correctable the figure, the more mysterious. And in English that uncorrectability is intrinsic, so that what might intelligibly start out as a transferred epithet turns into something else because we cannot tell it has been transferred. *Ibant obscuri sola sub nocte* becomes the type of the difficult hypallage at least partly because the formulation is already a little unbalanced. The substantive qualified by the epithet *obscuri* is left to be understood, and the re-exchange, being less readily available, is less rationalisable. The line makes its readers anxious.

Where the mechanism of transposition is obvious no one is likely to complain. Johnson indeed is overly comfortable with it. When Warburton raises a problem about the inadequately characteristic force of 'dark-working' as applied to sorcerers in Shakespeare's 'dark-working sorcerers . . . soul-killing witches' in the *Comedy of Errors*, Johnson proposes simply that the epithets are 'misplaced' – by which he means, I think, that they are deliberately transposed. Though they go by and large unremarked, his own poetry is full of obvious transpositions. In the *Vanity of Human Wishes* we get 'the busy scenes of crowded life' for a plausibly more accurate 'crowded scenes of busy life', but here the adjectives mean almost the same. So tempting to Johnson was this doubling of what look like utterly conventional noun and adjective combinations, that he allowed himself – certainly in what's supposed to be an impromptu version of some verses by Pierre Charles Roy – the absurdity of writing about ice as 'treacherous pleasure's flow'ry ground'. The doublings need not however be of near-synonyms. In another example from the *Vanity of Human Wishes* there is a hint of paradox: 'cheerful Wisdom and instructive Mirth'. The characteristic epithets for wisdom and mirth have changed places. Likewise, when Johnson writes of Dr Levet that he was 'Obscurely wise, and coarsely kind', he almost certainly means that he was 'coarsely wise' and 'obscurely kind'. He means that Levet's wisdom was homespun, that his coarseness was like the 'crassness' of Horace's Ofellus in *Satires* II.iii, *abnormis sapiens crassaque Minerva* ('Of mother wit, and wise without the schools' in Philip Francis's version). And he is remembering Addison's Cato's advice to his son to live retired and content himself 'to be obscurely good' (lines quoted in the *Dictionary*): he means that Levet was kind without the kindness being remarked, or he was kind in dark places – in 'misery's darkest caverns' his 'useful care was ever nigh'. No one troubles to make sense of the exchanged version; and indeed it may not be possible. Its near invisibility is a consequence of the power of the antithesis: the details of the paradox are rendered irrelevant.

Should it occur to us to worry about cases like these, we could have recourse, as Johnson himself did, to the notion that the epithets are 'misplaced'. But where there is no second noun hunting for an epithet, anxiety sets in again. The anomalous epithets become affronts to taste, as they were for Addison, or they become affronts to sense, as they were for Bentley. Despite his readiness to correct Addison's complaint about Ovid, he is steadily obtuse about figurative transfers when he meets them in *Paradise Lost*. Johnson appealed to 'misplacement' as a way round unconvincing emendations; Bentley took the opposite line and appealed to unconvincing emendations as a way round misplacements. Milton writes 'in wandering mazes lost' Bentley notes: 'I have read *wandering mazes* in some of our elder poets; but for all that, it's a vicious expression. For *mazes*, labyrinths, do not themselves wander; though those that enter, wander in them'. He reads: 'winding mazes'. Milton writes 'flow'ry brooks'. Bentley notes: 'Flow'ry *banks* is vulgar; but flow'ry brooks, as if the flowers grew in the water, is not easily met with'. He emends to 'silver brooks'. Milton writes 'dawning hills'. Bentley notes: '*Dawning Hills* are great rarities'. He reads 'Downs and hills'.

Not all tastes are affronted however. Among the 'elder poets' capable of solecisms like 'wandering mazes' is Spenser. ''Tis common with Spenser', writes his eighteenth-century editor Upton, 'to place his adjective in such a manner between two substantives, that it shall seem to agree with the latter, though in truth and propriety of construction it can agree only with the former. This occasions confusion if it be not attended to.' Upton carefully notes it: 'to see his sire and offspring auncient'; 'such ladies and such lovely knights'; 'a Tygre and a Lionesse / Are met at spoyling of some hungry pray'; 'tombling downe upon the senselesse ground'; 'he lay upon the humbled grass'. The confusions he carefully explicates are not errors of the printing house. Neither are they errors of taste. These are examples of what he calls 'synchysis', normally treated as a vice of style, but which according to Upton 'grammarians find in the best authors'. He does not call it 'hypallage', or any other standard rhetorical figure, as Trapp would have done, and so indicates that he is not quite happy to elide the confusion by thinking of it as a standard figure of speech. Something else is going on: something 'more than meets the ear', something beyond even Spenser's peculiar addiction to hybrid forms and more to do with a cast of imagination. Cleanth Brooks puzzles over the remembered days of Tennyson's weeper, 'Deep as first love, and wild with all regret'. Striking a Bentleyan pose, he fails to imagine days 'wild with all regret'. One could always justify the adjective, he says, as a transferred epithet on the model of Virgil's *maestum timorem* ('sad fear' for the 'fear that makes you sad'). And he suggests that some such rationalisation may have occurred to Tennyson. But he suggests also that it is not motivated as a transferred epithet, and that its effect on the reader is not an awakening to a grammatical convention, but rather to the sense that the weeper and her remembered days are the same thing.

Brooks is anxious not to explain away the anomaly, but to allow that the anagram of sense which Tennyson offers us may break up our way of thinking about things. Puttenham misplaces his account of hypallage among his 'auricular' rather than 'sensable' figures, as if it were a scheme contrived for euphony's sake and touching only the ear, rather than a trope, teasing us with a turn of thought. But that is because his account of it is offered by way of afterthought. He has been talking specifically about the scheme that works by exchanging grammatical accidents, which he calls 'enallage', in most grammar books indistinguishable from 'hypallage', but he believes it unillustratable in English (and indeed the examples, under 'permutatio', selected from elsewhere by Lee Sonnino, are unconvincing solecisms). We have no enallage, Puttenham says, 'but another sort of exchange which they had, and very pretty, we do likewise use, not changing one word for another, by their accidents or cases ... but changing their true construction and application, whereby the sense is quite perverted and made very absurd'. What literal English versions of the Latin do is replace that readily identified exchange of grammatical accidents with one where the word-order is upset and, Puttenham seems to say, loses touch with the unperverted sense of what's said. If I say 'they goes' you may correct what I say to 'they go'. If I say *ibant obscuri sola sub nocte*, you may correct what I say to *ibant obscura soli sub nocte*. But if I say 'they went dark under the lonely night'. I don't produce something that is instantly decodable. The grammatical intelligibility of an English sentence depends on its word order, and what I've said comes over in the first instance as a mere 'word-heap', a list of things indifferently alike – night, loneliness, dark, walking. You may suppose I am talking nonsense, or you may suppose that I'm inspired. The least likely thing for you to suppose is that I'm being clever.

As it happens Puttenham's examples of hypallage are of comic exchanges, all of them unfunny. But that is his peculiar limitation. It's true that Bentley's refusal to credit Milton's transfers of epithets comes from the suspicion that they are base; and it's admittedly true that the standard examples of the figure as they are given in Shakespearean commentary are of the kind represented in Bottom's 'the eye of man hath not heard, the ear of man hath not seen' or 'I see a voice'. They are examples taken from low characters who are not in control of their own rhetoric, Elbow in *Measure for Measure* ('do you hear how he misplaces', says Escalus to Angelo), Stephano in *The Tempest*, Dogberry in *Much Ado*. They are characters prone to malapropism, or on the edge of idiocy. When Puttenham looks for a way of describing it, he comes up with something base, but also magical. The figure is artless looking, like an ill-favoured child, but it is a fairy child.

I had rather have him called the changeling . . . alluding to the opinion of nurses who are wont to say, that the fairies use to steal the fairest children out of their cradles, and put other ill favoured in their places, which they called changelings or elfs: so, if ye mark, doth our poet, or maker, play with his words, using a wrong construction for a right, and absurd for a sensible, by manner of exchange.

Rhetorical figures are not condemned to the functions that grammar books prescribe for them. Quintilian thinks *metalepsis* a base figure and unfit for anything but comedy; but for Henry Peacham, in the *Garden of Eloquence*, 'it teacheth the understanding to dive down to the bottom of the sense'. The comic ineptitude that Puttenham focuses on can overtake itself and stifle laughter. And he offers one example that he evidently thinks of as pathetic: 'Madam, I set your eyes before my woes'. This means something other than would a mere mangling of 'I set my woes before your eyes'. Even if we were ready to recombine the elements in the sequence so that they readily yielded sense, we would be reluctant to do so, for there would ensue from the re-arrangement the sense of a lost possibility. And it amuses us, or moves us, to entertain the notion that 'setting another's eyes before one's woes' is a possibility. That is why Upton is nervous of Spenser's transfers, but values them.

There is sanction for the seriousness, for some people think this is how Virgil's Latin works anyway. From a variety of motives, he violates the expected logic of association between words. He habitually upsets our notions of how things might be combined with one another or opposed to one another, or of agencies and events or of which among events should be foregrounded and which recessed. The pretended subordination of one thing to another is illusory, and indeed we come to understand such formulations as presenting us with an arbitrary mere coordination of observations. This accords well with the prejudices of English readers of poetry. Or indeed with the prejudices of those affected by the manners of English poetry. One critic with a taste for symbolist poetry remarks that Virgil's only rudimentary syntax, as he thinks it, is typically characterised by failures of grammatical connexion, and that, underneath any intellectual or verbal pattern, its true organising principle is 'l'image primitive'. Discounting what is merely schematic in the notion of exchange, discounting indeed what is strictly figurative in its operation, he calls hypallage 'the attribution to something of a quality which it does not naturally possess'. Accordingly, he goes in for Virgil's 'primitive' and metaphorically suggestive mismatches: the 'heavy smelling centaury' in the *Georgics*, the 'black stench' of Latinus's burning capital in *Aeneid* XII, the 'breathable light' that Achaemenides swears by in *Aeneid* III. He makes Virgil a virtuoso of synaesthesia. Trapp enjoys the same effect. In *Aeneid* I, Venus carries Iulus to her Idalian retreat, where, in his translation, 'blooming jessamine around him breathes / With flow'rs, in fragrant shade' (*floribus et dulci . . . umbrâ*). He complains that the Delphin edition glosses the *dulci* as *gratâ* – merely 'pleasant' – 'in consideration, I suppose, that shade has no smell in it. But those must be ill acquainted with the genius of poetry, who do not know, that one of its greatest elegancies consists in transferring ideas from one adjunct to another. The flowers yielded both shade and sweetness and though the shade was not perfumed; the air, joined with it, was.' A scheme, a pattern of syllables – *dulci* instead of the expected *dulcibus*, for the safely expected fragrant flowers – has turned into a trope, a turn of thought. Hypallage in English might always be the vehicle of the absurd, but it might also always be something else 'founded upon the pleasure of change, and variety', as Trapp says, and also on the 'shifting of ideas, and comparing them'. The poets know that transposed or transferred epithets, attached to where they don't quite belong, are the source of Virgilian *sfumato* as well as of Ovid's deplorable wit or Shakespearean clowning.

BIBLIOGRAPHICAL NOTE

The rhetorical background is covered in Heinrich Lausberg, *Handbook of Literary Rhetoric*, ed. David E. Orton and R. Dean Anderson (Brill, 1998) and, with an early modern focus, in Lee Sonnino, *A Handbook to Sixteenth-Century Rhetoric* (Routledge and Kegan Paul, 1970). Illuminating accounts of relevant rhetorical anomalies are in Roman Jakobson's 'Two Aspects of Language and Two Types of Aphasic Disturbance' in *Language in Literature* (Harvard University Press, 1987) and, with a literary focus, in the essays by John Hollander collected in *The Figure of Echo* (University of California Press, 1981), and in *Vision and Resonance*, 2nd edn (Yale University Press, 1985). There are useful accounts of Pound's translating vagaries in John Sullivan, *Ezra Pound and Sextus Propertius* (Faber, 1965), and Gordon M. Messing, 'Pound's Propertius: The Homage and the Damage', *Poetry and Poetics from Ancient Greece to the Renaissance: Essays in Honour of James M. Hutton*, ed. G.M. Kirkwood (Cornell University Press, 1975). On Milton's style, F.T. Prince, *The Italian Element in Milton's Verse* (Clarendon Press, 1954) is still classic. *The Cambridge Companion to Virgil*, ed. Charles Martindale (Cambridge University Press, 1997), has essays of interest, especially those by Colin Burrow and James O'Hara; especially valuable is Nicholas Horsfall's essay on Virgil's style in his *A Companion to the Study of Virgil* (Brill, 2000). Two essays are devoted to Virgilian hypallage: E. Adelaide Hahn, 'A Source of Virgilian Hypallage', *Transactions of the American Philological Association* 87 (1956), 147–89 and A. Wankenne, 'L'Hypallage dans l'oeuvre de Virgile', *Les Etudes Classiques*, 17 (1949), 335–42.

Denmark, Sweden, and Liberty

Christopher Bentley

A few years after the 1689 revolution two men of significantly different backgrounds published accounts of the Scandinavian countries where they had served as envoys of the English crown.

Robert Molesworth (1656–1725), the son of a wealthy Dublin trader of English origin, was a prominent supporter of the Prince of Orange and was consequently attainted by James II's parliament on 7 May 1689, his property being seized. He fled to England and, after apparently undertaking a private mission to Denmark during 1689–90, he returned in 1692 as William III's envoy extraordinary. An irascible and tactless man, Molesworth disliked the Danes, despising them for being accomplices in their own oppression, and he quarrelled with them. According to an adversary, he seems also have indulged in some deliberate baiting of the Danish court, hunting on the king's preserves and driving on a road reserved exclusively for royal use. In 1694 he left Denmark abruptly, without the formality of an audience of leave.[1]

His *Account of Denmark* was published in London in 1694, and received considerable notice, being reprinted several times in a few months. The early editions are anonymous, though Molesworth's authorship seems to have been generally known. In the *Account* the fact that the author had lived in Denmark as English envoy is never mentioned and the uninformed reader might reasonably infer that the author had visited Denmark merely as a private citizen, with the degree of privileged access that might be granted to a person of quality. The author's indifference to Danish sensitivities seems especially undiplomatic. His lists of all Danish regiments, their strengths and commanders, and of the king of Denmark's ships, their guns and crew numbers, might possibly derive from sources readily available in Denmark, but look very like intelligence gathering.

Though Molesworth omits any mention of his diplomatic duties in Denmark, his narrative is not wholly impersonal. A few anecdotes place the author immediately in the story and are sufficiently circumstantial and evocative to suggest that he could have written a classic travel book, if that had been his priority. One personal recollection offers an unusual perspective on the short, hot Danish summer: 'In *Copenhagen*, during these three Months, they are constantly troubled with the Plague of Flies, which they endeavour to destroy by a poysoned Water; upon the laying of which in their Kitchins and Chambers, I have seen whole Bushels of dead Flies swept together in one Room.'[2]

None of these reminiscences is even remotely affectionate towards Denmark or the Danes. A personal anecdote in which Molesworth attempts to buy green geese – presented dismissively as a 'silly Story' and perhaps nothing more than a traveller's tale of differing values and mutual incomprehension – is used to illustrate the superstition and cupidity of the Danish peasantry (pp. 95–6).

Molesworth's concern is not to offer a traveller's or a diplomat's view of Denmark, but to recount how the Danes lost their traditional liberty and how they are kept in an oppressed and relatively impoverished condition. A warning to England is omnipresent. The beginning of Molesworth's preface establishes his priorities immediately:

> *Health* and *Liberty* are without dispute the greatest natural Blessings mankind is capable of enjoying . . . Yet these Blessings are seldom sufficiently valued whilst enjoy'd; like the daily advantages of the Sun and Air, they seem scarce regarded because so common, by those that are in possession of them. . . . so he that knows by *Experience* the trouble of a languishing Sickness, or the loss of his *Liberty*, will presently begin to have a right esteem of that which formerly he scarce thought worth his notice.
>
> This *Experience* is either what a Man learns by that which befals himself, or by making Observations on the condition of other People: the first is the common guide to the generality of Mankind, who are not apt to look beyond themselves . . . the second sort of Experience is the Instructress of wise Men: for the prudent will not fail to benefit themselves by the accidents that befal others, both in their *Health* and *Liberty*, by avoiding the occasions of them . . . . Want of *Liberty* is a Disease in any Society or Body Politick, like want of *Health* in a particular Person; and as the best way to understand the nature of any Distemper aright, is to consider it in several Patients, since the same Disease may proceed from different causes, so the disorders in Society are best perceived by observing the Nature and Effects of them in our several Neighbours.

The rest of this long preface is an essay on the preservation of liberty. Denmark is scarcely mentioned and Molesworth's observations are applied directly to England. The recommendation to study the political disorders of 'our several Neighbours' expands into a defence of foreign travel. Freedom to travel abroad is itself an amenity of a free society and is not universally enjoyed: 'In *Russia* and *Muscovy* . . . none are permitted to Travel upon pain of Death, except such as have special licence, which are exceeding few'. Where 'young Gentlemen' are concerned, Molesworth recognizes that the doubtful reputation of foreign travel is well deserved: 'We send them abroad Children, and bring them home great Boys, and the returns they make for the Expences laid out by their Parents, are suitable to their age: that of the Languages is the very best, but the most common is an affected Foppishness, or a filthy Disease, for which they sometimes exchange their Religion.' Their political values may also be corrupted: 'the Pageantry, Luxury, and Licentiousness of the more arbitrary Courts have bribed them into an opinion of that very Form of Government'. The foreign travel recommended by Molesworth

> is that of *Men*, who set out so well stock'd with the knowledge of their own Country, as to be able to compare it with others, whereby they may both supply it where they find it wanting, and set a true value on't where it excels: with this help such Travellers could not fail of becoming serviceable to the Publick, in contributing daily towards the bettering of our Constitution, though without doubt it be already one of the best in the World.

Here Molesworth takes a classic Whig view of the English constitution as an evolving system accepting incremental change, as opposed to a system based on the immutable claims of divine right, to be altered only by revolution. He views the 1689 revolution dispassionately, as a necessary restoration of freedom, and offers a sardonic assessment of what had been a turbulent century for the English:

> all that we pretended to by the late Revolution (bought with so great Expence, yet not too dearly paid for) was to be as we were, and that every one should have his own again; the effecting of which may be called a piece of good luck, and that's the best can be said of it. But must frequent Blood-lettings be indispensibly necessary to preserve our Constitution? . . . Methinks a method to preserve our Commonwealth in its legal state of Freedom, without the necessity of a Civil War once or twice every Age, were a benefit worth searching for, though we went to the furthest corners of the World in quest of it.

Besides travel by the judicious, Molesworth believes that education may be a preserver of liberty: 'Good *Learning*, as well as *Travel*, is a great Antidote against the Plague of *Tyranny*.' He dismisses foreign universities as having been captured by the clergy, who are defenders of absolutism.

By contrast, English universities 'are without controversie the best in the world'. However, their statutes are antiquated and in need of reform. Molesworth claims that 'those excellent men that of late years have been preferred in our Church (then which Set of Divines *England* scarce ever knew a better)' owe more to being 'very conversant with the World' than to their university studies, and that foreign travel and their experience of 'this Epitome of the World, the City of *London*', make them friends of 'Christian Liberty'. Along with worldly clergymen Molesworth believes that lawyers are often supporters of liberty because of 'their knowledge of ancient Practise, and the just Title which the People have to their Priviledges'.

In 'these latter Ages of *Slavery*' the freedom of the people has been destroyed or severely limited in most European states: 'at present nothing is so generally studied by the *Soveraign Princes* of the World, as the Arts of War, and the keeping of their own Countreys in the desired subjection'. English travellers go mostly to 'the more polish'd and delicious Countries of *France*, *Spain*, or *Italy*' where lifestyle, pleasant climate and food, and the cultural experience 'dazzle the Eyes of most Travellers, and cast a disguise upon the Slavery of those Parts'. However 'in the *Northern Kingdoms* . . . there appears little or nothing to divert the Mind from contemplating Slavery in its own colours', undisguised by climate or culture. Therefore Molesworth 'thought it might be of use to publish the following *Account of Denmark*, which I took care to be informed of upon the place with the greatest exactness possible, and have related fairly and impartially'.

A chapter of Molesworth's *Account* describes how the Danes lost their liberty in a royal *coup d'état* which destroyed their traditional representative institutions and replaced them with an hereditary, absolutist monarchy. Characteristically, the transformation happened at a time of national crisis. Denmark had fought a disastrous war with Sweden and had been deprived of her wealthiest provinces in the peace treaty. The army was not disbanded, could not be paid, and was becoming mutinous. The king appointed a meeting of the three estates, 'the Nobility, Commonalty, and Clergy', which began in early October 1660. The nobility insisted on their customary exemption from taxation and 'according to their usual practice debated how the Sums of Money requisite might with greatest ease and conveniency be levied upon the Commons, without the least intention of bearing any proportionate share themselves' (p. 50). One nobleman's provocative description of the commons as slaves ('the word in the *Danish* is *unfree*') led to all but the nobility withdrawing from the hall. Subsequently, some of the commons were manoeuvred into petitioning the king to declare himself and the monarchy hereditary, to relieve them from the exactions and pride of the nobility, for 'at the worst, they supposed they should only change many Masters for one' (p. 54). After further intrigue, perhaps ultimately directed from the court, the nobility are coerced into acquiescence: 'they saw they were no longer the Masters; the Commons were armed, the Army and Clergy against them' (pp. 61–2). A royal command to lock the city gates secured their capitulation by detaining them at a distance from their estates and supporters, and causing them to fear for their lives. Each member of the estates was then required to swear, publicly and with much ceremony, an oath of allegiance to the king as absolute and hereditary ruler. The revolution had been accomplished in four days.

Molesworth perceives the clergy as playing a discreditable, self-interested part in these events: 'having been hitherto kept under by the Nobility, they forecasted to have no other Superiour but the King, whose new Authority they engaged to maintain by the influence they had on the Consciences of the People; expecting with reason the like Favour and Protection from the King, together with an encrease of their Power' (p. 55). The nobility are blamed not only for precipitating the initial crisis over taxation but also for their collective cowardice in the face of intimidation by court interests:

> I have heard very intelligent Persons, who were at that time near the King, affirm, That had the Nobles shewed ever so little Courage in asserting their Priviledges, the King would not have pursued his Point so far as to desire an Arbitrary Dominion, for he was in continual doubt and dread of the Event, and began to waver very much in his Resolutions; so that their Liberties seem purely lost for want of some to appear for them. (pp. 72–3)

The consequences of loss of liberty in Denmark are extensively described by Molesworth. Excessive land-taxes have reduced the value of estates in most parts of the kingdom by three-quarters. Many landowners prefer to surrender some of their estates to the king rather than pay the tax assessments. Because of its diminished value 'there is no buying, or selling of Land here; for where an Estate is a Charge, there will be few Buyers' (p. 80). Molesworth recalls only one sale of land for money during the time he lived in Denmark, an estate bought by the queen for 16,000 crowns, which at the time of the revolution had been worth 60,000. Should a landowner decide to sell up and leave Denmark, and be fortunate enough to find a purchaser, one-third of the purchase price goes to the king. Some landowners are reduced to living in one corner of their ruinous country houses and rackrenting their tenants to ensure their own survival. As a consequence of depressed land values, there is a general depression in trade. The level of personal savings is very low and the 'Trading Towns and Villages' are in decay. Economic decline seems even to limit population growth: 'although this Countrey have a tendency to be extreamly populous, the Women being exceeding Fruitful, which is sufficiently proved by the vast Swarms that in former Ages, from these Northern Parts, over-ran all *Europe*; yet at present it is but competently Peopled; vexation of Spirit, ill Diet, and Poverty, being great Obstructions to Procreation' (p. 88).

In his preface Molesworth had asserted that 'a free Government' is more conducive to national prosperity. The *Account* frequently contrasts the present impoverished and oppressed Danes with the 'free and rich People' that they formerly were. Slavery has even diminished the personal qualities of the people: 'it creates a kind of Laziness, and idle Despondency'. Molesworth finds that ability and courage have declined: 'The Common People are mean spirited, not Warlike in their Tempers, as formerly.' Having degraded its people the government now despises and distrusts them: 'In *Denmark* the Natives are considered much less than Strangers, and are more out of the Road of Preferment; whether it be that the Court can better trust Strangers, whose Fortunes they make, than the Posterity of such whose Fortunes they have ruined' (p. 82). Commissions in the army and important posts in the civil administration are generally given to foreigners.

The absence of political rights and the preponderance of foreigners in positions of power would have tended to make the Danes a colonized people. The fact that the court and the nobility spoke German as a first language also suggests a social and cultural chasm between the ruling élite and the governed. Elements of this situation have existed elsewhere, for example in Norman England and nineteenth-century Russia, and are not compatible with a free society.

Cultural impoverishment is also among the consequences of loss of liberty. There is only one university in Denmark, and it is not well funded. Very few books are published, 'and those only some dull Treatises of Controversie against the *Papists* and *Calvinists*' (p. 255). Molesworth is dismayed to find the Danes sunk in the lethargy of intellectual uniformity. Nearly everyone is a communicant of the state church. Political dissent is equally unknown: 'there are no Seditions,

Mutinies, or Libels against the Government; but all the People either are or appear to be Lovers of their King, notwithstanding their ill Treatment, and the hardships they groan under' (p. 246). Molesworth is clearly puzzled by the quiescence of the Danes and attributes it, tentatively and not very convincingly, to the 'Equality of the Taxes', suggesting that subjects will complain less when all are uniformly overtaxed. Towards the end of the *Account* Molesworth has come to an even more dispiriting conclusion, where no explanation is attempted: 'I verily believe, the *Danes* do now really love Servitude; and like the *Cappadocians* of old, could not make use of Liberty if it were offered them; but would throw it away if they had it, and resume their Chains' (pp. 267–8).

Having considered the condition and attitude of the Danes, Molesworth reverts to the English revolution of 1689. His concluding assessment is more bleak than the view taken in the preface:

> the late King *James*'s Attempts to bring in Popery were the principal thing which rescued our Liberties from being entirely swallowed up; there seeming in his Reign, through the Interest and Dishonesty of some, the Dissoluteness, Laziness, and Ignorance of others, to have been . . . a general tendency towards Slavery, which would scarcely have been vigorously enough opposed, had he left the business of Religion untouched. (p. 259)

The Danish king had not attempted to subvert the state church, and had taken care to make common cause with the clergy. Freedom, in Molesworth's view, is a precarious condition, often threatened, not always desired by the people, and sometimes preserved only by the mistakes of its enemies.

The conclusion of the *Account* contains a clearly provocative comparison between Danish and Turkish absolutism. Molesworth was perhaps prompted to this by recording earlier the anxious words of a nobleman coerced into taking the oath of allegiance to the new government in 1660: 'he hoped, and trusted, that his Majesty designed nothing but the Good of People, and not to govern them after the Turkish manner' (p. 72). At this period, and for long after, the Turkish empire was generally considered to be the most oppressive government with a presence in Europe. Predictably, Molesworth finds the Danish rule to be worse. A number of laboured distinctions fail to convince, the most plausible being the claim that Christian subjects of the Turks are less heavily taxed than the Danes.

Not everything in Denmark is condemned. In what may be a rare concession to protocol, the present king and queen are always spoken of favourably. A potential embarrassment in a work so frequently critical of Denmark is dismissed in one sentence without comment: 'The King of *Denmark* has one Brother, *viz.* Prince *George*, born 1653 and married to her Royal Highness the Princess *Ann*, Sister to her Majesty of *England*' (p. 230). In his preface Molesworth had recognized that 'few Governments are so ill constituted, as not to have some good Customs. We find admirable Regulations in *Denmark*'. Chapter 15 of the *Account* describes these regulations. They include the 'Justice, Brevity, and Perspicuity' of Danish laws, 'all contained in one Quarto Volume, written in the Language of the Country'. As a consequence there are very few lawyers in the kingdom, and no prolonged, expensive lawsuits; though Molesworth carpingly suggests that 'since the King was resolved to empty the Pockets of his Subjects, it was not for his advantage to permit others to do it'. In Copenhagen the quality of goods sold by merchants is regulated, and adequate supplies of corn at a moderate price are required to be always available. The streets are kept clean and free of obstructions. Chimney-sweeps are obliged to keep a register of their jobs, and no naked flames are permitted in the streets. Molesworth finds the regulation of the apothecaries to be especially commendable. They are appointed by the College of Physicians, their numbers are limited, and their shops throughout Denmark are visited two or three times a year by the magistrates, accompanied by the physicians. During these visits their stock of drugs is inspected, and those that are ineffective or have deteriorated are destroyed. The prices of drugs are fixed at moderate rates and the apothecaries 'keep exact books of what they sell, to whom, and by whose Prescription' (p. 244).

Molesworth asserts that 'the like Regulation would not only agree with, but consummate the happiness of a rich Country; and this Instance of *Denmark* makes it evident that such a Regulation is practicable' (p. 234). The rich Country is evidently England, but Molesworth does not perceive that the regulations he praises are an outcome of Denmark's controlling, oppressive state, and that their implementation would in fact be altogether less practicable for England's liberal, *laissez-faire* government. In the Denmark Molesworth describes are the roots of modern European states, sustained by high taxation and omnipresent state power, where the common good, as defined by political élites, generally pre-empts individuals' rights.

Molesworth's Danish experience and the publication of the *Account* seem to have precluded further diplomatic appointments. His estates were restored after the reconquest of Ireland. At various times he was a member of both the Irish and the English parliaments, and of the Irish privy council. In 1719 he was created Viscount Molesworth. Swift addressed the fifth of the *Drapier's Letters* to him as an Irish patriot, placing him in a list of 'Dangerous Authors, who talk of Liberty as a Blessing, to which the whole Race of Mankind hath an original Title, whereof nothing but unlawful Force can divest them'.[3]

John Robinson (1650–1723), a Yorkshireman whose father 'appears to have been in a humble station of life', studied at Oxford and about 1680 became chaplain to the English embassy at the court of Sweden. He later filled the post of envoy extraordinary and remained abroad until 1709. Unlike Molesworth, Robinson was a successful diplomat, enjoying considerable influence and trust at the Swedish court.[4] His *Account of Sueden* (1694), apparently published a few months after Molesworth's *Account of Denmark*, was offered to the public as a companion to the earlier work. Facing the title-page is a full-page advertisement for the third edition of Molesworth's *Account*, and 'The Publisher to the Reader' links the two works: 'The kind Reception which the Publick has given to a late Book, call'd, An *Account* of *Denmark*, (whereof Three Large Editions have come abroad in less than Three Months) encouraged me to seek after an Account of *Sueden*, I found all sorts of People desirous to be inform'd in the state of this other *Northern* Crown.'[5]

No doubt well aware of the controversial nature of Molesworth's *Account* (the Danish envoy in London had protested to William III on behalf of his government), the publisher of both works places Robinson's *Account* in a different light: 'You will find here a Relation of Matter of Fact only, though I will venture to say, a very Exact one; and such as I doubt not but will be very Entertaining to the Reader'. Molesworth had written a treatise on liberty and the threats to it, using one unfortunate nation as an extended example. Robinson is more circumspect, and does not attempt political or philosophical extrapolation. His book is shorter than Molesworth's and part of it is occupied by an epitome of Swedish history from earliest times. Like Molesworth, he published anonymously and makes no mention of his diplomatic appointment. Indeed, the author is never mentioned in Robinson's work. His writing is detached and neutral, without Molesworth's hostility. One observation suggests a nascent aesthetic response to the Swedish countryside: 'In the *Summer* season the Fields are cloathed with variety of Flowers, and the whole Country overspread with Strawberries, Rasberries, Currants, and the like, which grow upon every Rock' (p. 18).

Molesworth had asserted that 'Every one ought to know how great the Rights of the *People* were very lately in the *Elective* Kingdoms of

Sweden and *Denmark*, and claimed that now the '*Swedes* treat their own Subjects' as badly as the Danes (p. 269). Unlike Molesworth, who arrived in Denmark some thirty years after the revolution, Robinson witnessed most of the recent political changes in Sweden. As in Denmark, a national crisis provided the occasion. A war with Denmark and her allies had exposed deficiencies in Sweden's military preparedness and had depleted her resources. In 1680 the king 'call'd together the States of the Kingdom', blamed elements of the nobility for the unsatisfactory conduct of the war, and reduced their privileges. 'The Clergy, Burghers, and Peasants, were easily persuaded, That the Miseries they had suffered, proceeded from the too great Power of the Nobility; that the King could never be too much trusted . . . besides, they were glad of an occasion of humbling the Nobility, who in Prosperity were always imperious' (p. 96). Heavy land-taxes and income taxes were imposed on all classes. Crown lands formerly sold or given away were reunited to the crown, either by questioning the titles of their present owners or by imposing such confiscatory taxes that the owners were forced to surrender them to the crown. Assemblies in 1683 and 1686 completed the creation of an absolute monarchy. A 1680 declaration that the king's coronation oath obliged him to rule the kingdom according to law was 'further explained' wholly in the royal interest: 'his Majesty was not thereby tied to the Laws then in being, but might alter the same, and add thereto such Constitutions, as he thought most useful for the present State of the Kingdom' (p. 107).

Robinson believes that the king's personal popularity contributed to the success of this revolution. He also claims that the king maintains his autocratic rule partly by conciliating the Swedish Lutheran clergy, 'because the *Priests* have very great and uncontroulable Interest and Authority among the Common People (who only can make Disturbances) and can at their pleasure inflame, or appease them' (p. 112). This alliance of mutual self-interest inevitably recalls Molesworth's comments on the Danish Lutheran Church. Robinson is usually a more cautious writer than Molesworth, but he is not loath to condemn the Swedish revolution and the king who instigated it. The 'excessive Affection' that the Swedes had for their king 'gave him an opportunity to lay the Foundations of as *Absolute* a *Sovereignty* as any Prince in *Europe* possesses' (pp. 96–7). By excessive taxation 'the King recover'd a very great Revenue, tho with the Impoverishing of most Families in *Sueden*, and many of them, such whose Ancestors, and themselves also had spent their Lives and Fortunes in the Crown's Service' (pp. 102–3). The

Swedes are frankly described as 'an Oppressed People' without rights or recourse.

Like Molesworth, Robinson suggests that a kind of national apathy is among the consequences of oppression. For example, Sweden could be self-sufficient in corn 'if the Inhabitants were industrious, above what necessity forces them to'. Trade is mainly in the hands of foreigners, 'most of the Natives wanting either Capacity or Application'. Government policy is to encourage trade and manufacturing, and Robinson drily observes that 'great Wonders are expected from it; but doubtless there is much more in their Imaginations, than will ever be found in the Effect' (p. 160).

The permanent quartering of soldiers is a form of exploitation possible and perhaps indispensable in an oppressed nation. Every farm in Sweden is required to house, feed, clothe, and pay a small allowance to a soldier. This is effectively another form of taxation, and the people are also forced to endure the continued proximity of those who are the primary instrument of their oppression. (Molesworth also mentions the burden of quartering in Denmark, where households are 'constantly plagued with insolent Inmates'.)

Robinson's *Account* attracted less attention than Molesworth's and does not seem to have hindered his diplomatic career. As a recognized authority on Swedish affairs of state, he responded to Gilbert Burnet's request for a 'particular Character' of the king of Sweden.[6] On his return to England Robinson received preferments in the Church, culminating in his appointment as bishop of London.

It is difficult to say whether either Molesworth or Robinson had knowledge of the other's work while writing his own. Molesworth's *Account of Denmark* was probably written shortly before publication. Robinson's publisher speaks of being 'so Fortunate as to light on this Account in *Manuscript*, written some few years ago by a very Able and Learned Gentleman; and hearing that several Copies of it were got abroad, I considered it might at last chance to come forth in Print less Correct than at present I undertake to give it the World, whom I pretend to oblige by a very Accurate Edition'. This reads like conventional trade language, and may not reveal the true circumstances of publication. What connects the two works is that both appeared shortly after a revolution in England to preserve liberty, and that in each an envoy of the English crown – one a far more polemic writer than the other – describes and condemns the recent destruction of liberty in a neighbouring Protestant kingdom.

NOTES

1. For Molesworth's life, see *Dictionary of National Biography* and Caroline Robbins, *The Eighteenth-Century Commonwealthman* (1959; rpt. New York, 1968), pp. 91–2.
2. *An Account of Denmark, as It Was in the Year 1692* (London, 1694), pp. 11–12. Subsequent references to this work are given after quotations in the text.
3. *Drapier's Letters*, ed. Herbert Davis (1935; rpt. Oxford, 1965), p. 108.
4. For Robinson's life, see *Dictionary of National Biography*.
5. *An Account of Sueden* (London, 1694). Subsequent references to this work are given after quotations in the text.
6. Quoted in Burnet, *History of His Own Time*, 2 vols (London, 1724–34), II, pp. 535–6.

'A Political, Practical Character'

John Lucas

In November, 1862, a group of men dubbed as 'the proscribed of all the Nationalities of Europe' gathered at Kilburn cemetary. They were there to attend the burial of the French republican Simon Bernard, who four years earlier had been accused of involvement in the 'Orsini Plot' to assassinate Louis Napoleon. Bernard was in 1858 living in exile in London, but the French authorities applied for him to be extradited to France to stand trial along with Orsini and others, most of whom were to be executed for their parts in the bungled assassination attempt. Bernard was brought to trial at the Old Bailey on a charge of 'wilful murder' (when grenades were thrown at the Emperor, several bystanders were killed), a charge of which he was found not guilty and formally acquitted. The British authorities therefore refused to hand him over to the French. According to the official records of the trial:

> Evidence was given that the iron shells of six grenades, similar to the three exploded and to two others found on the scene of the attempt, were made in Birmingham in November 1857 to the order of one Allsop; that about the same time the prisoner purchased in London explosive chemicals similar to those with which the two unexploded grenades were charged; that he procured grenades resembling these two grenades, and according to some witnesses including them, to be conveyed from London to Brussels, and thence to Paris; that he also forwarded to Paris two revolvers, afterwards found in the possession of the persons who threw the grenades; and that he was instrumental in inducing one of them, a destitute Italian, to go over from London and take part in the attempt.[1]

It is no part of my present purpose to enquire into the trial or its outcome, other than to note that although the circumstantial evidence against Bernard was strong and that he undoubtedly knew Orsini, an Italian exile who had spent some years in London, no English jury in 1858 would have been other than sympathetic to anyone accused of trying to blow up the French Emperor. The following year, indeed, such intense anti-French feeling was whipped up by the rumours of yet another invasion from across the channel that Tennyson was prompted to publish an absurd poem in *The Times* about the need to defend our island home ('The War'), and Queen Victoria addressed an estimated crowd of 200,000 volunteers in Holyrood Park.

We probably know as much as we need to know about mid-nineteenth-century Francophobia.[2] We know rather less about the group of internationalists who met at Kilburn that day in late 1862. There are few accounts of the time they spent in London, and fewer still of their connections with English radicals. This is to be regretted, not only because we have for too long been fed as true stories of English insularity which are belied by the hospitality shown to so many political exiles (Francophobia doesn't mean xenophobia), but because any adequate account of the period will need to recognise just how internationalist English radicals then were. This applies to working-class radicals as much as to those from the middle and upper classes.

Among the exiles at Kilburn were the Russians Bakunin and Herzen, very probably the Italian Mazzini and Frenchman Alexander Ledru-Rollin, as well as Charles Bradlaugh, George Holyoake – both of whom gave orations at Bernard's grave-side – and the poet James Thomson ('B.V.'). Still others, including Louis Kossuth, would have been there in spirit, all of them forming the 'proscribed' who in Bradlaugh's words 'mustered round [Bernard's] coffin to do him honour'.[3]

Meetings in London of these and other exiles had become part of an established pattern some years before Bernard's death brought them together at Kilburn. The exiles met informally in each other's houses. But there were more formal meetings. To take a couple of examples. In February, 1854, the American consul, Mr. Saunders, gave a banquet for a dozen of the 'principal foreign refugees in London'. Among those who attended were Herzen, Garibaldi, Mazzini, Kossuth, Ledru-Rollin, Worcell, plus Sir Joshua Walmsley MP (invited because of his well-known radical sympathies), and the American Ambassador, James Buchanan. At the conclusion of the dinner, a toast was proposed to the 'world republic'. It was drunk in punch largely composed of Kentucky bourbon, and Herzen, who drank from the punch bowl first, had to warn his fellow guests that:

> 'I, yes, I, a Russian, have burnt my palate, my throat, and my whole alimentary canal; and what will it be like for you?'. . . I alone passed up my empty cup and asked for more. My chemical affinity with the alcohol raised my prestige enormously in the eyes of the consul.

'Ah, yes!' he said, 'It is only in America and in Russia that people know how to drink.'

And there is another still more flattering resemblance, thought I.

It is only in America and in Russia that they know how to flog bond-slaves to death.

Almost exactly a year later, on Tuesday, 27 February 1855, a grand meeting was held in St. Martin's Hall. The handbill advertising it announced 'COMMEMORATION OF THE GREAT REVOLUTIONARY MOVEMENT OF 1848 ALLIANCE OF ALL PEOPLE', and promised 'An international soirée followed by A Public Meeting', and listed as invitees 'the following distinguished representatives of European Democracy':

FRENCH: Louis Blanc, Victor Hugo, Barbes, Felix Pyat, Ledru-Rollin, Raspail, Eugène Sue, Pierre Lesoux.
GERMAN: Kinkel, Marx, Ruge, Schapper.
ITALIAN: Bianciani, Saffi, Mazzini.
HUNGARIAN: Teleki, Kossuth.
POLISH: Worcell, Zeno-Swientoslawski.
RUSSIAN: Herzen.
ENGLISH: W. Coningham, J. Finlen, Cooper, Mayne-Reid, J. Beal, Gerald Massey.

At the bottom of the handbill appeared the names of ERNEST JONES, President, Alfred Tallandier, French Sec., Dombrovski, Polish Sec., M. Bley, German Sec., and Bruce Chapman, English Sec. There was one final piece of information: 'Tea on Table at Five. Doors open for meeting at half-past seven, to commence at Eight. Double tickets 2s. 6d; Single ditto, 1s 6d; meeting ditto 3d.'[4]

Other such meetings were a regular feature of London life during the middle and later years of the nineteenth century and they testify to three matters of considerable importance. First, they show how truly international a city London was. Secondly, they show how hospitable at least some of the English were to republican ideas. Thirdly, they make plain that the old canard about England never having possessed an intelligentsia is nonsense. These matters between them necessarily rebuke commonplaces about 'Victorian' England which are still offered as though unchallengeable: that it was insular, solidly monarchical, and bone-hard philistine.

It could of course be asserted that I am doing no more than pointing to the fact that while these refugees, exiles, the 'proscribed', are clearly republican intellectuals, they are nevertheless exotics, and that the natives among whom they make their homes continue to form a society of 'beef, bibles, beer and bishops'. The term 'intelligentsa' was coined to account for a specific historical phenomenon. The *OED* defines the word as follows: 'The part of a nation (orig. in pre-revolutionary Russia) having aspirations to intellectual activity, a section of society regarded as possessing culture and political initiative; the members of this section of a nation or society, intellectuals.' Yet it will hardly do to confine this phenomenon to Russia. Marilyn Butler glances at its equivalent in her study *Romantics, Rebels and Reactionaries*, when she identifies a sort of informal movement occurring throughout Europe at the turn of the nineteenth century but most intensely realised in Prussia: 'young burghers who went to university and stayed on, because there were no jobs – the bitterest and perhaps the best educated middle class in Europe'. Such estrangement produced a literature of protest, although as Butler admits 'it is notable that even the *Sturm und Drang* generation is not politically radical in the same *practical* sense as some of the youthful artists of France and England. In Germany political activism is not possible; there is no substantial, unified polity to act against' [My italics].[5]

This was emphatically not the case in Russia. In *Ends and Beginnings*, Herzen identifies a new 'type' which he says developed first in Petersburg, where, in the early 1840s, 'a group of young, gifted men, extremely intelligent and extremely well educated, but nervous, morbid, and hard to please' made its appearance. Herzen is sympathetic but finally damning in his judgement of this type.

> Between their overrating of themselves and their appreciation by their neighbours the disproportion was very great. Society will not accept notes of hand for the future, but demands completed work in return for the ready money of recognition. They had too little power of hard work and perseverance; they only had enough of each to understand and assimilate what had been worked out by others.[6]

Given this, and the recognisable appearance of the type Herzen defines in Dostoevsky's and Turgenev's novels, as well as Chekhov's plays, it may seem quite wrong to speak of the London exiles as comprising an intelligentsia. Herzen and the rest did not merely have ideas about politics, they did their best – sometimes indistinguishable from the worst – to put their ideas into practice. This was the very reason they had been forced to flee to London. But this is to say no more than that the *OED*'s definition applies perfectly well to them and that the identification of the term 'intelligentsia' with impractical theorists (those 'armchair marxists' in the formulation so beloved of the *Daily Mail*) will not do. As the briefest resumés of their careers show, all those who gathered at Kilburn, who dined with the American Consul and who met at St. Martin's Hall, had in different and unusually striking ways provided evidence of 'political initiative'.

The Italians Garibaldi and Mazzini were indeed popular heroes in England. Wherever they went they attracted crowds and they each had a large number of admirers. The reasons for this adulation are not entirely clear to me, but they must have something to do with the fact that Byron and Shelley, themselves heroes of nineteenth-century English radicalism, had both supported the cause of Italian independence; and that to the English imagination Italy represented the Romantic South, ready to let the warm love in. Garibaldi (1807–80) wasn't often in England but on his few visits he seems to have been received as a blend of Robin Hood, Byron and Che Guavara *avant la lettre*: swarthily handsome, impulsive, attracted and attractive to beautiful women, forever on the move, and, with a small but loyal band of warriors, able to outwit and even defeat entire armies. Some of the legends that became attached to him had their basis in fact. His life story is almost impossibly Romantic. Born in Nice, the son of a tailor, from a comparatively early age he became involved in nationalist politics. In 1834 he joined the Young Italy Movement, tried to help capture Genoa, was himself captured, condemned to death, but escaped to South America where he became leader of a guerilla band in the rebellion of Rio Grande against Brazil, and eloped with and married a beautiful Creole woman, Anita Riveira de Silva, who bore him three children. When he returned to Italy in 1848, he and his army of volunteers 'performed notable feats against the Austrians' and the following year he joined the revolutionary government in Rome, 'voted for a republic, drove back the French force and routed the Neapolitans'. Then came the fight-back, which eventually forced Garibaldi into retreat (during which Anita died), and after the Austrians and French regained all they had lost Garibaldi made his way to New York. There followed visits to England in 1854 and again 1862, where history reports that he 'was received by the public with wild enthusiasm'.

As for Mazzini (1805–72), the founder of the Young Italy Movement, who had been born in the city he attempted to liberate, after the debacle of 1834 he escaped to Switzerland. Three years later the Swiss expelled him and he arrived in London. While in England he was put under government surveillance, and in 1844 was able to prove that his letters had been opened and their contents communicated to Italy's rulers. News of this 'raised a storm of indignation throughout the country'. He returned to Italy in 1848 to lead the movement for Italian independence, but following the reverses of 1849 was once more forced into English exile. In London he continued to work for his dream of a united and independent Italy, and he also helped in the formation of the republican European Association.

Chief among those who came together to create the Association was Louis Kossuth (1802–94). Kossuth had led the Hungarian rising in 1848 and after its collapse fled to Turkey where he was imprisoned, although the Turks charitably refused to send him back to Hungary. In 1851 he arrived in London, where we are told 'he was received with respect and sympathy'. He stayed in England until 1859. One of his friends in exile was Alexander Auguste Ledru-Rollin (1807–74), also a member of the republican European Association, who had arrived in London in 1849 after the failure of an insurrection against Louis Napoleon in which he had been deeply involved.

Other French exiles in London included Louis Blanc (1811–82), socialist and historian, whose *Organisation de Travail* (1840) denounces competitive industry and argues for the establishment of cooperative workshops to be subsidised by the State. His *Histoire de Dix Ans 1830–1840* not merely made a devastating attack on the Orléans dynasty, it provided a thorough-going argument against monarchies. Having escaped to London in 1848, Blanc spent the following years completing a history of the French Revolution and writing for French journals. Félix Pyat (1810–89), journalist and communist, signed Ledru-Rollin's 1849 appeal to the French people to arm themselves before he escaped to Switzerland, then Brussels and finally London, where he became a member of the 'European Revolutionary Committee'. Eugène Sue (1804–57), was by the time he arrived in London in 1851 famous as a novelist, in particular for *Les Mystères du Peuple* (1849), which had been condemned by the French courts as immoral and seditious.

Of the Germans, Gottfried Kinkel (1815–82) was involved in the revolutionary movement of 1848, imprisoned in Spandau, made a daring escape and came to London, where he taught German until, in 1866, he was appointed Professor of Art and Archaeology at Zurich. He was joined in London by Arnold Ruge (1802–80), who had also been involved in the revolutionary efforts of 1848, and who some years earlier had helped to found a journal for the Young Germany movement and begun a bookselling business in Leipzig, where he published a treatise on the need for democratic politics, entitled *Reform*. And of course there are Marx and Engels. Marx settled in London in 1849, the year after his activities on behalf of the revolutionary movement on the Rhine. He arrived in England as co-author of the *Communist Manifesto* (1848), which he had written in collaboration with Engels, with whom he had established his life-long friendship at their initial meeting in Brussels in 1844. Four years later the pair were in the Rhineland, writing for the *Neue Rheinische Zeitung*, and starting to organize working-class resistance. After a period spent with the revolutionary army in Baden (1849) Engels returned to England (1850).

Finally, Herzen (1812–70). As a young political radical he had spent years in prison and, later, exile in Russia, and after getting out in 1846 and wandering across Europe, he arrived in London in 1851. Among his other activities he edited one of the most famous of all journals, *The Bell (Kolokol)*, which was smuggled into Russia and there 'read by every section of educated society (including the Tsar's own officials)'.[7] In 1863, however, Herzen made the mistake of aligning himself with the Polish cause of independence from Russia. For this, he was denounced by his erstwhile Russian sympathisers, who, though they yearned to throw off the Tsarist yoke, saw no reason why Poland should be allowed to throw off the Russian yoke. Herzen's decision to back the cause – most passionately argued in exile by Bakunin – led to the collapse of readership for *The Bell*. It should be said that Bakunin (1814–76), born near Moscow of a noble family, was condemned to death for his part in the revolutionary movement in Germany, 1848–49, then given up to the Russians, sent to Siberia in 1855, from where escaped to Japan, to finally arrive in England in 1861.

Bakunin's influence on international anarchism belongs to the later years of the nineteenth century, but he deserves a mention here because he is part of that continent-wide movement of the intelligentsia against various monarchist and anti-democratic forms of government which characterises the century's middle years. And it really *was* an intelligentsia. Only Garibaldi can be thought of as purely a man of action. A glance at the records of the others is enough to reveal that they were formidable intellectuals, and that most were writers of great distinction, as well as political activists. What had England to offer by comparison? Very little, it might seem. Byron and Shelley were dead. Tennyson, probably affected by the glamour of Byron's reputation, had been briefly in Spain during 1830, intending to fight for the abortive Spanish Revolutionary movement. But events at home, especially the Chartist demonstrations during the 1830s and 1840s, dampened the radical fervour of many middle-class intellectuals and writers. Few in 1848 shared any great desire to help democratic causes in continental Europe. Nor did they have much to say about events in Ireland. In short, there seems to be precious little evidence of a section of English society 'possessing culture and political initiative' in a manner to rival that of the exiles who began to arrive in London as the after-events of 1848 took hold across Europe. And a very good thing too, one of the most influential spokesmen for culture would add. Matthew Arnold famously thought that culture should have nothing to do with politics. In 1853, when he published a deeply-considered Preface to his *Poems*, Arnold went out of his way to detach writing, specifically the writing of poetry, from action. Poetry ought to be above the smoke of the market place. The poet will not therefore

> maintain a hostile attitude towards the false pretensions of his age; he will content himself with not being overwhelmed by them. He will esteem himself fortunate if he can succeed in banishing from his mind all feelings of contradiction, and irritation, and impatience; in order to delight himself with the contemplation of a heroic time, and to enable others, through his representation of it, to delight in it also.[8]

I used to think that when he came to write this passage Arnold had English writers specifically in his sights. Now, I'm not so sure. A hostile attitude towards the false pretensions of the age was after all what had brought many foreign writers to London in the years between 1848 and 1851, when Arnold wrote 'Dover Beach'. In that poem, looking across the English Channel to where 'the light/Gleams and is gone' he imagines himself and his lover on a darkling plain 'Swept with confused alarms of struggle and flight, /Where ignorant armies clash by night'. Most commentators take the ignorant armies to be those of warring religious creeds or of doubt. But they could just as easily be warring political creeds, and indeed 'flight' was literally all that was left to those who in 1848 had fought for democratic causes throughout Europe and who avoided the punishment of restored reaction by escaping to England.

This being so, we can say that while English intellectuals did not 'present their lives' at the events of 1848, England itself was remarkably hospitable to political dissidents needing safe harbour. And this may be part of a more general hospitality. Ross McKibbon's recent assertion that 'no other major country in the last hundred years has been so culturally open' could well be extended to include politics.[9] When in 1855 Herzen sent Carlyle a copy of *On the Development of Revolutionary Ideas in Russia*, which had just been published in London, Carlyle replied:

> For my own share I confess I never had, and have now (if it were possible) less than ever, the least hope in 'Universal Suffrage' under any of its modifications: and, if it were not that in certain deadly maladies of the body politic, a burning crisis may be considered as beneficent, I should much prefer Tzarism itself, or Grand-Turkism itself, to the sheer Anarchy (as I reckon it sadly to be) which is got by 'Parliamentary Eloquence', Free Press, and counting of heads.

He nevertheless ended his letter by hoping that 'you will call some day when you are in town' because 'I [will enjoy] once more a little talk with an estimable man of sense, which is always a pleasure to me'.[10] It would be difficult to find a better example of openness than that.

But while Carlyle was prepared to be on friendly terms with democrats, he was clearly no friend to democracy. Nor was Arnold. Both men were set four-square against the hopes that had inspired the events of 1789 and which, it was usual to argue, had prompted the uprisings of 1848. And here we come to a crucial matter. Neither Carlyle nor Arnold could see that he had anything to gain from the new energies emerging in Europe. On the contrary, they had, as they saw it, much to fear. It is therefore scarcely surprising that both men should be hostile to the claims of Chartism, which was, when all refinements are done with, an essentially working-class movement. Most historians agree that Chartism, especially the great rising of 1839, was as near as Britain came to revolution in modern times, though they inevitably disagree as to how near that was. It isn't part of my present purpose to enter this debate. I want merely to note that 1848, the time of the third Chartist petition, which in anticipation at least seemed the most urgently critical of all threats to the fabric of English society, also in anticipation promised to be uniquely divisive. Marx claimed that had Byron and Shelley lived to take part in the events of that year, Shelley would have still been on the side of the people whereas Byron would have gone over to the governors.[11] Perhaps. Perhaps not. But few English intellectuals were especially sympathetic to the Chartist cause.

Few, that is, who came from the middle or upper class. And this is the key issue. For intellectuals were supposed to come from these classes. And this is why, I suspect, there has always been an assumption that England lacked an intelligentsia. An intelligentsia is, after all, against the political and cultural establishment. It is dissident, oppositional, it wants to overthrow the old order. But intellectuals in England were the establishment. I am using the word intellectual to include those who had (typically) gone to university, who were men of letters, contributors to the many serious journals which distinguished English cultural life during the long nineteenth century: churchmen, scientists, politicians, historians. For all their differences they were a remarkably homogeneous group. To be sure, they argued among themselves, but what they had against each other was less remarkable than what they had in common. And it is notable that none of them was at Bernard's graveside, none attended the American Consul's dinner, none was at St. Martin's Hall on 27 February 1855.

Yet Englishmen *were* at all these places. And to register who they were is then to realise that the conventional assumption that England lacked an intelligentsia in the nineteenth century comes about because we have been pointed in the wrong direction. (I except the groups gathered round the *Westminster Review*, and *Household Words*.) Look again at those English participants in the GREAT REVOLUTIONARY MOVEMENT OF 1848 ALLIANCE OF ALL PEOPLES, or those who, seven years later, gathered at Kilburn cemetary: Thomas Cooper, Gerald Massey, Ernest Jones, Charles Bradlaugh, G.J. Holyoake, James Thomson. Nearly all working-class, deeply involved in radical, even revolutionary politics, opposed to and by the political establishment. An ignorant army, perhaps? Not at all. The merest glance at their life histories ought to disabuse us of any belief that these men, who mingled at their ease with the exiles already named, were an illiterate rabble or had at best stuffed themselves with undigested scraps of learning. Auto-didacts they may have been, but we should remember that just behind the term as it is, or anyway, *was* used, lurks a half-repressed sneer which at its most benign softens into condescension. When Lord David Cecil called George Eliot an auto-didact, he meant that she was too much in earnest, too serious. She lacked the easy polish that comes to those born into a cultured family and which may be given a final buff by a university education. I imagine Cecil would have found Cooper, Massey et al. wholly unpolished. As Mrs Skewton says of the young Florence Dombey, whom she finds to be in a dreadfully 'unfinished' state, 'it shows what a little cultivation will do'.

In the nineteenth century there grew up among what might be called the culturally orthodox a practice of scorning the 'seriousness' of those who hadn't 'naturally' acquired culture. Dickens knew himself to be the frequent object of such scorn, even if he was unaware of Mill's calling him 'that creature', or Arnold's murmuring that he was quintessentially middle-class (i.e. philistine) 'bone of its bone and flesh of its flesh'. Hence Dickens's contempt for Henry Gowan in *Little Dorrit*. Gowan dabbles in art, he does a little thinking; but on the whole he 'knows' in his amateurish way that all art and ideas are in the end a matter of gentlemanly 'taste' and well-nigh worthless. *Mutatis mutandis*, Gowan can be compared to Will Ladislaw. Both men are dilettantes, though Ladislaw learns to be far more than that. But it seems to me not merely inevitable but proper that Dickens and George Eliot recognised that much that passes for intellectual life was (and still is) predicated on assumptions that connect class and education. Gowan points out that he had certain 'prospects washed and combed into my childish head when it was washed and combed for me, and I took them to a public school when I washed and combed it for myself' (*Little Dorrit*, Bk 1 Ch. 34).

The men whose names I have listed above represent a small fraction of those who taught themselves foreign languages, made themselves conversant with philosophy, theology, science, and art, who wrote, and edited the writings of others, and who spoke, lectured and debated at public meetings. There is no need here to go into detail of their intellectual achievements, nor of their publishing records. It is, however, necessary to provide an outline of their accomplishments, if only to show how impressive these were.

Thomas Cooper (1805–92), for example, wrote an autobiography which tells much about his passion for acquiring languages, including Hebrew. It also touches on his writings, including the at-one-time famous *Purgatory of Suicides*, a vast poem written while he was serving two years in prison for sedition (1843–5). Cooper was in addition the author of treatises and novels, of which *Seth Thompson the Stockinger*, also written while he was in prison, is perhaps the best known. It is far superior to Disraeli's *Sybil* or Kingsley's *Alton Locke*.[12]

Like Cooper, Ernest Jones (1819–69) spent time in prison. Although not of working-class background – his father was an officer in the British Army and equerry to the Duke of Cumberland – Jones began publishing fiction and poetry of an increasingly radical persuasion from the later 1830s. He became a much admired public speaker for the Chartist cause, and it was his advocacy of physical force to bring about change that in 1848 led to his arrest and two-year imprisonment. While in prison he wrote an epic poem, *The Revolt of Hindostan*, whose Shelleyan title sufficiently indicates its politics. (According to rumour the poem was written in his own blood, on leaves torn from a prayer-book.) Jones was passionately against Cooper's more meliorist approach to change. He was an all or nothing man.[13]

So, at least in his earlier days, was Gerald Massey (1828–1907). The son of a canal boatman, Massey left school at the age of 8 and began work in a silk factory, where he put in daily shifts of 11 hours. Seven years later he moved to London, took up with Chartists, began to read voraciously and to write poetry, including at least one poem much quoted in later years, 'The Song of the Red Republican'. (It begins 'Fling out the red Banner! In mountain and valley/Let Earth feel the tread of the free once again'.) In 1849 the Chartist printer John Bedford Leno employed Massey to edit *The Spirit of Freedom*, 'the working man's paper', and in the same year he published *Voices of Freedom and Lyrics of Love*, a collection of poems which brought him to national attention. (George Eliot is supposed to have at least partly based Felix Holt on Massey.) In 1851 he was among the group of radicals who welcomed Kossuth to England, and from then on he became a champion of Hungarian, Italian and Polish nationalism. In later years he also spoke up for women's rights, remarking on one occasion that 'We mean for woman to have perfect equality with man, social, religious and political, and her fair share in the equity which is of no sex.'[14]

Massey was one of the few radicals in my list who escaped prison. No such luck for George Jacob Holyoake (1817–1906). Born in Birmingham into an artisanal family, Holyoake became sufficiently well-educated to teach mathematics for some years at the Mechanics Institute of his native city. By the late 1830s he had taken on the secretaryship of Garibaldi's English supporters and was editor of *The Reasoner*. It was this which got him into trouble. *The Reasoner* promoted the cause of secularism. In 1841 Holyoake was charged with atheism, then an imprisonable offence. He was found guilty and jailed. There is not much doubt that the charge against him was trumped-up and had more to do with his radicalism than his disbelief. Imprisonment had the unintended effect of reinforcing both Holyoake's radicalism and his atheism; his later works include *History of Co-operation in Rochdale* (1855–72), *Limits of Atheism* (1861) and *Sixty Years of an Agitator's Life* (1892).

Holyoake was for a time close to James Thomson ('B.V.', 1834–82), because Thomson was employed by Charles Bradlaugh (1833–91). Although neither man was old enough to have taken part in the Chartist movement, both were companions of many who had done so, and by the late 1850s both had become radicals, republicans, and free-thinkers.

Like the others mentioned here, both were formidably well-educated and culturally enlightened. Thomson, born of working-class Scottish parents in Glasgow, was sent to school in London (the Caledonian Asylum) and subsequently taught himself French, Italian and German. He earned a precarious living as a journalist, writing for Bradlaugh's *National Reformer* and *Secularist*, edited by George Foote.

Bradlaugh famously came up against the law when in 1880 he was denied his Parliamentary seat because he refused to swear the oath of office. He had experienced earlier run-ins with officialdom, most notably perhaps in 1869, when the government prosecuted his *National Reformer* for non-compliance with the security laws. Moreover, as a militant republican and free-thinker he was a man who, as John Crangle notes, seemed 'an archetypal Radical to his contemporary adversaries'.[15]

Not all of the men described here were extreme radicals. Not all were working-class. Not all went to prison. But they form part of that radical continuum that can be traced back to the late years of the eighteenth century (and behind that of course to the period of the Commonwealth), and that first becomes important in the nineteenth century in the circle that in the 1830s and 1840s gathered round W.J. Fox and his journal, *The Monthly Repository*. From that and from Fox's *Lectures: Addressed Chiefly to the Working Class*, published in four volumes in 1845, other journals developed, including Dickens's *Household Words*, which began publication in 1850.[16] There, Dickens makes common cause with fellow-radicals and the issues that engaged their attention. In his proposal for the journal, he writes that *Household Words* will call 'upon the working class to turn the "Indifferents and Incapables" out of Downing Street and Westminster and force the government to remedy the ills from which poor men suffer'. True, he also seems to urge reconciliation rather than opposition: *Household Words* will, he says, oppose 'radical, national, religious and class prejudice'. But if he thought that would appeal to the liberal élite who made up much of the self-appointed cultural and political establishment, he was wrong. Mill and Arnold regularly curled the lip at any mention of his name. And there were plenty more where they came from. Mill and Arnold are still habitually linked as exemplars of the best kind of English intellectual life in the nineteenth century. F.R. Leavis famously claimed that such life 'co-ordinates itself round John Stuart Mill' and that only Arnold can be linked to Mill, for 'although he is in so many ways unlike Mill, he too stands for intelligence (as the contrast with Carlyle brings out)'.[17] It would be good to think that most commentators might feel uneasy about this confident and ignorant generalisation. Yet I am not aware that there has been much recognition of the fact that a true English intelligentsia is to be found among those radicals whose careers I have touched on above and who, in common with others I have no space to discuss, were not disabled by the Arnoldian retreat from active oppositional politics. Such politics were of course anathema to Arnold. Hence the following:

> At first sight it seems strange that out of the immense stir of the French Revolution and its age should not have come a crop of works of genius equal to that which came out of the great stir of the great productive time of Greece, or that of the Renaissance, with its powerful episode of the Reformation. But the truth is that the stir of the French Revolution took a character which essentially distinguished it from such movements as these. These were, in the main, disinterestedly intellectual and spiritual movements; movements in which the human spirit looked for its satisfaction in itself and in the increased play of its own activity. The French Revolution took a political, practical character.[18]

These words, from the essay on 'The Function of Criticism at the Present Time', will sufficiently indicate why Arnold would see no intellectual distinction in those who aligned themselves with the cause of radical republicanism and whose commitment to their ideas not only put them in opposition to the cultural and political establishment, but often put them outside the law and into prison. Of course they disagreed among themselves, sometimes ferociously. Of course they changed their minds. In this as in other ways they are identical with all those exiles who arrived in London in the period that falls roughly between 1840 and 1850, but they are unlike in that where the exiles were mostly university educated and even from aristocratic backgrounds, the English radicals weren't. As we have seen, this didn't prevent them from becoming formidably well-educated, but it did mean that they weren't of the class from which the English expected—and still perhaps expect – to derive an intelligentsia.

This expectation, pernicious, debilitating and at the last contemptible, is, or was, shared by others who have written about nineteenth-century artisanal radicals. In her book *The Industrial Muse*, Martha Vicinus mocks Gerald Massey in a manner that suggests she sees him as offering himself as a bit of rough for middle-class ersatz radicals.

> The middle-class literati saw the craggy well-built Massey as a prototype success story, made a bit more delicious by his righteous indignation at the sufferings of the less fortunate. Favourable reviews soon led Massey out of radical circles and into a career as a lecturer, specializing in mesmerism and phrenology.[19]

No mention here of Massey's commitment to the causes of European nationalism and women's rights, let alone the work he did for both. It is therefore worth noting that Martha Vicinus asked me to meet her sometime in the very early 1970s, when she was on a visit to England from Indiana University, where I had taught during the summer of 1968, and where she had a reputation as a campus radical. In the months I was at Indiana I became friendly with Orlando Taylor, a black academic who was trying to establish a series of scholarships to help impoverished black students enrol at the university. A good cause, and I for one was pleased to help a very little by giving Orlando the car I'd bought for the duration so that he could sell it in order to raise funds for his proposed scheme. After my return to England I'd written to him a few times, but all my letters had been returned with a note to the effect that he'd 'Gone Away'. It seemed natural to ask Vicinus if she could tell me what had happened to Orlando. 'Oh,' she said, 'he didn't get contract renewal.' 'Why on earth not?' He'd obviously been a highly intelligent man and was by all accounts a gifted and a conscientious teacher. She agreed. 'But he was always pushing his views in people's faces. You make enemies that way.' 'But what about his friends? Didn't they protest?' She shrugged. 'There wasn't much point', she said. 'Anyway, he's got some sort of post at Howard' (the university set up for black students in Washington D.C.). Vicinus clearly didn't regard the university's treatment of Orlando as in any way her concern. I wasn't therefore surprised that when her ill-written book appeared it should try to make fun of radicals who lived by and for their ideas.

NOTES

1. *Reports of State Trials*, NS, vol. VIII, 1850–8, published under the direction of the State Trials Committee, ed. John E.P. Wallis, HMSO, 1898, p. 887.
2. For Francophobia see my essay on 'Love of England' in *Heart of the Heartless World*, ed. David Margolies and Maroula Joannou, London, 1995, especially pp. 138–42.
3. See Tom Leonard, *Places of the Mind: The Life and Work of James Thomson*, London, 1993, p. 103.
4. E.H. Carr, *The Romantic Exiles* (first published 1933), Harmondsworth, 1949, pp. 161–4.
5. Marilyn Butler, *Romantics, Rebels and Reactionaries: English Literature and its Background, 1760–1830*, Oxford, 1981, p. 73.
6. Alexander Herzen, *Ends and Beginnings*, ed. Aileen Kelly, Oxford, 1985, pp. 400–1.

7. Kelly, p. xv.
8. Matthew Arnold, *Poetical Works*, ed. Tinker and Lowry, Oxford, 1957, pp. xxix–xxx.
9. See *London Review of Books*, vol. 23, no. 13, 5 July 2001, p. 13.
10. Carr, *The Romantic Exiles*, pp. 427–8.
11. I am grateful to David Brooks for directing me to the source of this remark, which is to be found in a newspaper article on Shelley by Eleanor Marx and her husband Edward Aveling. The article is excerpted in *Marx/Engels, On Literature and Art*, Progress Publishers, Moscow, 1976, pp. 320–1.
12. For Cooper, see his own *Life*, with an introduction by John Saville, The Victorian Library, Leicester, 1971; Dorothy Thompson, *The Chartists: Popular Politics in the Industrial Revolution*, Aldershot, 1984.
13. For Jones, see articles in the *Encyclopaedia Britannica* and in Thompson above.
14. For Massey, see *Biographical Dictionary of Modern British Radicalism*, vol. 3, 1870–1914, A–K, ed. J.O. Baylen and N.J. Gossman, Hassocks, pp. 336–9.
15. As above pp. 108-9.
16. For this see my essay 'Past and Present: *Bleak House* and *A Child's History of England*' in *Dickens Refigured*, ed. J. Shad, Manchester, 1996, especially pp. 139–46.
17. Leavis's claim is made in the introduction to his *Mill On Bentham and Coleridge*, quoted by Edward Alexander in *Matthew Arnold and John Stuart Mill*, London 1965, p. 28.
18. *Lectures and Essays in Criticism*, ed. M. Super, London, 1962, pp. 262–3.
19. Martha Vicinus, *The Industrial Muse*, London, 1974, p. 102.

Towards the Real: A.B. Paterson, the Bush and the Boer War

Ken Stewart

Paterson's fame and reputation as a bush balladist and 1890s nationalist, the main reason for his cultural and historical importance, have overshadowed or distorted his literary significance as an old-fashioned Romantic poet.[1] Much of his verse and journalism reflects and parallels a personal quest for exhilaration, whether within nature or through 'masculine' adventure. Even in a poem found unfinished at the time of his death in 1941, 'Air-fight over France', he rejects the claim that the twentieth century offers 'no romance', 'nothing to stir the blood'.[2]

His first published ballad was also a war poem, 'El Mahdi to the Australian Troops' (*Bulletin*, 28 Feb. 1885).[3] The Sh'ite Muslim El Mahdi had a month previously led a successful rebellion against the Egyptian occupation of the Sudan, during which Khartoum was captured and the Victorian hero General Gordon was killed. El Mahdi chastises 'fair Australia, freest of the free' for siding with benighted Mother England against the rebels in this 'unholy war'. Gordon's military successors are ridiculed in a pretentious and unwitting rehearsal of some of his Boer War poems, but by 1900 Paterson was to find any public proclamation of his criticism of British foreign and military policy more problematic.

During the interval, 'the Banjo' had become Australia's most popular poet.[4] Since he published in the *Bulletin*, and championed the bushman, the bush, and the (white) underdog, it is perhaps not surprising that literary, cultural and military historians have sought to find in his Boer War writings endorsement of their too hasty suspicion that these dispatches and rough ballads are essentially shallow glorifications of war as masculine adventure, exercises in jingoism, 'big-noting' and cultural cringing, and translations to the war-zone of the bush ideal in which the Australian soldier becomes a Clancy among the kopjes (prefiguring the iconic bushman-digger of World War I). As well, Robin Gerster argues, Paterson 'could hardly be more obsequiously supportive of the Australian role in assisting Mother England', and 'was amongst the first to link the established local hero, the bushman, with conventional conceptions of martial prowess'.[5] 'The mythical properties which were ascribed to the bushman by the literary nationalists clustered around the *Bulletin* . . . reappear in Paterson's portrait of a soldier who combined resourcefulness, stoicism and independence with skilled equestrianism . . .'[6]

This intertwining of Paterson's verse and prose with that amorphous monster 'the masculine bush legend' leaves us much to unscramble, and to modify. The 'legend' itself is ambiguous, and is I suggest more helpfully understood not so much as a consistent monolithic construction, as a contest comprising at least two *opposing*, in some respects incompatible, masculine ideologies or aesthetics. The first, represented broadly by Paterson (and, for example, Randolph Bedford), consists of a local masculinising of traditional romantic individualism, and the bush (as explored by Marilyn Lake);[7] the second, articulated particularly by Henry Lawson, encompasses certain homosocial and originally working class codes and forms of behaviour, and favours a realist aesthetic. There is some interplay between the discourses: Lawson's texts sometimes move in Paterson's direction, and *vice-versa*; but generally the homosocial element and 'mateship' are absent from Paterson's celebrated texts before the Boer War – or have, in effect, been 'added' to them as part of the process of social production, through the medium of the *Bulletin* and later radical nationalist texts. The nomadic loners Clancy, the Jolly Swagman, the Man from Snowy River and the Castlereagh Traveller are thus appropriated and reshaped for a collectivist cause, and their underdog status is redefined in more specific class terms than Paterson's texts spell out or than he apparently intended.

Before 1899, Paterson did not write about 'mateship', rarely used the word 'mate', and seldom focused on 'the pair'; his oppositions are between 'folk' or 'society' and the individual. There are virtually no married couples, wives or individual women in his ballads of this period, whereas in Lawson the heterosexual partnership of marriage is almost as prominent as homosocial 'mateship'. Paterson's romanticism celebrates 'imagination', 'freedom', 'spirit'; it evokes reverie, dream, personal individual experience; it sanctifies solitude and exhilaration; and it prefers 'nature', landscape and rustic 'folk' to urban pollution and noise.[8]

In their celebrated verse 'feud', Lawson manipulated Paterson into an untenable (though heartfelt and popular) defence of the Arcadian bush as 'real'. Lawson was writing 'The Drover's Wife' at the time, and it is likely (though I have not seen the case argued elsewhere) that he perceived the story as a calculated rebuttal of Paterson's idealised drover, Clancy. Into his verse debate Lawson incorporated arguments, phrases and images which find their way as well, verbatim or modified, into 'The Drover's Wife':

> Bush where there is no horizon! Where the buried bushman sees
> Nothing. Nothing! but the maddening sameness of the stunted trees!
> Lonely hut where drought's eternal – suffocating atmosphere –
> Where the God forsaken hatter dreams of city-life and beer
> . . .
> Land where gaunt and haggard women live alone and work like men
> Till their husband, gone a-droving, will return to them again.[9]

His satirical treatment of Paterson's comfortable urban bachelordom anticipates in some respects Marilyn Lake's critique of the masculine ideal of romantic freedom:

> Would you like to change with Clancy – go a-droving? Tell us true
> For we rather think that Clancy would be glad to change with you
> And be something in the city; but 'twould give your muse a shock
> To be losing time and money thro' the foot-rot and the flock,
> And you wouldn't mind the beauties underneath the starry dome
> If you had a wife and children and a lot of bills at home.[10]

Perhaps the strongest evidence of the ideologically popular need to transmute Paterson's romanticism into a (somewhat degraded) homosocial version of the 'bush legend' is the commercial metamorphosis of 'The Man from Snowy River' from a ballad celebration of the equestrian demi-god spirit of an 'underdog' stripling loner into, in the 1980s, a blockbuster film resembling an American advertisement for Marlboro cigarettes, in which a complex new plot gives the previously unnamed 'man' a new bland personality, a handsome, strong appearance, a close 'mate' and homosocial friendships, as well as a heterosexual romance leading to marriage. The recipe is repeated in the self-styled 'novelisation of the film' by Elyne Mitchell, and in the television series of the 1990s.[11] (At the Sydney Olympic Games opening ceremony, it will be remembered, *myriads* of men from Snowy River wearing 'Driza-bone' capes rode gregariously through the stadium.)

Immediately after the outbreak of the Boer War in October 1899,

Paterson negotiated with the *Sydney Morning Herald* to employ him as a war correspondent; in the event, several reports were also published in the Melbourne *Argus*, and the Reuters international agency commissioned him as well. The troopship S.S. Kent, carrying 130 Australian soldiers, and horses, weapons, clothing, food and medical supplies, left Albany, Western Australia, on 30 October, amid chiacking and revelry on shore and abroad. After thirty days of weary steaming, the east coast of South Africa was reached at Port Elizabeth; but after only one hour in port the *Kent* steamed on to Cape Town, which, except for the prominence of black labour, was 'all just like Sydney'.[12] Three days later the Australians made a hot, slow and tedious journey, forty-eight hours by rail, to the interior and the warfront. For Paterson the expedition began optimistically: in the cause of civilisation and the Empire he was to report the war to his countrymen. To us a century later, the jigsaw of dispatches that were to document the next nine months and thousand miles of the expedition northward towards the centre reads at some moments disarmingly like a novel Joseph Conrad was about to write titled *Heart of Darkness*.

During this demanding itinerary, Paterson rode and camped in war zones at the front line, virtually as a soldier. Continually under threat, on one occasion he was slightly wounded by a ricocheting bullet. He was with the troops for the advance on Carlsberg (which he reported 31 December), the relief of Kimberley (reported 17 February 1900) and the surrender of General Cronje, ancestor of the less honorable cricket captain. From Bloemfontein he proudly reported that he had won a race on his reliable Australian colt against two other war correspondents who, like himself, were 'seeking the honour' of being first to arrive:

> Once in the town we slowed to a walk, and were warmly welcomed by the townsfolk, who all shook hands with us, and hoorayed as though they liked having their town captured.[13]

There he met with Rudyard Kipling, before joining the clashes against the Orange Free Staters, and eventually the Transvaal Boers.[14] He reported the capitulation of Kroonstad (12 May), of Johannesburg (30 May) and eventually of Pretoria, and on 28 July the defeat of the Orange Free State army.[15]

The experiences of war he reported were diverse: monotony, privation, pain, valour, resourcefulness, desperation, folly, despair, conviviality, panic, bonding with mates, meetings with officers, military leaders, celebrities; occasional jubilation, relaxation; continuing frustration, uncertainty, hope for an end to the fighting; disgust at the incompetence of British officers and leaders, and the shallowness of the 'Piccadilly generals' and the aristocracy. Ironically, the realist aesthetic, homosocial values, and themes and characterizations more often associated with Lawson's writings, begin to inhabit his prose, and verse; 'mate' is now an unaffected, ordinary word; the social and domestic behaviour of rural men and women under great duress and privation, especially that of poor Boer farmers, is compassionately observed; class struggle and poverty become issues.

The bushman/soldier had been idealized in Australia long before the Boer War, for example by William Lane, who in his racist invasion-scare novel *White or Yellow? A Story of the Race War of A.D. 1908* (serialised in the *Boomerang* in 1888) had depicted the redemptive martial powers of Australian soldiers rallying from the Bush and outback in predictably heroic terms. The use of official labels during the African war itself, such as 'the Australian Bushmen's Contingent' and 'the Bushmen's Corps', in practice valorised the Bush type and countrified the urban volunteers; while writers such as the Melbourne *Argus* columnist-cum-poet John Sandes, and later J.H.M. Abbott in *Tommy Cornstalk*, prefigured C.E.W. Bean's digger-bushman far more exaggeratedly than Paterson, whose approach is more temperate and analytical, and frequently designed to counter extravagance or question stereotypes and popular fallacies. He observed, for example, that the origins of Australian soldiers, whether urban or rural, did not affect their visible skills, and were imperceptible in their physical appearance. Nor was the country, in the African setting at least, inherently superior to the city: distinguishing between Transvaalers and Free Staters, for instance, he observed that 'if there is any difference at all, the Transvaalers are the more civilised and cultivated', which 'is easily understood when it is remembered that the Transvaal is the mining country and has a large city – Johannesburg – in its midst, while the Free State is purely a farming community. When the Free State want to mix in the world of civilisation, they go up to Johannesburg'.[16]

As Australia's virtual laureate at the front, Paterson was increasingly caught in a dilemma brought about by the disparity between perceived patriotic duty towards the public, the Empire and the morale of the troops, and his growing awareness that the morality and conduct of the war and the incompetence of British military leaders could not be given unqualified support. Some of his ballads were written for the troops, and were sung or recited by them in camp, or on the march or ride: these are often self-conscious and racist braggadocio or jingo, designed to lift morale. Other verses and dispatches, spurred by the public glorification of war, and by the initially unexpected protraction of hostilities, moved him to write bitter satire. He allayed a nagging conscience, perhaps, by arguing in favour of mercifully hastening an inevitable victory; and dealt practically with his dilemma by carefully selecting the venues for his publications, and by controlling the content of his critiques and timing their appearance in print. Though continually critical, he is careful and restrained (and also more 'heroic' or jingoistic) when writing for the conservative press, and more savage in the anti-Boer War *Bulletin*. Some of his critiques were held back until delivered during a controversial lecture tour on his return to Australia, or until they appeared in the verse collection *Rio Grande's Last Ride* (1902). The most extreme anti-war verses remained in manuscript until his grandchildren published them in 1983.[17]

The fluctuation and seeming inconsistency in Paterson's war writings, then, is attributable to the variety of roles and identities he felt required to assume, and to his own ambivalence. Riding with the troops, wearing the khaki, admired by the men and the officers, involved in military strategy and in the broader public war effort, he doubtless felt himself to be 'almost' a soldier, governed by military obligation to his 'mates' and their managers. In this incarnation, quasi-soldier rather than commentator or critic, he evidently felt obliged as a matter of tactics to fan in verse the self-esteem of, for example, the Cape Mounted Rifles, and the Queensland Mounted Infantry.[18]

The new homosocial quasi-Lawsonian Paterson, now in support of a cause and of his mates, encourages cooperation, compassion and awareness of the class hierarchy separating 'us', the Australians, from 'them', the 'Piccadilly generals'. Paradoxically, this 'mateship' intensifies, as awareness of the Boers' resourcefulness, kindness and integrity is acknowledged, into an implicit respect for the underdog that extends beyond national boundaries to the enemy soldiers as well. His originally untested stereotype of the Boers as uncivilised rednecks, 'only part human', is rejected, as gradually and cumulatively, all common soldiers – 'the men' – whether Australians, Tommies or Boers, are (in terms of human respect rather than military loyalty) recognised as the true 'underdog'. Although he considers the Boers somewhat less adept and practical as soldiers, lacking the Allies' shooting skills, and more pampered in their expectations and habits owing to their use of black servants, his celebration of Australian skills and resourcefulness is generally observed analytically, and should be perceived within a wider context, against his recurring *attacks* on military vainglory, 'big noting', the use of war for personal aggrandizement, profit and decoration, on war as a grand adventure and on the British military aristocracy.[19] The admiration for *Boer* courage, tenacity, resourcefulness and tactical guile has not been acknowledged by those who accuse him of puffing the Australians.

The transition towards a Lawsonian aesthetic is discernible even on the long initial train journey to the interior:

> All the way up we passed through open country, not a tree to be seen, except what were planted in rows on a few farms . . . there is no water to be seen and the herbage is a sage-like bushy scrub a few inches high. Looking out of the train windows . . . A few sheep. . . . All day long it is as hot as the hottest day in Bourke, and at night the temperature falls to about 50 degrees [Fahrenheit].[20]

Naauwpoort is described as:

> a frightful place – just a lot of small galvanised iron houses and a dust storm. Sometimes whole mule wagons drive into each other in the dust, not being able to see one yard ahead.[21]

Such echoes and replications of Drover's Wife country, or of Lawson's Bourke or Hungerford, are more common than the occasional reminders of the sunlit plains; for Paterson, a Boer homestead is 'absurdly like an Australian homestead in every way. Sheep yards, horse yards, cultivation paddocks – everything reminds one of Australia'.[22]

Now he is at the front, stressing once more that there is no glory in soldiering, and no exhilaration:

> Out all day in the hot sun, out all night on public duty or patrol. . . . Everyone gets as dirty as a badger, with dust that is flying, and we had a storm one night that flooded the tents and stained everything with muddy water. . . . The reader may not understand why we do not attack the Boers, but it would be like marching up the side of the Great Pyramid to attack a force of unknown strength. It might be magnificent, but it wouldn't be war.[23]

The Canadian voluntary contingent, he reports, 'largely composed of wealthy men, who have volunteered for the sake of seeing some service', have not perceived the true nature of war: '. . . soldiering is not an amusement. Out all day in the sun, up all night on watch, hungry, sunburnt, thirsty, and unspeakably dirty, there is no glory about it'.[24]

A dispatch from Arundel dated 21 January 1900, records an interview with 'our friend the enemy', Olive Schreiner, the celebrated Afrikander author of *The Story of an African Farm* (1883), whose brother was Premier of the Cape Colony. Paterson had never previously paid such publicly respectful attention to a woman's views. Schreiner argued that the impulse of the Australians 'to show the world that when the mother country got into a war the colonies were prepared to take their place beside her' was naïve: 'This is a capitalists' war. They want to get control of the Rand and the mines.'[25] The exploited Boers, she predicted, would not surrender until overwhelmed, and their guerrilla resistance would protract a struggle resulting in appalling carnage and loss of life.

The capitalist ownership of land and the exploitation of farmers had long been an issue which concerned Paterson. Ten years previously he had published *Australia for the Australians*, a pamphlet in which he advocated land nationalisation, adapting to an Australian economic and geographical context the Single Tax arguments of Henry George (with a significant modification, entailing the rejection of free trade in the local situation).[26] Although he had by the mid-nineties put George aside, Schreiner was stirring the memory and vestiges of his radicalism, and he refused to make Cecil Rhodes, whom he later saw at Kimberley, into a hero. 'She says openly what most South Africans think', he writes in a display of considered tolerance, 'and it is always well to hear both sides'. At first he reassured his readers that 'the English are too humane to care about levying reprisals by destroying homesteads and leaving [the guerrillas'] wives and children without shelter'; throughout the course of the dispatches he is anxious to disprove (or at times to concede) that Schreiner is a Cassandra. When the British generals began to burn farms and to hold Boer women and children in camps, torturing and blackmailing their captive husbands, and forcing families to flee to the mountains, he was forced to concede that her prophecies had been fulfilled.[27]

Paterson's 'Australian nationalism', like that of his contemporaries, was inseparable from a sense of radical kinship (filialness and 'brotherhood' are variants of this familial trope), a shared nationhood with the British. At the commencement of the war, voicing the official line, he proclaims:

When we hear our brethren call,
Sound a clear reveille,
Then we answer, one and all,
Answer that the world may see,
Of the English stock are we,
At their side we still will be,
Sound a bold reveille.[28]

The profound racial connection cannot be affected by political differences, social structure, political ideology or policy, or by aversion for English practices and military incompetence. As 'With French to Kimberley' uncompromisingly proclaims, 'those who fight the British Isles must fight the British race!'[29] Consequently, as Paterson's respect and even personal liking and compassion for the Boer farmers and soldiers increased, all his humane faith had to be channelled singly into the hope for a rapid British victory to curtail carnage and suffering. The problem was, he speculated, that the English could not communicate successfully with the Boers, personally, politically or militarily, since they lacked sensitivity and diplomacy. In effect Paterson's writings now reflected his fluctuating optimism, disillusion and eventual despair of the 'merciful' outcome he sought.

At Cape Town a victory seems imminent: the problem will be sensitive relations with the defeated, as 'after England has beaten these Boers she will still have a sullen and discontented [African] population'.[30] After Colesburg, and despite heavy Boer losses, he is more aware of guerrilla tenacity, but believes the enemy 'must break down . . . before long'.[31] After the talk with Olive Schreiner, and several military setbacks, he believes England will 'certainly want every one of the 120,000 men in the field', and is disheartened by this 'slow and expensive business'.[32]

> It is the most depressing thing I know to go up on the kopje and see the horses stiff in death, and trace the long lines of human blood over the stones, each showing where some wounded men had made for shelter. When one remembers that the wounded men were some of one's own best friends, small wonder that some of us cared to stay too long on the kopje.[33]

By early February, during the invasion of the Orange Free State, Paterson is conceding, and to some extent excusing, the destruction of Boer farms, but he clings still to a belief in the integrity of British generals Roberts and Kitchener. When the Presidents of the Free State and the Transvaal protest that British troops are 'blowing up farms with dynamite and behaving like barbarians', he agrees that they have 'blown up a farm or two' but claims 'only where necessary for safety to clear away cover from the enemy'.[34] The troops are under orders not to loot or destroy, or 'needlessly leave women homeless'. By late February, after French's successful dash to Kimberley, he is still 'prophesying a steady end to the war', as if that outcome is possible and imminent, but he also marvels at the defiance of Cronje and his men, who look 'as if they had just come out from a fire' and 'knew they had made a phenomenal resistance against the odds – 50,000 men against 3,000'.[35]

The ambivalence of the war writings is strikingly illustrated by the contrast between Paterson's idealised, heavily 'British' literary ballad 'With French to Kimberley', which eulogises the courage and skills of 'the world wide Empire's sons', and his sober prose dispatch of 17 February concerning the entry into Kimberley:

> The people were half starved, and had been limited to a quarter of a pound of horseflesh a day; they had been hiding in holes in the ground, and sleeping in the ditches for fear of shells. Poor wretches: no wonder they cheered. . . . They all rushed at the General's horse to caress him, they cried, they waved their hands and ran alongside the line. . . . The General hurried off to arrange an attack next day. . . . The blacks are all around our camp eating the horses that fall weak and are shot. They fling themselves on them like a crowd of vultures, and in minutes there isn't a scrap left.[36]

After Bloemfontein, and buoyed by its siege, he is still unaware of the realities of guerrilla warfare – that captured or empty townships are not necessarily the evidence of imminent victory. He has 'no doubt' that the Free State will 'placidly' and 'loyally' accept the English rule, provided that the Boers are not turned off their farms.[37] Nevertheless, a few weeks later he is lamenting the prolongation of the war 'for a year or two' [!], and complains against the convention preventing the Allies from taking African horses from farms as remounts.[38]

Kroonstadt, Johannesburg and Pretoria are captured: on 17 June, without a trace of intended irony, Paterson records that 'the capture of Pretoria does not appear to have ended the war'.[39] A week later, Boer General Christian de Wet attacks, and the end of the war is put back 'six months at least'.[40] Disillusion increases, and despite earlier arguments he admits:

> We burnt a house belonging to the Boer Commandant as a means of inducing him to . . . lay down his arms. The women were given 15 minutes to get their effects out of the house; they lost their heads, cried pitifully, and brought out all sorts of useless things – vases and photographs, and so on [!] – instead of bedding and eatables. Then the house was burnt and the army moved on. No doubt it is an advisable step but when you see it done it is a different matter. When you really see women and children turned, homeless and crying, out on the open veldt – well, you want to be home and done with the war. Let us hope that it may be the means of bringing the war to an end.[41]

In one of his final dispatches, Paterson concludes at last that 'the Boers are certainly bearing out the prediction of Olive Schreiner' that the taking of Pretoria would mark not the ending but merely a new phase in the war, and that 'while rebels are at large, and the Boers are threatened with transportation, the war will drag on for a great while in guerrilla fashion'.[42] The war was to continue for another two years, and the British and their allies were to lose many more lives than their eventually defeated opponents; but Paterson now left South Africa. It was time to make a shift.

Beneath an energetic, closely observed, pictorial surface realism, Paterson's dispatches reveal, like a diary, the process of his personal discovery both of War in general and the distinctive nature of the African War. They chart the emotional dynamic of his hopes, delusions, insights and rationalisations, and his eventually overriding determination to achieve honesty and clear-sightedness. The war poems are like accompanying illustrations, often in caricature, sometimes indicative of a conscience hidden from the public because it was, Paterson felt, too dangerous or personally disturbing to be revealed. Generally more remarkable for their sometimes astonishing personal, biographical and historical interest than for their literary merit, they are to the reader today a curate's egg, of which the 'good parts' are epigrammatic lines, bitter quips and satirical jibes, expressions of contempt towards the glorification and self-interested exploitation of war, and black comic whimsy. If we read the poems carefully, and in conjunction with the dispatches, we discover echoes and less extreme or less exaggerated counterparts in the prose reports. Taken together, Paterson's prose and verse are revealed, on balance, as more emphatically '*anti*-war' than bellicose or even nationalistic. Since the 'extreme' poems that were not published during the war can frequently be related to experiences that were described in the prose correspondence, it is impossible to conclude that Paterson merely wrote bush-war propaganda. Indeed his early departure from the war zone indicates, in the context of his journalism, that he had become (in the words of one of his verse characters) 'fed up'.[43]

In 'Our Underpaid Army', his target is hysterical social adulation of war 'achievements', together with privilege, sinecure and incompetence amongst the British officer class:

And nowadays each little cheap success
Is quite enough to set the country yelling,
With big black headlines in the daily press
And D.S.O.s thrown out like pom-poms shelling.
With people drinking, Mafficking, and bawling,
Our frenzied self-laudation is appalling![44]

The 'eye-glassed impotent from Piccadilly' receives the highest financial reward for the grossest incompetence:

> But business training! Why, they never had one!
> If sent to buy a pie they'd buy a bad one!

'That V.C.', published in the *Bulletin* (19 May 1900), exposes contemptuously the quest for heroic recognition ('big noting') and financial reward for war 'achievements' by revealing the spurious side of 'mateship'. A soldier seeking glory and reward fails to persuade a wounded comrade to leave his foxhole:

> 'You get up on my shoulders, mate
> And if we live beyond the firing
> I'll get the V.C. sure as fate
> Because our blokes is all retiring.'
> 'It's fifty pounds a year,' says he,
> 'I'll stand you lots of beer and whisky'
> 'No,' says the wounded man, 'not me,
> I'll not be saved, it's far too risky.'

'On the Trek' (written 1900, published in *Rio Grande*, 1902), also subversively deploys pastoral and mateship legendary against the glorification of war: 'khaki soldiers travel like a mob of travelling sheep' and

> When the dusk and the excitement and the novelty are dead
> And you've seen a load of wounded once or twice
> Or you've watched your old mate dying – with the vultures overhead
> Well, you wonder if the war is worth the price.[45]

'Now Listen to Me and I'll Tell You My Views' (*Bulletin*, 29 March 1902) vilifies the Tory press for its propagandist 'shriek' against Afrikaner generals ('De Wet is a madman, and Steyn is a liar, and Kruger a pitiful cur!'), and courageously redirects the rhetoric upon the English:

> And let us join the bloodthirsty shriek, Hooray for Lord Kitchener's 'bag'!
> For the fireman's torch and the hangman's cord – they are hung on the English Flag!
> In front of our brave old army! Whoop! The farmhouse blazes bright.
> And their women weep and their children die – how dare they presume to fight!

> For none of them dress in a uniform, the same as by rights they ought.
> They're fighting in rags and in naked feet, like Wallace's Scotchmen fought![46]

'Our Own Flag' (written 1900) goes further, not only *blaming* the English, but also advocating (despite the connections of Empire and of race and blood) the ultimate act of rejection – imperial (and in the deepest racial sense, national) separation. The contract to 'stand by' the English flag, 'right or wrong', is to be jettisoned: 'deep in our hearts' is the truth that we fought not for the British but 'for the sake of a fight'; in the future we 'will carry our own flag up to the front'.[47] But perhaps the most potentially controversial (and of course only recently published) is the balladic monologue 'I Joined A Contingent', in which a Falstaffian deserter who has enlisted for the pay, promotion and pastime of Boer hunting, defends his pragmatism with the evidence of his own survival. 'Spoken' prose voice-over 'asides' using Australian codes of humour are employed to elicit a jocular understanding for the extreme underdog position of the malingering deserter:

> Yes you can talk about your V.C. and all that: Wait till you've heard a bullet go wheeuw, close past your head. The officer shouted 'Forwards, Forwards', so I lay there and said to myself, 'well he doesn't want me – I'm not a forward, I'm a fullback'.[48]

Although this jeu d'esprit is scarcely the literal realism of the dispatches, what is most arresting and effective in the war verses is nevertheless a product of the focus on the real war. The reader is directed by comic strategies of withering satire or whimsical grimness not towards a world of escape, to another place like that of the Geebang Polo Club or the innocent abroad from Ironbark, or even to an African equivalent of sunlit plains and drovers replacing soldiers on horseback, or of gallant and wonderful victories. The tragedy, Paterson makes clear, is that the world depicted is this one.

NOTES

1. This case is argued in detail in my essay 'A.B. "Banjo" Paterson' in S. Samuels (ed.), *Dictionary of Literary Biography, Volume Two Hundred Thirty: Australian Literature, 1788–1914* (Detroit, etc., Gale, 2001), pp. 285–301. The present essay is a revised version of the 2000 Barry Andrews Memorial Lecture ('Banjo Paterson and the Boer War') delivered at the Australian Defence Force Academy in October 2000.

2. See Rosamund Campbell and Philippa Harvie (comp.), *Song of the Pen. A.B. 'Banjo' Paterson: Complete Works 1901–1941* (Willoughby, N.S.W., Ure Smith Press), 1991, pp. xxv–xxvi.
3. See Rosamund Campbell and Philippa Harvie (comp.), *Singer of the Bush. A.B. 'Banjo' Paterson: Complete Works 1885–1900* (Willoughby, N.S.W., Ure Smith Press), 1991, p. 41.
4. Paterson did not sign his poetry with his own surname until his first collection, *The Man from Snowy River and Other Verses* (Sydney, Angus and Robertson), appeared in 1895. The best known of his several pen names during the previous decade was 'The Banjo', and critics and biographers are usually quick to point out that by his own admission he chose the name of a favourite racehorse. What has been overlooked, of course, is that to infer (as is often done) that the name was selected without regard for its balladic and musical connotations is a non-sequitur.
5. Robin Gerster, 'War Literature, 1890–1980', in Laurie Hergenhan (gen. ed.), *The Penguin New Literary History of Australia* (Ringwood, Vic., Penguin Books, 1988), p. 341. See also Gerster's *Big-noting* (Melbourne, Melbourne University Press, 1987).
6. Gerster, 'War Literature, 1890–1980', p. 341.
7. Marilyn Lake, 'The Politics of Respectability. Identifying the Masculinist Context', *Historical Studies*, vol. 22, no. 86 (1986), pp. 116–31.
8. For closer discussion of individualism and romanticism in 'Clancy of the Overflow', 'The Man from Snowy River', 'Waltzing Matilda' and 'A Bushman's Song' see Ken Stewart, 'A.B. "Banjo" Paterson', note 1 *supra*.
9. 'Borderland', *Bulletin*, 9 July 1892. (Later re-titled 'Up the Country'.)
10. 'In Answer to Banjo and Otherwise', *Bulletin*, 6 August 1892.
11. Elyne Mitchell, *The Man from Snowy River: The Novelisation of the Film* (Sydney, Angus and Robertson, 1982).
12. *Singer of the Bush*, p. 465.
13. Ibid., p. 571.
14. Ibid., pp. 582–4. The interview with Kipling is notable particularly for Paterson's scepticism towards him, his contempt for Kipling's urge to 'get some revenge out of the Boers for men we've lost', Kipling's impracticable plans for irrigation of the veldt, and Paterson's remark: 'I said that our men did not think the country worth fighting over.'
15. Ibid., pp. 675–8.
16. Ibid., p. 605.
17. Ibid., pp. 455–698, *passim*.
18. 'Cape Mounted Rifles', *Singer of the Bush*, p. 505, and 'Queensland Mounted Infantry', *Singer of the Bush*, p. 524.
19. See below.
20. *Singer of the Bush*, p. 471.
21. Ibid.

22. Ibid., p. 473.
23. Ibid., p. 475.
24. Ibid., p. 477.
25. Ibid., p. 523.
26. A.B. Paterson, Solicitor, Sydney, *Australia for the Australians: A Political Pamphlet, Showing the necessity for Land Reform, combined with Protection* (Sydney, Gordon & Gotch, 1889).
27. See, for example, *Singer of the Bush*, p. 668.
28. 'The Reveille', *Singer of the Bush*, p. 461. First published *Sydney Mail*, 6 January 1900.
29. 'With French to Kimberley', *Singer of the Bush*, p. 689; f.p. *Sydney Morning Herald*, 29 September 1900.
30. *Singer of the Bush*, p. 469.
31. Ibid., p. 509.
32. Ibid., p. 529.
33. Ibid., p. 525.
34. Ibid., p. 526.
35. Ibid., p. 536. 'One good defeat will bring peace much nearer – Olive Schreiner notwithstanding.' Compare this with a dispatch some five months later (14 July): The Boers never make a stand now—they fight from ridge to ridge, always having a way of escape when our men get too close; and the troops are asking themselves whether they are to follow the Boers all round Africa for the rest of their lives. The Boers are certainly bearing out the prediction of Olive Schreiner, who stated to the writer at Capetown quite early in the war that after we got to Pretoria they would begin to give trouble. One cannot help admiring their pluck and determination. All the stories about Boer savagery are nonsense. To the eye of an English globe-trotter, they, no doubt, seem pretty tough and uncouth, and so would a lot of Australian backblock settlers; but, as a matter of fact, the Boers are a very commonplace lot of farmers and settlers. (*Singer of the Bush*, p. 668.)
36. Ibid., p. 546. Note, however, that Paterson's compassionate and respectful attitude towards the Boers does not extend to the Kaffirs, or 'niggers' as he terms them. His racist contempt has been misrepresented by biographers, who disregard it or depict it as merely characteristic of the period. Paterson's attitudes were clearly more callous than those of most of his journalist and literary contemporaries. See Stewart, A.B. "Banjo" Paterson, op. cit., p. 297, and Paterson, 'The Kaffir Question' in *Singer of the Bush*, pp. 603–4.
37. *Singer of the Bush*, p. 572.
38. Ibid., p. 600.
39. Ibid., p. 650.
40. Ibid., p. 655.
41. Ibid., p. 661.

42. Ibid., p. 688. See also pp. 679–80.
43. 'Fed Up', *Sydney Mail*, 26 May 1900, repr. in *Singer of the Bush*, p. 580.
44. The reference is to the much publicised relief by General Roberts and his army of the Cape Province town of Mafeking (later renamed Mafikeng) which had been besieged by the Boers from 12 October 1899 to 17 May 1900. *Singer of the Bush*, p. 548.
45. Ibid., p. 663.
46. *Song of the Pen*, p. 59.
47. *Singer of the Bush*, p. 686.
48. Ibid., p. 694.

Zarathustra's 'Statue': May Fourth Literature and the Appropriation of Nietzsche and Lu Xun*

Mabel Lee

Nietzsche (1844–1900) reviews his life and works in the preface to *Ecce Homo*, claiming that with *Zarathustra* he had given mankind the greatest gift it has ever received (Nietzsche, 1888: 219). He is certain of *Zarathustra*'s transcendent beauty and as if fearful of its misappropriation, he repeats Zarathustra's warning: 'Beware lest a statue slay you' (N, 1888: 220). However, at the time, it is unlikely that he could have imagined the nature and extent of the extraordinary cultural transcendence *Zarathustra* would achieve in China some decades later.

The writer Lu Xun (1881–1936), who through his short stories laid the first foundation stones of China's modern literature in the period known as May Fourth (1915–22), was dubbed by his contemporaries as 'China's Nietzsche'. This resulted from a reference to his 'Tolstoy Nietzschean thinking and Wei-Jin style of writing' by Liu Bannong (1891–1934) (Cao nd: 43). While the Nietzschean label has remained with Lu Xun and has resulted in countless studies on Lu Xun and Nietzsche, the Tolstoy (anarchist) and Wei-Jin (Daoist individualism) labels have largely been ignored. The present study asserts that Liu Bannong's brief description encapsulates essential elements of Lu Xun's persona and aims at addressing the anarchist element in Lu Xun's intellectual makeup as well as investigating how anarchist and Nietzschean elements coalesce because of his underlying commitment to Daoist individualism. In this study, the transmission of Nietzsche to China is recontextualised in a continuum of two-way intellectual intercrossings between China and Europe. In the process some 'statues' such as those of which Zarathustra speaks will be observed.

It is maintained that whereas a younger cohort of May Fourth writers had chosen to appropriate Nietzsche (in preference to Tolstoy and anarchism) as a modern icon, political weapon, or 'statue' for their cause to re-invent Chinese literature, this was not the case with Lu Xun. For Lu Xun, as for Nietzsche, literature is universal and timeless. Neither is Nietzsche a 'statue' for Lu Xun, despite his admiration of the philosopher. His 'statue' is the nation and it is this 'statue' which slays the writer Lu Xun (cf. Lee, 1982a and 1998; Gao, 1990: 27 and 1993). However, as the author of the first exemplary works of 'modern' literature in China, Lu Xun in turn was also appropriated to the cause of the young writers. This zealous double appropriation of Nietzsche and Lu Xun as 'statues' has distorted people's understanding of Lu Xun's view of literary creation.

Lu Xun's existential being may best be described as Zhuangzean-Nietzschean. His notion of literature may be elucidated by *Zarathustra* which in Nietzsche's words is 'born out of the innermost wealth of truth, an inexhaustible well to which no pail descends without coming up again filled with gold and goodness. Here no "prophet" is speaking, none of those gruesome hybrids of sickness and will to power whom people call founders of religions' (Nietzsche 1880: 219). This notion of literature is confirmed in Jungian terms as the visionary poet's expression of the primordial unconsciousness (noting that Jung is informed by Daoism) (Clarke 1992 and 1994). It is suggested that apparent similarities in the thinking of Lu Xun and Nietzsche may lie in their tapping of the same 'inexhaustible well': what Jung calls the primordial unconsciousness that has its origins in Daoism.

Jung acknowledges his debt to Daoism but Nietzsche research to date is only beginning to establish archival evidence of Nietzsche's knowledge of Daoist texts (see Cheung 2002: 14, fn 7; cf. Figl 1991). Notwithstanding, numerous detailed and meticulous comparative studies have suggested remarkable similarities and mirror reflections (e.g. Hall 1984; Ames 1984 and 1991; Chen 1991). The present study works on the assumption that it is highly improbable that Nietzsche was not familiar with the French translations of Daoist texts published after the Chair of Sinology was established in Paris in 1814 (Schipper 1995), as Nietzsche was known to have been a Francophile (Parkes 1991b: 4). Furthermore, it should be noted that German thinkers from Leibniz to Schopenhauer have to varying degrees been inspired by the philosophical traditions of China (cf. Clarke 1994: 6–7), and that their philosophical systems constituted the intellectual matrix in which Nietzsche developed his ideas.

It is asserted that apparent similarities in Lu Xun and Nietzsche may therefore to some extent be traced to cultural intercrossings: in the early nineteenth century of Daoism to Europe, and in the early twentieth century of European anarchist thinking and Nietzsche to China. The suggestion is that Lu Xun's notions of the self and the individual (Daoist individualism) were re-affirmed by European anarchist thinking as well as Nietzsche's *Zarathustra*. However, it would seem that a significant reason for similarities lies in the fact that both were writers of powerful intellects, uncompromising cultural critics who were deeply engrossed with the existential issue of the challenges of socialised existence for the individual.

Industrial capitalism in nineteenth-century Europe further empowered the minority and disempowered the majority: for the disempowered majority, the person of the individual was reduced to an integer of labour resource for insatiable machines. Backed by military might, industrial capitalism spilled into the non-industrialised world in search of raw materials and markets, spawning colonies and forcing nations such as China to open for trade. During the 1880s and 1890s, the depredations of capitalist industrialisation on human society came to be actively addressed throughout the industrialised world by anarchist, socialist, utopian movements, and by the bold pronouncements of Nietzsche.

The political activism of European anarchism appealed to Chinese revolutionaries, as did the familiar ring of Daoist equality in its utopian belief in human equality and dignity which emphasised the right of individuals to basic needs as well as to develop their full potential as human beings. Alongside Nietzsche, the writings of Tolstoy, Kropotkin, Bakunin, Malatesta, Proudhon and Stirner served to re-affirm, regenerate, and to reformulate traditional notions of the self and the individual as contained in Daoist thinking.

As noted above, Daoist texts became known to the intellectual world of Europe from the early years of the nineteenth century. My contention is that Daoist equality because of its 'otherness' came to be internalised in European critiques of its own culture and that it was subsumed in the intellectual matrix out of which much of modern European thinking has grown. The familiarity of residual Daoist traces thus explains the appeal of both European anarchism and Nietzsche for Chinese intellectuals when they encountered these at the beginning of the twentieth century. Remade and repackaged with European labels, Daoist individualism assumed a Western modernity that authorised and legitimised its attacks on China's traditional culture, blamed as the reason for China's failure to meet the challenge of the industrialised nations of the world.

When neighbouring Japan (which had joined the industrialised world by the 1880s) emerged as victor in the Sino-Japanese War (1894–5) and the Russo-Japanese War (1904–5), Chinese intellectuals became acutely aware of the nation's predicament. Confronted by the impending loss of territorial sovereignty, the exploitation of resources and the annihilation of the Chinese race, Chinese students began to flock to Japan to acquire the modern (i.e. Western) knowledge needed to save the nation. Significant numbers of students were also drawn to Europe despite the fact that there they were even more lowly regarded than in Japan. A Chinese anarchist noted in London: 'People say that the Chinese are useless, fit only to serve as work animals for the white race' (Zhang 1908).

In Japan the negative effects of industrialisation on Japanese society were already apparent and social and existential problems, as in Europe, increasingly became the major concern of the Japanese intellectual world. It was a dynamic intellectual scene throbbing with socialists and anarchists, and at the same time undergoing a Nietzsche craze, that Chinese students encountered on their arrival (see Ito, 1990). The Chinese scholarly tradition was strongly biased towards the humanities, hence often while pursuing studies in Western disciplines such as science, law and economics, many Chinese students instinctively looked to the literatures, histories and philosophies of the West. This humanities bias was reflected in their avid reading of Western thinkers, at first largely through Japanese interpretations and translations but soon, in some cases, by reading the original works. By the May Fourth period Chinese writers, including Lu Xun, were publishing their translations of large numbers of European and Russian writers as well as using these works as rough templates for their own creative writings.

In the last decade of the nineteenth century Tan Sitong (1865–98) observed that Confucian philosophy, used as state ideology, had progressively annihilated the self: it had robbed the individual of initiative and responsibility by inculcating slavish and hypocritical thinking and behaviour which had become endemic in all levels of society. Confucianism had achieved social harmony by emphasising inequality and, moreover, ensured the acceptance of the moral correctness of that inequality, hence according moral sanction to political authority. Tan Sitong identified personal autonomy and the empowering of the individual as the reason for the dynamism of the European powers (cf. Chan 1984). Chinese anarchists in Tokyo and Paris developed Tan Sitong's attacks on Confucian society with the help of Western anarchist thinking and by revisiting Daoist critiques on the sycophantic behaviour of Confucians who had aligned themselves with the bureaucracy. Importantly, the anarchists widely publicised these ideas. The notions of human equality, human dignity, and the value, freedom, and autonomy of the individual were established as goals for all of humanity and as an integral part of mainstream intellectual discourse endorsed by all progressive Chinese thinkers. By the May Fourth period these notions were 'not easily distinguishable as anarchist ideas, especially as the anarchists did not claim them explicitly for anarchism' (Dirlik 1991: 160–1).

These same notions, also found in the writings of independent thinkers of the past, had been expounded unambiguously in the Ming dynasty by Li Zhi (1527–1602), whose critical dissertations on Buddhist, Mohist and Daoist texts incurred the wrath of orthodox Confucians. He was vilified, slandered and finally silenced. Modern Chinese anarchists resurrected him from obscurity, hailing him as 'China's Bakunin'. For Li Zhi freedom of the individual and freedom of thought were paramount. The individual should not be a prisoner to the codes of morality dictated by society nor should he be deluded by personal gain. Instead, he should act fearlessly as his heart dictates. Li Zhi's goal was to destroy the boundaries between the noble and the humble, the rich and the poor, those with or without family ties, and also boundaries between the sexes (Bugong Chou 1907: 434–5).

By incorporating elements of European evolutionism, the anarchist Chu Minyi (1844–1946) provided Daoist individualism with an active edge and an emphasis on progress. He argues that civilised man is not the same as primitive man and, apart from eating and clothing himself he desires 'to investigate other phenomena, to conquer the natural world, and to strive to progress'. Man's intellect is highly developed and mankind therefore possesses greater sensitivity to pain and pleasure. If something does not suit he will adapt it: this has led to the inventions which have come about in the history of mankind. However, man is a composition of organic matter and therefore subject to the laws of nature, so he will inevitably die and decompose. Nevertheless, if he has the freedom to express himself in speech and in action and if he uses his time wisely and exerts his intellect to its potential, he may be considered as having accomplished his goal in life. The individual's freedom is sacrosanct. Chu rejects morality that is imposed by others, for him it is the individual who defines morality (Chu 1908: 191–3). However, in Chu's formulation of anarchist morality, the extension of knowledge is absolutely critical, for by the extension of knowledge the mind is enlightened and it is the enlightened mind that makes actions sincere. By defining 'the actions of sincere men as the morality of just men' Chu's notion of sincerity is similar to that of Song Confucianism (which had absorbed elements of Daoism). In the Confucianism of the Song dynasty, it is this notion of sincerity that deletes differences between individuals (cf. Metzger 1977), making it akin to Daoist equality (cf. Murakami 1987). Chu sees education as agent both for developing the propensity of the individual to sincerity of action and for human progress (Chu 1908: 194).

Anarchism, according to Chu, assigned to the individual the role of actively pursuing the full development of his intellectual and moral capacities. This would empower the individual to autonomous and independent thinking and action that, at the same time, would be 'sincere' (morally just). In this form of empowerment of the self, there is no difference from Daoist individualism or (when it is not aligned with ambitions to political power) philosophical Song Confucianism. However, the extension of knowledge by definition now included Western knowledge, thus passive Daoist individualism was transformed into a modern way of thinking which offered the means for creating a more just society. Indeed, Chinese anarchists of the time engaged in political activism, including terrorism, and anarchist ideals dominated the late-Qing revolutionary movement that toppled the imperial government in 1911.

Anarchist ideals of equality and Daoist individualism were widely publicised by the revolutionary propaganda machinery to such an extent that by the May Fourth period these permeated all intellectual discourse. This intellectual climate facilitated the appropriation of Zarathustra by young writers who set out to re-invent Chinese literature as a 'new' literature which addressed contemporary issues. (This new literature, China's modern literature, written in the vernacular language instead of the classical language, was much influenced by European literary models.) However, as this new literature had a clearly defined mission of social reform, it was at odds with Nietzsche's 'gift' of literature. China's contemporary issues were such that the intellectual climate was dominated by extreme nationalism, and Nietzsche's *Zarathustra* inspired heroism, romanticism, iconoclasm, and missionary zeal. As Japanese expansionism in China escalated and the nation became a 'statue', these Nietzsche-inspired sentiments fused and led to the heroic self-sacrifice of the individual for the collective. The survival of the nation was of paramount importance and it grew increasingly difficult to retain *Zarathustra*, even as a 'statue', as literature increasingly came to be used as a tool of political propaganda.

My claim that *Zarathustra* was no more than a 'statue' for May Fourth writers is substantiated by the fact that in the mid-1920s, only the Prologue and a few of the essays of the book existed in Chinese translation; the publication of Nietzsche's other writings came even later. The proposal by May Fourth writers to re-invent Chinese literature negated the universality and timelessness of literature and blinded them to what constituted literature. This self-inflicted blindness denied that the masterpieces of China's literary heritage too had tapped the 'inexhaustible well' of which Zarathustra spoke. Literary criticism did not exist as a genre in traditional China, but was articulated in scattered desultory comments in prefaces and essays, as is the case in the writings of Nietzsche (cf. Lee 1998).

The early years of the foundling Republic were fraught with instability as former revolutionaries struggled for political power in the real world. The anarchist ideals, acknowledged as utopian and unattainable in the short-run, constituted the common core of the various revolutionary utopias, and became the domain of idealist intellectuals and writers. The non-involvement of many former revolutionaries in post-1911 politics is partially explained by their anarchist tendencies but more so by their lack of political expertise and experience. It was at this point that Nietzsche's pronouncement 'God is dead!' and Nietzsche's *Zarathustra* came to be appropriated by May Fourth writers to bestir intellectuals from their inertia, despair and feeling of impotence. In what seemed to be a hopeless reality the individual could perhaps hope to achieve self-realization through literary and artistic creation. However, the interventions of international and domestic power politics steered Chinese intellectuals into supporting collective action which would further subvert the dignity and authority of the individual and work against the human equality envisaged in anarchism and the heights of intellectual and artistic freedom espoused in Nietzsche's *Zarathustra*.

Both anarchism and Nietzsche, restate the Zhuangzean notion of the unfettered self that is relevant to the core of literary creation. Literature is a personal endeavour, and while associated with widening perceptions that accompany the influx and reception of new ideas, it nevertheless remains the solitary act of the individual. At all levels of the creative act, it is the individual who retains absolute authority for the interpretation of his reality. This essential message of both Daoist individualism (and Chinese anarchism) and Nietzsche, however, is not confined to literature but embraces the total being of the individual.

Lu Xun has been categorised as China's Nietzsche because of his early essays written in Japan (see Yue, 1988–89; Ito, 1990). However, the fact that these essays show his approval of Nietzsche should not be misconstrued as Lu Xun's having read a large number of Nietzsche's works or in fact many pages of *Zarathustra* at that time, although he was seriously studying German at the time. It is likely that he had read some secondary sources in Japanese as well as four articles on Nietzsche in *Education World*, 1904 (see Cheung 1992). After his abortive attempt in 1907 to establish a literary journal *New Life*, he sensed a deep loneliness growing like 'a giant poisonous snake' around his soul and on his return to China in 1909 he virtually succumbed to inertia and despair (Lu 1922: 1: 417). The success of his short story 'Diary of a Madman' (Lu 1918) coaxed him out of his inertia and he subsequently translated the Prologue of *Zarathustra* (Lu 1920). By that time, a younger cohort of writers had already formed a vanguard and was actively engaged in formulating the guidelines for China's new literature.

Lu Xun's commitment was to a Zhuangzean-Nietzschean philosophy which embraced his total being, including his views on literature. In his existential outlook he is close to his teacher of classical Chinese in Japan, Zhang Taiyan (1868–1936). Whereas Lu Xun tends to cloak his ideas in the poetic symbolism and implied meanings of his creative works, Zhang Taiyan, a brilliant polemicist, clearly and cogently articulates his notion of the individual. In the following I have therefore 'borrowed' Zhang Taiyan to elucidate the nature of the Zhuangzean-Nietzschean individualism both he and Lu Xun embraced. Zhang Taiyan describes his own individualism as approximating Nietzsche's *Übermensch*. One of the most powerful intellects of his time, he affirms the importance of the subjective self, which he dissociates from self-interest. He castigates public morality, evolutionism, materialism, and Song Confucianism, for having eroded the autonomy of the individual.

In Zhang's view, modern man's insistence on material evidence has led to an obsession for concrete things and the denial of spontaneous human reactions. He resoundingly declares that the individual emerges naked into the world at birth with only an instinct to survive and an innate resourcefulness: 'He was not born for the sake of the world. He was not born for the sake of society. He was not born for the sake of the nation. He was not born for others. Hence he has no responsibility to the world, to society, to the nation or to others' (Zhang 1907: 10; see Lee 1983). On the other hand, he repudiates the Christian concept of God as being 'an almighty spirit who created man to propagate His species in order to bring Glory unto His Kingdom' because it abnegates the autonomy of the individual to a Superior Being. This, he says, is the basic difference between Christianity and the teachings of Laozi and Zhuangzi which state explictly that man is independent at birth and is not born for others: 'If a Creator does not exist then there can be no one giving orders. . . . My actions derive from an innate love and not because some regulation stipulates it' (Zhang 1908: 3; see Lee 1983).

Zhang Taiyan thus eloquently articulates the essential link between Daoist individualism, Nietzsche, and modern Chinese anarchist thinking. There is no conflict in the existential message for the individual. As European intellectuals from the nineteenth century onwards read translations of original Daoist texts, their Chinese contemporaries read the originals, as well as two thousand years of literature inspired by those ancient texts. Even the Song Confucian texts had incorporated the existential ideas of Daoism. Although traditional Daoist thinking had evolved over the centuries there nevertheless remained a timeless existential core which was transmitted back to China through the writings of European anarchists and Nietzsche.

By the time Lu Xun encountered Nietzsche's writings as a student in Japan in the early years of the twentieth century, he was already widely read in China's traditional literature. While in Japan he was also exposed to European and Chinese anarchist writings, revolutionary writings, and not least the powerful writings of his teacher, Zhang Taiyan (see Lee 1983). While there are substantial differences between Lu Xun and Zhang Taiyan, a strong similarity exists in their uncompromising defence of their personal integrity, sincerity to the self, and commitment to a Zhuangzean-Nietzschean style of being. This aspect of their personalities rendered them, as well as Nietzsche, incapable of being effective political individuals: they were supreme in their independence of the crowd, or the collective. Zhang Taiyan for example boldly wrote the preface to Zou Rong's anti-Manchu booklet *Revolutionary Army* and was imprisoned for three years in the International Settlement in Shanghai. Released in 1906, he was immediately taken to Tokyo to assume editorship of *Minbao*, the propaganda newspaper of the Chinese Revolutionary Alliance; by 1908 he had totally fallen out with its leading members. A few years later, he had the temerity to offer unsolicited advice to Yuan Shikai (1859–1916), the most powerful man in China, to abandon plans to re-establish the monarchy with himself as the emperor. Zhang found himself under house arrest for another three years of his life, only to be released after the death of the dictator (see Lee 1983).

Lu Xun states that while he did not subscribe to the idea of a revolution in literature, he had written the stories collected in *Outcry* (1923) because he sympathised with the young writers' goal of social reform. He was in a sense complying with the wishes of these enthusiastic young writers, but only because their goals seemed at the time to coincide with his own (Lu 1932: 1, 455–7; see Lee 1982: 146). His 'Diary of a Madman' had instantly made him a celebrity, the hero of Chinese youth. However, while little understood by them, both Lu Xun and Nietzsche became 'statues' for Chinese youth. Based on his powerful writings in *Outcry* and in a later collection *Hesitation* (Lu 1926) Lu Xun was appropriated by the youthful writers promoting a 'new' Chinese literature. However, his participation in May Fourth literary groups was, in fact, marginal.

As in the case of Zhang Taiyan, Lu Xun was a loner, unable to conform to the collective will. His commitment to a Zhuangzean-Nietzschean philosophy was total and can be seen in his act of choosing to abandon creative writing, an act which he knew would leave him like a 'corpse with its heart gouged out', as described in his prose-poem, 'The Epitaph' (Lu 1925). The 23 prose-poems Lu Xun wrote between 26 April 1924 and 10 April 1926, published as a collection with the title *Wild Grass* (Lu 1927), remain amongst the finest examples of China's early modern poetry. At the same time, *Wild Grass* is a poignant dirge written as Lu Xun makes the choice to end his creative life: an act which may be attributed to his uncompromising commitment to a Zhuangzean-Nietzschean philosophy of the self (see Lee 1982 and 1990).

In 'Autumn Night' (Lu 1924), the first of the *Wild Grass* poems, Lu Xun already perceives a bifurcation in his persona, symbolised in the two date trees whose branches stretch up to pierce the night sky (the total persona of Lu Xun), making it wince with pain. One of the date trees represents Lu Xun the writer, and the other the intellectual Lu Xun who has a responsibility to the nation (Lee 1982: 148). This bifurcation of the persona can be explained in Jungian terms. The creative being is a human being with a personal life but simultaneously he is an impersonal creative process:

total persona of Lu Xun), making it wince with pain. One of the date trees represents Lu Xun the writer, and the other the intellectual Lu Xun who has a responsibility to the nation (Lee 1982: 148). This bifurcation of the persona can be explained in Jungian terms. The creative being is a human being with a personal life but simultaneously he is an impersonal creative process:

> Art is a kind of innate drive that seizes a human being and makes him an instrument. The artist is not a person endowed with free will who seeks his own ends, but allows art to realize its purposes through him. As a human being he may have moods and a will and personal aims, but as an artist he is 'man' in a higher sense—he is 'collective man'—one who carries and shapes the unconscious, psychic life of mankind. To perform this difficult office it is sometimes necessary for him to sacrifice happiness and everything that makes life worth living for the ordinary human being. (Jung 1944: 192–5)

Jung identifies Nietzsche as a visionary poet who taps the primordial unconsciousness. The visionary mode of creation derives its existence from the 'hinterland of man's mind' and is a primordial experience beyond man's understanding, but it has psychic reality and therefore physical reality. The artist or writer penetrates to 'that matrix in which all men are embedded, which imparts a common rhythm to all human existence, and allows the individual to communicate his feeling and his striving to mankind as a whole' (Jung 1944: 196–8).

Jung refers only to the artist or writer who must sacrifice the goals of normal life in order to pursue the calling to create. In Lu Xun's case the other choice is painfully made: to cause his creative self to suicide and to deny himself the possibility of achieving the Nietzschean joy of creating a *Zarathustra*. In concluding, I suggest that in writing the poems of *Wild Grass* Lu Xun had drawn from the 'inexhaustible well' from which *Zarathustra* was born. Significantly, in June 1924, he wrote several studies on the Daoism-inspired Wei-Jin writer Ji Kang (224–63) as well as a preface for *Ji Kang's Collected Poems*, a textual research project he had started in 1913. On 15 September 1924 he wrote 'Autumn Night', the first of the *Wild Grass* poems, and then a few days later on 22 September he began translating *Symbols of Suffering* (1924), by Kuriyagawa Hakuson (1880–1923). In this work Kuriyagawa systematically explores literary creation within a Nietzschean framework (see Lu 1981: 16, 14–15; Lee 1982: 156–62). Literature had a specific meaning for Lu Xun and he did not want the creative writings that had given him Nietzschean ecstasy to be tarnished by the polemical writings he knew he had to write. His decision to sacrifice his creative life was for a 'statue', the nation, to which he had committed himself many years ago in Japan when he had solemnly declared: 'I offer my blood as a sacrifice to the Yellow Emperor' (Lu 1903).

REFERENCES

Academia Sinica, Institute of Modern History, ed., *Essays from the Conference on the Early History of the Republic of China*. Taipei: Academia Sinica, 1983.

Ames, Roger (1984), 'Coextending Arising, Te, and Will to Power: Two Doctrines of Self-Transformation'. *Journal of Chinese Philosophy*, 11: 113–38.

Ames, Roger T. (1991), 'Nietzsche's 'Will to Power' and Chinese 'Virtuality' (De): A Comparative Study'. Parkes 1991a: 130–50.

Bugong Chou (Enemy of Injustice) (1907), 'Li Zhuowu xiansheng xueshuo' (On the Teachings of Mr Li Zhuowu). Yang 1978: 434–9.

Cao, Juren. (n.d.), *Lu Xun pingzhuan*. Hong Kong: Dongxi wenhua shiye chubanshe.

Chan, Wai-sim (1984), *An Exposition of Benevolence: The Jen-hsüeh of T'an Ssu-t'ung*. Hong Kong: The Chinese University Press.

Chen, Guying (1991), tr. James Sellman, 'Zhuang Zi and Nietzsche'. Parkes 1991a: 115–29.

Cheung, Chiu-yee (1987), *Nicai yu Lu Xun sixiang fazhan: Nietzsche and the Development of Lu Xun's Thought*. Hong Kong: Qingwen shuwu.

——— (1992), *Nietzsche in China 1904–1992: An Annotated Bibliography*. Canberra: The Australian National University.

——— (2001), *Lu Xun: The Chinese 'Gentle' Nietzsche*. Frankfurt am Main: Peter Lang.

Clarke, J.J. (1992), *In Search of Jung: Historical and Philosophical Enquiries*. London: Routledge.

——— (1994), *Jung and Eastern Thought: A Dialogue with the Orient*. London: Routledge.

Chu, Minyi (1908), 'Wuzhengfu shuo' (Anarchism). Gao 1984: 161–211.

Davis, A.R. and Stefanowska, A.D. (1982), *Austrina: Essays in Commemoration of the 25th Anniversary of the Founding of the Oriental Society of Australia*. Sydney: Oriental Society of Australia.

Dirlik, Arif (1991), *Anarchism in the Chinese Revolution*. Berkeley: University of California Press.

Figl, Johann (1991), tr. Graham Parkes, 'Nietzsche's Early Encounters with Asian Thought'. Parkes 1991a: 51–63.

Findeisen, Raoul David (1997), 'The Burden of Culture: Glimpses at the Literary Reception of Nietzsche in China'. *Asian and African Studies*, 6, 1: 76–91.

Findeisen, Raoul D. and Gassman, Robert H. (1998), *Autumn Floods: Essays in Honour of Marián Gálik*. Bern: Peter Lang.

Gálik, Marián (1971), 'Nietzsche in China (1918–1925)', *Nachrichten der Gesellschaft für Natur- und Völkerkunde Ostasiens*, 110: 5–47.

Gao, Jun et al. (1984), *Wuzhengfuzhuyi zai Zhongguo* (Anarchism in China). Changsha: Hunan renmin chubanshe.

Gao, Xingjian (1990), 'Bali suibi' (Jottings from Paris) in Gao, 1996: 21–8.

——— (1993), 'Guojia shenhua yu geren diankuang' (Nation as Myth and Insanity for the Individual). *Mingbao yuekan*, 114: n.p.

——— (1996), *Meiyou zhuyi*. Hong Kong: Cosmos.

Ito, Toramaru (1990), Xu Jiang, 'Lu Xun zaoqi de Nicaïguan yu Meizhi wenxue' (Lu Xun's Early Nietzschean Views and Meiji Literature'. *Wenxue pinglun*, 1: 135–47.

Jung, C.G. (1944), tr. W.S. Dell and Cary F. Baynes, *Modern Man in Search of a Soul*. London: Kegan Paul, Trench, Trubner & Co. Ltd, 7th impression.

——— (1995), *Jung on the East*, edited with an introduction by J. J. Clarke. London: Routledge.

Lee, Mabel (1982), 'Suicide of the Creative Self: the Case of Lu Hsün'. Davis and Stefanowska 1982: 140–67.

——— (1983), 'Chang Ping-lin's Concept of Self and Society: Questions of Constancy and Continuity After the 1911 Revolution'. Academia Sinica 1983: 193–228.

——— (1985), 'From Chuang-tzu to Nietzsche: On the Individualism of Lu Hsün'. *The Journal of the Oriental Society of Australia*, 17: 21–38.

——— (1998), 'Gao Xingjian in Conversation with Two Dead Poets from Shaoxing: Xu Wei and Lu Xun'. Findeisen and Gassmann 1998: 401–14.

Lu, Xun (1903), 'Ziti xiaoxiang' (Inscribing My Own Portrait). Zhou 1980: 24.

——— (1918), 'Kuangren riji' (Diary of a Madman). Lu 1981: 1, 422–33.

——— (1922), '*Nahan* zixu' (Author's Preface to *Outcry*). Lu 1981: 1, 415–20.

——— (1923), *Nahan* (Outcry). Lu 1981: 1, 415–570.

——— (1924), 'Qiuye' (Autumn Night). Lu 1981: 2, 159–60.

——— (1925), 'Mujiewen' (The Epitaph). Lu 1981: 2, 202–3.

——— (1926), *Panghuang* (Hesitation). Lu 1981: 2, 5–155.

——— (1927), *Yecao* (Wild Grass). Lu 1981: 1, 159–225.

——— (1932), 'Zixuanji zixu' (Preface to *An Author-Selected Anthology*). Lu 1981: 4: 455–7.

——— (1981), *Lu Xun quanji* (Collected Works of Lu Xun). Beijing: Renmin wenxue chubanshe.

Nietzsche, Friedrich (1888), *Ecce Homo*. Nietzsche 1969: 222–335.

——— (1969), *On the Genealogy of Morals and Ecce Homo*, ed. with commentary by Walter Kaufmann. Toronto: Random House.

Metzger, Thomas A (1977), *Escape from Predicament: Neo-Confucianism and China's Evolving Political Culture.* New York: Columbia University Press.

Murakami, Yoshimi (1987), 'Conceptions of Equality and Human Nature in Taoism', in Siriwardena, ed., 1987.

Parkes, Graham (1991b), 'The Orientation of the Nietzsche Text', in Parkes 1991a: 3–19.

Parkes, Graham, ed. (1991a), *Nietzsche and Asian Thought*. Chicago & London: The University of Chicago Press.

Schippper, Kristofer (1995), 'The History of Taoist Studies in Europe'. Wilson and Cayley 1995: 467–91.

Siriwardena, R., ed. (1987), *Equality and the Religious Traditions of Asia.* London: Frances Pinter.

Wilson, Ming and Cayley, John, eds. (1995), *Europe Studies China*. London: Han-Shan Tang Books.

Yue, Daiyun (1988–9), tr. Cathy Poon, 'Nietzsche in China'. *The Journal of the Oriental Society of Australia*, 20 & 21: 199–219.

Yang, Tianshi (1978), 'Shehuizhuyi Jiangxihui ziliao' (Research Materials on the Association for the Study of Socialism). *Zhongguo zhexue*, 1: 373–451.

——— (1983), 'Shehuizhuyi Jiangxihui ziliao: xu' (Research Materials on the Association for the Study of Socialism: continued). *Zhongguo zhexue*, 9: 461–510.

Zhang, Taiyan (1907), 'Da Tiezheng' (Reply to Tiezheng). *Minbao*, 14: 1–10, photo. repr. Zhongguo kexueyuan lishi yanjiuso disansuo 1957: 113–22.

——— (1908), 'Si huo lun' (On the Four Delusions). *Minbao* 22: 1–22, photo. repr. Zhongguo kexueyuan lishi yanjiuso disansuo 1957: 1–22.

Zhang, Ji (1908), 'Mr Zhang Ji's Letter from London'. *Hengbao*, 4, 28 May, Yang 1983: 498–503.

Zhongguo kexueyuan lishi yanjiuso disansuo comp. (1957) *Minbao*. Beijing: Kexue chubanshe.

Zhou, Zhenfu. (1980) *Lu Xun shige zhu* (Lu Xun's Poetry with Annotations). Hangzhou: Zhejiang renmin chubanshe.

*This paper has been developed from research carried out for 'Nietzsche Appropriated: Towards Establishing a New Literary Tradition During the May Fourth Period', a paper presented at the International Symposium on Nietzsche and East Asia, 26–9 September 1998, organised by Ostasiatisches Seminar de Universität Zurich.

Proust and His Biographers

Don Anderson

In his monthly 'Word from the Chair' (*Newswrite*, September 2002) Michael Wilding observed that

> one of the perennially fascinating questions that novels always raise is that of the origin of the characters. Are they totally fictional, or are they based on real people? . . . Garner [recently] remarked to me that she had never seen the point in making up characters. I feel much the same way. One of the functions of literature is that of assisting the understanding of life; and you are likely to understand more if the characters you read about are based on actuality.

Michael drolly recalls our erstwhile colleague Stephen Knight's Flann O'Brienish suggestion, based on a sense of comic outrage at the *romans-à-clef* of Michael himself and Frank Moorhouse, that the characters' 'originals' should form a union and go on strike to try to achieve better pay and conditions. Speaking as one of those paranoid 'originals', I offer the following essay about Proust's 'originality'.

> *To paraphrase Proust's biographer George Painter, the books are often unforgettable, but the reader may never know what it is he can't forget.*
>
> Andrew O'Hagan

There are, however, things that I will never forget about Marcel Proust. His school chums called him *prout*, or 'fart'. Perhaps appropriately, his Latin master's name was 'Cucheval', or 'horse's arse'. He was in the habit of tipping the staff at the Paris Ritz no less than 200 per cent. In January 1914 he listened from home to the Paris Opéra production of *Parsifal* by means of a device known as the 'theatrophone'. One night in 1916 he collected members of the Poulet string quartet at 11 p.m., had them driven to his apartment, where at 1 a.m. they performed César Franck's quartet for him. Told by his doctors to avoid alcohol, but convinced that beer was not alcoholic, Proust consumed considerable quantities of it. His father, typical of members of his haut-bourgeois class, sent his shirts from Paris to London to be laundered. (Vladimir Nabokov's father sent *his* from St. Petersburg to London.) All these items of information are trivial, and there is something vulgar about my insisting upon them. But I wanted to get your attention, also to suggest that there is something prurient if not dishonourable about our, about our age's, heightened interest in literary biography. To put it another way: I am prepared to wager that more have read David Marr's eminently readable biography of Patrick White than have persevered with one of White's demanding novels.

All the gossipaceous information in the preceding paragraph comes from Jean-Yves Tadié's magisterial *Marcel Proust: a Life* (1996; trans. 2000.) This is an anything but vulgar, merely gossipy biography, of which Edmund White, author of a splendid small biography of Proust (1999), says boldly: 'This is the best biography I've ever read.' Assuming White has read Leon Edel's *Henry James* and Richard Ellmann's *James Joyce*, this is a very big claim. Tadié, in his Preface, alerts us to the fact that he is writing a biography of the book rather than of the man:

> taking into account those things that only the work of an editor permits him to know – the history of the manuscripts and of the work as it goes through the process of being written; *the true biography of a writer or an artist is that of his work* [emphasis added]. Proust said of Ruskin: 'The events of his life are intellectual ones and the important dates are those in which he perceives a new art form'.

Celebrating Tadié's achievement, White observes:

> Whereas George Painter's amusing two-volume biography of the 1960s, the standard life of Proust until now, relied almost exclusively on memoirs by Proust's contemporaries, Tadié's book benefits from a whole library of subsequent scholarship, including the publication of more than 20 volumes of correspondence. Tadié has made a thorough study of Proust's manuscripts as the editor of the four-volume Pléiade edition of *A la recherche du temps perdu* and of six volumes of *Etudes proustiennes.*

White's referring to Painter's biography as 'amusing' is not kindly meant. In his Bibliography to his brief life (that 'brief' *is* meant kindly, and White need hardly apologise for the corrective 'homosexual bias of [his] little book'), White claims that 'Painter seems almost obsessed with discovering who were the "originals" of Proust's characters, which can make for tiresome reading'.

Tadié, invoking Roland Barthes, points to the crucial methodological flaw in Painter's work, a flaw which also characterises Leon Edel's truly great, for other reasons, biography of Henry James. We might call it the 'biographical circle'.

We read a biography that is transfused by the novel, in which entire pages of Proust's work are spilled out, but without his style. Painter's success, as Barthes has shown, lies mainly in this impression it gives of reading a novel, one that is both about a life and a work, avoiding the immense effort required to read *A la recherche du temps perdu*. Unfortunately, the novel is to biography what the historical novel is to history.

It is crucial to Tadié's work that 'not a single love letter [by Proust] has yet been unearthed'. Prurient biographers have not felt this to be a constraint. Tadié accuses Painter of 'vulgarizing' the 'grimmer legends' that surround Proust (the desecration of maternal/paternal photographs, which figures in the novel, for example). Of the celebrated, and celebratedly unsuccessful, high meeting of High Modernism, between Proust and James Joyce, Tadié observes in a curt note: 'For a somewhat over-embellished account of this evening, see Painter'.

George D. Painter's *Marcel Proust: a Biography* appeared in two volumes, the first in 1959, the second in 1965. (A revised and enlarged one-volume version was published in 1989. I have used the first edition.) The dust-jacket of Volume 2 carried plaudits for Volume 1 that sound like a roll-call of the London literary eminences of 1965: Pamela Hansford Johnson, Cyril Connolly, Stuart Hampshire, Angus Wilson, Anthony Powell, Robert Speaight. Admittedly, no sane publisher puts negative comments on a book's cover, but is something more at stake? Has there been a significant shift in taste or, indeed, in sophistication with regard to literary biography? Should one be too hard on Painter, given that he was early in the field? (Though note that he failed to interview sources many of whom, as Tadié points out, were alive at the time.)

For many of us, the most egregious characteristic of Painter's book, which is symptomatic but more instantly discernible than its local habitations, may be found in his 'Indexes', of which there are two. 'I. Persons and Places', and 'II. Characters and Places'. A note to the Indexes reads:

Two separate indexes are provided, the first of real persons and places, the second of fictitious characters and places in Proust's novel, *A la Recherche du Temps Perdu*. In order to facilitate the tracing of discussions in the text of Proust's models in real life, cross-references from each index to the other have been given, where applicable, in capitals and parentheses. For this special purpose the two indexes should be used in conjunction with one another, and with the corresponding indexes in Volume One.

Thus, under 'I. Persons and Places', one may read: 'Agostinelli, Alfred (ALBERTINE)'; 'Montesquiou, Comte Robert de' (CHARLUS)'. Under '2. Characters and Places', one finds: 'Albertine (AGOSTINELLI, Alfred; ALTON, Colette d'; BAUCHE, Mlle; CHEVILLY, Marie de; FINALY, Marie; IDEVILLE, Helene d'; MORNAND, Louisa de; NAHMIAS, Albert; NORDLINGER, Marie; ROCHAT, Henri.)'; 'Charlus, Baron Palamède de (DOASAN; LA ROCHEFOUCAULD, Comte Aimery de; LORRAIN, Jean; MONTESQIOU, Robert de; SAGAN, Prince Boson de; WILDE).'

It is evident that such simplistic equivalences are anathema to Barthes and Tadié, whose life of 'Proust' is essentially a biography of a novel, of its conception, gestation, birth, and effects. Surely *that* index entry would have affronted Oscar Wilde who wrote to Edmond de Goncourt in 1891:

> French by sympathy, I am Irish by race, and the English have condemned me to speak the language of Shakespeare. . . . The English public, as usual hypocritical, prudish and philistine, has not known how to find the art in the work of art: it has searched for the man in it. Since it always confuses man with his creations, it thinks that to create Hamlet you must be a little melancholy, to imagine Lear, completely mad.

This would appear to be a lesson that biographers of eminences of the *fin de siècle* and Modernism failed utterly to observe.

Proust's opposition to the critical methods of Daudet, of Goncourt, of Sainte-Beuve ('It's all very unintelligent.') would have made Painter's biography anathema to him. With regard to Agostinelli and Albertine, Proust wrote in his notebook: '*Vitally important*: when I say that Albertine, etc., have posed for me, so have others whom I can't remember; a book is a vast cemetery in which one is unable to read the faded names on most of the tombstones.' In 1918, Proust inscribed a copy of *Swann's Way* to Jacques de Lacrettle, in which he gave him the *clefs* or keys to the novel, while at the same time asserting that 'there are no *clefs* to the characters in this book; or rather there are eight or ten for each one them'. This may give some comfort to biographers of the Painterly persuasion; it should, at the same time, serve as a cautionary injunction. Yet we ought not forget Picasso's remark to Jean Hugo, reminiscent of Oliver St. John Gogarty's regarding James Joyce : 'Look at him, he's keeping his eye out for models.'

Perhaps the most economical, trenchant, and only apparently para doxical statement regarding the Modernist author/character (Joyce / Stephen Dedalus; Proust/Marcel, the Narrator) nexus was made by

The work is not an autobiography, the narrator is not Proust the person and the characters never existed except in the author's mind. Let us not, therefore, go into the author's life. It is of no importance in the present case and would only cloud the issue, *especially as the author and the narrator do resemble each other in various ways and move in much the same environment* [emphasis added].

But literary biographers cannot take this advice which is, perhaps, a death sentence. Even very fine, delicate, discriminating literary biography – Leon Edel's *Henry James*, for example – is implicated in the biographical circle, which may be virtuous or vicious, and may be stated thus: events in the life (as seen by the biographer) generate events in the fiction, the explication of which validates citing events in the life. Richard Poirier sees James Atlas's biography of Saul Bellow (2000) as an example of the vicious: 'When evidence is wanted to show that Bellow tried to blot out the reality of his mother's death, it is drawn not from his life, however, but from little details in his fiction, read as if they were details in his life.'

Literary biography, of which Atlas's and Painter's may be taken as examples, appeals to the worst in us. It excites our prurience, appeals to our lust for gossip and, worst of all, is often taken as a substitute for the complex, delicate, and demanding works of fiction begat by the biography's subject. No wonder authors have tried to prohibit or inhibit such biographical activity – consider W.H. Auden and J.D. Salinger, for example. (See Ian Hamilton's *Keepers of the Flame* for an informative and entertaining account of how eminent authors have endeavoured to avoid or influence biographers and biographies.)

Tadié observes of Proust's relations with Robert de Montesquiou, whom Painter offers in his index as an equivalent for the Baron de Charlus in the novel, that 'conversation does not require transcription, but metamorphosis: so many memoirs – as well as *romans-à-clef* – have failed because their authors have not realized this'. 'Metamorphosis' is a term as insistently associated with literary Modernism as it is with Ovid, and it may be peculiarly appropriate here in drawing attention to Proust's concerns and their differences from the emphasis on 'transcription' in the immediately previously dominant aesthetic modes, particularly realism and naturalism. The metamorphosis of an incident in the author's life into a crisis in the novel requires, at the very least, tact and discrimination in the biographer.

Such metamorphoses of course occur, Tadié acknowledging that the following event in Proust's life begat an extraordinary passage in *A la recherche*. As 1902 drew to a close, Proust's private life was dominated *recherche.* As 1902 drew to a close, Proust's private life was dominated by Bertrand de Fénelon's departure for Constantinople. So distraught was Proust, he spent his nights weeping and, as soon as he had taken his Trional to help him sleep during the day, accused his mother of allowing the servants to make a noise.

> Thanks to you, I was in such a state of nerves that when poor Fénelon came with Lauris, because of something he said – extremely unpleasant I have to say – I flew at him with my fists (Fnelon, not Lauris), and not knowing what I was doing, I seized the new hat he had just bought, trampled on it, tore it to pieces and then ripped out the lining. As you probably think I'm exaggerating, I enclose a piece of the lining so that you can see I'm telling the truth.

Consider how that biographical episode has been transformed, metamorphosed, in the incident involving the narrator and the Baron de Charlus in *The Guermantes Way*, recalling that neither Fénelon nor Lauris is mentioned against Charlus in the Index to Painter's biography.

Kenneth Tynan once famously said of Beckett's *Waiting for Godot* that it was the play 'in which nothing happened . . . twice'. Depending on which edition or translation one is reading, it might be observed, almost truthfully, that *Remembrance of Things Past* (Proust detested the English title) is the novel in which nothing happens three, or four, or twelve times. It certainly seems like this in the two hundred page dinner-party held by the Duc and Duchesse de Guermantes during which nothing happens, many times. After the dinner, very late in the night if not early in the morning, the narrator keeps an appointment with Proust's sacred monster – at times he reminds one of the Minotaur – the Baron de Charlus, who behaves towards him with superb (cf. Latin *superbia,* pride) rudeness or, as one commentator observes, 'like a madman'. Consider the narrator's response to this, which breaks his crisis, and possibly the reader's tedium.

> But at that moment the idea of madness never even entered my head. There was in him, according to me, only pride, in me there was only fury. This fury (at the moment when M. de Charlus ceased to shout, in order to refer to his august toes, with a majesty that was accompanied by a grimace, a nausea of disgust at his obscure blasphemers), this fury could contain itself no longer. With an impulsive movement, I wanted to strike something, and, a lingering trace of discernment making me respect the person of a man so much older than myself, and even, in view of their dignity as works of art, the pieces of German porcelain that were grouped around him, I flung myself upon the baron's new silk hat, dashed it to the ground, trampled upon it, began blindly pulling it to pieces,

of M. de Charlus, which continued to sound, and, crossing the room to leave it, opened the door.

How's that for a transformation? How's that for a metamorphosis? Q.E.D. That is without a doubt the best hat scene I have read, better even than that in Joseph Conrad's *The Secret Agent*. That is without a doubt the finest interaction between a human character and an inanimate object since Diogenes dealt with his tub at the Siege of Corinth in Book III of Rabelais' *Gargantua and Pantagruel*. And it both is and *is not* the incident that involved Proust and Fenelon. One can imagine that for the eminently scientifically-minded and informed Proust, as for Joyce, the word 'parallax' would have been of the first importance.

One might use Peter Robb's words regarding Graham Robb's biography of Rimbaud to recapitulate the argument so far. Having observed that the pre-eminent French poet Yves Bonnefoy's 'rigorous account of Rimbaud's life as revealed in his poetry' is the antithesis of Graham Robb's in being 'dry, Frenchly abstract, humourless, and fairly hard going unless you are interested in Rimbaud's poems', Peter Robb adds:

> But it constantly leads back into the poems and never makes the mistake of interposing itself between the reader and Rimbaud's art. Graham Robb resourcefully mines in Rimbaud's work a rich lode of buried autobiography, but his method doesn't always allow room for recognition that the poems amount to more than sources of personal information or intellectual statements. The very nature of the biographical undertaking is at issue here. (*The Best Australian Essays 2001*, ed. Peter Craven.)

It would be a dereliction to fail to mention André Maurois' 1949 study *The Quest for Proust*, which Jean-Yves Tadié says has been 'forgotten'. This, if true, is a pity, for despite being a relatively early critical biography, Maurois' book displays an acute and discriminating reader. It also includes information which I have not encountered elsewhere. According to Maurois, Proust regretted that his book should not have been announced, as was that of his contemporary Paul Morand, with a showcard bearing the words NOT FOR YOUNG GIRLS! This, perhaps perversely, recalls Henry James's lament (1880), instigated by the publication of Emile Zola's *Nana*.

> The novel, moreover, among ourselves [English and Americans], is almost always addressed to young unmarried ladies. This fact, to a French storyteller, appears, of course, a damnable restriction. . . . Half of life is a sealed book to young unmarried ladies, and how can a novel be worth anything that deals only with half of life?'

Did Proust wish to protect young unmarried ladies from his novel, protect his novel from them or, perhaps, incite them to read it despite, if not because of, the prohibition?

Maurois' *Quest for Proust* provides also a benign example of how a strong literary style dominates its readers and interpreters. Who has not, somewhere during *The Golden Bowl*, started to think in Jamesian sentences? Has not something similar happened to readers of *Absalom, Absalom!* ? Proust's metaphors, many of them derived from the natural sciences of his day, are justly celebrated for their length and complexity, their truth to Proust's conception of human subjectivity and his role as a realist of that subjectivity, if that is not an oxymoron. Having observed that the role of metaphor for Proust 'is to give strength to the Spirit by forcing it to renew its contacts with the Earth, its mother', Maurois, some eighty pages later, executes a Proustian metaphor of his own.

> The effect of the war [1914–1918] on the novel was profound and surprising. When the life of the world is proceeding normally, a book breaks free of its author as soon as it is published: the umbilical cord is cut, and new stimulus produces new works. But because *La Recherche du temps perdu* [sic] could not appear, it went on developing in a pathological manner. All the cells of that magnificent and monstrous body proliferated at will. As in one of Piranesi's engravings, growing things and creepers burst through the walls of the original construction.

One might say of Proust's gigantic novel, as one might of Joyce's *Ulysses*, that it was not so much written as re-written. Unsurprisingly, Maurois will have nothing of Albert Feuillerat's opinion (1934) that *A la recherche* is characterised by a 'monstrous quality of excess'. Proust was literally killing himself by working all night on the proofs of *The Captive*, dictating 'additional matter':

> Someone having been so foolish as to tell him that the brain functions best on an empty stomach, he refused all food in order that *La prisonnière* should be worthy of the earlier volume. There is something sublime in this sacrifice of a mortal body to an immortal book, in this act of transfusion in which the donor deliberately chooses to shorten his life that the characters who are dependent on his gift of blood may live.

Perhaps I am alone in thinking that this points to the supererogatory status of literary biography, or at least of some kinds of literary biography, or to literary biography of some kinds of books. Marcel Proust owned no books, but borrowed them, claiming to lack space and that they would gather dust and aggravate his asthma. Yet he foisted an biography, or to literary biography of some kinds of books. Marcel Proust owned no books, but borrowed them, claiming to lack space and that they would gather dust and aggravate his asthma. Yet he foisted an enormous book upon the world. Yet a further irony: the only reason for finishing *Remembrance of Things Past* is in order to read it, again.

BOOKS CONSIDERED IN THIS ESSAY

André Maurois, *The Quest for Proust* (1949; trans. Gerard Hopkins, 1950).
George D. Painter, *Marcel Proust: a Biography* (2 vols, 1959, 1965).
Jean-Yves Tadié, *Marcel Proust: a Life* (1996, trans. Euan Cameron, 2000).
Edmund White, *Proust* (1999).
Marcel Proust, *Remembrance of Things Past* (3 vols, 1981, trans. C.K. Scott Moncrieff, Terence Kilmartin, Andreas Mayor).

I.A. Richards and the Crisis of Imperialism

David Brooks

'I.A. Richards and the Crisis of Imperialism'? The conjunction sounds bizarre. What can a respectable Anglo-American literary critic have to do with anything as exotic as the 'crisis of Imperialism'? The two terms seem to come from contexts so remote that they cannot have any connection.

In *The Destruction of Reason* Georg Lukács traces the rise of irrationalism in Germany from the end of the French Revolutionary period to the Imperialist period, specifically to the period of the rise of Nazism. He sees this irrationalism as having its origins in Romanticism, particularly in the thought of Schelling, and as running through the work of Schopenhauer, Nietzsche, the 'Life-Philosophy' of Dilthey, Simmel et al., to the existentialism of Heidegger and Jaspers, until it culminates in 'National Socialist Philosophy'. It is with this historical account that I intend to connect Richards, however unlikely the connection may seem at first sight.[1]

By the destruction of 'reason' Lukács is not thinking merely of intelligence in general. First, he is thinking of the distinction between the Understanding and Reason in post-Kantian philosophy. Under standing here means analytics, induction, deduction, definition and division, everything that usually falls under formal logic. Reason means what has come to be called dialectics, the thinking that breaks down the fixed distinctions of the Understanding, the thinking that produces and then overcomes contradictions, the thinking that insists on the unity of opposites. Reason in this sense is important to Lukács as he is a Marxist philosopher for whom the Hegelian heritage in Marxism is to be embraced and not rejected. Irrationalism thus involves anti-dialectics.[2]

Second, for Lukács as a Marxist, Reason means materialism, or realism concerning material objects, the insistence that there is a material world independent of consciousness, and that it can be known.

Irrationalism, then, comprises all forms of philosophical belief that are anti-materialist in this sense.[3]

It is *not* these characteristics of irrationalism with which I shall be concerned in this paper. It hardly needs to be said that Richards as a denizen of Cambridge is a devotee of analytical empiricism, and is suspicious of anything that smacks of dialectics.[4] And, as an empiricist, Richards rejects materialism as metaphysics, and adheres to phenomenalism, the doctrine that we can know sensible appearances but not what, if anything, lies behind them.[5] Anti-dialectics and anti-materialism are relevant to Richards' pragmatism, which he developed from the 1930s onwards, but in this essay I shall only be concerned with Richards' positivism, which was at its strongest in his thought in the 1920s and early 1930s.

In connection with Richards' positivism what I shall be concerned with is the rest of what for Lukács constitutes irrationalism, viz., intuitionism, an 'aristocratic epistemology', and myth-making. If understanding and reason are both marginalised, then the only faculty for knowing is intuition (hence the association of this irrationalism with Romanticism). To place all emphasis on intuition suggests that the possibility of knowledge must vary with the quality of the mental powers of individuals, one person's sensibility being greater than another's. And so, as in Romanticism, the genius, the extraordinary individual, is privileged, in contrast to a rationalist conception of knowledge as science, where knowledge is conceived as a collective historical project of the human species as a whole. Moreover, if, according to the anti-materialism present in this irrationalism, all we can know is mere phenomena, and not a real material world, or if we see intuition as transcending, mystically, mere sense experience, then these irrationalist positions encourage the belief in 'myths', in constructed world-views, which go beyond all rational evidence, and whose justification can only be mystical or emotive.[6]

For Lukács this whole intellectual current is based on socio-economic and political developments, and specifically on the changing state of the struggle between social classes. In Lukács's view the French Revolutionary period encouraged the rise of the bourgeois doctrine of progress, as in the work of Herder and Hegel. With the roll-back of the revolutionary movement, the subsequent feudal reaction promotes the first phase of irrationalism, as in the work of Schelling, Schopenhauer, and Kierkegaard. 1848, the year of revolutions, sees the entry of the proletariat into the revolutionary arena for the first time, in the rising of the June Days.

Defeated in 1848, the Paris proletariat again seizes power in the Commune of 1871. With the appearance of the proletariat as an organised and revolutionary body the European bourgeoisie abandons its doctrine of progress, and goes over to reaction and irrationalism. The period of Imperialism proper is the climax of this whole development. The phase of irrationalism that moves from Nietzsche and Dilthey to Heidegger and Jaspers has for its implicit opponent the dialectical materialism, and communist idea of progress, of the labour movement, specifically of the German Social Democratic Party, the Second International, and subsequently the Third International. This phase is inevitably intensified by the Bolshevik Revolution in 1917.[7]

For the Imperialist period Lukács suggests some international parallels to developments in Germany. The parallel cases he sketches are Croce's idealist philosophy in Italy, Bergson's life-philosophy in France, and William James's pragmatism in the USA.[8]

In Lukács's view irrationalism was most strongly developed in Germany because of Germany's *backwardness* in capitalist development. This backwardness keeps the German bourgeoisie weak, and makes it dependent on the absolute monarchy, so that its politics and world-view become reactionary. The corollary of this is that the strength of irrationalism varies from country to country in accordance with the level of capitalist development, and the corresponding strength or weakness of a country's bourgeoisie in its ongoing struggle with the proletariat.[9]

Although Lukács briefly discusses the American context of William James's pragmatism, he says nothing of Britain. And it is easy to see why. From Lukács's view of the inverse correlation between the development of irrationalism and the development of capitalism it follows that Britain, with its advanced capitalist development, would *not* be a country in which irrationalism was prominent. And this deduction is of course verified by the hegemony of positivism and empiricism in Britain. One would not expect a country whose representative mid-nineteenth century philosopher is J.S. Mill, and whose philosophy in the Imperialist period is dominated by Bertrand Russell and G.E. Moore, to be a close parallel in irrationalism to the Germany of Nietzsche, Heidegger and Jaspers. And at the level of the class struggle in Britain the British bourgeoisie is protected by the spoils of empire, the incorporation of the labour movement on the basis of those very spoils, and by the jingoism of successful imperial expansion. At the most fundamental level we must distinguish between, on the one side, Germany, Austria-

Hungary, and Russia, where the bourgeois revolution is still to take place, and where a revolutionary situation is really developing in the years prior to WWI, and, on the other side, Britain, that had its bourgeois revolution two hundred and fifty years earlier, and that subsequently developed as a bourgeois society, with its relatively smooth development punctuated only by the merely political revolution of 1688, and by nodal political reforms since then (1832, 1867, etc.). In Britain there could be no developing revolutionary situation. In the years around WWI when Central and Eastern Europe are falling into the revolutionary abyss, the best that Britain can manage is the constitutional crisis over the powers of the House of Lords in 1911. So, from both a philosophical, and a socio-economic point of view, Britain would seem to be quite rightly ignored by Lukács.[10]

But no social formation, and no ideological formation, is ever quite stable, homogeneous, and non-contradictory. In nineteenth-century Britain the very strength of capital, and of its corresponding positivist philosophical culture, calls forth a Romantic opponent in the system of literature and the arts. The ongoing ideological struggle between the two sides is represented by the well-known opposition of Bentham and Coleridge. Mill offers to mediate between the two sides, but from the standpoint of the dominant side, that of positivism. This is also the situation of Richards. In the Imperialist period the philosophers remain strongly positivist. But against them the world of literature and the arts brings forth Romantics and irrationalists, in the like of Yeats, Lawrence, Eliot, and the Bloomsbury followers of Croce and Bergson. Richards' project, like Mill's, is to mediate between positivism in philosophy and Romanticism in literature and the arts, and, like Mill, he undertakes this task firmly from the standpoint of positivism. But as we shall see, the very strength of British positivism, within its own boundaries, forces British Romanticism into the same kind of irrationalism as Lukács describes for continental Europe. Ironically and paradoxically, Richards' thought, while paying homage to positivism as the hegemonic philosophy in Britain, comes to exhibit the same sort of Romantic irrationalism that Lukács shows to be the ideological symptom of the Imperialist crisis in Europe.

At the socio-economic and political levels there is of course no revolutionary situation, as there is in Central and Eastern Europe. But Britain around WWI is nonetheless going through its own capitalist and ideological crises, losing its economic hegemony with the rise of the USA and Germany, rescued from WWI only by American military power, and horrified by the human catastrophe of the war. In the interwar years liberalism, with its idea of progress, is in crisis, and the liberal intelligentsia, of which Richards is a representative figure, are torn between the traditional faith in science and rationalism, and the Romantic obscurantism of the kind of Yeats's theosophy, Eliot's Christianity, and Lawrence's quasi-Nietzschean myths. Richards is not just an *eclectic* in his thinking, trying to combine positivism and Romanticism. He is a contradictory figure, who swings irrationally from side to side.

My discussion in this essay will cover only Richards' early positivism, which belongs to the nineteen-twenties and early 1930s. A complete study of Richards' thought in relation to the crisis of Imperialism would have to look at his pragmatism of the 1930s, and his rapprochement with Plato and idealism in the 1940s. But this cannot all be done in an essay of this length.

Positivism against Romanticism

Richards' anxieties for society, in the years after the First World War, belong, as is well known, to the tradition of liberal humanism. According to Richards' updating of the classical liberal humanist view, science has finally undermined religion, and without religion to form the minds of individuals the populations of the West have become demoralised, and consequently the cohesion and stability of society are in danger. Since science itself cannot minister to the emotional needs of human beings, various irrationalist philosophies that privilege feeling over reason (e.g. those of Bergson and Croce) and various pseudo-religions (e.g. those of Yeats and D.H. Lawrence) have arisen to fill the void left by religion. As a liberal humanist in the tradition of Arnold, Richards believes that poetry, or the arts generally, can and should take over the role of forming minds, from religion. But in the current situation the rise of irrationalism threatens both science and poetry. For Richards it is necessary to preserve *both* science and poetry. Science is necessary to the technical and material basis of civilisation. It also provides the standards of all adequate thought. Poetry is necessary to ensure the 'health of the mind' of individuals, and so, indirectly, to preserve the social order.[11]

The situation after WWI is exacerbated by the rise of mass culture and mass propaganda. Richards is anxious about both what he takes to be a decline in popular *taste*, and by the possibilities of influencing the minds of whole populations, in an irrational way, by modern techniques, already put to use during the war. More generally, the speed of social change has accelerated, and the change in our social and material circumstances makes it ever more urgent to change our mentality and behaviour. For Richards, as a modern Benthamite, a Utilitarian, this means especially abandoning any traditional religious or moral beliefs that are inconsistent with our ever expanding scientific knowledge. Since psychology is not yet a well developed science, and since ethics, as a traditional branch of philosophy, is sterile, the burden of adapting our minds to ongoing social change must fall to poetry.[12]

But for Richards, if both poetry and science are to be preserved against the threats of irrationalism, they must be separated from each other. The ways in which poetry and science are mixed together, in metaphysics, in theosophy such as Yeats', in the kind of speculations that Lawrence makes about the cosmos, and in propaganda, are themselves a species of irrationalism. The task then is to segregate poetry and science from each other. Segregated, they can co-exist, and both perform their function.[13]

To segregate is to prevent each side from interfering with the other. In this principle of non-interference we can discern the spirit of positivism, and of its political homologue, liberalism. For positivism thought is essentially analytic. It takes to pieces, it separates. For liberalism the assumption is that human affairs will run smoothly if left to themselves, provided that the different kinds of activity do not get entangled and confused. For liberalism freedom is essentially negative. The only interventions into social life that are permissible are those aimed at removing obstacles and blockages, so that things may continue on course, of their own accord. So, in Richards' project to save both poetry and science, *and to save them from each other*, we can see positivism oriented against irrationalism, oriented against the metaphysics of feeling, against the revival of myth, against everything that Lukács describes as the 'destruction of reason'.

Just how Richards separates poetry and science is so well known that I will only sketch an outline here. Science and poetry are identified with different functions of language. Richards divides linguistic functions into the referential and the emotive. Science is identified with referencing, while poetry is identified with the emotive function. Keeping science and poetry apart, therefore, becomes a matter of keeping apart two different uses of language.[14]

Once this semiotic move has been made, a further, psychological move can be made to give an account of the emotive function of poetry.

Richards offers his famous, or notorious, model of the mind as an energy system, in which impulses are organised so as to enter into relations of equilibrium at different levels of complexity. Poems, and indeed all forms of emotive discourse, are held to organise and reorganise the psychic energy system, largely unconsciously. Good poems, then, are those that organise the system of impulses with maximum integration and least 'waste'. Bad poems, cheap fiction, and propaganda organise the mind in crude ways, confining people to low levels of responsiveness, and condemning them to confusion and frustration.[15]

According to this schematisation, 'truth' and 'knowledge', as involving genuine references to the world, belong to science, while poetry and the arts have no truth or knowledge in the literal sense. What are imagined, wrongly, to be their truth and knowledge are just illusions arising on the basis of good emotional organisation, that is, organisation that is maximally 'efficient'. People may feel that they are in contact with truth in the experience of a great poem, but they are wrong. However, this does not matter because all real knowledge belongs to science, and the real value of great poetry is to organise the psyche. Thus, by means of these semiotic, psychological, and epistemological doctrines Richards segregates science and poetry. He has, as he thinks, created an instrument to protect science from metaphysics and irrationalism, to protect poetry from the hegemony of science, to oppose the effects of mass culture, and to deconstruct propaganda.[16]

All this is familiar. What is less familiar is the prior negative critique of aesthetics that Richards had to make before he could put forward his positive doctrine.

In his early critique of aesthetics Richards acknowledges that criticism must draw upon philosophy for its theoretical resources. But bad philosophy will lead to bad criticism.[17] Richards approaches this situation as a Cambridge positivist, hostile to all forms of idealism, metaphysics, and Romantic irrationalism. As a positivist, Richards assumes that science has a monopoly of real knowledge, that science provides the standards of adequate thought because of its clarity and precision, and that one day all the sciences will be unified into a single system.[18] Philosophy must become scientific. But this can only be a transition to the blessed state where philosophy is in fact displaced by science. Philosophical aesthetics, therefore, must be criticised from the standpoint of a scientific philosophy, but this must mean a philosophy that points beyond itself to a scientific aesthetics.

In the years after WWI British aesthetics is dominated by Croceanism, and for Richards to put literary criticism on a sound theoretical basis means overthrowing the influence of Croce. This is the function of the early polemical essays against Roger Fry, Clive Bell, John Middleton Murry, and Herbert Read.[19] Croce's aesthetic system is condemned as a mindless pursuit of synonyms. According to Richards, in Croce's philosophy 'Art' is identified with a series of concepts, so that all the concepts, including art, lose their specific, distinctive character, and so become meaningless: Art = Intuition = Expression = Feeling = Imagination = Fancy = Lyricism = Beauty. These semantic identities represent the philosophical enemy for Richards. His whole effort in his early semiotics is to disambiguate the vague terms of the philosophical tradition, terms that are vague precisely because they are confusedly ambiguous. Croceanism, it seems, erects this ambiguity into a principle of theoretical construction, thus producing worthless theory.[20]

Richards is especially concerned with Croce's concept of Expression, which by being identified with Intuition, seems to equate *word* and *thought*. If this distinction is lost, then language becomes unanalysable. 'Expression', then, must be subjected to a multiple definition to expose its ambiguities, lest these ambiguities infect criticism. For Richards 'expression' must be analysed into its *causal* and *semiotic* elements. What this means, of course, is that Croce's philosophical aesthetics must be replaced by scientific psychology and semiotics.[21]

But as with the whole nineteenth-century positivist tradition stemming from Feuerbach this means not just *abandoning* philosophy but '*translating*' it into empirical human sciences, into psychology with Feuerbach, into psychology and semiotics with Richards. The result of this critique is, firstly, to translate Croce's concept of Expression into Richards' semiotic doctrine of communication, the 'transmission' of experiences from one mind to another, or rather their coding and decoding by sender and recipient, by means of external signs. Secondly, it is to translate Croce's Intuition into Richards' mechanistic psychology. Thus, Croce's Idealist Expressive-Intuitive nexus is turned into the terms of Richards' positivism, into the language of visual and aural percepts, of mental and material 'events', of stimulus and response, and of impulses, their magnitude, and their equilibrium. Romantic and Idealist philosophy is thus appropriated and transformed into positivistically conceived science, according to the idea that physics provides the model for all the sciences.

But *translation* suggests that the two sides, Idealist-Romantic philosophy and Positivism, are not such clearly opposed antagonists as

Richards' positivist assumptions suggest. Richards' anti-irrationalist project is about to turn on its head.

POSITIVISM AND ROMANTICISM

One of the Idealist philosophies that Richards appropriates and converts into his own psychological terms is the Confucianism of the Chinese sage Mencius. Why should a positivist like Richards be attracted to anything as exotic as ancient Chinese philosophy? The explanation – or at least part of it – perhaps lies in the *specific* complex of desirable mental states that Richards wishes to find in Confucianism. For, what he finds there is not just the general idea of a well organised psyche. It is, quite specifically, equilibrium, serenity, equanimity, rest, acceptance, love, and compassion.[22] These are not the mental states of the 'active life', of world mastery or world transformation. They are rather those of the 'contemplative life', of withdrawal from the world, of spiritual self-perfection and social quietism. In this combination of spiritual perfectionism and political abstentionism we can see what Lukács calls in his German Romantic philosophers 'religious atheism'.[23] The modern world has undermined the traditional religions (as Richards continually emphasises), but the conditions of modern life, i.e. the conditions of monopoly capitalism, preserve in existence the religious need. Hence in the late nineteenth and early twentieth centuries the rise of secular philosophies imbued with religious sentiment and performing the same social and psychological functions as the religions that they offer to displace the philosophies of Nietzsche and Heidegger in Germany, and their mythopoeic equivalents in the Anglophone world, the speculations of Yeats and Lawrence. At first sight Richards seems to be – is explicitly – opposed to this development. But his opposition involves complicity. Like other twentieth-century Romantics Richards wishes to find himself in the Other of Oriental philosophy. He will convert that philosophy into his own terms, but after the conversion the substance of the philosophy remains as *attitude*. Richards will preserve the attitude, and the social function that the attitude is designed to serve; and he will discard the metaphysical *belief* that originally supported the attitude. It is explicitly to this end that Richards constructs his positivist-emotivist doctrine of 'belief'. There are two kinds of 'belief', that which can be verified, as in science and our everyday practical engagements with the world; and that which merely serves as a support for a desirable attitude. The second of these is merely a fiction, and now the time has come for this to be recognised.[24] Richards recommends that we adopt Confucius's ethics and psychology, without adopting Confucius's metaphysics. And what Confucius's ethics and psychology will promote in us is: equilibrium, serenity, equanimity, rest, acceptance, love and compassion. We will cultivate our souls, and not concern ourselves too much with the social and material world.

And so in Richards we can see a bizarre parallel with Lukács' Romantic Irrationalists. Richards is one too, *but from within positivism*. What this means for Richards' liberalism is of course a very considerable weakening from the activist, social reforming liberalism of the mid-nineteenth century, the liberalism of Shelley, of Arnold, and of Mill. In Richards' withdrawal from the arena of social and political reform we can see a manifestation of the general crisis of liberalism in the early twentieth century. The crisis of Imperialism produces Heidegger, and the cult of Kierkegaard in Lukács' German-speaking world.[25] In England it produces Richards' positivistically formulated Romanticism, with its spiritual perfectionism and its political abstentionism. Both the German and the English phenomena arise out of the same crisis.

From Utilitarianism to Intuitionism

In his essay on 'The God of Dostoyevsky' (1927) Richards suggests that there are two ways to resolve a conflict in the psyche. One way is that of the 'philosopher', and consists in finding a *thought* that reconciles the opposing sides. The second way is that of the 'artist', and this consists in finding a way of *feeling*, or an *attitude*, or an *action*, in which the conflicting impulses can combine and cooperate.[26] But, according to Richards' positivism the philosopher is wrong to suppose that his problems can really be solved by thought. Problems of science and mathematics can be solved by thought, but not those of philosophy. For Richards 'nearly all' the problems of philosophy and theology cannot be solved by thought.[27] They belong to the other group of problems, that are not really conceptual problems at all, but are instead practical problems requiring a solution in the form of emotional organisation, attitude, or action. They merely appear to be conceptual problems, but this appearance is an illusion. Richards' doctrine of the two kinds of 'belief' enters the scene to reduce questions of metaphysics and morality (such as those with which Dostoyevsky was obsessed) to psychological problems of finding the right life-attitude. All this is a manifestation of Richards' positivism.

It is in this context that we have to consider Richards' commitment to a Benthamite, Utilitarian view of morality, social policy, and human self-formation. The Benthamite Richards, as we have seen, believes that all religious and moral beliefs that interfere with the efficient adaptation of the psyche to changing social and material circumstances should be abandoned. For Richards what is important is the organisation of the psyche, and not metaphysical beliefs about God, Man, and the Universe. However, whereas for Bentham the search for new social policies and new norms of behaviour was one of deliberation and calculation, for Richards it becomes one of instinct and intuition. As we have seen, Richards believes that in the modern world, given the decline of religion and of communal traditions, it is literature and the arts that must play the primary role in forming minds. But as a Romantic, Richards believes that this process of psychic formation must take place largely *unconsciously*.[28] It is this belief that makes Richards' Benthamism with regard to human self-formation suddenly appear as Romantic Intuitionism. We are to form our own minds, but no longer by any rational calculus, rather by the unconscious organisation of the impulses making up our psyche, under the influence of poetry and works of art. While Richards may talk in quantitative terms about the maximally efficient organisation of impulses, on the thermo-dynamic model of an energy system, all this leads nowhere. There is never any question of making measurements. In practice Richards is just as Romantic as Shelley in wanting the psyche to be formed unconsciously. Once again we see that from *within* positivism Richards is taking up a position similar to the Romantic Intuitionism that Lukács finds in his European irrationalists.

The parallel between Richards and the European Romantics can be taken even further. We have seen that for Richards the function of the appreciation of literature and the arts is not just aesthetic. Its role is not just the cultivation in human beings of taste and discrimination in matters artistic. Nor is its role confined to promoting psychic harmony and well-being. For Richards there is no distinction between the responses that we give to works of art and literature, and the responses that we give to the problems of living generally, the problems of social relationships, or even the problems of political life.[29] This means that although Richards' doctrine begins as a theory of literary criticism, or as a poetics, it immediately transforms itself into a contribution to ethics and politics. Training in aesthetic discrimination takes over the role of training in morality and politics. Richards explicitly equates skill with poetry with skill with life.[30] According to Richards, 'the judgment that a passage [in a poem] is good is an act of living. The examination and description of its merits is an act of theory.' He continues, 'What Coleridge says here applies to all our choices, moral, philosophical, or political. There is no measuring such virtue in any theory.'[31] From statements like this in Richards' early work of the 1920s and early 1930s it is clear that Richards is retreating from any rational theory of ethics and politics into Intuitionism. It may be that for Richards the basis for intuition is constructed by the unconscious influence of poems and works of art, but the result is nonetheless that moral and political decisions are to be taken on the basis of feeling. We have an immediate sense of rightness, whether in reading a poem or in considering some moral or political quer ion, and it is in this way that we make what Richards inappropriately calls our 'choices'. 'Choice' no longer means deliberation, the examination of evidence, thought, reasoning – it means instinctive, impulsive responses. Romantic irrationalism arises from within positivism.[32]

Spiritual Perfectionism

For Richards ethics and politics are to be modelled on poetics. This means that all the problems of life are to be solved by faculties of taste and discrimination. The task is to produce more mature, more discriminating, more responsive individuals. And the means by which this is to be done is an education in the appreciation of literature and the arts. 'The raising of the standard of response is as immediate a problem as any, and the arts are the chief instrument by which it may be raised or lowered.' 'Finer adjustment, clearer and more delicate accommodation or reconciliation of impulses in any one field tends to promote it in others,' and literature engages 'the most widespread systems [of impulses], those active in our responses to human beings, and to the exigencies of existence.'[33]

But the corollary of this doctrine is, literally, an élitism, and it is at this point that the dependence of Richards' project upon the distinction of the élite and the masses becomes clear and explicit. Civilisation is threatened by commercialism, and its by-product, populism. There is a real danger of the 'tyranny of the majority' over expert opinion. There is a potential, via commercialism, for popular taste to overthrow trained discrimination.[34] Richards' educational project, therefore, has two prongs, the raising of the level of popular taste, and the education of a cultivated élite.[35] But the former clearly depends upon the latter.

The élite is to be trained in such a way that it develops a responsiveness to life, that is the most balanced, the fullest, the clearest, the least confused, that literature and the arts can facilitate. Looked at from the standpoint of lived experience and cultural tradition, this means the cultivation of sensitivity, insight, self-knowledge, freedom from self-deception, and so on. But for Richards, as a positivist, mere experience of the arts is not enough. What is required is a *technique*. What in general the technique is to promote is the presupposed tendency of the human mind to order itself, or rather the technique is to promote the habit of *allowing* the mind to order itself, the habit of non-interference with the mind's supposed natural process of self-growth, self-completion. This habit Richards calls 'sincerity'. 'Sincerity, then, is obedience to that tendency that "seeks" a more perfect order within the mind.'[36] 'Obedience' suggests a spiritual discipline, an art of self-fashioning, within 'religious atheism'.

For his conception of this art or technique Richards turns again to Confucianism, which again he 'translates' into his own terms. The standard of sincerity, says Richards, is the sincere emotion that we already possess. What Confucius says is that 'in hewing an axe-handle, in hewing an axe-handle, the pattern is not far off [i.e. in our hand]'.[37] Richards takes this analogy to imply that our standard for a perfectly sincere response is the sincere response of simple sensation, about which we cannot be mistaken. We all hate a bad smell. Our response to a bad smell gives us the required experience of transparent honesty about our own mental states. We must bring this degree of honesty to the higher levels of our mental life. And so from bad smells Richards passes to his notorious technique of Pascalian meditation. In order to cultivate in ourselves sincerity concerning life in general, we must meditate upon the most universal and profound existential themes – 'man's loneliness, the facts of birth and death, the inconceivable immensity of the universe, man's place in the perspective of time, and the enormity of his ignorance'. Although Richards' quotations to illustrate these themes come from T.S. Eliot, Yeats, and Bradley, as well as Pascal, the themes themselves are clearly Pascalian. In this respect Richards parallels the European existentialists who abandon Pascal's religious faith, but adopt Pascal's conception of the human condition deprived of God.[38]

It will be apparent that Confucius provides for Richards both the idea of psychic well-being that is the *goal* of the educational project, and the idea of the *means*, the technique, by which the goal is to be reached. Moreover, we can see not only that Richards was attracted to the philosophy of the 'good life' that Confucianism offers, but also that there is an affinity between the status of Confucianism as a mandarin ideology, and the 'élite theory' within which Richards' specific educational projects are located.

Confucius thus is melded with Pascal, Pascal with existentialism, existentialism with Romantic humanism. From Pascal's religious faith Richards passes to the Romantic faith in the spiritual influence of the arts. But this is no longer just the ethical humanism of Arnold. It has become a mirror of the Heideggerian contemplation of mortality. What for Heidegger is authenticity is for Richards sincerity. What for Heidegger is *das Man* for Richards is 'social automatism', the mechanical responses that vitiate human life.[39] Richards' conceptions are more residually nineteenth century than Heidegger's, but the mood, the attitude, the world-view, is the same, and both in Britain and in Germany it arises out of the same global crisis of imperialism.

Political Abstentionism

Richards' spiritual perfectionism is connected with his peculiar attitude to politics in the 1920s and early 1930s, an attitude which reflects the crisis of liberalism in the interwar years, and which expresses yet another slide of Richards' thought between opposites, this time a slide between liberalism and conservatism. One can describe this by saying that on the one hand Richards' spiritual perfectionism seems to be at first sight a simple recoil from politics, but that on the other hand it must come to be seen as a substitute for politics, or even as politics in another form.

In *Science and Poetry* (1926) Richards speaks of poetry as the means by which we can adjust more effectively to our increasingly chaotic social environment.[40] Characteristically, Richards makes no mention of any socio-political project to *change* that social environment. This is not just a slip. Richards' conviction is that socio-political projects are to be abandoned in favour of the spiritual therapy provided by the arts. In his little known essay 'Nineteen Hundred and Now' (1927) Richards identifies with his own generation, of whom he says, 'We feel a need for order in our own minds *before we can set about ordering the affairs of men in general* . . .' (my italics).[41] And in his essay 'What is Belief?' (1934) Richards speaks, with some complacency, of 'his generation's' revolt against pre-WWI 'creeds'. Richards thinks of his generation as being content to live 'without beliefs'.[42] The creeds that Richards is thinking of are not just religious. They include the political creeds of pre-WWI liberalism and socialism. For Richards H.G. Wells, rationalist and socialist, is no longer an influential thinker. His rationalism and socialism have become obsolete for the interwar generation.[43]

How Richards' élite theory pertains to the social and political problems of the interwar years can be seen in his remarks on Forster's *Howards End*. Richards attributes a 'sociological thesis' to Forster, but this is sociology that turns out to be ethics in disguise.[44] In Richards' view Forster's sociological thesis is that the wretchedness and crudity of the denizens of the lower orders, such as Leonard Bast, are due to the 'separation and antagonism of people of vision and people of action', the separation and antagonism of the 'able, competent, practical, effectual' people, like the Wilcoxes, and the 'speculative, contemplative, critical, and imaginative' people, like the Schlegels.[45] This then is Richards' substitute for class analysis: the moral condition of the proletariat is due to the estrangement of the utilitarian and aesthetic fractions of the liberal bourgeoisie. The implied solution to this political-social-*moral* problem is that the liberal bourgeoisie should become reunified. And this is evidently to be achieved by Richards' project of aesthetic education. Under the influence of the arts the élite will become both sensitive and effective, and so will be able to improve the conditions, material and spiritual, of the masses. So while this is from one point of view the abandonment of specifically social and political analysis, it is from another point of view politics in disguise – politics reconceived as spiritual guidance. The recourse to Confucius becomes more intelligible. To summarise: politics is reconceived as ethics; then ethics is reconceived as spiritual discipline, as the cultivation of sensibility.[46]

But if this is a project for the liberal bourgeoisie, it is a project that is no longer liberal, but rather conservative. In his essay on Dostoyevsky Richards shows no interest whatever in projects of social reform or revolution that might bear on the pain and suffering of humanity, with which Dostoyevsky was obsessed.[47] This is striking, given that while Richards was writing this essay a revolutionary government in Russia was trying to deal with the problems inherited from Dostoyevsky's time. For Richards what we derive from reading Dostoyevsky is not a more urgent concern with the problems of the social and material world; it is rather an attitude of *acceptance*. When we read Stavrogin's story: 'feelings and impulses for which we have no better names than horror, despair, shame, desolation, pettiness, futility, doubt, and fear get, not pushed out of sight, but somehow reconstituted so as to become parts of a possible way of accepting existence. In other words we find a way of life.'[48]

Acceptance is also what we learn from Hardy. Once again Richards sounds like Heidegger, and the political implication is conservative: 'The comfort of forgetfulness, the comfort of beliefs, [Hardy] has put both these away. Hence his singular preoccupation with death; because it is in the contemplation of death that the necessity for human attitudes, in the face of an indifferent universe, to become self-supporting is felt most poignantly. Only the greatest tragic poets have achieved an equally self-reliant and immitigable acceptance.'[49]

The crisis of imperialism undermines the liberal social order. The *sentiment* of liberalism remains, but the political content of liberalism – to change the social world so that it becomes more rational and more free – has to be abandoned. It is replaced by the political content of conservatism. The world as it is is to be accepted.

This conservatism is the result of Richards' Romantic Irrationalism. As we have seen, Richards presents the odd but striking picture of a Romantic whose irrationalism arises within positivism. Positivism and Romanticism are bound together in a contradictory relationship, both complementary and antagonistic. But to conceive this it is necessary to think dialectically, like Lukács. To do *that* was outside Richards' intellectual horizon.[50]

NOTES

1. Georg Lukács, *The Destruction of Reason*, translated by Peter Palmer, 1980 (orig. publ. in German, 1962), pp. 3–33. Hereafter *DR*.
2. *DR*, pp. 6–7, 97–104, 133–55.
3. *DR*, pp. 6–7, 21–2, 109–28.
4. I.A. Richards, *Coleridge on Imagination*, London, 3rd edn, 1962 (orig. publ. 1934), p. 166. Hereafter *COL*.
5. C.K. Ogden and I.A. Richards, *The Meaning of Meaning: A Study of the Influence of Language upon Thought and of the Science of Symbolism*, London, 10th edn, 1949 (orig. publ. 1923), pp. 55, 82. Hereafter *MM*.
6. *DR*, pp. 10, 24–6, 30–2, 95–100, 116–21, 129–55, 414–16.
7. *DR*, pp. 6–8.
8. *DR*, pp. 17–33.
9. *DR*, pp. 16–18, 37–91.
10. Lukács briefly mentions Bertrand Russell, and the early Wittgenstein in his

Epilogue 'On Post-War Irrationalism', but these figures do not enter into his main argument.

This is not the place to argue the impossibility of a *socialist* revolution in Britain in the Imperialist period. The issue is obviously contentious.

11. I.A. Richards, *Principles of Literary Criticism*, London, reset edn, 1967 (orig. publ. 1924), Preface (dated 1928), and pp. 209–10 (hereafter *PRINC*); *Science and Poetry*, New York, 1926, *passim* (hereafter *SP*); *Complementarities: Uncollected Essays*, ed. J.P. Russo, Manchester, 1977, pp. 169–77 (hereafter COMP).
12. *SP*, ch. 1; *PRINC*, pp. 22–3, 24–7, 43; *MM*, pp. 17–19.
13. *PRINC*, Preface, and pp. 209–10; *MM*, pp. 82 n. 1, and 159.
14. *PRINC*, ch. 34; *MM*, pp. 149–59.
15. *PRINC*, chs 7, 11, 12, 14, 16, 24, 25, 31; *SP*, chs 2, 3.
16. *PRINC*, chs 32–5; *MM*, pp. 150–1, 156–7.
17. *COMP*, pp. 12–13.
18. *PRINC*, pp. 68, 206–14; *COMP*, pp. 5–6, 13–15.
19. *COMP*, chs 1, 2, 3, 6, 18.
20. *PRINC*, p. 201 and n. 4; C.K. Ogden, I.A. Richards, and James Wood, *The Foundations of Aesthetics*, New York, 2nd edn, 1925 (orig. publ. 1922), pp. 43–5 (hereafter *FA*).
21. *COMP*, pp. 13–15, 180–1.
22. *FA*, p. 13 and ch. 14; I.A. Richards, *Mencius on the Mind: Experiments in Multiple Definition*, Richmond, 1997 (orig. publ. 1932), pp. 17, 41, and 65–85. The idea of acceptance is introduced in connection with Dostoyevsky, as I shall show later in this essay. But it is introduced as an essential characteristic of the poetics that is read out of, or into, Confucianism.
23. *DR*, pp. 211–16, 446–51.
24. *COMP*, pp. 24–36, 198–9; *PRINC*, pp. 219–26.
25. *DR*, pp. 489–517.
26. *COMP*, p. 150.
27. *COMP*, pp. 150–1.
28. *PRINC*, p. 43.
29. *PRINC*, chs 2, 7, 8; *COL*, p. 140.
30. I.A. Richards, *Practical Criticism: A Study of Literary Judgment*, London, 1964 (orig. publ. 1929), pp. 319–21. Hereafter *PRAC*.
31. *COL*, p. 140.
32. Richards polemicises against Intuitionism, particularly in connection with Croce, but this does not alter the fact that his own Romantic view of value and response ends in Intuitionism. See *PRINC*, pp. 76–8, 201, and n. 4.
33. *PRINC*, pp. 184, 185.
34. *PRINC*, pp. 25–6.
35. *PRINC*, pp. 25–7. For European élite theory see DR, pp. 29–30.
36. *PRAC*, p. 288.

37. *PRAC*, pp. 284, 289.
38. *PRAC*, pp. 289–91, and 291, n. 1.T.S. Eliot famously criticised Richards' account of sincerity in his Charles Eliot Norton lectures of 1932–3. See *The Use of Poetry and the Use of Criticism*, London, 1964 (orig. publ. 1933), pp. 131–4.

    For Lukács on the relation of Pascal to Romantic Irrationalism see *DR*, pp. 114–16.
39. *COMP*, pp. 162–3. For Lukács on Heidegger see *DR*, pp. 489–517
40. *SP*, pp. 95–6.
41. *COMP*, p. 172.
42. I.A. Richards, *Poetries: Their Media and Ends. A collection of essays by I.A. Richards published to celebrate his 80th birthday*, ed. Trevor Eaton, The Hague and Paris, 1974, p. 238.
43. *COMP*, p. 171.
44. *COMP*, p. 164.
45. *COMP*, pp. 165–6.
46. For European parallels, see *DR*, pp. 501–8 (Heidegger) and 519–20 (Jaspers).
47. *COMP*, pp. 148–58.
48. *COMP*, p. 157.
49. *SP*, pp. 82–3.
50. In the 1940s Richards takes up an interest in 'dialectic' as a result of his rapprochement with Plato. But this 'dialectic' turns out to be merely analytics. It has nothing in common with the dialectical tradition of German Idealism and Marxism. See I.A. Richards, *How To Read A Page*, London, 1943.

Christina Stead's Politics

Jennifer Gribble

Writing to Florence James in January 1952, Clem Christesen, editor of *Meanjin*, asks, 'by the way, could you tell me what are Christina Stead's politics?'[1] The question was prompted by the comment of Arthur Levy, an Australian working in UNESCO in Paris, that a 'Letter from Paris' Stead had submitted to *Meanjin*[2] was 'hopelessly inaccurate'.[3] Published without attribution as part of a round-up of news from abroad under the title of 'The Uneasy Chair', Stead's Paris letter mainly concerned itself with the 'present local stir' of the quarrel about communism that had made the decisive and public rift between Camus and Sartre. In 1951, in *L'Homme revolté*, Camus emerges as a critic of dogmatic Marxism, particularly in relation to the Soviet political labour camps. In the controversy generated by the review of Camus' book in Sartre's journal *Les Temps modernes*, Sartre remains a firm supporter of Stalin.

Stead's letter is not so much inaccurate as disengaged. Written at the last minute, as a long-delayed and brief reply to points raised by Christesen, and with the promise of a further 'small critical article', it is a somewhat breezy dismissal of both existentialists as examples of post-war 'middle class pessimism', detecting temporising and indecision in Sartre's attitude to the party. Elsewhere in the letter, however, she discusses the Moscow Nineteenth Congress. The enthusiasm with which she reports favourable remarks in a variety of British, European and US papers 'for the first time, about the five year plan . . . observing, as a reality, the immense productive power of Russia, and of China', reflects as much a pacifist as a pro-communist position: 'This means that their policy is and must be peace, many of these non-Communist observers say; and it would be insensitive not to feel a great breath of relief, in a war-terrorized world.'

Christesen was later to nominate Stead for a Creative Arts Fellowship at the ANU in Canberra, an award she took up in 1968, and he and his wife Nina were to become Stead's firm friends. But back in 1952,

Christesen, like many other Australian literary figures, knew little of Stead. His question about her politics suggests that, unlike Hazel Rowley, he did not read Stead's Paris letter as 'pro-Communist'.[4] Rowley is one of a number of recent critics who find Stead's last, posthumously published novel affirming a 'pro-Stalinist vision': 'She completed *I'm Dying Laughing* in the 1960s, well after Stalin's atrocities had become public knowledge; the main characters are communists and the novel's timespan is 1935–1950, yet unlike many novels of the period by leftists, it contains no attack on Stalin.'[5]

Central to the achievement of *I'm Dying Laughing* is its interest in the way in which ideology informs and shapes narrative. And however summarily Stead seems to dismiss the debate between Camus and Sartre, I find evidence in the novel that not only is Stalinism subjected to critique, but that the very terms of that critique tacitly acknowledge the debate she reports in the *Meanjin* letter. A letter from The Hague in 1953 suggests that she was further revising the novel while weighing up her reactions to the death of Stalin.[6]

One way of understanding Stead's repeated protestations that she was not an adherent of any political party is that she wished it to be understood that the way in which a novel thinks about politics is more complex and diverse than the way in which she may have placed views on record in her letters, for example, or in essays. I shall, however, argue that even those views elicit no univocal meanings. Indeed, on the question of Stead's politics, Rowley herself seems ambivalent. On the one hand, she is inclined to credit Stead with a mind of her own, which gave rise to 'impatience with the eternal Marxist talk around her ears',[7] on the other, 'she always remained loyal to Bill Blake's Marxist vision'; 'Blake's faith in Stalinism never wavered, and if Stead had private doubts, she would never say so publicly'.[8]

That way of putting it diminishes the integrity of Stead's politics, and takes no account of what Jameson has taught us to call 'the political unconscious'. It is not surprising to discover that the two published letters in which Stead focuses explicitly on Stalin bear the marks of her struggle to articulate her own views in response to her closest personal relationships and in particular, to the views of her husband. As a novelist she would always explore stated views as psychologically situated. In the letter of 17 March 1953, in which she reports her revisions to the manuscript of *I'm Dying Laughing*, she attempts to explain to her brother and sister-in-law in Sydney, Gilbert and Sheila Stead, why the death of someone widely perceived to be the anti-Christ could seem a significant event in twentieth-century history, and, for Bill Blake, an event to be mourned. The letter is as interesting for what it does not say as for what it says. For Bill, Stalin had been the focus of a Marxist utopian vision centred on the Soviet state. There is a gentle irony in Stead's account of Bill's walk into the centre of The Hague, where he found that only the embassies of Canada and the USA had not hung their flags at half-mast:

> Bill was so upset when he saw a funeral director's car outside the Czech's palace, he thought someone had become ill and died of sorrow! But it was merely to bring decorations for the reception. As to the death of Stalin, that was a very great event, so strange and so close to millions! Lenin established the revolution but the socialist state has lived and been firmly founded with Stalin and for example all Gilbert's life, practically, he has been there. But there was a curious feeling I had and a lot of people had I am sure of a sort of powerful guard of men coming forward into the middle ground with Malenkov a little in advance and standing there, stalwarts. In a way for the first time the Soviet statesmen appeared to be there: if Stalin appears to some to have been anti-Christ, to a lot of others he stood for the Soviet world: a childish but comfortable way of feeling, which also arose in his interesting and apparently good-natured sane wise mind. . . . It will take a *long time* for Stalin to leave the world; he is so firmly fixed in it.[9]

In the debate about whether Stalin was indeed the anti-Christ, Stead takes no sides. Her own response hovers between registering something like the 'great man' theory of historical change and a significant detachment in assessing Stalin's significance. She notes a 'feeling', characterised as 'curious', that behind the curtain, powerful, somewhat shadowy presences will forward the revolution for which Stalin has seemed to stand. But the belief that he represented Soviet achievement is seen as 'childish but comfortable'. The odd leap in her next thought, 'which also arose', leaves some room for ambiguity. A reference to Stalin's way of feeling about his role? Surely not to Bill's? The effect of addressing conflicting views – Stalin as saviour, Stalin as enslaver of child-like belief – is apparent in the syntax. Unambiguous, however, is the qualification that Stalinist thinking was only 'apparently' good-natured and sane.

The second letter, to Edith Anderson, 14 November 1956, follows the Soviet invasion of Hungary in November 1956:

> Don't let politics faze you, is Bill's opinion . . . . Many intellectuals who regard party activities as 'part of my picaresque life' are jumping off the Train at this station. It's quite a clean-out of the soft element . . . . Bill and I were discussing the curious traits of intellectuals, the liberal bourgeoisie – why are they so immoral? For they are. To jump off every time you're threatened is immoral. Of

course it's hard for an unromantic like myself to realize these people are sincere when they think feudalism changes to cynicism by soft methods: but they are.[10]

About which Rowley comments:

It was, Stead admitted, only Bill's opinion, and in politics she would only ever echo him. To regard those who jumped off the locomotive of history as immoral was understandable in previous years (though a bit preposterous coming from someone who had never clambered on the train), but after 1956, it was difficult to defend this position. Yet from now on, Stead and Blake were more impatient than ever with those who criticized the USSR.[11]

Her assumption that Stead would entertain no criticism of Stalin seems to depend on Stead's disdain for Sartre, after his denunciation of the invasion. Stead had, however, seen Sartre as a temporiser from the time of the Paris letter: 'a smart pedlar with a few varied goods in his pack; he is not selling any of them particularly until he sees which line takes'. Stead's own attitude in this letter is by no means easy to gauge. In so far as she 'echoes' her husband's views she seems to be reporting from that domestic space of shared talk, a long habit of apparent compliance which prevented 'breaking up the happy home'.[12] She clearly shares his scorn for phoney radicals, communists by life-style choice rather than solid conviction. And many felt able in conscience still to remain on 'the train from the Finland station', in Lenin's famous image, after Kruschev's exposure of Stalin's crimes seemed to promise hope of liberalisation in the USSR. Stead's self-characterisation as an 'unromantic', or pragmatist, has the effect of muffling the point that in describing the progress of the Soviet Union she sees it not as a journey from feudalism to socialism, but from 'feudalism' to 'cynicism'. It is not difficult to read this slip of the pen as an involuntary betrayal of a point of view different from that reported as Bill's unquestioning loyalty.

This is not to deny Stead's life-long Marxist sympathies. It is merely to anticipate my argument that Stead turns to art to explore what she senses is an as yet un-negotiable assessment of the crimes of the Soviet state. She is able, in *I'm Dying Laughing*, to find a way of allowing that assessment to emerge. And it is also salutory to remember that the disclosure of Stalinist atrocities has brought with it its own version of historical forgetting, suppressing and distorting the appeal of a Marxist utopia to the imaginations of a whole generation of Western intellectuals, some of whom never recovered from the feelings of betrayal involved in getting off the train. Remembering Stephen Murray-Smith, Manning Clark said:

To his chagrin and dark, undying pain, he found the Communist Party asked humanity to pay too high a price for the sake of some future harmony, for they were manuring the soil with human blood for the sake of some far-off event, that they were deciding for us what we should read and think.[13]

But as late as 1961, Bill Blake remained committed to 'the Celestial Vision':

Not all the mistakes of Socialism, not its crassness, vulgarization, bureaucracy, tyranny, errors in humanity as in theory, can ever cause me to lose the Celestial Vision and I am not by nature Apocalyptic, Utopian or Messianic. I see the millennium as Marx saw it, a struggle, ever widening and ever deepening.[14]

He and Stead looked now to the German Democratic Republic as a place in which that vision seemed realizable.[15]

Entangled in Blake's Marxism are significant paradoxes. There was a period of his life when he found it possible to be both Marxist and banker, and a period when Blake and Stead belonged to a Marxist milieu in Hollywood that felt able to justify feeding capitalism's celluloid dreams. Albeit under pressure, Blake in 1954 absolutely repudiated his communist affiliations: 'I was a member of the Communist Party in New York, New York from about March 1938 to April 1939. . . . I am not now in politics, have no political affiliations, belong to no organizations whatever, have not for many years. I am not and was not a member of the Communist Party except for the period mentioned above.'[16] Stead never joined the party or admitted to being 'party', despite the left-wing sympathies her journalism and novels record. She became disaffected with *New Masses* and ceased to write for it in 1938, turning her attention instead to her novels as an exploration of political commitment. In attempting her appraisal of Blake's 'celestial vision' in *I'm Dying Laughing*, it is the gap between Marxist beliefs and the economic imperatives of a capitalist cultural background, the gap between ideology and its local and historical realizations, the entanglement of idealism in individual psychology, that interests Stead. This entails a moral sifting finer than any available to the letter writer or the essayist, and from a vantage point beyond the immediately pragmatic. 'We read her', Michael Wilding writes, 'in order to be true'.[17] 'I felt I had to write "the truth" – and this is it, expressed in my own way',[18] she wrote of this final, unfinishable novel. As her writer-protagonist, Emily Wilkes, points out, this is the writer's unique duty and role:

'If we don't tell the truth, what's our function? . . . I know it's like shouting "What is Truth?" in the middle of a cocktail party. We get into money habits and we forget the tremendous responsibility a writer has to tell the truth . . . tell it with all the skill and ability and experience – he has – to rise above himself – not like I'm doing, Stephen, going down to the sodding level of my grandfather. To be better than he was for the sake of others. That's a funny thing, but every night I wake up and I think, I want to be better than I am by nature. To be a writer in an age where the truth will set us free means to be a writer of the truth; or to be an utter, utter, decadent damned soul'. She put her arms on the table and cried. At this Stephen turned round and shouted uneasily, 'For God's sake that's enough drama'.[19]

Stephen's ironic undercutting of Emily's outburst, and the self-placing reiteration of 'truth', registers Stead's own recognition of how truth-telling is mediated through the social and psychological dispositions of the teller. Being 'better' and 'rising' are particularly entangled moral and social signifiers. Emily is based on the life and work of Stead's Marxist friend Ruth McKenny. But Stead's commitment to telling the truth as she saw it extends beyond the desire to celebrate and to analyse the life of her friend. There is more wry self-projection in the portrait than has generally been recognised.[20] Emily's analysis of 'the American dilemma', her conflict between socialist conviction and the need to survive, and indeed indulge herself, within the capitalist economy, underlines Stephen's observation: 'I never met a communist yet who wasn't fighting for a bourgeois way of life for himself, his family and the rest of mankind' (p. 92). The 'hand-to-mouth existence' the Howards live in Paris permits a flamboyant opulence quite beyond the spartan existence of Stead and Blake for most of their lives. But Stead, like Emily, often felt burdened by her bread-winning responsibilities. The personal betrayals that underlie Emily's larger political ones also find a parallel in Stead's own life: 'Said to Walt [diary code name for Blake] "it wasn't the cat that hurt me, it was Elie [code name for Peter Kelly], he withers and blasts all the women he's close to". Walt said "Cut out that Elie stuff and stick to me. I never did you any harm"',[21] words almost directly echoed in Stephen's attitude to Emily's romantic dalliance with the charismatic comrade Vittorio. While drafting *I'm Dying Laughing* Stead's letters record that she is drinking excessively and suffering from unrequited love for the unresponsive Kelly. Telling the truth involves a ruthless self-scrutiny, and that is why Emily, like Stead, is constantly drawn to the autobiographical mode. 'The truth' can reside, ultimately, nowhere but in human accounts, and accountability.

Stead's attempt to tell it, in this novel, is perhaps most explicit in the meta-discursive scene that opens Part Two. Its very subject is history: history as suppression and forgetting, history as a tissue of gaps and absences. Against the on-going commitment of the Howards and their friends to the Russian revolution there is registered the history of Soviet 'betrayals', which they are aware of but unable to accommodate. Geering's chapter title 'Two Lists', points up the counter-balancing of this list with the Howards' list of 'requirements' (prescription drugs, refrigerator, deep freeze) as they prepare to abandon America and set up house in post-war Paris. Arraigned at a dinner party by Hollywood party members for their 'ultra-left posturing' and Emily's 'unreasonable self-indulgence, the exploitation of her own personality' (p. 100), and terrified by the probability of their being called up by the Investigating Committee into un-American Activities, they begin their drift into self-destruction. With Des Canby, British reporter, and their friends Axel and Ruth Oates, they discuss their liminal position, and its consolation of possible return: 'we're standing now where you stood a few months ago .... When you left the Party but left the door ajar to get back if need be.' To which Canby is reassuring: 'Well, you've had so many chances to step out and you didn't, why think about it now? You just want to step out for awhile. Good idea. Have a holiday' (p. 183). Emily and Stephen pride themselves that they are still on the train from the Finland station while others, Stead's 'soft element', had been getting off 'at every whistle stop'. Strange emotional currents are let loose as Canby opens up 'the crimes of the Soviet Union. I know the full calendar.' He himself seems 'bored'; the Oates begin to laugh, the Howards are embarrassed. Betrayal, Canby insists, is woven into the very fabric of Marxist history, and those 'who woke up one day to find the Soviet Union had betrayed them', would seem to have ample justification for betraying in turn: 'Do you know how often the Soviet Union has betrayed?', he asks.

There follows, in Emily's words, 'a canticle'. Canby frames it as a 'catalogue' – Don Giovanni's famous aria is explicitly invoked: 'mille e tre, mille e tre', sang Des Canby (p. 185). What is at issue for the speakers is how the historical record is to be read by those who, with individual agendas, 'romantics and mystics and people like ourselves', are looking for 'new energy, a new aim for the revolution'. What is at issue for the novel is how the listed betrayals might be understood in terms of individual histories and the larger sweep of the revolutionary history of humankind. The recital at every point raises the question of who, exactly, is being betrayed. Whatever the intended ironies of the speakers,[22] no detail of the case against the Soviet Union is omitted, from Lenin's 'betrayal' of the Allies and democracy in 1917, to the 'mock democratic elections' that established him as 'the new dictator' demanding 'dictatorship', not 'liberty' of the proletariat, the murder of Lenin, the party purges, the 'betrayal of the greatest revolutionist, Trotsky', the 1926 Soviet constitution giving more votes to the industrial workers in the cities than to peasants:

Emily said, 'And 1927, Trotskyists expelled from Russia, Stalin became a grisly murderer, though *no one was shot* . . . all the old fighters, the romantic revolutionists who had shed so much of their own blood, didn't recognize the revolution once it was organized as a state. Yes. They got off the train in shoals at every station, giving the ticket-collector their paid-up tickets to the real revolution. . . .

The three men were still laughing heartily. Throwing dates and historical events, long famous, to each other. Emily had sunk into reflection. Towards the end she listened to them again. 'In the Pacific war, she failed to declare war on Japan, leaving us to bear the brunt of the war. She won the war, she could not have done so, but for the large American lendlease aid and she is showing total ingratitude to the only country who saved her from extinction, the USA'.

Axel said, 'And what about the twenty-five million to forty million slave labourers – figures vary with passions – exterminated or worked to death in prison camps, the biggest slave system known in human history, not excluding the Romans and the Nazis?'

Emily said slowly, 'Well, honestly there have been moments when my heart failed. By golly, what a canticle you have made! We talk about the crimes of the USA, but well, with that list, put that way, we've got a shining morning face compared with them – at least you can't blame readers of the morning papers for thinking so. And to think we're losing our shirts and our face, standing up for such a nation, such betrayals of all that's dear to the romantic hearts of the parlour pinks. It's quite a record, isn't it? It wouldn't look good set down in black and white and pasted on the walls of the town. But we all have a terrible record, looked at that way. Think of the British. Well – heigh-ho! History doesn't bear scrutiny.' (p. 184)

Although all speakers, including Emily, are attempting a degree of irony, it is difficult to sustain the view that Stalin is somehow valorised in this discussion. Dramatically, and in terms of its creation of personality and mood, it subjects political loyalties to the scrutiny of that history Emily glimpses but cannot yet confront. The historical record is allowed to speak for itself, in a way that challenges the would-be denial of the ironists: 'Stalin became a grisly murderer'; 'the biggest slave system known to human history, not excluding the Romans and the Nazis'.

Stead charts Emily's ambivalence: 'we've got a shining morning face compared with them – at least you can't blame the readers of the morning papers for thinking so'. Her qualification implies that perhaps this sense that US crimes are overshadowed by those of the Soviet Union is just a product of the Western press; perhaps those who cannot recognize the revolution 'once it was organised as a state' were only 'parlour pinks' after all, the 'soft element' of which Stead writes in her letter. But Emily is reflective and anxious as she tries for some even-handed response to the 'canticle': 'we all have a terrible record. . . . Well – heigh-ho! History doesn't bear scrutiny.' This is manifestly a betrayal of her moral and professional duty to investigate the facts, and there is a parallel made at the end of this chapter between the deflection of her best instincts as a writer and the over-riding of her instincts as a mother when she persuades herself that her much-wanted child should be aborted as they prepare for the journey to Europe: 'all foetuses that come to nothing, the abortions, are defective' (p. 187). The 'record', Emily admits, 'wouldn't look good set down in black and white and pasted on the walls of the town'. But that is exactly the effect of this scene: Stead as novelist seeks to set the record straight, projecting, in Emily, some of her own tensions of comittment, but subjecting them to the impartial historical vantage point evoked in the passage's long historical sweep. Beneath the pro-Stalinist orientation of the speakers is registered the repressed, and perhaps, as Jameson would argue, the 'unrepresentable' history of the Soviet state. History is seen as an interplay between 'the record', in so far as it can be known through its politicized mediations, and the attitudes of those who live it.

It is this vantage point towards which Emily strives in her 'magnum dopus', *Trial and Execution*: 'we are all being tried and all go to our execution' (p. 409). The opportunity for betrayal expands as the Howards' capitalist life-style entraps them within the European post-war black market. As they move inexorably towards the final betrayal of their communist convictions and their friends, Emily now attempts to see these betrayals in the light of the battles that have shaped her world, catastrophic upheavals succeeding one another in America, France, Germany and Russia : 'all these haunted holes in history, through each of which a man or woman fell, shot, starved, self-murdered to despair. And each man is a history, you can't talk about history: we are history, each thudding heart' (p. 210). Tales of the concentration camps are brought to them by eye-witnesses: Jews betraying Jews in order to survive; their friend Suzanne accused of letting burn 'hundreds of babies, hundreds of women . . . mangled and tortured and burned alive and – for her one life' (p. 282). Emily vividly calls up the horror of revolutionary France: 'the terrifying memory of the furies, clawing at the cobblestones, their feet gaping with festering wounds, dirt ground in and scarred everywhere, filling the air with their rotten breath, spoiling the gilt with their fierce dirty paws . . . shouting, jeering, lusting, and bad, bad, as conquerors are always bad, jealous, mean, and justified eventually by history' (p. 423). And she is made to reappraise her heroicisation of Cicero as the enemy of tyranny and dictatorship, the model for the republicans of the French Revolution. Jean-Claude, her son Christie's tutor, produces a catalogue of his sins 'so odious that his misfortunes came as the punishment of unpardonable faults into which he was plunged by the mistakes of a mind too weak to overcome the crises in which his generation struggled . . . his need for money, urgent bills and a pack of creditors always after him' (p. 331). The corruption of the ancient Roman finds its parallel in the corruptions of the Howards, and this, in turn, mirrors the betrayals of the Soviet Union, as the catalogue precisely suggests.

Shoshana Felman and Dori Laub, in *Testimony: Crises of Witnessing in Literature, Psychoanalysis and History*, see the twentieth century as 'the age of testimony. If the Greeks invented tragedy, the Romantics the epistle and the Renaissance the sonnet, our generation invented a new literature: that of testimony.'[23] They see Camus' *The Fall* as 'a book about how art inscribes (artistically bears witness to) what we do not yet know of our lived historical relation to events of our times'.[24] *The Plague* then inaugurates 'an age whose writing task (and reading task) is to confront the horror of its own destructiveness, to attest to the unthinkable disaster of culture's breakdown'.[25] And this is also surely Stead's task in *I'm Dying Laughing*. Through Emily, she shows the process by which, in Felman and Laub's words 'our own historical forgetting' is given 'the power to address us'.[26]

In his letter to Sartre in *Les Temps modernes*, Camus wrote: 'He who believes *nothing but history* is walking towards terror . . . he who believes nothing of history is authorizing terror.'[27] The clash between the two existentialists on which Stead reports to *Meanjin* revolved around their different diagnoses of, and approaches to, history. Camus' *L'Homme révolté* is a critique of authoritarian Socialism, 'the principal revolutionary experience of our era', and sees the labour camps as an example of the historical degeneration of legitimate political revolt. Sartre remained (until 1956) an apologist for Stalinism, seeing it as offering a totalising legibility for the Russian revolution.[28] Camus, on the other hand, saw the totalising impulse of an historicism that believes it can account for everything to be as pernicious as the totalitarian impulse of anti-historicism. Camus reproaches Sartre that he is literally 'making silence'; that in not pronouncing upon Stalin's camps, he is shrouding their reality in silence. The enduring product of his thinking on these issues is *The Fall*, in 1956. The suicide scene the judge-narrator has witnessed and from which he has retreated in silence, and which is only at last acknowledged during his prolonged monologue in the presence of an anonymous listener, functions as a metaphor for history as the assertion, and reassertion, of silence. This 'aggregate of the vices of our whole generation in their fullest expression', to quote Camus' epigraph from Lermontov, figures the holocaust and the Soviet labour camps as that about which silence reasserts itself among contemporary European intellectuals. As Felman and Laub comment: '*The Fall* 's reflections upon "knowing" and "not knowing" are translated into actions, and what they in fact mean is the practice and the theory of history. . . . Narrative has thus become the very writing of the impossibility of writing history.'[29]

The catalogue of Soviet betrayals in *I'm Dying Laughing* is a reflection comparable with that of Camus, on 'knowing' and 'not knowing' and on history as that which 'gives our own historical forgetting the power to address us'. The novel suggests Stead's more considered response to the debate about which she has been so dismissive in *Meanjin*. Her novel anchors her reflections on 'knowing' and 'not knowing', on silence and history, within the lived experience of her protagonists. They are vividly, painfully destroyed and they destroy. After Stephen elects to silence himself in suicide, Emily drifts into death by slower means, unable to complete and to publish her witness to what she has seen, in much the same way as Bill Blake's death and Stead's desolation silenced them both.

Martin Malia, in his recent book *Russia under Western Eyes*, makes the point that the Soviet party-state was in essence a Western political idea, a utopia, whose eclipse represented 'a burnt-out fantasy, a moral black hole, an anti-world'.[30] Among the spate of historical appraisals that have followed the collapse of communism in the Soviet Union is *The Black Book of Communism: Crimes, Terror, Repression*, edited by Stephane Courtois, which argues that communism should be regarded as the defining characteristic of 'the short twentieth century that began in Sarajevo in 1914 and ended in Moscow in 1991', for it 'predated fascism and left its mark on four continents'.[31] The book's attempt to subject communism to moral assessment and judgement, together with its high estimates of the deaths in camps and gulags, made it the subject of controversy on its appearance in France in 1997. For the French historian of revolution, François Furet, in *The Passing of an Illusion*, analysis is inseparable from judgement.[32] Inga Clendinnen, in *Reading the Holocaust* , argues not only that moral assessment is the historian's task, but that it is the historian who can best evoke readerly reflection and critical evaluation: 'Secular "professional" historical writing, the writing which declares itself not or not primarily art, is open to interaction, selection and revision, all processes which art, in its necessary absolutism, rejects.'[33]

I have argued a contrary view in this discussion. It is through art that Stead discovers what she wants to say about communism in our time. Through the embodiment of ideas in personality and action, the juxtaposition of points of view and historical movements, she subjects to critique ideas about which she is elsewhere ambivalent. The reader of *I'm Dying Laughing* is challenged by that critique, moved by the human suffering foregrounded in its tragic process. And so, precisely because it is a work of art, and a considerable one, Stead's novel, begun at the mid-century, takes an authoritative place among the political reassessments of communism that are only now beginning to emerge.

NOTES

1. Clem Christesen to Florence James, 3 vi 1953 (Meanjin Papers), quoted Hazel Rowley, *Christina Stead: A Biography* (William Heinemann Australia, Port Melbourne, 1993), p. 388.
2. *Meanjin* XI, 4, 1952.
3. Quoted Rowley, op. cit., p. 388.
4. Ibid., p. 388.
5. 'Christina Stead: Politics and Literature in the Radical Years, 1935–1942', *Meridian* 8, 2, 157. In an interview with Robert Dessaix, *24 Hours* July 1993, she refers to 'Stead's well-known loyalty to Soviet Russia and her refusal to credit the rumours of its crimes.' Cf. Judith Kegan Gardiner, *Rhys, Stead, Lessing, and the Politics of Empathy* (Indiana University Press, Bloomington and Indiannapolis, 1989), p. 80: 'Despite its completion two years after Stalin's atrocities became public knowledge, *I'm Dying Laughing* does not attack the Soviet Union.' And Angela Carter 'Laughter in the Dark', *The Guardian*, 27 iii 1987, 21: 'Stead takes the validity of the ideology for granted.'

6. Letter to Sylvia and Gilbert Stead, 17 iii 1953: 'I have done a fair amount of work here and hope to send one MS off this month . . . the second novel is about American literary life and struggle especially the terrible life-and-death struggle now on.' *A Web of Friendship: Selected Letters 1928–73*. R.G. Geering, ed. (Angus and Robertson, Pymble, 1992), p. 134.
7. 'Politics and Literature in the Radical Years', 157.
8. Rowley, *Biography*, p. 394.
9. Geering, op. cit., 134.
10. Quoted Rowley, *Biography*, p. 411.
11. Ibid., p. 411.
12. Letter to Stanley Burnshaw, 29 ix 1938, quoted Rowley, 'Politics and Literature', 154.
13. *Overland* 112, October 1988, 8.
14. Letter to Stanley Burnshaw, 11 x 1961, quoted Rowley, *Biography*, p. 424.
15. Ann Blake, *Christina Stead's Politics of Place* (Nedlands, University of Western Australia Press, 1999), p. 161.
16. Quoted Chris Williams, *Christina Stead: A Life of Letters* (McPhee Gribble, Melbourne, 1989), p. 208.
17. 'Christina Stead's Puzzleheaded Girl: the Political Context', G. Barnes, J. Gunn, S. Jensen, L. Jobling, eds., *Word and Wordsmiths: A Volume for H.L. Rogers* (English Department, University of Sydney, 1989).
18. Letter to Leda and Stanley Burnshaw, 10 xi 1966, Geering, op. cit., p. 272.
19. Christina Stead, *I'm Dying Laughing*, ed. R.G. Geering (Virago, London, 1986), p. 120.
20. Judith Kegan Gardiner, op. cit., p. 81, for example, states that Emily is 'a woman writer *not* modelled on her author'.
21. Quoted Rowley, *Biography*, p. 369.
22. Brigid Rooney, *Gendering the Revolutionary Subject: the Role of Marxist Thought in Christina Stead's Authorial Production*, Ph.D. thesis, Macquarie University, March 1997, p. 328, notes that the 'unthinkable' is met by 'parodic laughter, ritualistic group attack'. Rooney reads the scene as a 'textual undermining of revolutionary certitudes' but sees it, 'finally, in its reasserted attention to closure and unity' attempting 'to stave off the full implications of such a crossing into post-holocaust and post-revolutionary terrain'.
23. (New York, Routledge, 1992), p. 5.
24. Ibid., p. 180.
25. Ibid., p. 114.
26. Ibid., p. 164.
27. 'Lettre au Directeur des *Temps Modernes*' *Les Temps modernes*, 1952, quoted ibid., p. 174.
28. Ibid., p. 173.
29. Ibid., p. 185.

30. (Harvard University Press, Cambridge Mass., 1999), quoted Nicolas Rothwell, *The Weekend Australian*, 11–12 August, 2001, Review 2.
31. Ed. Stephane Courtois (Harvard University Press, Harvard, 1999), quoted ibid., Review 2.
32. (University of Chicago Press, Chicago, 1999), quoted ibid., Review 2.
33. (Text Publishing, Melbourne, 1998), p. 204.

Michael Wilding's Short Stories: A Speculative Note

Robert Yeo

To read Michael Wilding for the first time and to review *Somewhere New: New & Selected Stories* (1996), is to be struck by variety – of genres and of strategies. Many stories were experimental beyond the modernist and suggested many post-modern preoccupations.

In earlier stories like 'Odour of Eucalyptus' and 'Hector and Freddie' he had shown that he could write the traditional short story that met the demands of the form as laid out by early masters like Sean O' Faolain, Frank O'Connor and H.E. Bates. Their magisterial pronouncements had, in some quarters, hardened into laws during the hegemony of New Critical practice. Take, for instance, O'Connor's dictum: 'There are three necessary elements in a story – exposition, development and drama. Exposition we may illustrate as, "John Fortescue was a solicitor in the little town of X", development as, "One day Mrs Fortescue told him that she was about to leave him for another man", and drama as " 'You will do nothing of the kind,' he said."'

The Oxford Book of Short Stories chosen by V.S. Pritchett, published 1981, established a canon. O'Faolain, O'Connor and Bates first published their critical books in 1948, 1962 and 1972 respectively and their writings through the years, assumed the force of edicts that ensured that the short story must have well-observed beginning, middle and end, must be, in short, well-constructed. Pritchett's selection largely concurred.

Well, Wilding is frankly not interested, at least not in the form defined in this holistic way. His stories are often and deliberately inconclusive. There is no attempt to manipulate both the story and the reader into near resolution, and this is shown as early as 1972 in the story 'Somewhere New' which ends in an almost throwaway manner.

Just before he disappeared into the street I called out, 'Do you have his address? Where did he go?'

'Oh America,' he said, looking back into the doorway.[1]

What interests Wilding is not the extrinsic need of winding up the story but the intrinsic need to seize the moment, to render accurately the conglomerate of idea-cum-feeling as it is born, grows, progresses and passes. In other words, he is fascinated by process. This is shown in the self-consciousness that characterises many of these stories. Consider the beginning of the story 'The West Midland Underground'.

The West Midland Underground goes from . . . to . . .

Or should I say went? Should I have said went? Should I be saying went? Or even will go. May go. Could go. Could have gone. Was to have gone. Is to go. Is to have gone? Is it possible to say is to have gone? Are there certain tenses that do not exist, may not, cannot, will not, did not; though now do? Perhaps the impossible tenses are needed for the impossible background. Perhaps the hitherto impossible tense will bring into being the hitherto impossible West Midland Underground.[2]

Obviously, the narrator at the very beginning of his wanting to tell a story, becomes preoccupied by the word 'goes' and he is not prepared to proceed until he has sorted out the grammar of his feeling. He is obviously aware of this tense and allows it to flow its linguistic course because he is not really keen on the story as unfolding structure but in the immediate ripple of the sentences which make up the essential artistic units as they render instantly the indissoluble mix of idea-feeling. If there is a larger unit than the sentence, it is the paragraph.

This self-consciousness is about the act of writing. Writers feature frequently as narrators and protagonists and they ruminate and agonise over writing. The writers could be real, like Jack Kerouac, or fictional. 'Bye Bye Jack, See You Soon' has a second paragraph which begins:

What's Kerouac? I didn't even have my copy of *On The Road* then.[3]

And the third paragraph starts:

What's kerouac? Kerouac is a registered code name, like Kodak ® or Coca-cola ©.[4]

Intertextuality and allusiveness, as this example shows, are among Wilding's wider strategies, wider in the sense of going beyond the sentence. Embedded in his texts are literary quotations, references to writers (mostly) and books which challenge his readers to make the necessary connections. The most obvious is the modernist insertion of lines from poems and novels ('The horror, the horror') for the purpose of ironic commentary. And there are allusions to the cultural and artistic icons of the sixties (Kerouac, Jon Silkin, Norman Podhoretz, to name just these) as well as to some of its defining political acts like the Kennedy assassination, Vietnam, CIA-hatched conspiracies, etc.) Another kind of intertextuality is the subversion of the familiar fairy tale, for example the Snow White story, for trenchant critique of contemporary sexual mores, as in 'The Phallic Forest'. Wilding had successfully attempted a variation of this previously, by collaging for his own ends material from Jane Austen and John Cleland in 'Emma: Memoirs of a Woman of Pleasure'.

Experience, he is saying, is an integrated process and there are no divisions between the person who reads D.H. Lawrence and who smokes hash. Time passing is a stream of experience carrying in its wake assorted styles in deliberate disjunction or ironic proximity going apparently nowhere (if the traditionalist expects it to go somewhere, narratively speaking) and frequently stopping (not ending) inconclusively. It is not surprising, therefore to find line drawings instead of words to describe the indescribable as in 'The Silence of the Seer' or documentary material, e.g. a dictionary definition of a word inserted in a matter-of-fact way, as in 'Their Mind Keeping On Working'.

A few of the stories have English settings. (Wilding was born in England and later moved to Australia, Sydney, as a young man.) The English stories, very likely autobiographical, record with an almost unbearable mix of nostalgia and guilt, the British class consciousness that made the young boy, in 'Class Feeling', feel ashamed of his father's working-class roots. These stories were probably written before the Sydney stories and both show some continuity of concerns both artistic and thematic. Mordant criticism of the sex-and-drug culture of the sixties and comic send-ups of cross-cultural encounters are found in the latter.

One is tempted to classify his stories but it is better to describe his techniques because they point to his understanding of aspects of post-modernism which he could and did use successfully. This point will be taken up later.

Reading again his short fiction (which is mainly but not entirely the subject of this essay) I find no reason to revise my views. But having read more and other writings relevant to the fiction, some things about Wilding seem inescapable to me. The first is that one can read Wilding's stories critically, without reference to his life, as the preceding section did. But the numerous revealing interviews he has given, since 1975, the metafictional nature of his short fiction and the appearance of *Wildest Dreams* in 1998, make such an approach inadequate. It is not enough just to read Wilding; one has to read Wilding on Wilding. Read the interviews, read the selective memoir and see how they illuminate the fiction. See how the life weaves in and out of fiction in an indeterminate way, the real enriching the fictional, the fictional crossing with the real. Hans Hauge has suggested, for instance, that *The Short Story Embassy* be read as 'an autobiography'.[5]

The life has seen a passage. It is not the more usual journey of the writer from the ex-colony to the imperial centre but the reverse, from England to Australia. In 1963, Michael Wilding, fresh from Oxford, took up a teaching post in Sydney, returned to England briefly, went back to Sydney and stayed. Bruce Clunies Ross correctly describes him as an 'immigrant writer'. 'In a sense,' Clunies Ross continues, 'Wilding is a writer in voluntary exile, a common enough condition for twentieth-century artists, especially Australians.'

> However, his is a reversal of the usual pattern; instead of gravitating from the periphery to the center of culture, he has moved tangentially from the English provinces to the new world. Inevitably, this has helped shape his work.
>
> He was a young writer when he came to Australia and his work might have developed quite differently had he remained in Britain. For most of the sixties he hovered between England and Australia, and this is reflected in his first collection, *Aspects of the Dying Process.* Since then his work as a writer, critic, editor and publisher, has been increasingly a contribution to Australian literature. He is an exile who has become an artist of his adopted country.[6]

While he has noted the reverse journey, Clunies Ross has not suggested, to the best of my knowledge, that the exile was a wrenching decision forced upon Wilding. It was accidental; and not to any Australian city but to Sydney, Australia's most urbanised centre, an environment he found exciting. The contrast between the provincial, poor, class-ridden decay of his boyhood and adolescence in the West Midlands and the urban, cosmopolitan and egalitarian character of Sydney was enormous.

Yet, his first book *Aspects of the Dying Process* (1972) had nothing to say about the life he left behind and little to say directly about the passage. The exception is 'Odour of Eucalyptus', which is a passage story, one of a few about the transition experience, the trip from England to Australia that is both physical and psychological. The blurb of *Aspects of the Dying Process* described the author as 'an Englishman, at present a Senior Lecturer in English at the University of Sydney' and this description is augmented by a photograph of a handsome young man in jacket and tie. At that time, 'an Englishman' was probably a convenient label. Wilding did not like easy labels. It is not difficult to see why his stories defied easy categorisation. In fact, he expressed reservation about being seen as an Australian writer in an interview in 1986 with Giulia Giuffré (GG):

> GG: Do you see yourself as an Australian writer?
>
> MW: I didn't realize, when I decided to be a writer, how closely that is associated with nationality and political ideology. I thought you could just be a writer. I'm not happy about being identified with a particular nation group. In any case, Australian nationalism is a delusion. It seems to me a culture can only come out of economic realities, but Australia doesn't control its own economy. It's part of a colonial multi-national economic structure. So how can it have its own national art?[7]

In a relatively long writing career that began formally in 1972 with the publication of his very first book *Aspects of the Dying Process*, it is less useful to discuss Wilding's transition as that of a young English writer gradually becoming an Australian one. Later writing will qualify the notion, emphasising and de-emphasising, augmenting or denying. At the same time, his metafictional strategies will perform the same functions and make easy explanation difficult. Thus, by the time he came to write what eventually became *Wildest Dreams,* which his publisher described as a selective memoir, published in 1998, the transition could be seen from the point of view of the protagonist, the young Englishman, Graham, who sails willingly from England to Sydney: 'He was glad to fly, surrendering the old world was what he was doing, so surrendering the last of those sea voyages was a double surrender, about which he was perfectly happy. But to fly, that was to belong immediately to the new world . . . '[8]

Surrendering the old world for the new world – this idea will encompass that of the Englishman-to-Australian transition as well as that of the centre to the margin move. It reverses the America to England passages of Henry James and T.S. Eliot, the surrender of the new world for the old. Wilding has admitted to James as an important influence in a 1998 interview. At the same time, he disclosed how he moved away from the written Jamesian style into something more conversational as

. . . reading to an audience encouraged the development of a more colloquial style that directly engaged readers. Not everything I've written works well when read aloud, some of it is very much for the printed page. And as I was developing this through having to do a lot of lecturing, I decided that since I was having to give lectures, then I would put the work into developing new ideas in them so that they could be published. This in part involved adopting a style that would work both as a lecture and in print. So out of the lectures emerged a more accessible style. Otherwise I might have gone the other way into Henry James or Joyce or something like that.[9]

Sometime in the mid-1990s, having learnt about his English beginnings, the trip to Australia, literary life in Balmain and teaching in the University of Sydney, I remarked that he had lived an interesting life and would he consider writing his autobiography? He did not answer then and I did not press him. A few years later, he sent me an answer and it was *Wildest Dreams*. Reading it in early 1999, one year after it was published, and in the same year later reading his actual account of his early years in the University of Sydney called *Among Leavisites* (*Southerly* 59, 3 & 4, 1999, 67–93) I was struck by the fact that Wilding is not one to do the obvious. Autobiography, the unadulterated life, would have been too easy; and if it was to be book length (*Wildest Dreams* has 310 pages) it might have been too much – Wilding taking his life *that* seriously, moving predictably from A–Z. That was not his style; casting life as selective memoir allowed for distancing, for eschewing the first person narrative which could be inward and cloying. At the same time, it allowed him to deconstruct events in ways that were non-linear and fluid, as this quotation shows:

It was a scenario and he followed it, wrote about it, read it. In which order? The model had permeated through so many texts, he could not have cited any specific one at that point, though it was another ten years before he read the archetype, *Lost Illusions*. But he knew what it was to be the young writer arrived in a metropolis, unknown yet there to be known, the writer's growth the discovery of the metropolis, objective correlative, homology, or only subject.[10]

Thus, his penchant for metafictional modes would incline him more towards writing where the line between the real and the fictional remains deliberately indeterminate. This would enable him to exploit the narrative strategies that came from both life and art. One moves seamlessly into the other and vice versa. *Among Leavisites,* his essay on his early years in Sydney University, has the features of a realist, traditional short story, with its sharp dialogue, suggestive characterisation and suspenseful plot ups-and-downs.

Scrutiny of Wilding's selection and arrangement of stories in both the individual volumes and the three selections points to obvious non-observance of chronology and to deliberate witholding as part of his evolving narrative strategy. Two stories, extremely revealing in a very autobiographical way as they deal with early life in Worcester where the author was born, did not appear until *Reading the Signs* (1984) the fourth of his individual collections; the stories are 'Reading the Signs' and 'Class Feeling'. Both, as well as an important third English story called 'Canal Run', are not found in his first selection of his hitherto published stories called *The Man of Slow Feeling* (1985); only 'Reading the Signs' appeared in *Great Climate* (1991), the selection that was published by Faber in his native England. Finally, they were both included in his third selection *Somewhere New* (1996), fifteen years after the appearance of his very first book in 1972. Such apparent delay to include obviously autobiographical stories and their later, almost step-by-step inclusion, point to an initial rejection of the English past and show acceptance of, with *Great Climate* published in 1991, the inevitability of the passage from the old to the new world; with acceptance came the recognition of the impossibility of reversal. Again, as Clunies Ross has observed, 'He is an exile who has become an artist of his adopted country'.[11]

The two stories must be read as a pair or, with 'Canal Run', as a trio. 'Canal Run' and 'Reading the Signs' are realist, but not 'Class Feeling'. Already experimental concerns, intrusive, process-oriented, as well as the obvious, developing 'general leftist position' (in his own words), had begun to show:

> But when you asked again – and at the same time you were diffident about it, you were asking as if you really felt it was asking for something, as if I had to put myself out for it, asking again because you thought I'd said Yes and then not bothered or forgotten, and I hadn't forgotten – that time I intended to write a story for you. . . . And all this business of barmaid and waitress heroines in the suggestive half-light of our provincial wide-boy pubs is to show you this different life – this life that even so isn't really my life; but I can't pretend it is and push it forward as a punch in the face of the bourgeoisie, especially your cultured and literate bourgeoisie.[12]

If I were assembling a Collected Wilding and wished to show his development, a case could be made for starting out with these stories, 'Reading the Signs', 'Canal Run' and 'Class Feeling'. Wilding may not approve, given his preference for non-sequential timelines; but a new reader, approaching his vast and varied corpus, will gain invaluable entry into it. I would go on next to include what may be described as 'passage' stories about people involved in the cross-cultural crossing from England/Europe to Australia which reprise the old world to new world journey, like 'Odour of Eucalyptus'. 'The Phallic Forest' which deconstructs a familiar fairy tale and the collagic 'Emma: Memoirs of a Woman of Pleasure' will be part of this group of stories. It shows the range expanding, the appropriation of European and American models adapted to Australian locations. They prepare the reader for the stories which successfully deploy many of the techniques of post-modernist fiction and place Wilding squarely in the international stream of authors who were changing the way short stories got written. Masters of this genre, like John Barth and Donald Barthelme, come to mind. In Australia, Wilding was there from his very first book and, as earlier noted, with stories like 'Somewhere New' (1972) and 'The West Midland Underground' (1975); a phase continued with 'The Word She Types', 'The Silence of the Seer', 'Their Minds Keeping on Working', 'Bye Bye Jack, See You Soon', and 'Stuck on the Mesa', all from his second book, and resumed unabated up to *This is For You* published in 1994.

In *Postmodernist Fiction* (1987) McHale writes, 'A number of post-modernist books are illustrated, either with photographs or with drawings lifted or collaged from other sources, or, more rarely, with drawings from the authors themselves'.[13] Such a practice is apparent in Wilding's 'The Silence of the Seer' where the abstract drawings deepen the satiric irony. McHale refers to the work of the American novelist Richard Brautigan who often blurs the distinction between the real and the figurative; his example comes from Brautigan's 'The Tokyo-Montana Express' but this quotation from *Trout Fishing in America* (1967) is just as effective.

> 'I wonder what Hemingway's up to,' I said to myself. I looked inside the magazine and turned to the pages about his death. Trout fishing in America forgot to tell me about it. I'm certain he knew. It must have slipped his mind.[14]

In this extract, Brautigan does not make out the difference between the real (a person) and the figurative (trout fishing in America); the man who loves trout fishing in America and the activity, which is trout fishing and which symbolises an alternative, open-air, informal lifestyle, are fused. Here is Wilding, in the story 'Sex in Australia from a Man's Point of View', but transported to an Australia beach:

> We were lying on the beach when we saw sex in Australia from a man's point of view, coming low over the horizon, just clipping the top of the waves, doing

that limping in on a wing and a prayer routine, two wings, it was a biplane, one of those old canvas and struts amphibious biplanes that had been continually in the wars, ripped again without a doubt.

'Lily,' I said, 'there's sex in Australia from a man's point of view just clipping the tops of the waves.' [15]

This essay has focused, in a limited way, on Michael Wilding's short stories as an example of one author, out of several in Australia, whose practice is marked by many features which are recognisably post-modernist. That there are others in his adopted country is obvious from a reading of *The Oxford Book of Australian Short Stories* (1994) which he selected and edited. In the introduction, Wilding writes:

> The late 1960s and the 1970s were an exciting time for Australian short fiction. There was a lively sense of change and renewal. There was a sense of breaking through into new possibilities, both in formal aspects and in subject. There was a new emphasis on sexuality, there were confrontations over permissible vocabulary, and there was a focus on contemporary urban experience replacing the preoccupation with the outback that the earlier nationalists had tended to privilege.[16]

The liberality of his selection acknowledges this fact. To review his output in short fiction is to be aware how easily he mixes his genres in ways that stretched the short story internationally, especially in the second half of the last century. The extent of Wilding's contribution to some of the magazines which carried experimental writing of the day testifies to his cosmopolitanism.

Ralph Cohen's essay about postmodern genres is indirectly useful about Wilding's achievement. Cohen writes:

> The initiation or use of one genre is determined by its relation to others. If writing were always identical, there would be no kinds and no need for generic distinctions. . . . And if each piece of writing were different from all the others there would be no basis for theorizing or even for communication. But since one piece of writing tends to be based on other pieces – some theorists refer to genres as families of texts with close or distant relatives – a genre offers the most extensive procedure for dealing with this phenomenon. It not only inquires into the reasons for intertextuality; it inquires into the significance of the combinatory procedures that result from it.[17]

I ended my review of *Somewhere New: New & Selected Stories* in the *New Straits Times*, published in Kuala Lumpur, by saying that for both Malaysian and Singapore writers of the short story, whose stories are largely realist and modernist, Wilding is essential reading. This essay, then, is also written for them and for their readers; and also for myself, as a reminder of challenges of writing and reading fiction today.

NOTES

1. Michael Wilding, *Aspects of the Dying Process* (University of Queensland Press, St Lucia, Queensland), 1971, p. 11.
2. Michael Wilding, *The West Midland Underground* (University of Queensland Press, St Lucia, Queensland, 1975), p. 1.
3. Ibid., p. 3.
4. Ibid., p. 4.
5. Hans Hauge, 'Michael Wilding, Post-Modernism and the Australian Literary Heritage', *Overland* 96 (1984), 50–1.
6. Bruce Clunies Ross, 'A New Version of Pastoral: Developments in Michael Wilding's Fiction, *Australian Literary Studies*, X1 (1983), 182–94.
7. Giulia Giuffré, 'An Interview with Michael Wilding' , *Southerly* 46 (1986), 313–21.
8. Michael Wilding, *Wildest Dreams* (University of Queensland Press, St Lucia, Queensland, (1998), p. 1.
9. Ian Syson, 'After Libertarianism: An Interview with Michael Wilding', *Australian Literary Studies* (May 1998), 280–2.
10. *Wildest Dreams*, p. 4.
11. Bruce Clunies Ross, op. cit., 189.
12. Michael Wilding, *Reading the Signs* (Hale & Iremonger, Sydney, 1984), pp. 48–9.
13. Brian McHale, *Postmodernist Fiction* (Routledge, London, 1987), p. 187.
14. Richard Brautigan, *Richard Brautigan's Trout Fishing in America, The Pill versus Springhill Mine Disaster, and In Watermelon Sugar* (Houghton Mifflin Company/Seymour Lawrence, Boston, 1989), p. 89.
15. Michael Wilding, *Somewhere New: New & Selected Stories* (Central Queensland University Press/McBride's Books, 1996), p. 95.
16. Michael Wilding, *The Oxford Book of Australian Short Stories* (Oxford University Press, Melbourne, 1994), p. xv.
17. Ralph Cohen, 'Do Postmodern Genres Exist' in Niall Lucy (ed.), *Postmodern Literary Theory: An Anthology* (Basil Blackwell, Oxford, 2000), p. 296.

Tichborne Redivivus
Re-Viewing Michael Wilding's Fiction

Brian Kiernan

'That's why people write fiction,' he said. 'So no one's ever really sure whether it's true or not. It gives you a let out.'

She turned her eyes to his bookshelves.

'Is your fiction true?'

'I'll give you some,' he said. 'You can work it out for yourself.'

This exchange comes towards the end of Michael Wilding's *Wildest Dreams* (1998). His protagonist, Graham, is teaching creative writing at a campus in California, and has just been praising his most talented student for the naturalness and honesty of her stories. Concerned, she hastens to inform him that they are not literally true; to which the ever-adroit Graham responds that they have what really matters, 'the sound of truth'.

Truth in fictions and truth in more sweeping narratives, social, political, ideological, are sustained, intersecting concerns for Graham as he progresses (if that is the right word) from impressionable young littérateur and aspiring novelist freshly landed in Sydney to disillusioned middle-aged academic and writer washed up on an alien shore. Despite the publishers describing it on the cover as 'a selective memoir', *Wildest Dreams* is, of course (as we always say), fiction. Don Graham has elaborated its homage to Balzac's *Lost Illusions*, that sprawling, classic realist study of a young provincial's literary ambition at the mercy of publishers, reviewers, booksellers in the Paris of the 1830s and 1840s; and it is otherwise imbued with Wilding's characteristic literary allusiveness and wry authorial detachment.[1] But still, like the fictional Graham's student, readers might well be curious as to how closely this fiction relates to its author's own career.

They should feel encouraged in their curiosity because, as Robert Yeo argues in his contribution to this volume, if we read the interviews

Wilding has given over the years together with *Wildest Dreams* itself, we can more fully appreciate how 'the life weaves in and out of fiction in an indeterminate way, the real enriching the fictional, the fictional crossing with the real'. The autobiographical dimension to this novel about writing, being published and publishing others, reviewing and being reviewed, promoting, distributing and teaching writing invites a retrospective glance at Wilding's career in all these areas – but most importantly his career as a writer of fiction, because many of the varied fictions that preceded *Wildest Dreams* constitute part of the reality it refers to.

Readers familiar with these earlier fictions will recognise the kinds of stories Graham imagines himself writing after his arrival in Sydney as being like most of those in Wilding's first collection, *Aspects of the Dying Process* (1972). Graham, we are told in *Wildest Dreams*, was at that time 'torn between Lawrence and Sillitoe and the proletarian tradition, and the conscious artifice of Henry James. Or between the provincial celebrations of George Eliot and the exotic expatriation of Durrell' (pp. 20–1). For Wilding himself, Durrell and James seem to have had the edge on the other contenders, because most of the stories in *Aspects*, certainly the most frequently reprinted, are about discovering, as though exotic, à la Durrell, the environs and hedonistic life-style of contemporaries in Sydney. Simultaneously they present, à la James, the hesitancy of the central consciousness – sometimes a first person consciousness, sometimes third person (and sometimes also called Graham) – over what exactly he has encountered, experienced, achieved in what to him is the unfamiliar, but beguiling, sub-culture of his new country's youthful, and lustful, bohemia. In these stories, a latter-day Christopher Newman meets not the decayed aristocracy of the Old World but the Sydney 'Push'.

Their readers also meet some of the memorable characters who will reappear, sometimes under different names, in many of Wilding's subsequent fictions – first of all 'Joe', drawn from close associate and rival writer, Frank Moorhouse, and 'Dexter', who may owe something to Gareth Powell, the publisher of soft-porn magazines (like *Sire* in the novel) in which stories by both Wilding and Moorhouse appeared. Recognition of the fiction's truth to such real-life models was part of the pleasure for audiences (often including the models themselves) when many of these stories were first 'published' at readings – a medium which emphasised their aural or performable qualities. But as well as reintroducing characters and situations familiar to readers of his preceding fictions progressively throughout *Wildest Dreams*, Wilding goes further and engages in self-referentiality (or auto-intertextuality?) by incorporating elements from his earlier work into Graham's story.

The first story in *Aspects*, the often anthologised 'Somewhere New' – based on the young Wilding's experience of meeting Charles Higham, then literary editor of the Sydney *Bulletin*, later biographer of Hollywood stars, and co-editing with him the anthology *They Came to Australia* (1967) – is reworked in *Wildest Dreams* to become Chapter 3, 'Life in Review'. But even before this, the opening of Chapter 2, 'Bachelor Writing', could very well stir the memories of readers familiar with Wilding's writings from when his career was at the same stage as Graham's is at in the novel. The chapter begins with Graham meeting one of Joe's girlfriends, Lisa, at a WEA conference. This elaborates a detail from 'Joe's Absence', that wonderful evocation of the perverse pleasures to be gained from an Other's texts. In it, the narrator's voyeuristic thrill at reading through the absent Joe's jealously-guarded, pristine manuscripts with Joe's girlfriend, and their defilment of them in the process, substitute for the sexual betrayal both have been flirting with. The Graham of that story in *Aspects* also recalls being attracted to one of Joe's girlfriends, there called Lydia, at a conference. Later in the same chapter of *Wildest Dreams*, readers may recognise that Graham's flirtation with yet another of Joe's girlfriends, Angie, both incorporates and extends 'From His Apperceptiveness of the Terribleness of Things' which appears in the collection of previously censored stories, *The Phallic Forest* (1979). Clearly, such echoes from Wilding's fictions since his first collection establish that Graham's career in *Wildest Dreams* as writer, critic, publisher, academic is a selective, and comic, version of Wilding's own since the late 1960s.

When *Aspects of the Dying Process* first appeared during the years of countercultural resistance to the war in Vietnam and the not unrelated emergence of a self-proclaimed 'new' fiction – leading some reviewers to make shorthand reference to a contemporary realistic 'Wilding-Moorhouse' genre, as earlier generations had referred to the 'Lawson-Furphy' tradition – it was understandable that its representation of youthful, inner-urban lifestyles attracted most attention. Revisiting the collection in the different context, and with the hindsight of today, one notices stories that did not neatly fit those interests of reviewers then: the Jamesian-titled and Gothic 'The Altar of the Family', the early-Jamesian (but Lawrentian-titled) 'Odour of Eucalyptus', the arachnophobically Gothic 'As Flies to Wanton Boys'. But even the more realistic stories were less focused on the there and then than on the narrators' or protagonists' uncertainties about the situations, especially the sexual situations, they find themselves in. Wilding's first novel, *Living Together*, also published in 1972, projects (comically for the reader) such confusions into an extended reversal of roles: over its course, Paul, initially the hapless butt of Martin's sexually-smug superiority, metamorphoses – thanks to ego-building assistance from Nina, Kate and Marianne – into the dominant male.

Wilding's second and ampler collection, *The West Midland Underground* (1975), displays a much wider, indeed virtuoso, command of genres. As Robert Yeo observes in his contribution here, some stories, like 'Canal Run' and 'Jealous of Ali', set in England and in adolescence, would seem to have been written before those collected in *Aspects*. The majority though exhibit the generic variety, and hybridity, characteristic of the 'new writing' that Wilding, with Moorhouse and others, was then promoting. The first and the title story of the collection is a collage that yokes together some of the author's heterogeneous memories and interests, ranging from local historical myths recalled from his childhood in Worcester to a manic contemporary fantasy of having short stories broadcast over taxi radios, and contains much else along the way. Like 'Bye, Bye, Jack. See You Soon', which presents a narrator 'writing instant experience' whose personality also draws together disparate elements, this is a good example of a short story as performance piece. However, other cool and impersonal voices narrate many of the stories in the collection, notably those favourites of anthologisers 'The Man of Slow Feeling' and 'The Words She Types'. The first exemplifies a strain of speculative and fabulistic fiction that runs throughout *The West Midland Underground*; the second another (though not mutually exclusive) strain, of self-reflexivity or writing about writing.

In Chapter 2 of *Wildest Dreams*, 'Bachelor Writing', Graham recalls that his early conversations with Joe about 'literary business, the business of getting published' were not recorded because they occurred before 'the self-reflexive moment'. The impact of this 'moment', together with the influences of American, South American and European fabulists on the 'new writing' in Australia, especially among those published in *Tabloid Story*, the supplement edited by Wilding, Moorhouse and others and hosted by various journals, is clearly registered in *The West Midland Underground* collection and Wilding's second novel, *The Short Story Embassy*, also published in 1975. As well as employing a Burroughs-like cut-up technique in some stories, such as the performance pieces mentioned above, Wilding seems to be paying homage to Borges in 'The Silence of the Seer' and, drolly, to Richard Brautigan – or the absence of Brautigan – in 'Lost on the Mesa'. In the novel, the 'embassy', with its Earlier Brautigan potting shed, Borges library, Henry James carpet, O. Henry guest suite, G.K. Chesterton refectory, Maugham veranda and Pat Hobby construction room, is a veritable house of fiction.

Its permanent residents are three short story writers defying a monolithic, covert cultural establishment that they suspect is based in Melbourne. These ambassadors for 'new writing' are the gruffly counter – countercultural Wendel; the highly literary, tormentedly suspicious Lazlo; and Valda, New Age princess and Lazlo's lover (but, he wonders, only his?). The novel begins with the arrival of a stranger, Tichborne, at the embassy's Gothic portico (but on a bright and summery day). A reviewer who has published on Wendel in a Melbourne-based journal which cannot be named in Sydney, Tichborne moves in to involve himself vicariously, if obtusely, in the creative life of the three ambassadors, even though Lazlo has suspected immediately that he is an agent of the secret establishment's Literary Police. By the end he has mysteriously disappeared [Alas! poor Tichborne . . .]; the Literary Police have shut down the Short Story Cab Radio transmitter (shades of 'The West Midland Underground'); and Lazlo, who believes that short stories predict the future, unlike novels which chronicle the past, is left dreading the fire that recent writings have foretold.

Narrated in brief episodes from the very different points of view of the four characters – despite Lazlo's belated insistence that it is *his* novel, even though it keeps slipping out of his control – *The Short Story Embassy* mocks the omniscient narration conventionally attributed to traditional realism. Like Graham in *Wildest Dreams*, each of the three writers is preoccupied with the relation of fiction to reality, or truth, yet none sees that relationship in the same way. Nevertheless, an historically-minded commentator would have little difficulty in recognising the real life situations and relationships being caricatured, with self-caricature to the fore. Approached as a *roman-à-clef*, the novel is full of disguised references to Wilding's, Moorhouse's and Vicki Viidikas's actual writings around the time it appeared. A particularly convoluted example is when Wendel quotes Wilding quoting Joe who is quoting Hemingway (p. 97). Is Wendel slyly signalling his awareness that the author has cast him as Joe in other fictional contexts? As with much else here, readers must feel lost in a hall of fictional mirrors, abandoned by author-ity, left to work it out for themselves, as Graham in *Wildest Dreams* encourages his student to do.

Lazlo and Wendel are variations on the dominant and recessive male personalities who compete in many of the earlier stories (the long story 'Hector & Freddie' in *The West Midland Underground* is an extended, hilarious example). In these stories, the dominant male is usually called 'Joe', as he is in *Wildest Dreams*. Like Joe, the Wendel of *The Short Story Embassy* is adept at inducing anxiety and confusion in others, and at meeting their responses with heavy put-downs. His name, and Lazlo's, invite speculation. Is 'Wendel', with its echo of Grendel, intended to suggest an ogre-ish presence? And could 'Lazlo' have been inspired by Lazlo Toth, the naturalised Australian who fleetingly achieved international ignominy by attacking Michaelangelo's *Pietà* with a hammer?

Such caricaturing of actual writers, situations and settings is cast in a highly individual mode, a crossing of mock-Gothic mystery (or should that be 'post-Gothic', as in *Academia Nuts*?) with the paranoid espionage thriller to involve the reader in the characters' shared, but also their separate, preoccupations – or paranoias. There is much in *Wildest Dreams* about 'paranoia' as the catch-cry of the Vietnam War years. Australia's involvement in the Vietnam war, itself the consequence of *official* fears of an international communist conspiracy, polarised the nation and provoked 'paranoid' reactions – what could be believed, who could be trusted? Even before then, prominent, and influential, American novelists had been asking how could they write plausible fictions about public suspicions that spun out towards fantasy: was John F. Kennedy sharing Marilyn Monroe's favours with a Mafia boss; had the Mafia and the CIA joined forces to assassinate him (and her)? Classic realism had assumed a normative society, if only for its heroes and heroines to rebel against. Increasingly, American novelists (Burroughs, Pynchon, Roth, Vonnegut . . .) had enlisted 'low' genres – science-fiction, crime and espionage thrillers, pornography – to devise appropriately paranoid modes and so unsettle expectations of a neat congruence between realism and reality, between a stable mode and a schizoid world.

For Graham in *Wildest Dreams* – in Chapters Twelve and Fourteen, 'Nigredo' and 'The Fishing Club', which together recall the title story in the 1988 collection *Under Saturn* – the political novel he would like to write has become impossible in this world in which, for instance, the CIA traded arms for drugs in El Salvador. Not only would the plots that he has perceived so pellucidly under the stimulus of marijuana seem delusory but if he employed them in fiction no one would publish him. However, despite his laments, Graham's unpublishable paranoid ravings against feminism/post-structuralism/abstract expressionism as CIA global conspiracies *have* now been published, in Wilding's objectively narrated, ironically detached, and, in mode, predominantly realistic comic novel. What readers of *Wildest Dreams* alone would not suspect from it, though, are the kinds of playful, 'paranoid' fictions that Wilding was publishing around the time that Graham in that novel is elaborating his marijuana-induced insights into global conspiracies.

At the imaginative centre of *The Short Story Embassy* and its 'sequel', the suite of interrelated stories *Scenic Drive* (1976), is, as Bruce Clunies Ross has neatly put it, 'an underlying concern with being exploited and controlled in another's fiction'. Here self-reflexivity, writing about writing, and anxieties about covert conspiracies are inventively, and comically, combined as the characters write about their fears of others' writing, and their own. For Clunies Ross, though, *The Short Story Embassy: a novel* is 'nothing like a novel, as it is ironically subtitled', and he very informedly points to a wide range of precedents throughout Western literature for the non-realistic genres Wilding was drawing on around this time.[2] Nevertheless, the irony he perceives in the subtitle also depends on an equally historical recognition of the then-contemporary, local as well as international, reactions against realism – the embrace of 'irrealism', 'surfiction', 'fabulation', the 'anti-novel' and other formulations (which were soon to be subsumed under the category of 'metafiction', before eventually being replaced by that even more undiscriminating term 'post-modern fiction'). Considered as an anti-novel, *The Short Story Embassy* calculatedly plays with – if only to play against – readers' expectations of mimesis and resolution. Perhaps, though, the ultimate turn of the anti-realist screw might be leading readers to suspect that the literary comedy has been fantastically projected from real or true-to-life experience and leaving them to try to work out for themselves what this experience was?

Finding a form to express experiences that seem unwritable within the conventions of realistic fiction can also be seen as the impulse behind *Pacific Highway* (1982). Though not subtitled 'a novel' as (however ironically) *The Short Story Embassy* is, it can also be readily identified as an 'anti-novel' within the broad stream of then-contemporary experimental fiction that evaded traditional categorisations, often by crossing them. It has a set of characters who interact throughout and react to the environmental and politico-cultural threats, as they perceive them, to what should be their idyllic hippie way of life on the far north coast of NSW. All is mediated through the consciousness of a self-reflexive and (as Bruce Clunies Ross has again elaborated) very literary narrator.[3] This narrator begins with a brief, declarative description of the weather, and immediately comments on what he has written; he ends 158 pages later by musing on the manifold meanings of 'plot', and whether expectations of it in narrative might not be conditioned by capitalism. Two clues to what happens, and what does not really happen, in between are hinted at by a reference to Richard Brautigan's *A Confederate General from Big Sur* and a more than a page-long quotation from de Quincey's *Confessions of an English Opium Eater.*

Brautigan's title encapsulates generic and historio-geographical hybridity–no realist would so defy conventions and readers' expectations as to situate a Confederate general in California. (And Wilding's title, if we ignore the initial capitals and look beyond the specific reference, is also worth contemplating – a *pacific* highway?) In Wilding's semi-tropical, quasi-paradisal location there are incongruous elements, stereotypes from another culture and literary tradition: a half-timbered pub with its horse-brasses and peacocks on its lawn; a pair of equestriennes fully kitted-out, right down to their County accents; the Women's Institute meeting in the Puginesque Gothic School of Arts in the fields (not the paddocks) where the cleaning lady leads the hymn singing; the village fair on the vicarage lawn. . . . These for the narrator typify the way of life of the wider community, those he calls the 'midlanders' – a way of life which is as much under threat from development and pollution as is that of his immediate circle of drop-outs from late twentieth-century industrialisation and conformity. But could the narrator be projecting his own personal and literary coordinates onto this community? When the hippies seek to return to the pub there are only trees where they imagined it had been. The horsey girls can probably be assumed to be 'real', but whether they were as frisky with each other as the narrator lubriciously imagines we'll never know. There is, the others tell him, no cleaning lady, so how could she lead the hymn singing in the School of Arts, which anyway no one has ever seen before? And what about the narrator's vision of a satanic pier and conveyor-belt delivering wood-chips to a freighter? A fog obscures it, and when it lifts the beach is seen to be as pristine as ever.

Readers can recognise (perhaps better a second time around) that much the narrator recounts issues from his consumption of hallucinogenics, as in that often-excerpted incident 'Sex in Australia from a Man's Point of View'. But just how much? Where in his account of events does the actual end and his paranoid perception of it begin? And could his suspicions that global conspiracies are behind unwelcome developments in this otherwise near Arcady or Eden be justified? Instead of being transported into Asiatic scenery, as was de Quincey after the visit of the Malay, and, famously, 'kissed, with cancerous kisses, by crocodiles, and . . . laid, confounded with all unutterable abortions, amongst reeks and Nilotic mud', the narrator's waking nightmares are of all forms of ecological degradation, and he is predisposed to assume the worst, in the beginning mistaking natural phenomena – foam on the beach, the redness of the pool – for chemical pollution. Readers are taken immediately into the narrator's hallucinations, both those filled with foreboding and those with euphoria. There is no implied authorial voice controlling the narration, as there is in the presentation of Graham's THC-induced revelations of global conspiracies in *Wildest Dreams*. Here, readers must seek to distinguish the 'real' situations from the narrator's distorted perception of them (though this is not to say that these perceptions are any less real for him).

Although, unlike Lazlo, this narrator seems to have total control over his narrative, the comedy it generates implicitly distances readers, and the real author, from his account. He is convinced that a recently arrived figure of mysterious authority, Major-General Darling, has been teamed with a covert CIA operative, the anthropologist Doctor Dai, to ensure that the local entrepreneur, the builder Mr Boon, is able to proceed unhindered with his 'developments'. These caricatures of the Authoritarian, the Foreign Agent, and the Capitalist are children's story-book villains, humours . . . and most humorous, especially when they dress up in funny hats. But they are also menacing as when, wearing assorted military head-gear, they sweep into the fair and execute the bears (bears?!). Or does the narrator on a trip imagine this, as he imagines so much else; is he fantastically projecting his fears onto these malevolent rustic clowns? Not that the narrator is the only one to hallucinate. Rose-Marie imagines she has been abducted by aliens and, very gratifyingly, molested sexually. But the narrator, ever-suspicious, always relentlessly rational in his own way, is unconvinced: surely the imagined 'aliens' must have been US test pilots?

Bureaucratic persecution is another form of, as well as stimulus to, paranoia. Does cutting down the sign that Major-General Darling has had put up to prohibit entry to the beach at night constitute no more than acknowledgement of his authority? The apogee of bureaucratic absurdity, a true Catch 22, is reached when the hippie recyclers, who have no garbage to dispose of, are intimidated into going in search of some, so that they can take it to the tip and get a receipt to prove that they have not been dumping refuse illegally. In its distinctive mode, or blend of genres, *Pacific Highway* engages comically with at least some of those 'paranoid' preoccupations with surveillance and control that Graham in *Wildest Dreams* is convinced he could not get published if he wrote them down. Like *The Short Story Embassy*, but unlike *Wildest Dreams*, it does so by taking readers 'inside' the experience of paranoia.

To return to the end of *Wildest Dreams*: immediately before Graham's concluding exchange with his most talented student, another, a young man, tells him how he would like to write about the victim of a CIA experiment to chemically program his memory for espionage. Graham responds, 'It's hard to write about that sort of thing . . . People just think you've flipped.' This could very well be an oblique allusion to the inventively 'paranoid' comic fictions Wilding himself, along with many others (though theirs were not always comic), was writing in the 1970s and into the early 1980s. While fear of surveillance, infiltration, surreptitious control and other paranoid preoccupations (or are they perceptions?) permeate his next novel, *The Paraguayan Experiment* (1984), its genre is predominantly historical-documentary realism, a genre engaged with more extensively in *Raising Spirits, Making Gold, and Swapping Wives: The True Adventures of Dr John Dee and Sir Edward Kelly* (1999). In both, the narrator and therefore the readers observe the characters' obsessions and suspicions from outside. This is also the case with Graham's in *Wildest Dreams* – which is itself an historical-documentary account in many ways, not least because it alludes to so much of the author's previously published fiction. But while the story of Graham, and how he is not able to write a political novel (a novel which Wilding in fact writes for him), invites readers to work out for themselves how much of this fiction is true, they will not get from *Wildest Dreams* a full sense of the comedies its author was writing in those dark years Graham found so sterile. For that they will have to go back to Wilding's earlier books, as, of course, *Wildest Dreams* invites them to do.

NOTES

1. Don Graham, 'Michael Wilding's Lost Illusions: the Balzacian Underpinnings of *Wildest Dreams*' in Fran de Groen and Ken Stewart (eds), *Australian Writing and the City*, Association for the Study of Australian Literature, [Sydney], 2000, pp. 138–43.
2. Bruce Clunies Ross, 'A New Version of Pastoral: Developments in Michael Wilding's Fiction', *Australian Literary Studies*, XI, 1983, 182–94. See also his 'Paradise, Politics, and Fiction: The Writing of Michael Wilding', *Meanjin*, I, 1986, 19–27; and 'Lazlo's Testament: Or Structuring the Past and Sketching the Present in Conemporary Short Fiction, Mainly Australian', *Kunapipi* I, 2, 1979, 110–23.
3. Bruce Clunies Ross, 'A New Version of Pastoral', 101-3.

The Problematics of Pierre Bourdieu's Concept of Art in Respect of the Theatre

Maria Shevtsova

The concept of art in Bourdieu's theory is predicated on his argument concerning 'field' (*champ*) and is essentially inseparable from the latter. His theory is formed by a multidisciplinary approach encompassing philosophy, anthropology, sociology, economics and politics but which, by its focus, is most appropriately described as a sociology of culture. Culture, for Bourdieu, is not purely a matter of artefacts, or of artistic 'products' or *objects d'art* in the realm of what in *La Distinction* (1979) he identifies as the culture of the élite. Nor does it primarily involve the surface events produced by manners, customs and habits, as specified by anthropologists, although this anthropological, everyday-life perspective is fundamental to Bourdieu's thought. It is, above all, a *practice*, by which term Bourdieu refers to the processes of doing rather than to the results of what is done. Culture, in other words, is a momentum in which social agents of action act. What they produce through action, whether the behaviour patterns named 'manners' or the material constructs going by the name of 'artefacts' or 'art', is integral to this momentum. Bourdieu's objective, by homing in on the doing and making – practice – that constitute art, is to accentuate its social character and thus prise it away from the conceptual framework in which formalism and philosophical idealism of one kind or another hold sway.

The anthropological residue of Bourdieu's eminently sociological outlook on the source, place and purpose of art – and on its character in relation to the collective structures that define 'society' itself – has to do with his early research which was ethnographic and conducted in Algeria. It was here that he studied the relationship between rural work and community organisation and the impact of colonialism and the economic structures peculiar to it on traditional methods of farming. Thus his research gave rise to 'sociologised' accounts of ethnographically inspired observation such as the collaborative *Travail et travailleurs en Algérie* (1963) and *Le Déracinement* (1964) as well as the single-authored publications *Esquisse d'une théorie de la pratique* (1972) and *Algérie 60* (1977); and his analysis showed how economic changes not only set into contradiction the ways of working of the Kabyle, but permeated their ways of doing and perceiving in the course of their daily relations with each other. Everyday life was, then, far more than an expression of manners and customs that had been adopted and transmitted passively though time. It was imbricated actively in the whole social dynamic and was acted upon by social agents whose capacity for agency, precisely, generated the conflict between the old and the new, the indigenous and the colonial, and the various forms taken by labour (*travail*) in relation to culture understood as daily life. Bourdieu's conception of practice, which applies to a wide range of purposeful activities from tilling the soil and investment banking to writing novels, emerges from this context of ideas.

The example of investment banking, although not explicitly proposed by Bourdieu, is implicit in his discussions of economic capital, financial transactions being integral to this capital which he distinguishes from cultural capital, social capital and the remaining types of capital he claims coexist at any given historical moment without being possessed equally by the same social groups. That is to say, that holders of one type of capital are not necessarily, at the same time, the beneficiaries of other types: those, for instance, with economic capital are not automatically endowed with the capital of culture (1979). This argument as to the imbalance of the various capitals is Bourdieu's bulwark, as he sees it, against the economism of Marxism and its deterministic correlation between the economic base and the superstructure to which culture allegedly belongs. By the same token, his absorption of the notion of labour into that of practice, which is consistent throughout his writings, similarly articulates his critique of Marxist economism, now specifically of its overdependence, when defining labour, on such notions as exploitation and surplus value. Investment banking serves the purposes of this discussion in that it highlights the direction taken by Bourdieu. Albeit not labour, least of all in the Marxian sense of the term, investment banking is nevertheless brought about by agency, which, in Bourdieu's schema, is indispensable for any kind of practice. Bourdieu's disagreement with Marxism is merely one facet of his overall view and is complemented by his attack on structuralists and post-structuralists. Contrary to these thinkers, who were his contemporaries, and notably Michel Foucault with whom he has some affinity, Bourdieu incorporates agency in his theory. Moreover, in still greater polemic with them, he gives it priority as an analytical and explanatory principle for all social phenomena including the exercise – agency, again – of power which, notably in Foucault, is an agent-less, as it were anonymous function of systems of control.

Practice, however, is not the mere fact of, say, writing novels. It is integral to specific infrastructural and what might be termed symbolic networks – 'symbolic' in the sense in which, for example, values, signs, representations and perceptions create meaning and indicate social evaluation but are not material, as are machinery or administrative and managerial systems. And these networks, which are particular to particular activities, are part and parcel of whichever field of activity is designated by this or that practice, giving such categories as the literary field (in which the process of novel writing, publishing, distribution and critical reception occurs), the political field, the juridical field, and so on, all of them homologous to some extent since no practice can operate entirely on its own. The viscosity of society prevents it from doing so. Bourdieu's centre of interest where the arts are concerned is painting and literature, theatre receiving scant attention from him for reasons to do with his familiarity with the former rather than with any assumption that his theory is unsuitable for it.[1] Yet his theory is actually more than pertinent for the study of the theatre. The theatre is not only a practice in the strongest sense of the term since it relies on *performance*, which is a process of doing *par excellence*. It is also a collective practice *par excellence*, since its works, particularly when it comes to stage productions, rely on being made by a group of people – directors, actors, scenographers, musicians and technicians, among others. As a field, the theatre is a prime case of multiple agencies producing the constructs known as 'art'.

One of the prominent aspects of Bourdieu's notion of *champ* is its non-reducibility to anything that may be related to it. The theatre, according to this precept, cannot be scaled down, say, to literature by virtue of the fact that dramatic literature is incorporated in the field of the theatre as a whole. A second major feature of Bourdieu's definition is that a field cannot be reduced to a practice homologous with it. Thus, the theatre, which is functionally homologous with, say, economics in that it depends on the financial, market, distributional and other forces involved in a given economy cannot be reduced to a matter of economic operations. Reducibility is not possible, Bourdieu argues, because each field 'assumes a completely specific form at its very core' (1987:167).

It is essential to observe that the term 'arts' used above could well be replaced by that of 'cultural practices', which is not only Bourdieu's all-embracing terminology for different activities, but is also his generic category for creative-artistic endeavour *in toto*. His purpose in using it is to identify art as a *cultural* activity, hence necessarily a social one generated by, and open to, social pressures. Bourdieu thereby calls into question the idea that art is ruled solely by the principles of composition immanent to it. This premise, central to the philosophy and history of aesthetics, finds its extreme expression in the ideology of *l'art pour l'art*, which is Bourdieu's preferred point of comparison and contrast for a sociological-materialist approach to the issue (1979: 50–1; 1992a: 140, 188–9). This issue, as Bourdieu sees it, cannot be confined to the problem of aesthetics concerning what *constitutes* art, but must ask *why* it is constituted in this rather than that fashion – its Why? superseding compositional rules or the apparently disinterested motive of art for no other purpose than its own sake.

Bourdieu's response to the question regarding the differentiation between the forms of a particular art field is in two tiers: the first distinguishes between the field of art and other fields of activity; the second concentrates on distinctions within a field for which Bourdieu elaborates what might be called the *champ* nexus, that is, the knot tying together the three principles of 'position', 'disposition' and 'position-taking' (*prise de position*) that govern the players of a *champ*. Thus, according to Bourdieu, artists occupy different positions in the cultural field, as do lawyers, politicians, and so on, in their respective fields. The position held by its holder virtually determines this holder's *disposition*. By 'disposition' Bourdieu refers to such things as outlook, expectation, selection, evaluation and acquisition of knowledge and insight through exposure to art and culture generally, which, he argues, is inclusive in 'taste' (1979). Position and disposition undersign the holder's *prise de position* in respect of the field, that is to say, how she/he assesses it, situates it, places herself/himself in it and takes a position on it, as she/he might take, say, a political position or a moral one (1987: 175).[2] All this concerning artistic fields helps to explain why, in the case of the theatre, the profession is not uniform, and why theatre practitioners generate an immense variety of styles, approaches and attitudes over and above their differences as individuals. They do so, following

Bourdieu, because the tripart nexus of position-disposition-taking position provides the *objective* conditions in relation to which artists practise their art. And this, given Bourdieu's argument that art is not personally inspired but socially generated makes a field a space of 'objective relations' between artists. This could be put very crudely by saying that how artists work and are distinguished from each other depends on their place in 'the system' of the field and how they define and view their place in it.

Where issues of stylistics and artistic qualities are concerned (my terminology), Bourdieu argues that the *prises de position* as regards artistic *modes d' expression* (Bourdieu's terminology) correspond to the different positions that practitioners hold in a field. In other words, practitioners' choice of genres, forms and styles and how they practise them defines their position in the field as a whole. One might think, here, of the hierarchical distinction perceived by Bourdieu between classical music and jazz. Classical musicians presume that they hold a more elevated position than jazz musicians in the field of music, and are presumed by society at large to have greater distinction because the genre itself is assumed to have a higher status (1964b: 61–5; 1979: 95–6). Another example, this time in the theatre, would be the distinction Bourdieu claims lies between 'serious theatre', such as the theatre of national houses, and boulevard theatre (1979: 260–5) which, he argues, was initially established by the ruling cultural élite and was subsequently maintained by it, with the result that the rest of society adopted the same evaluative scale.

Bourdieu argues, in addition, that the status accorded to a genre depends on the channels through which it is distributed. These channels ensure as well as perpetuate the genre's station in the gamut of genres available in any one historical period. Thus, if Bourdieu's point regarding serious and boulevard theatre were developed, we would find that the venue where a certain type of theatre is performed conveys the latter's place in the hierarchy. The example of France, where Bourdieu collected the empirical data sustaining his theory, serves this discussion well. Entertainment theatre of the kind performed in Parisian boulevard venues, which are invariably private theatres, would not appear in the higher-status national houses of the Comédie-Française or the Odéon. It would appear least of all at the Odéon since its change of identity in 1983 as the Odéon-Théâtre de l'Europe, a nationally funded theatre to showcase Europe and facilitate exchanges between European theatre professionals whose work is deemed to be of a high quality by peers.

The theatre's artistic policy, despite its political agenda regarding the European Union, is not exclusive to the European Union, but its mission as an institution, and, therefore, also as a venue, precludes boulevard theatre of any kind and, most of all, its most commercial, low-quality manifestations.

Nor would entertainment theatre be considered for the publicly financed 'serious theatre', that is, such art houses as the Théâtre des Amandiers, a municipal theatre that rose to fame through the productions of Patrice Chéreau, its artistic director, who has since turned his creative efforts to film; the Théâtre du Soleil, where, for thirty years, Ariane Mnouchkine has produced some of the most innovative work of late-twentieth century world theatre; the Bouffes du Nord inaugurated by Peter Brook in 1973, where he has explored the principles of poetry, simplicity and immediacy in the theatre as has virtually no other director of the past fifty years and where he has built an awesome international reputation, leaving behind an unparalleled legacy in Western Europe on the art and craft of acting and directing. While these directors, their teams and their work (Mnouchkine alone has a company as such) built up the symbolic capital of their houses, their houses, in turn conferred distinction upon them – future, on the spectators who came to performances there and basked in the reflected glory of the venues elevated to the status of their occupants.

If venues and the type of theatre performed in them are ordered hierarchically, what these art-house instances demonstrate is that theatre practitioners are classified accordingly. Directors of commercial theatre on the boulevards cannot hope to aspire to the status of a Chéreau, Mnouchkine or Brook since their positions in the field are defined in relation to each other and the whole field by virtue of the 'What?' and the 'Where?' of their respective practices. Moreover, pecking orders regarding 'What?' and 'Where?' vary according to the artists working in a designated field. Bourdieu, as usual, takes the field of literature and observes that its genres may be ranked by the literary reviews in which they are published and which, *ipso facto*, define the positions of their authors (1987: 175). This – extrapolating from Bourdieu – gives positions ranked as superior, inferior, or somewhere in a potentially broad middle range.

Positions are also defined by what Bourdieu terms 'more exterior indicators' such as social and geographic origin, by which he means that artists who have emerged from the lower social classes or from the regions rather than the metropolis occupy less prestigious positions in the field. He argues, moreover, that the 'objective relations' at issue 'determine or orient the competitive relations' that, in his example of literature, an author has with other authors (1987:165). Despite his specific example, for Bourdieu, these 'objective' and 'competitive' relations govern any and every field, artistic or not. Allusions to competition, rivalry, tension and conflict abound in his writings, making his image of field rather like that of a battlefield, as Bernard Lahire, not a friendly critic of Bourdieu, observes with some irony (1999: 24). Lahire also notes that with the concept of field Bourdieu attempts to resolve the issue of the social division and function of labour, which has been central to French sociology since Durkheim (1999: 26–30). His interpretation sheds some light on how Bourdieu subsumes the question of labour under his theory of practice in order to affirm that practice (and not labour, as in Marx) defines social activity and differentiates between different activities. By the same token, it is practice that defines different fields differently, and, as well, drives all types of art.

Now, care must be taken not to turn Bourdieu's argument into a matter of mechanistic correspondence between elements by which position x would correspond with disposition y, without mediation, deviation, subtlety or ambiguity. For, although Bourdieu insists that a field is a *network* – an image implying the subtlety of interweave and texture – his determination to establish its *objective* workings has a critical consequence, that of privileging the objectivity of processes to the detriment of any subjective intervention in them which is proper to agency. In other words, Bourdieu runs the risk of eliminating the subjective components that are caught up in a field from the situation altogether; and subjectivity is necessarily embedded in dispositions, irrespective of how dispositions are shaped objectively by the available variety of practices in the field. These components include such personalised features in an art network as an artist's temperament, which, if not always discernible, and certainly not quantifiable, filters through a work, nevertheless. It is clear that, for Bourdieu, art is made in complex circumstances that restrict artists and rein them in. Which is why, in his optic, art cannot be understood as the outcome of an artist's volition, free will and free choice. Nor can art be the outcome of individuation through, for example, such individuated attributes as inspiration, talent, genius, imagination, emotion and temperament. It cannot be any of these, given, especially, the invasive role played by 'objective relations' in all matters to do with art.

What is not completely clear, however, from Bourdieu's body of writings, speaking chronologically about them – thus up to and including *Les Règles de l'art* published in 1992 – is the time when, and the place where, an artist's individual qualities affect the process of making art, and how these qualities impact on it. The artist's individual contribution and, consequently, her/his particular creativity, must necessarily play a part somewhere in this process. If it did not, all artists in the same or similar tripartite nexus of position-disposition-position-taking that is operative within their field as a whole would do nothing more than reproduce each other, in serial fashion. Differences of form, style, skill, technique, feeling, approach, and so on, would appear from one nexus to the next, but not *within* each nexus. Yet, in the reality of practice, such differences do, in fact, exist.

Given these differences, which are empirically observable, there must exist, then, a margin of relative freedom for inspiration, talent, and other qualities not inherent in 'objective relations' within the determinants of position-disposition-position-taking. To acknowledge the presence of subjectivity and individuation in the cultural field does not discount in the slightest the 'objective relations' constituting this field. Furthermore, acknowledgement along these lines does not desocialise the subjectivity of socialised agents of action: agents are not less social for having subjective dimensions. In fact, they are capable of individuation only because they *are* social beings, and are individuated only because they can be differentiated *within* the collectivity and *from* the objective social relations that constitute it.

Bourdieu's quasi-exclusive emphasis on the objective relations integral to a cultural/artistic field is based, of course, on his critique of the 'philosophy of consciousness' (1992a: 253) at whose heart lies 'the subjectivism which sees action as a deliberate accomplishment of a conscious intention, as a free project of a conscience positing its own ends and maximizing its utility through rational calculation' (1992b: 96). The 'free project' of 'conscious intention' is exactly what, to his mind, underlies subjectivism and makes it a false proposition. Consequently, subjectivism is nothing more that a variant of the various types of idealist philosophy that posit the idea of the artist as an isolated, asocial being – an unexplainable 'creative genius' (1992a: 262). Bourdieu's criticism does not stop here. If he polemicises against subjectivism and its variations, he does not spare an objectivism that deletes all notions of agents and agency from consideration – structuralism, as noted above, being a case in point.[3]

Yet, the problem that arises from Bourdieu's own version of 'objectivism', that is, of actions that are both objectively given *and* have agents of actions (the two virtually defining a field), is its relative lack of recognition as to how the subjectivity of agents interferes in action and organises and *transforms* it. In other words, what I am suggesting is that Bourdieu's conception of objective relations is essentially *systemic* and, as such, is open to the charge of objectivism of the kind that he condemns, irrespective of his inclusion of agents and agency in the equation. A chronological reading of Bourdieu shows, in fact, that he becomes increasingly aware of this problem (and is possibly indirectly replying to criticism of him on these grounds) when, in a rare personal note, he refers to himself as an 'objective observer' able to explore without indulgence 'the most obscure regions of my subjectivity' (1997:12). He also observes, this time on an impersonal note, that sociology 'cannot be reduced to an objectivation incapable of giving its place to the effort of agents to construct their subjective representation of themselves and their world' (1997: 225). This reformulation in terms of *representation* of selves and world introduces a stronger sense of subjective image-making and creative intervention than appears in Bourdieu's earlier writings.

We now need to pursue a little further, as regards the theatre, the interrelationship between what is objectively given and the subjective responses to it implied, but not fully articulated, by Bourdieu's notion of position-taking.[4] What needs to be stressed, is that the subjective element involved in this interrelationship entails an act of interpretation, that is, how a position is taken in the very moment when the position-taker interprets *both* the field *and* the position that she/he is taking. This interpretative aspect of the process – 'transaction' would be the Bourdieusian term for it – is an area that Bourdieu passes over rather too quickly, and requires closer attention. It is particularly important for understanding, for example, how directors make formal-stylistic choices – in other words, work artistically on a specific stage production. What this means is that they do not simply take a perspective – *prise de position* – on the field of the theatre, but take it, primarily, on the particular task at hand, which, although field-related is not pinned down by the field or dictated to by it. Directors' creative choices, intentions, pursuits and decisions may be reactive to the field to a certain degree, but are *proactive* above all else. And this proactivity, which is embodied through the bodies of actors in a production, is rarely as cognitively-based, rational and rationalised as supposed by Bourdieu's three-pronged schema of position-disposition-position-taking. It involves, to varying degrees of intricacy, the ludic, emotional and libidinal dimensions of creativity, as well as its subconscious impulses and drives. This goes some way to explaining why directors, in conversation with professionals as well as spectators, may claim that they were unaware of having done something attributed to them. Or why – Peter Brook being a prominent example – they may claim that they did not start out with a clear idea of what they were looking for, but explored the possibilities until something looked 'right'. Or why they speak, as Brook often does, of following their intuition rather than a specific theatrical precept, conception, or vision.[5]

The very idea of a stage production as a coherent, unified whole emerged with the rise of the modern director at the turn of the twentieth century. Stanislavsky, as is well known, was a pioneer of this new development, which has continued to be made flesh by practitioners until the present day. It could well be argued that, historically, the director's responsibility for an orchestrated ensemble gave the director's practice the legitimacy of authorship and ownership. Furthermore, the status of the director's role, together with the higher stakes placed on the process of directing, conferred upon productions the status of veritable artistic creations. Emphasis on creation and, as well, on creativity – the cornerstones of Stanislavsky's work in the theatre – shifted perception. A production could no longer be perceived as mere 'entertainment', which was a remainder from the nineteenth century that had been inherited, in any case, from an earlier notion of *divertissement*. Nor could it be a mere *object d'art*, a decorative *thing*. It breathed and grew, and changed with time like a living organism. Furthermore, it demanded recognition as serious work. This claim, fuelled with great energy by Stanislavsky, was sustained by such pioneer directors of the first half of the twentieth century as Meyerhold, Vakhtangov, Copeau, Artaud and Brecht, who, besides Stanislavsky, prioritised the actor's play (*igra*, *jeu*), demonstrating that it was purposeful invention in purposeful work, based on effort, craft, discipline and dedication.

Awareness of these historical factors is essential for understanding one aspect, at least, of what is 'objectively given' in the field of the theatre by the theatre for today. What was nothing less than revolutionary at the beginning of the twentieth century had become, one hundred years later, something of a tradition and, certainly, a foundation of contemporary mainstream theatre.[6] This theatre, moreover, could be called establishment theatre, if not the theatre of the establishment, by virtue of the fact that it has been appropriated by cultural élites both inside and outside the theatre, and to boot, by international cultural élites who, by internationalizing it and, thus, de-nationalising it, have made it appear to be their exclusive terrain. With this having been said, however, the field of the theatre, as its stands today, continues to alter as its pioneers continue to be reference points for new exploratory work – reference points that endure even when they are overturned or rejected by emerging experimental and avant-garde individuals and groups. The myriad of types of theatre generated in the second-half of the twentieth century in relation to them, whether a positive or negative attraction, can be suggested by a few: performance art, happenings, community theatre, street theatre, site-specific theatre, 'invisible' theatre (Augusto Boal), 'ritual theatre' (Jerzy Grotowski), and the 'third theatre' and 'barters' (Eugenio Barba).

In addition, this myriad has spawned hybrid genres of one kind and another in which physical theatre, dance, acrobatics, musical theatre, opera, circus and the visual arts, as distinct from the performing arts, merge. The encounter between the visual and the performing arts, for example, gives performance art and, as well, installations in which objects and performers interact. Digital and multi-media art, which are frequently included under the label of visual art, also combine with performers. The dynamics of the process is such that not only does it expand the perimeters of the field of the theatre, but also challenges its achievements. Nor does this field easily convert to the much broader notion of 'performance' to which, in recent years, academic inquiry has devoted considerable energy, consolidating the claims of 'performance studies' in its distinction from 'theatre studies' (Carlson, 2001; Shevtsova, 1999). It could be argued, in fact, that 'performance studies' has become a noticeable contestant in the intellectual study of the theatre quite intentionally and, by doing so, illustrates Bourdieu's contention as to how competition and rivalry are inherent in any field, while all players in it take position and vie for supremacy. How all this comes out in the wash in the future will become history. The essential point to be made here is that the players make the play ('art' or whatever new terms supplant it), and the 'objective relations' of their interplay can only be established with the help of their continual subjective intervention.

NOTES

1. Bourdieu's few references to the theatre are to be found in *La Distinction: Critique sociale du jugement*, Paris: Minuit, 1979, pp. 260–5; *Les Règles de l'art: Genèse et structure du champs littéraire*, Paris: Le Seuil, 1992, pp. 170–5: 'La Production de la croyance: contribution à une économie des biens symboliques', in *Les Actes de la recherche en sciences soçiales*, 13 (February 1977), 12–23.
2. It is essential to note that here, as elsewhere in my text, I am glossing and interpreting Bourdieu's thought and not translating him verbatim or even approximately. When I translate directly from Bourdieu, these translations appear in inverted commas, according to scholarly convention.
3. In this Bourdieu echoes Bakhtin who, with the collaboration of the 'Bakhtin Circle', published under the name of Voloshinov [Volosinov], an incisive argument against 'individualistic subjectivism' and 'abstract objectivism'. This argument cleared the ground for Bakhtin's theory of dialogism and all its attendant concepts, not least that of social agent. See *Marxism and the Philosophy of Language*, translated by Ladislav Matejka and I.R. Titunik, Cambridge, Mass.: Harvard University Press, 1986, pp. 45–63. Bourdieu consistently critiques these two philosophies, but see, particularly, his succinct formulation in *Méditations pascaliennes*, Paris: Le Seuil, 1997, pp. 225–6. As regards his critique of structuralism, it can be noted that Bourdieu did not escape structuralism's influence, especially not in *La Reproduction* (with Jean-Claude Passeron), Paris: Minuit, 1970.
4. It is doubtful, however, whether 'position-taking' encompasses the broader idea of 'subjective representation of themselves and their world' which emerges from the 'later' Bourdieu quoted in my preceding paragraph. I am suggesting that Bourdieu's thought undergoes a subtle shift in the late 1990s.
5. Still claimed by Brook as a pervasive theme of his most recent publication *Threads of Time: A Memoir*, London: Methuen, 1988 and reiterated in a public discussion at the Young Vic, London, 1 February 2001.
6. As Meyerhold observes: 'At first you are an arbitrary innovator, and then a silver-haired founder of tradition'. See Aleksandr Gladkov, *Meyerhold Speaks, Meyerhold Rehearses*, translated and edited by Alma Law, Amsterdam: Harwood Academic Publishers, 1997, p. 159. Meyerhold's remark is à propos of Chaliapin: 'Few people know how wilfully Chaliapin manipulated the score of *Boris Godunov*. In the "mad" scene he needed time for his extraordinary improvised acting: there he played an entire segment without singing. But the orchestral part was too short. Then he asked the conductor to repeat in this place the so-called "chimes" music . . . Once I heard *Boris* on the radio and I caught in the "mad" scene those same "chimes". That means they had become a tradition.' This is, indeed, a neat way of putting the issue.

REFERENCES

Bourdieu, Pierre with Alain Darbel, Jean-Paul Rivet and Claude Seibel (1963), *Travail et travailleurs en Algérie*, Paris and Amsterdam: EHESS-Mouton.

Bourdieu, Pierre and Abdelmalek Sayad (1964a), *Le Déracinement: La Crise de l'agriculture traditionnelle en Algérie*, Paris: Minuit.

Bourdieu, Pierre and Jean-Claude Passeron (1964b), *Les Héritiers*, Paris: Minuit (*The Inheritors*, trans. Richard Nice, Chicago: Chicago University Press, 1979).

——— (1970), *La Reproduction*, Paris: Minuit .(*Reproduction in Education, Society and Culture*, trans. Richard Nice, London: Sage, 1977).

Bourdieu, Pierre (1972), *Esquisse d'une théorie de la pratique*, Paris: Droz (*An Outline of a Theory of Practice*, trans. Richard Nice, Cambridge: Cambridge University Press, 1977).

——— (1977a), 'La Production de la croyance: contribution à une économiedes biens symboliques', in *Actes de la recherche en sciences sociales*, no.13, pp. 3–28.

——— (1977b), *Algérie 60: Structures économiques et structures temporelles*, Paris: Minuit (*Algeria 1960*, Cambridge: Cambridge University Press, 1979).

——— (1979), *La Distinction: Critique sociale du jugement*, Paris: Minuit (*Distinction*, trans. Richard Nice, London and New York: Routledge and Kegan Paul, 1986).

——— (1980), *Le Sens commun*, Paris: Minuit (*The Logic of Practice*, trans. Richard Nice, Cambridge: Polity Press, 1990).

——— (1987), *Choses dites*, Paris: Minuit (*In Other Words: Essays Towards a Reflexive Sociology*, trans. M. Adamson, Cambridge: Polity Press, 1990).

——— (1992a), *Les Règles de l'art: Genèse et structure du champ littéraire*, Paris: le Seuil (*The Rules of Art: Genesis and Structure of the Literary Field*, trans. Susan Emanuel, Stanford CA: Stanford University Press, 1996).

Bourdieu, Pierre with Loïc J.D. Wacquant (1992b), *Réponses*, Paris: Le Seuil (*An Invitation to Reflexive Sociology*, Chicago: Chicago University Press, 1992).

Bourdieu, Pierre (1997), *Méditations pascaliennes*, Paris: Le Seuil.

Brook, Peter (1998), *Threads of Time: A Memoir*, London: Methuen.

Carlson, Marvin (2001), 'Theatre and Performance at a Time of Shifting Disciplines', in *Theatre and Interdisciplinarity*, ed. Maria Shevtsova, *Theatre Research International*, vol. 26, no. 2, pp. 137–44.

Gladkov, Aleksandr (1997), *Meyerhold Speaks, Meyerhold Rehearses*, ed. and trans. Alma Law, Amsterdam: Harwood Academic Publishers.

Lahire, Bernard (1999), *Le Travail sociologique de Pierre Bourdieu*, Paris: La Découverte.

Shevtsova, Maria (1999), 'Bells and Alarm Clocks: Theatre and Theatre Research at the Millennium', in *Theatre Research International*, vol. 24, no. 1, pp. 98–108.

Volosinov, V.N. (1986), *Marxism and the Philosophy of Language*, trans. Ladislav Matejka and I.R. Titunik, Cambridge', Massachusetts: Harvard University Press.

Literary New Chums: Michael Wilding and Marcus Clarke

Laurie Hergenhan

I don't remember exactly when I first met Michael but it was sometime in early 1966. I was on the staff of the English Dept of the University of Tasmania and was spending the year temporarily attached to the University of Sydney, one of my alma maters. James McAuley of Hobart had made the arrangement with Sam Goldberg, I suppose because he was ostensibly the head and because McAuley felt some intellectual affinity with him, though they were hardly ideological mates. I arrived at the time when the Sydney Department was divided into two camps – one under Sam and one under Gerry Wilkes who had been a junior lecturer when I studied there in the early 1950s. By chance, then, I was nominally of the Goldberg party so far as teaching duties were concerned, but through sympathies and some former friendships (notably with Peter Edwards who had been a fellow doctoral student with me at the University of London) I felt that I belonged more to the other party, if not really to either. Through my training at Sydney and London I was mainly interested in both the critical and historical study of literature and in an 'open' approach, though this did not affect my teaching at Sydney one way or the other and I took little interest in politics. As Michael was later to say this was my general attitude (though he has not held it against me). Goldberg was personally kind and welcoming to me as were his staff. I formed no lasting friendships with them (though I did maintain a friendly contact with him), except for Axel Clark, who taught next door to me in the Botany building. Not that alignments mattered much to me or to other people's view of me. I was not politically useful, to either side, so I was free to move between the lines. No one bothered to recruit me and I noticed only undertones of war. You might say I was of the Goldberg party, the rebels, 'without knowing it', a bird of passage with fortunes not affected by the split, unlike Andrew Reimer and Michael who have both left memoirs of these fraught days.

So except for the main outline of the battle I didn't take much interest – it was not a darkling plain for me but a time of freedom.

Michael was the main and lasting friend I made in the Sydney Department, though I was also friendly with Terry Sturm who later moved to New Zealand. Both were from overseas and their interests included, as well as the range of English and American literatures, a keen involvement in the contemporary Australian writing scene, especially the Sydney one. As I had become editor of *Australian Literary Studies* in 1963, this became a continuing link with Michael – through his contributions and advice – though my knowledge of him was very limited at this time. Frank Moorhouse remarked that his friendship with Michael indicated a connection as writers between gown and town as he saw it, academia and journalism, which made them 'serviceable to one another'. In a way, a similar if limited mutual helpfulness might be said to be part of my lasting friendship with Michael, revolving around *ALS* as well as common interests and outlook. As I recall it, we were both open-minded and enthusiastic about things.

Although there was a disparity of age, he (and Terry) seemed to me to stand out as having a freshness and range of outlook. They were young and just setting out on their careers I felt a link, having only started my academic career in later 1960 and my interest in Australian literature in 1963 (not a part of my Sydney education).

Michael was co-editor of the short-lived Sydney University journal, *Balcony*, and published in it an article of mine on Victorian censorship of George Meredith – who was the subject of my Ph.D. thesis and an author who has never gained high acceptance. Any editor who would publish two articles in a fledgling magazine on Meredith (the other was by Peter Edwards) must be broad-minded, I thought. Michael was to publish on Meredith much later himself, typically on the political novel *Beauchamp's Career*, admired by Jack Lindsay.

At this time at Sydney University I did not see anything of that part of Michael's life that I was later romantically to consider 'bohemian'. He invited me to a party at a house backing onto Lane Cove River, where I was supposedly to meet Charles Higham, but he didn't turn up. Michael later told me that Higham was a model for the protagonist in the ironic 'Somewhere New', one of the best stories in *Aspects*, showing a scepticism of the 'new' that he was to be associated with.

Michael went back to England 1967–8, returning in 1969. When we took up our association again he contributed articles to *ALS* and we found we had a common interest in Marcus Clarke. He was allowed to be a 'classic' but of little or no relevance to the current studies of literature or to modern times, though I had been encouraging articles on him in *ALS* and writing some myself. A small example, trivial as it may seem, shows how Clarke was regarded. I was working in 1968 in Melbourne on a selection of Clarke's uncollected journalism, whose extent and interest had been uncovered in Brian Elliott's neglected biography. I called in to the English common room of the University of Melbourne's Department of English as I had made some acquaintances with academics who had visited the Hobart Dept at McAuley's invitation. One greeted me with: 'Well how is – shall I say your 'research' – on Marcus Clarke, going?' Attitudes outside academia were different. For instance, Geoffrey Dutton generously arranged a Sun Books contract for the journalism, even though when I came to the delivery of the bulky ms the manager Brian Stonier cancelled it. The book was later to appear with UQP.

Michael was deeply interested in Clarke in the early 1970s. I remember fascinating discussions about Clarke in his house in Balmain where I stayed a couple of times. Here Michael had a cat called Marcus Clarke. Not your usual black cat, it kept its distance and had for me something strange, even preternatural about it. I was not involved in Michael's 'bohemian' life though I stood on the fringes a couple of times. Yet romantic as I was I compared it in my own mind with phases of Clarke's life, especially his early days in Melbourne as described in his nostalgic essay 'Austin Friars', the rooming-house of a motley group of people, including writers.

In writing this essay I had intended to continue in the memoiristic vein of this introduction, but when I came to think back on Wilding's (as I shall call him now) interest in Clarke I realised that there were connections between the two as writers which I had noticed in passing but remained only floating threads. This essay gave me a chance to pursue new perspectives. The memoir form, though it's still present, became secondary, a kind of random prompt from the past, throwing up suggestions and possibilities. It was with our mutual interest in Clarke, independently arrived at, and following Michael's return from London, that our friendship really firmed. Shortly afterwards he began his publications on Clarke, a monograph, many articles, an edition of *His Natural Life* and selected journalism (in the Portable Australian Authors series, later called the Australian Authors series, of which I was general editor), and much later, an edition of the complete stories, the only modern edition. I had carried over my interest in Clarke from the 1960s.

Michael and I joked about initiating a Clarke revival, and for a time it looked as though we had contributed to that, but while it did not happen in any spectacular way – as these things usually don't – along with the added contributions of other scholars our efforts ensured that his reputation did not remain as it had been – he is accepted into modern criticism, though of course he has always remained widely read.

I have come to think that perhaps Wilding saw much of himself in Clarke, showing a greater empathy than usual when one author writes about another, and conveying an affinity rooted in displacement from England and a determination to forge a career in literature in a new and lively society. Clarke became for Wilding an 'imagined counterpart'. No critic, as far as I know, has seen Wilding as having much kinship with 'migrant' or 'multicultural' writing, partly because so-called WASP writers were ironically excluded from these blanket categories, supposedly aimed at fostering diversity. Though migrant writing is useless as a label, some broad analogy with it is helpful in trying to place Wilding, especially in relating his work to that of Clarke. Clarke combined detachment with involvement, immersion in the different, fluid scene of post-goldrush days in Melbourne, as does the persona in Wilding's 'selective' memoir of the 'new' exciting times of the 1960s and after, *Wildest Dreams*. I don't intend to tie Wilding too closely to Clarke or the nineteenth century but rather to suggest that he found Clarke sympathetic to his aims and attitudes, along with modern English and American writers, especially D.H. Lawrence, who had moved among 'new' cultures. This connection illuminates Wilding's search for the new, a roving restlessness of mind that continually invokes the immediate environment yet reaches beyond it, as Clarke did, for larger connections.

Wilding's monograph (still the only one) on Clarke, *Marcus Clarke* (1977), selects those aspects that he saw as especially attractive. Literary historians have overlooked the way an extraordinary sympathy with Clarke's situation as migrant writer led Wilding to new insights into his own work and into a colonial culture that was at the time more disparaged than appreciated. The main thrust of the study is to see Clarke not as a one-book writer but as a thoroughly professional and successful man of letters, dedicated to writing about a new society. Wilding celebrates this 'range and achievement' of this 'extraordinarily prolific writer'. He was novelist and short story writer, dramatist, poet, historian, librarian, critic, editor, reviewer, journalist of many parts. This is the mark of what Wilding sees as an adventurous, committed mind. And he himself is adventurously prolific and active across the literary scene, as writer of novels, short stories, journalism, editor, publisher, reviewer, member of an influential literary circle of 'new' writers, he was concerned with the production of literature and the ways in which its power groups could block opportunities. Both writers used their knowledge of the marketing of literature to criticise the process. Hence Wilding's career as publisher and editor, and his amazing knowledge of contemporary publishing practice, in Australia and overseas.

As well, Wilding was interested in the way Clarke honed his skills as a *diverse* writer, an interest extending to the nuts and bolts: the recycling of material, the holding over of rejected material for later adaptation and incorporation. (Recently Wilding told me he learned these skills from Clarke.) Wilding also delighted in Clarke's 'internationalism':

> He was one of the first great internationalists of Australian writing – reading, responding to and drawing on an international literary culture, not a narrowly provincial one. And it was with his knowledge of that culture that he con sciously pioneered an Australian one, ensuring it drew on an international heritage. (p. 3)

Wilding did not see Clarke as a derivative writer, except in the sense that all writers are. Rather he adapted and transformed his models with literary flair. 'He lived in a period that has been labelled the "colonial" phase of Australian literature; but implications of a second-rate dependence are false for Clarke.' He was a popular yet sophisticated and 'literary' writer who used allusiveness to mine his new subject-matter and to give it resonance. He was 'local and international in the best tradition of our writing', as is Wilding. Each work of the latter is a setting out in a new direction through experiment, transformation of genre and style. This is a quality insufficiently appreciated in his work because it depends on a subtle allusiveness. (Bruce Clunies Ross's article on the Arcadian element in *Pacific Highway* is an exception).

Wilding admired the way Clarke tied his writing to Australia (while noting the absence of Aborigines, a sign of this 'racism and ethnocentricity'), he points out the contrast to nationalism:

> The danger of that nationalistic approach that says, 'we have all the materials we need for literature in this new society' is a constricting insularity. The writers draw on fewer and fewer materials, non-insular connections are rejected, and we are left with a myopic survey of a few worn-out acres. Clarke's stress however is one of internationalism. He is asserting that Australia's material has as much romantic material as other histories – he is putting it on a par with other

national myths, and he is stressing the cosmopolitan nature of that early history. (pp. 13–14)

Like Clarke, too, Wilding draws on historical, not just contemporary models in terms of style and social theme, a quality also stimulated by his academic immersion in the range of literature in English. In Clarke's neglected short stories, for instance, Wilding carefully traced experimentalism across a range of genres and styles—realism, romance, Gothic, sketches, fabulation, the supernatural, the speculative, the documentary. Or as he put it in summary: 'there are, at least three distinct strands of story writing. There are his realistic stories and sketches of up-country life; there are his formula magazine stories, melodramatic, plotted, sensational; and there are his experimental, metaphysical and fantasy stories' (introduction to *Stories*, p. xii).

The blending of the historical and the contemporary in Wilding's own work is called up in a comment on Clarke's story 'Human Repetends' remarking that besides having 'gloomy autobiographical themes . . . it is also a powerful exercise in what De Quincey called "unutterable and self-repeating infinities", a genre that has emigrated from English writing but is alive and well and living in South America'. Again, Wilding sees the story 'Cannabis Indica', one of Clarke's 'drug stories', as 'a genuine literary experiment, as a piece of real innovation' (*Stories*, p. xxx). In discussing another story he notes experiment again, 'the self-referentialism and closed loops of the writer conscious of his own process of writing' (ibid.). Here and elsewhere Wilding could be talking about his own work.

On first coming to Wilding's critical writing on Clarke, especially the stories and lesser novels, a reader might think that for some reason, some soft spot for his subject perhaps, he is too 'easy' on him, passing over the infamous charge of Clarke's 'fatal facility'. But this would be to misunderstand Wilding's approach. He is not concerned to give a staid 'faults and strengths' picking-over and summing up found in some conventional criticism, but rather to approach Clarke as one fellow writer to another and to put the best face on his underestimated, *pioneering* achievement without feeling any need to be apologetic. Besides, as a writer, Wilding appreciates the sheer inventiveness and prodigality of Clarke, including the necessary 'formula' and more routine work. If the stories seem to others more uneven than Wilding allows, this is not a point to niggle about for the stress is on reinstating Clarke as a *professional* writer:

> Yet if we look at the full range of Clarke's stories of the 1870s, we can see a plurality of form and traditions. Then there was an internationalism, an eclecticism, a richness of literary culture: which became reduced to the single, utilitarian, insular, aggressively anti-experimental, philistinely parochial 'write Australian' line: something caused not so much by the nationalistic nineties writers, but by the new nationalistic theorists, critics and publishers and magazine editors from the 1930s through the 1950s. (*Stories*, p. xiii)

This is a good statement of Wilding's own credo from the 1960s, as both an Australian and international writer. Clarke shows up clearly as a model here.

While Wilding touches on dark sides of Clarke's short life, his self-destructiveness and melancholy, he may understate it in his aim to recuperate Clarke; but he is perceptive in pointing out and possibly expressing something of himself that expatriatism was always a theme in Clarke and that, while he nurtured hopes of returning to England,

> his base is firmly in Australia; he writes as someone committed to be there, not as a visitor or tourist or unwilling exile, not as the stock fictional figure come out to make a fortune to be able to run home and buy back the family estate. Clarke showed no likelihood of ever making a fortune. But that was because he was enjoying the life he was leading – immersed in it as a real experience, not perched on the sidelines wanting to leave. These were the hectic days of Clarke's bohemian life, when he was writing brilliantly and prolifically and mixing in a world of similar literary and journalistic talents. . . . As an editor he published and encouraged those writers who established a literary culture in Australia. They were people he was close to, members of that erratic literary Bohemia in which he lived his life. (p. 6)

There were other sides to this Bohemia, as Clarke admitted:

> The morning was spent in scribbling, the afternoon in tobacco, the evening in dinner, theatre and gaslight. I fear we did not lead virtuous lives. I am sure we were often out of bed after the small hours. I know that Madame Gogo and Lisette de Jambejolie assisted in the spending of the *Peacock*'s [*Argus*'s] money. (p. 6)

In such comments I can hear undertones of some of Wilding's own literary ideals and subjects, contributing to, and arising from his sympathy with Clarke. Wilding was himself to cultivate and write about the 'new' literary Bohemia of Sydney – 'le ghetto de Balmain' – from the 1960s onwards. Clarke distinguishes in his journalism between an 'upper' Bohemia of writers and artists and a 'lower' one, the down-and-outs of Melbourne, whom he feared he might one day join. The depiction of these outcasts and their counterparts, the convicts, stirred Wilding's radical sympathies.

Wilding was particularly interested in Clarke's short stories drawing on Australian history, *Old Tales of a Young Country*, a title suggesting Hawthorne's *Twice Told Tales*.

> Clarke was trying to do for Australia the sort of thing Hawthorne had done for America; consciously to create, to draw attention to the romantic past, the archetypal characters and situations. . . . But searching out materials for literature in a new land resulted in a far more violent world of action than Hawthorne presented. (p. 11)

For Wilding, then, it was not, as Henry James said, that the literary soil of America in the mid-nineteenth century was not deep enough to produce good literature, but rather that imaginative writers there and in Australia had to deepen the soil by their own efforts – the relative shortness of history was not necessarily a drawback. Clarke was demonstrating the falsity of Frederick Sinnett's charge that there were no materials of romance for the writer in this 'young country' of Australia.

Wilding's most concentrated contribution to writing the history of Australia is *The Paraguayan Experiment*, also a literary experiment in documentary realism, a favourite mode of Clarke's. But this is not the only point where Australian history is drawn into his work and outlook. When he is recalling his early days in Sydney, in *Wildest Dreams*, 'trying to connect with the magic circle of publication, of acceptance, of recognition, of acclaim', Graham realises that he has actually anticipated some of the strategies of literary survival he was later to admire in Clarke:

> This was the apprenticeship, the learning time, working on the scraps and margins, picking up skills, picking up the confidence of familiarity, continuing that confidence of the weekly essay, the rapid concentration, the focus, the sleight of hand, the fatal facility that Francis Adams had detected in Marcus Clarke. (p. 41)

The 'fatal facility' is ironic; Graham adds that Clarke was to die at 35. Even though this literary acquaintance was yet to come, as Graham acknowledges, it is foreshadowed by way of an epiphany or premonition he experiences while walking through Sydney, a glimpse of the local history he will go on to discover and connect with:

> These weren't stories Graham knew at the time. This was the literary history he was to discover. As he grew into the present he became conscious of the literary

past. The flat, dusty walls of the brick city in the dusty sun filled out, developed the depth of a past, emanated the romances of former hopes, lost futures, offered sites of all those imaginary possibilities, backdrops of desire, settings for anecdotes in its eating houses, pubs, streets. (p. 41)

This is a remarkable moment and image in Australian literature. Usually, if the city yields moments of vision it is of a transcendental nature as in Brennan, or of a pastoral beauty, as occasionally in Lawson and Louis Stone. And in migrant literature it is usually the 'foreign' past that protagonists bring with them and nurture. Graham himself recalls this in describing old Chinese men in Dixon Street cafes – Sydney's Chinatown – who had never 'integrated with this wide south land', remaining prisoners of toil or of dreams (p. 69). Graham's connection with Australia's past is unusual too. Many migrant writers from whatever origins are concerned mainly with the past they carry with them, it can become a burden and overshadow a new start.

In *Wildest Dreams* Graham calls up *Lost Illusions* of Balzac (Clarke's 'prince of novelists') as the literary 'archetype' of his memoirs. They follow the graph of the innocent drawn to the big city to begin a literary life that he hopes will lead to fame but leads instead to disillusion and defeat by the pressures of a closed market place (p. 4). Balzac has accordingly been taken as the main model, even though Graham stresses that he read it 'later' when its message had already 'permeated through many texts'.

There is another model, closer to home, the life of literary new chums learning their colonial experience. This is there fragmentarily but forcefully in Clarke's life and writing. Most ostensibly it is an inevitable, satirical literary subject to hand as well as serio-comic personal experience. The typical 'new chum', common to colonial literature, the inexperienced, opinionated Pom, is a joke to the superior locals who often pull his leg. Clarke wrote specifically of these new chums as 'The Peripatetic Philosopher' and elsewhere, their class superiority, their dependence on 'home', their recoil from the new. They sink or swim, often 'disappearing' from the fashionable Melbourne scene. In exceptional cases, says Clarke, they go to work up-country, as he did, reaching some reconciliation with their past and their expectations with the realities of a new world. But there was also the case of Clarke, the literary new chum, serving his apprenticeship then surviving, indeed excelling as a professional writer. This is the development sketched in Wilding's Clarke, showing him not so much adapting or assimilating to, as imaginatively transforming his new experience and milieu through the writing process, with help rather than hindrance of the culture he has brought with him. Hence his up and downs, 'the shifts and struggles' – the false starts, the experiments, the variations on a theme, the recyclings.

It is easy to pick up an echoing framework in *Wildest Dreams* as it consciously and wryly adapts and updates its materials of 'the literary life'. There is the arrival (by air), the light, the warmth, the harbour, the initial sense of freedom, Kings Cross and its restaurants and bookshops (with leading American and UK magazines – 'these worlds of allusion' – he had not seen in his home town in the English Midlands), ferries ('a word on ferries . . . another Mediterranean or Asiatic note.'), reviewing, his first literary job, and other aspects of apprenticeship, and chapters on familiar topoi: mateship, libertarianism, the Vietnam war protest, the literary 'stockyard', festivals, 'publish and perish', and so on, Graham ending up, or left suspended, in the USA teaching creative writing. Graham was glad to be in Australia when 'Old Europe was softening', here dissolved away in the light and heat. But it is interesting that the sparse or dwindling 'continental' restaurants, that flourished in Clarke's post-goldrush Melbourne, were to flourish again in Sydney after Graham's arrival in the 1960s, as did the sidewalk cafes he had believed impossible because of the narrow streets. In other words, *Wildest Dreams* offers a version of the history of the near present, of what is now yesterday, as well as glimpsing the historical past, as did Clarke's work for its time.

Amongst the many contexts in which Wilding can profitably be read, then, is the life and works of the expatriate Marcus Clarke. Indeed it is one of the key perspectives. Clarke provided a literary model, a morale booster, and above all an analogue of a thoroughly professional writer, with a flexible, restless outlook, pursuing the new with the aid of the old, a young expatriate writer, beginning his acclimatisation but always nurturing his internationalism. Wilding would not be likely to say of Clarke, '*c'est moi*', but I think he would acknowledge him as '*mon frère*'. Theirs is one of the most fascinating connections – of 'imagined counterparts' – in Australian literary history.

Stories of Things Happening

Bruce Clunies Ross

There is nothing merely itself here. Only stories. Everywhere figures are enacting characters, enacting characters. Their stories are many layered, leading into other stories.

He'd seen it all before.

Standing at the window of the train from the south, staring into the dull glare of the winter afternoon, scanning the skyline between branches for glimpses of the towery city, he thought of Jude. Or may have thought, for Jude was often in his mind at the time. The train rocked through the shunting yards and slowed as it approached the station. His eyes dropped to tangled backyards; withered plants smudged with snow.

They carried baggage through the base and brickish outskirts, looking for domes, spires, towers. Grey light leaked between black tree-trunks. Across a dark standing pool – the canal – was a wall topped with revolving spikes. When he thought of Oxford later it was of high dark walls and dim yellow lights suspended in gloom. Yet these unprompted images immediately faded behind the pageant that flowed from his reading. He had arrived in a world he knew from stories and began to discover it was a world of stories. Fabulous. Young women with razor-cut hair and shiny black macs; flaunting fetish dances in bright-coloured shoes. There was a whole scene going; a great spiralling story hoard.

This is the staircase where Swinburne ran up and down in the nude. An angular pink body with flaming red hair was descending the stairs. But who was it chasing? Part of the story is missing. His tongue jammed on words that belonged in books. He watched himself waking in the Broad and nodded to the Emperors on their pillars outside the Sheldonian. Their features had eroded since the days of Zuleika and they did not respond. In Christchurch Meadow he heard fading resonances of Anthony Blanche declaiming *The Waste Land*. He wondered if there would be poplar stumps at Binsey, or traces in the ground where the roots had been. An aerial photograph might reveal their position to after-comers. It was a lifetime since they had been all felled but there might be people alive who had seen them growing. Would they have recognised the especial beauty of the poplars in the scene or applauded their felling as an improvement on nature? The beauty now is in the poem but we only have it because the poplars were felled.

In Adelaide he'd walked unaware that was treading on song-lines. The enchantment of stories was that they transported you somewhere else; away from the world you actually inhabited. He knew these imagined places so well he could speak of them as a familiar visitor, and Oxford, now that he was actually here, was amazingly recognisable. He could find his way around in it, yet it was somehow diminished. He could no longer imagine the place. It was invading his memory.

How strange it all was! He realised now why Billie was playing with Alice. It was not the fascination of girl-children or a scholar's delight in the innocent Freudian slips of the Victorians. Billie had found a role which enabled him to exist in a world where everyone was looking in the mirror. His own reflection was superimposed on the ghost of Jude. Its presence was powerful outside the high wall of Balliol just by the Martyrs' Memorial and whenever he passed that way it greeted him like a familiar. He was just turning into the Broad after one of these encounters when he felt a soft plop on his head, dropped by a pigeon from the colony in the great plane tree in St. Michael's churchyard.

'What a knockout!' laughed Billie and inflated it into a scene in his ironic romance of their lives. There had been shouted introductions as Billie passed beneath Linda's window in Walton St and when they met again in College he was unresistingly drawn into the ongoing fantasy through which Billie's Oxford affairs were conducted. It mainly consisted of episodes of subjective humiliation narrated with disingenuous candour, even in the account he gave of his viva.

'I overslept and had to dress in a hurry. It was when I stumbled into the Schools that I realised I wasn't wearing my own shoes. The dons were doffing their mortar boards. I stood waiting for their puerile questions but they just sat there expecting me to flash my willy. I was sick with nervousness. If I'd opened my mouth I would have puked all over them.'

Even so he assumed that it would be polite to back out of the room but when he tried to step backwards he left the shoe behind. He stared down at his short slender foot and experimentally re-inserted it in one of the tightly laced size fourteens in which he was standing, and then, keeping his heels on the floor, began to shuffle backwards, doffing his mortar board as he retreated. During the long, slow slide back to the door he kept repeating the gesture like an entropic vaudeville entertainer. That is the story he told (or something like it) but Billie had an uninhibited imagination – as if the imagination could be anything else. Its wildest flights depicted him as the victim of bizarre and obscene practices by the dons which he described with finely detailed verisimilitude. Robert was shocked. 'I never fart,' he announced in his clipped Scottish accent. They raised their eyes admiringly and turned him into a story.

Propelled only by a preoccupied headlong stride on his unsteady feet Robert is returning from the Bodleian. His duffle coat is toggled asymmetrically. In the Porter's Lodge he picks up a letter, tears it open, throws it away, stares absently at the envelope for a few seconds and then screws it up. He is thinking about numerology and the mathematical stanza in the *Faery Queen* when it hits him. Of course! It is an exercise not in planar but in solid geometry. People are gathering on the steps of the Hall, among them Billie and Blackjack Fowler, volubly explaining something to Bruce. Robert slips around the edge of the garden to his room and starts to scribble elliptical notes in his customary style on the sheet on his desk. He is halfway down the other side when Bruce knocks at his door, enticing him out for coffee. Robert signs the paper.

'Wotcher writing? Is that your thesis?' Robert's eyes desperately check the papers scattered around his room to make sure his thesis is safely hidden. 'Just answering a letter.' He is already folding it and forcing it into an envelope. 'Came today from my parents.' He addresses the envelope and puts it in his pocket, where it slips through the lining and joins the ball-point pens, small change, pencil stubs, matches, paper clips, shampoo sachets and lost keys which weigh down the lower edges of his tweed jacket. About a week later Bruce manages to remove it for weighing. 'It will make you round-shouldered carrying all that around on your back.' Billie is dipping into the lining, holding up his finds between dainty fingertips.

'What's this?'

'Shit. A letter home. I forgot.'

Robert rushes out to post it. Three days later his mother rings to find out why he is signing his letters home 'Yours faithfully, R. M. Cummings.'

Robert would protest that none of this is true. That is not how it happened. The story robs him of his identity but only he knows that, and this is not his story. Perhaps Robert could hold on to the distinction between stories and what happened, and Billie could ceaselessly spin out the romances that enabled him to survive where everyone is playing someone in a story, but he could not find any bearings. He began to wonder whether he could know anything but the story; or rather, he had to admit that he might know what happened but the moment he tried to externalise it, it became the story of what happened. Michael understood this instinctively and often wrote stories that revealed things did not happen as they were supposed to happen. In those days they discussed stories as if they were revelations, not of truth, necessarily, or of what was really happening, but of something hidden in the events, perhaps even from the storyteller. Things were not as they seemed. He was moving in a border zone between the actual and the imaginary, except that being there blurred the distinction. It was a dangerous situation. Unless he was to disappear in its interstices like the third policeman he needed a story.

'And what' inquired the Baroness, 'do you propose to do about your accent?' He demonstrated phonetic expertise. 'Mole' and 'pole' could be pronounced so that they did not rhyme with 'moll' and 'poll'. At the time he was ready to compromise, at least in the classroom. The students did not come to an expensive language school in Oxford to learn to speak English like Australians. There was no need to flaunt it like Margaret trying to buy mice at Palms in the market.

Teachers were expected to attend court before and after classes. It was not formulated so crudely, of course, but he was beginning to catch on to the allusiveness of English, or at least, Oxford conversation. Backlit in a broad bay window the Baroness watched from behind her desk while the four or five teachers positioned themselves at carefully judged distances from her and each other. The idea seemed to be to form a balanced semicircle across the centre of the room which served as her study, library and secretarial office, with Felix, the Director of Studies, on her right. When they were all nicely arranged, facing her across the desk, the Baroness opened the conversation.

'I happened to overhear one of the students – it was that noisy Frenchwoman Mallard – use the phrase "read a book". But one can't read a book, Mr Lawton. You read *in* a book.'

'Indeed, Baroness.'

She emitted a satisfied plume of smoke through upwardly pursed lips, the holder angled to balance the ash on the tip of her Balkan Sobranie. Her head was long and skull-like, eyes deeply sunken in the sockets, wide mouth inaccurately glossed in red. Heavy pendants hung from sagging earlobes. She looked exactly right for the daughter of the Kaiser's ambassador to Turkey during the First World War, which, according to the story, she was.

'I assume you recommend my exercises in the use of prepositions, Mr. Beauchamp.'

Paunchy Felix focused on a point in the air between them.

'Certainly Baroness.'

'And what are you planning to do about this strike?' Her speech was slow, smoky, sybilline.

'Unfortunately my party no longer holds office, Baroness. There has been an election.'

'What difference does that make? The country can't go on without the mail. The army will have to be called in.'

'Quite, Baroness.'

There was not, as far as he could detect from his position on the other side of the room, the trace of a flicker in Felix's eye. Would the soldiers be delivering letters or shooting the postmen? He did not pose the question while the other teachers were deploring the effects of this new Labour government. Felix may have noticed his craven silence but turned the subject by asking how he found the teaching, after the first day. 'Ah yes,' said the Baroness. 'Did you have enough to keep them occupied for two and a half hours? You have to keep introducing new material to keep their attention. Everything depends on that.'

He had been given an impressive demonstration of this by Felix, for whom teaching English was simply a matter of playing the part he had been given at birth and refined as a secret agent in France (that, at least, was the story). He dressed as a careless dandy and played the fool seriously from the conviction that it was an English privilege. This was all he needed to teach foreign students the language. It was a game which required verbal felicity and had to be played with intelligence as an amusing alternative to collecting the vintage fire-engines in which he sometimes arrived at the school, though the Baroness preferred them not to be parked outside the gate in Banbury Road. 'L'ours,' sniggered Mlle Mallard, 'Winnie l'ourson.' He discreetly cultivated the persona among the students and stamped the few who met his exacting standards by teaching them the meaning and use of the word 'persiflage'.

Oh yes. This actually happened. Felix, the Baroness and the Language School certainly existed but they belong in someone else's story. Their very existence kept Evelyn Waugh's Oxford in place. It was still actually *there*, and trying to tell their stories only trapped him in it. Everywhere he went, people were rehearsing stories. It was as if this was the only mode of existence, yet the place must have contained people for whom the stories were . . . just stories. Were they deluded, hidden in someone else's stories or lost because they had no story? The complicated rules and customs of the place were deceptive conventions of fiction. Was it necessary to know them to read the stories and have an existence here? At the time there seemed no other way. Deconstruction had not crossed the Channel. Oxford philosophy was a perfect resistance. Being invisibly embedded in the stories made it the most impenetrable Oxford story of all. He was entranced, yet disoriented by the discovery when, he attended lectures, that Gilbert Ryle took all his examples from *Alice in Wonderland* and P.G. Wodehouse.

And then one night late there was a banging on the door of the house they rented in Woodstock High Street. Margaret answered it and he heard a loud voice explaining 'This is Clancy. And Michael.' They had nowhere to sleep. There were two rooms in the attic, so they took them in, and that's how he met Michael.

Some time later they returned; in the meantime the attic had been let but it was summer and their lodger was away. They could retire to the same bed. It was three or four o'clock in the morning when he was jolted out of heavy sleep by banging on the stairs and a voice, not whispering, not actually yelling, but exclaiming, repeatedly, varying the sequence.

'This is ridiculous.'

'I don't understand it.'

'What is going on?'

Margaret, already wide awake, got up to sort it out while he shrank into the bedclothes, pulling the blankets tightly around his head. The exclamations continued through Margaret's calm negotiations. There were sounds of footsteps stumbling downstairs and low muttering. Did she advertise the advantages of a pre-warmed bed and actually introduce the lodger to their guests?

'Nic, this is Michael, and Clancy, and this is, er . . .'

'Marianne,' said Margaret.

Marianne! But what was she doing with Nic? She was no stranger to that bed but the last time she had slept in it, as far as he knew, was with Billie whom she accompanied when he came back from the States at the beginning of summer. Billie had returned to Harvard alone for another of the examination ordeals with which he punished himself and Nic had taken Marianne to see Dartington. A bad sign.

An elaborate version of this incident forms the climax of *Living*

Together but that is Michael's story. When whatever it was that happened, happened, he was in the middle of it while I (it's time to drop the mask) was hiding under the bedclothes hoping it wasn't happening. Michael's story is the text of what happened for all readers and perhaps a few will guess that something lies behind it, but there are six whose reading will elicit other stories.

'This actually happened,' we will say.

'But that is not how it happened.'

'Really?'

'Well, no, we can't say what really happened.'

Our stories will come tumbling after Michael's, like footsteps downstairs in the dark.

Marianne returned to America and at least briefly, according to his letters, to Billie's bed under the huge blow-up of the Liddell sisters. Nic disappeared. Robert moved into the attic. Michael and Clancy came to live in the flat above the shop across the road and we became the centre of their view. Perhaps it was while gazing through the window, writing in his thick folio notebooks, that Michael began to compose the story of *Living Together*. We don't know.

By the time he came to share our house in Woodstock, Robert had become a figure in an ongoing narrative. Perhaps it had happened to all of us by then. We existed only in others' stories. But Robert's had become canonical and we treated him according to its rules. We could never match the absolute concision of his speech though we tried to parody it. When exact words were not available he remained silent, or would rush off in the middle of a conversation and return mutely pointing to a passage in an open book. Perhaps he was amused to watch the way it deflected the conversation. He cultivated his friends by supplying them with recondite references and stayed up all night reading about Spinoza, papyri, jurisprudence, early Greek poetics, deontic logic or Hermetic philosophy. Was all this somehow finding its way into his thesis? That was his secret. We tormented him by threatening to discover it. Robert allowed us to play with him this way but he often escaped and stayed out all night or crossed the road to talk to Michael about Marvell and pineapples. That is the story but perhaps they were actually discussing harassment by fiction and how to resist it.

Living Together is dedicated to Robert but is set in Sydney slightly later than the Woodstock years. In retrospect it seems that the three inhabitants of the house in the High Street were seen as somehow living together. Billie's letters arrived covered in crude drawings representing us as the holy family; Michael was creating narratives which exposed how living together worked through stories which turned out to be exercises in power. We were on the cusp of a transition – flower power was imminent – but our lives were still rooted in the earlier 1960s; the time of Michael's Oxford stories. The timing and location of *Living Together* is a move which encourages speculation about the degree to which the cultural disruptions of the late 1960s rebounded from the cities of the New World where values derived from the old were diverging. The centre of it all is alleged to be Haight-Ashbury, and its glamour blinded most of us to the contribution of Sydney libertarianism to the way things were changing. I wish now I had realised this when I met the editors of *Oz* slumped on the floor of Michael's flat talking about Germaine. Sydney was the right setting for *Living Together* but in my reading it is counterpointed over a Woodstock *cantus firmus*.

Musing on the way it transformed us I cannot distinguish memories of stories from memories of things happening, but that is how it was in those days. Michael would bring his stories across the road for us to read but we never discussed them as artist and critic, or one as the other. Our talk traced the paths of stories between truth and lies; between revealing and concealing, and the way they made both possible. We could never be sure, but nor could we exist without stories. We followed their tributaries and digressed at intersections, discovering behind every incident, every passage, another story *ad infinitum*. Attempts to explain what actually happened produced more stories. We silently wondered what they revealed and speculated about whether they were disinformation.

Michael insisted that stories did not reflect the world; they were part of it, just as physical objects were. Of course. Or were they, rather, ways of knowing? But that would trap us in a world of narrative when actual events were happening out there. Atoms and planets were orbiting, couples were loving, continents were shifting, *coups d'état* were being planned. Billie's letters now were full of war; people were dying of fire. The difficulty was in telling it. We are afloat in an ocean of story, navigating a passage between Scylla and Charybdis; between succumbing to someone else's story and subjugating others to our own. Michael's long story of Hector and Freddie is a chart of this dangerous passage.

It was among the typescripts in a spring-back binder which he brought across Woodstock High Street, and when I read it then I detected something behind it; not myself, or Robert or Billie but a couple I had been observing in the Bodleian. Singly they might not have attracted attention. Only when I realised they were companions did I begin to speculate about them. One was neatly formed with a strictly measured walk, brushed, clipped hair and the ghost of a moustache. He dressed in subdued, well-fitting clothes including the dark overcoat, which hung over his shoulders like a military cloak. The other was larger and very ill-proportioned; his shaggy haired head wobbled on a thin neck with a protruding Adam's apple; his arms and hands flapped without co-ordination – he could never have worn a cloak – and his steps on unmatched long feet were irregularly syncopated. He wore highly polished light tan shoes, corduroy trousers and jacket in different shades of brown, and a check viyella shirt with coarsely woven woollen tie. I was slightly acquainted with him because we had both been employed by the Baroness during the summer. His name was Claude Bates; his companion, I learnt from frequent allusions, was Adrian.

We hardly knew them. I don't think I had ever heard Adrian's voice, though I imagined it above medium pitch, precise and self-assured, quite unlike Claude's, which I knew from our brief attendance at the court of the Baroness, was always breaking. He was unsure of his accent which constantly switched between midlands and elocutionary. This did not seem to bother the Baroness. I watched Adrian and Claude having whispered conversations but I was never aware of Claude's arrival in the library. He was always already there when Adrian marched down the long southern wing of the Upper Reading Room possibly concealing a swagger stick under his cloak. Claude would have already secured two desks and laid out their books.

In the Upper Reading Room there was a mute fellowship which depended on eye contact and being noticed. Its members had a certain speculative knowledge and curiosity about each other but this remained unconfirmed because they never communicated by other means than momentary glances and oblique allusions. One could never be sure who the members were. Only a few would notice and be noticed noticing. Adrian and Claude were not among them. They were my story until Hector and Freddie produced a shock of recognition which reversed the experience of arriving in Oxford. It interacted with perception and memory rather than a world submerged in literature. The complication is that Michael's is a story of stories – and I always misremember its title as 'The Story of Hector and Freddie' – which shows that they are part of the world rather than reflections of it. It would be trite to suggest that Adrian and Claude are behind Hector and Freddie. I know they are not. Watching them in the Bodleian, I had no more than mused on their story. I had not invented one. Now, in 'Hector and Freddie', I had a story for them, but beyond that, an account of how living involves narrating and narrating is an exercise in power.

Perhaps this is better narrated than explained and that is what Michael's stories are doing. They precede and pre-empt the strident vulgarity of theory with stylistic finesse. The three long Oxford stories are important because, in different ways, they undermine the power of traditional narratives which seductively reinforce Oxford's role as an enchanted playground for the privileged. In Michael's stories, Oxford is depicted from the perspective of characters outside that world. His handling of this perspective is complex. The Oxford of the traditional narratives is neither directly rejected nor disregarded. There are fine moments in the stories when the characters walking in the Parks, for example, sense a fleeting pastoral harmony in the place, but this is not envisaged as distinctive of Oxford; it is consistent with the recurrent pastoralism of Michael's stories.[1] It marks a subtle but important displacement of Oxford in fiction. Connections with narratives which sustain the idea of Oxford are severed in two stories firmly located in the early 1960s[2] whose protagonists are not enchanted by Oxford, even if they fleetingly feel in place there. Their prevailing feeling is of isolation. At the beginning of their story, Hector decribes Freddie as looking 'like he was in purdah', and in 'Among My Books' the narrator points out the similarity between Cathy's story and his own, 'except in the degree of loneliness'. It is 'a simple enough story of a lonely child in a provincial city, a child with no brothers or sisters, who was clever, and went to the local grammar school, and who was now lonely in another provincial city, pursuing a higher education'.

'Hector and Freddie', 'Among My Books' and 'Writing a Life' are different in mode and style, but they share attributes and qualities with all Michael's fiction. His stories are characterised by precise attention to their stylistic and tonal range, and style is functional in his work. The reader of 'Writing a Life', for example, is enticed into savouring the style which Edwin creates out of the idiom of the donnish spinster Olivia. This is given a delicate twist at the end as it subtly modulates into the tone of Cressida, the student with whom Edwin is planning to escape the illusions of Oxford. The management of fine stylistic gradations in the Oxford stories (as in all Michael's work) is enhanced through their allusiveness which derives from the realisation that stories are part of the world, not merely reflections of it. They are created in a domain of narratives to which they inevitably allude and in Michael's stories this is accepted and developed. The allusions which lace his writing are therefore not puzzles to be solved and are generally not hidden or cryptic. It often does not matter whether the reader identifies them; what matters is the suggestion or intrusion of a hint from another text. For example, there are allusions to work of Henry James scattered throughout Michael's writing. He is introduced as 'old HJ' in the long Jamesian paragraph which opens 'Writing a Life' with an introspective discussion of precisely the matter I am trying to explain here (so perhaps you should drop this and turn to the story) and his style comes to the surface intermittently. The passage describing the protagonist's first approach to Olivia's grand North Oxford house (*Under Saturn*, p. 172) faintly echoes Tichborne's description of his arrival at *The Short Story Embassy* (p. 7) which, Michael pointed out, alluded to a passage at the beginning of the governess's narrative in *The Turn of the Screw*. The allusions here do not procure an effect by being identified. Their function is to convey an awareness that telling a story inevitably implicates the narrator in pre-existing narratives.

The allusiveness of the Oxford stories is hinted in their titles (though not quite perfectly unless '*The Story of* Hector and Freddie' as I misremember it is allowed for the sake of argument) which indicate a conscious engagement with the creation of narrative in stories, writing and books. 'Among My Books' is, at least at first glance, the most straightforward of the three, a subjective first-person narrative by a man about his relationship with a woman. Both are students and the Oxford they inhabit is described with lots of gritty detail. It is not quite an example of dirty realism but a love story which implicitly subverts the images presented in such books as *Zuleika Dobson or an Oxford Love Story*, a satirical fantasy which assumes an enchanted Oxford where love quickens in the idyll of the summer. The Penguin edition, 'published in celebration of the Author's eightieth birthday, 24 August 1952' contributed to the preconceptions with which I arrived in Oxford. In the earlier reprint of 1946, Max Beerbohm had included a prefatory note suggesting that 'my fantasy was far more like to the old Oxford than was the old Oxford like to the place now besieged and invaded by Lord Nuffield's armies' (a battological mouthful from an alleged master of style). 'Among My Books' is set in that invaded Oxford, not in an idyllic summer, but in the midst of the harsh winter of 1962–3, and the two characters, living in frigid rooms, have to go to bed together for warmth as well as for sex. It is an Oxford love story retold from the perspective of a character who would be invisible in the world of *Zuleika Dobson* and its subversive effect is reinforced through deliberate ambivalences in the narrative tone as the passiveness of Cathy, who can be seen as the narrator's negative double, traps him into recursive moral reflection and betrayals in his efforts to confront their relationship candidly.

'Writing a Life', first published in *Under Saturn*, 1988, has a more complex narrative texture, permeated with allusions and formal indications of its invention. These are justified by their thematic function, for this story about writing a life and the practice of writing itself is firmly based on a triangular plot. The significance of writing in this story is apparent in its style, for in contrast to 'Among My Books' which evokes a colloquial voice which could be telling the story spontaneously, 'Writing a Life' opens on a long Jamesian paragraph which could only be composed in writing. This involves a complication, implied in the subject of the paragraph as well as its style, for it concludes with an intricate discussion of voice and its representation. The story begins with Edwin, the narrator, musing on the problem of imitating the voice and conversational idiom of Olivia, a donnish spinster with a faded literary reputation, and it develops as a portrait of Olivia composed by representing her speech. However, Edwin's reflections make the reader aware that this is not to be taken as spontaneous. The art in this case is not to create the illusion of a speaking voice; it lies in the formation of a literary style based on the rhythms, cadences and diction of Olivia's conversation. This is brilliantly achieved in the story by creating Edwin as an imperfect imitator of Olivia.[3]

In the stories which reflect the process of composition in their style and form, Michael makes a point of compounding narrative awareness with thematic motivation and this sets his work apart from that of the fictive experimentalists who have no stories to tell. 'Writing a Life' is Edwin's story of Olivia's story of Hugo's fiction (and lies) at the core of which is the relationship between Hugo and the decorative young man, who seem to have behaved like Edward Upward and Christopher Isherwood in transforming 'the events of the contemporary world into this fantasy world – events even of the very immediate world. Figures walking towards us, especially recognisable noteworthies, they would suddenly transplant into their imaginary country' (191). Just as, thirty years later, Billie would do with the dons, and with my collusion, our friends.[4]

In the story, Olivia, even with the help of Edwin's research, never manages to write the life of Hugo, but she imagines it as 'the best of critical analysis, the best of literary history, and the truest memoir'. I know this is not the best and the truest, Michael, but it is what I am attempting. Since 'Writing a Life' concludes a book you generously dedicated to me I am taking the liberty of appropriating some of Olivia's words from it: *What I would like is somehow to establish the nature of those days, the texture of our life then. That is why I work on it so slowly.*

'Hector and Freddie' uncovered the narrative texture of our lives and when I read it first in Woodstock, I realised that existence is not merely a matter of living in stories but of knowing the stories of the stories. I had been moving towards this since the disorientation of my arrival but in 'Hector and Freddie', the first of Michael's three counter-narratives to the glamour of Oxford, I found the bearings to plot a course among the stories in the world. I had already arrived when dialogism and deconstruction came along.

The train from Oxford was snaking through the Thames Valley in midsummer sunlight. Trying to ignore the don with an Oxford voice like an air-raid siren giving us his views on education, we watched the red-tiled towns flashing past and the pleasure boats cruising the quiet reaches of the river. Since Spring the streets had been full of young people in floral shirts and dresses moving to the tinkle of bells on long tassels around their necks. In the summer term they started going barefoot and some of the women appeared in see-through blouses. One or two attempted to enter the Examination Schools wearing open-weave fishnet subfusc under their gowns. We were leaving just as the blackberries began to ripen in Blenheim Park. On a last walk around Oxford, returning from the Parks I passed the long back wall of Keble. It was painted from end to end with the first grafitto I had seen; a larger than life brontosaurus, inscribed 'remember what happened to the dinosaur'.

NOTES

1. Such as West Midlands pastoral which I wrote about in 'A New Version of Pastoral: Developments in Michael Wilding's Fiction', *Australian Literary Studies*, 11, 2, 1983, 182–94 and 'Paradise, Politics and Fiction: The Writing of Michael Wilding', *Meanjin*, 45, 1, 1986, 19–27. What I said in the first about *Pacific Highway*: 'It does not actually recreate an idyll, but uses elements of the pastoral mode allusively, to hint at underlying contradictions and ironies which the protagonists themselves only partly comprehend' applies more accurately to the pastoral moments in the Oxford stories.

Perhaps it is also worth mentioning that Oxford is not only on the edge of Jude's Wessex; it is also marginal to the West Midlands.

2. The mid-point of a brief historical phase, after the end of the war and before the reimposition of new, ruthless forms of exclusion in the 1980s, when relatively more students arrived in Oxford on their academic merits, without the benefit of a privileged schooling, than is the case today.
3. There are great possibilities for some future graduate student to study the many and varied narratives between the sexes in Michael's stories.
4. Upward and Isherwood called their fantasy world 'Mortmere'. It is described in Isherwood's *Lions and Shadows*, 1938, and can be traced in the collection of Upward's writing published as *The Railway Accident and Other Stories*, 1969. I doubt whether Billie had heard of it.

The Voice on the Verandah

Don Graham

The American writer, the Canadian poet, and the Thai novelist had each appeared under the aegis of the new globalism at the Writers Conference in Brisbane, and Harry, the American, was certain he'd never see his international compatriots again, but here they all were, reassembled like a third-rate vaudevillian team, ready to read at 'Voices from Abroad', another Writers Conference, another festival, another week Down Under, Southern Cross Circuit. The one at Brisbane had been held in new modern buildings located right on the river that ran through the city, but here in Sydney, in the tatty old suburb of Rozelle, the site was at once historic and a bit dowdy, like a house where hippies had once lived, a large, two-story ramshackle structure with a comfortable, artsy feel to it, appropriate for a Writing Centre located on grounds that, for nearly a century, had been the home of an asylum for the clinically insane. A famous Australian poet who had written about birds had once been confined here, back in the nineteenth century. The birds he sang of could still be heard singing in the Sydney bush. Harry had heard them, admired them, but never seen them. Apparently they were the sort of birds to be heard but not seen.

Harry was betting that the Canadian poet would revisit the Greek travel memoir she had intoned in Brisbane, and the Thai novelist would chant of characters named Fa-ther and Son of Fa-ther and the dubious selling of children into prostitution. Harry himself was unsure what he was going to present. In Brisbane he had read 'American Narratives', an odd sort of piece linking cowboy poetry with the bombing of the federal building in Oklahoma City,which the Aussies seemed to like because it confirmed their ideas about America's propensity to blow itself up; or perhaps he would read something else entirely, something from his great laundry bag of unpublished manuscripts.

The Canadian poet began, as she had in Brisbane, with a colourful account of her life in a Greek village. Harry knew where it was going, and in anticipation, had told his friend Marvell, the conference convenor, to listen for the goat cries and the piercing whistle in the Canadian poet's reading, and sure enough, as she warmed to her material, shriekingly it sounded, her bell-blast bleat shattering the morning quiet, lending her story about simple Greek peasants that little frisson of delight that the audience, Harry could see, simply adored. Harry noted with pleasure Marvell's carefully averted gaze, an index of ironic pleasure.

Harry admired Marvell for many things, certainly for his writing, and especially for the fact that, alone among contemporary Australian authors, Marvell had never written a story about a Drover's Wife nor shown, so far as Harry could tell, any inclination to do so. Marvell's stories made Harry himself want to write; it was the conversion of instant experience into fiction that was at the heart of many of Marvell's stories that so appealed to Harry. But Marvell wasn't reading this morning, the vaudeville troupe was, and when the Canadian poet finished, the audience showered their love on her, and then the Thai novelist bounced to the podium, his face aglow, smiling, happy. He spoke of conditions in his homeland, lamenting the censorship restrictions that prevented him from using the 'F' word, unlike the free-for-all linguistic openness of Australia where, gesturing towards Marvell his hero, a writer was able, no, empowered, to have a go at whatever bloody-well came to mind, so long as, Marvell told them all later, it had nothing to do with sex; the new mob had seen to that. But the Thai novelist didn't really believe Marvell's demurrers; he was certain that everything would be different if only he could use the 'F' word. But he dared not use it, even here, so far from his own country. There were agents everywhere, he told Marvell later, who told Harry, who remembered how the happy face of the Thai novelist gave way to a furtive, hunted look once the reading was over, and still later, as the conference limped on, how the Thai novelist disappeared altogether.

Now came Harry's turn, and at the last moment, a vibration in the air, something, decided him against the Oklahoma story. There had been that odd experience the previous day. Severely hung over, Harry had caught the ferry to Manly at Circular Quay and enjoyed, as always, churning past the Opera House and the Bridge and on towards Manly. He loved the rolling plunge when the ferry struck the deep sea swells near the Heads, south of which, he always reminded himself, lay Antarctica.

After dining on crabs drowning in cream sauce, Harry had a quick pint and dutifully scribbled a few obligatory postcards to America. Then he boarded the boat for the return and, three minutes after it was to depart, the loudspeaker instructed everybody to disembark. The lady next to him said she'd been riding the ferries for thirty years and had never seen this happen.

It was very windy coming off the boat. The lady said it would blow a dog off a chain, and Harry reckoned it would. He waited around till the next departure, but there was none. Then one of the officials announced there would be no further boats leaving Manly today; there had been a bomb threat at Circular Quay. Buses carted everybody back to the city, taking another hour. The newspapers the next day carried no mention of this incident, and Harry had trouble convincing anybody that it had even happened. Except Marvell, who relished such stories. The suppression of news interested Marvell more than the news that was reported. Harry, too: they both loved tracing the motives and textures of real and possible conspiracies.

At the last moment Harry grabbed a few leaves from an unpublished piece he and Jamie had been working on, one of their collaborative efforts that so far remained unfinished, one of several, one of too many. It was a pity Jamie hadn't been able to come on this trip. The two of them enjoyed conferences so much. He missed her. He felt himself all at sea without her. He took a swig of Victoria Bitter, a little early perhaps to start in on the beer, 10:30 a.m., but he told himself to think of it as a nutritional boost, and, doing so, he felt better.

The last two nights had been very long. Two days ago when Harry had come down from Brisbane, elated at being back in Sydney and seeing his friend Marvell and the others, they had all gone to a pizza joint in Leichhardt, an Italian suburb where every other establishment was a restaurant or a front for dubious activities. In a gelato bar directly across from the pizza place, the containers of gelato were never opened, were merely props, it seemed, and all the tables were always occupied by young men in dark suits, speaking on cellular phones. Nobody ate gelato there, Harry remembered from his and Jamie's experiences back at the beginning of the decade when they had lived in Leichhardt. They hadn't been at all surprised when they learned from a local hairdresser who looked exactly like Olivia Newton-John that, not long before their arrival in Sydney, two men had been taken out in back of the gelato store-front and shot to death. The newspapers reported it as an 'execution style' murder. There were no arrests. The suburb where Harry and Jamie lived so cosily that spring was definitely of a criminal cast. The news reports showed cops receiving bribes in restaurants just round the corner, and across from the little house where Harry and Jamie lived, dwelt a handsome couple who were later convicted for selling jewellery, shoes, and other portable booty lifted from corpses in the funeral home the husband ran. It was still in operation, Harry had noticed on this trip.

That night at the pizza joint the problem wasn't criminals but a *poète maudit* who had attached himself to Marvell and his entourage, Harry and Marvell's wife and another man, a friend of Marvell's whose name Harry never did catch. They all piled into cars and drove over to the pizza joint, a favourite of Marvell's, and there, at a small, crowded table, they learned the full dimensions of madness of the *poète maudit* who had attached himself to them. He was young and extremely drunk although it was still early in the evening, and he grew quite belligerent. He wanted to know if Marvell's wife had a daughter, and when she said yes, then he wanted to know if he could fuck her. The 'her' floated in the air, malevolent. Harry drank extra to make up for the poet's behaviour, and although Marvell manoeuvred deftly to dump the poet on the other man at the table whose name Harry never did manage to take in, the damage had been done. Harry was drunk, though not belligerent, and the next day he paid for it. He staggered into the nearest pub where he ordered a VD. The lingerie barmaid, a young girl wearing almost nothing, didn't pick up the mistake because of Harry's accent, and so he escaped that blunder, and reordered, properly this time, a VB. He had three more in quick succession.

But the VB this morning wasn't helping nearly as much as he'd hoped.

At the podium, imposingly he hoped, he began to read a section from 'Continental Desire: An Academic Idyll', part of a first-person narrative of what academic life was like back in the States, back in Texas, back in Austin, back in Parlin Hall, where year after year he stood before a lectern talking. Often it was Parlin 105, a particularly ugly venue, gray walls, chairs in disarray (it was a time for circles in the academy), and a black board that hadn't been cleaned in the last decade. Here, two times a week, he held forth on whatever.

He read: 'Although postmodern pedantry is as didactic as any older, discredited expression of professorial authority, it masks its authority under the sign of openness. In practice it can make an act as simple as buying shoes into something frighteningly subversive. Exhibit A, from a published essay:

To explain the Lacanian distinction between need, demand, and desire, Josue Harari uses a story of what he calls the 'Imelda Marcos syndrome'. A woman who says to her husband, 'I want to buy a pair of shoes' does not articulate a statement of need, since her wish has no biological basis. The statement is, instead, a demand with an ostensible object (shoes), but the object obviously will not satisfy her since the demand is addressed to her husband, from whom she seeks some kind of recognition, triangulated through the screen of her request for shoes. This story indicates a desire, a demand for recognition and love, a demand that exceeds its apparent object(s). The shoe, the commodity, is the inadequate object of desire. In Lacanian terms, it is the *petit object a (autre)*, the metonymic and fetishistic object onto which desire for the Other cathects,

which is a new word, a characteristic of this kind of prose,

only to be further displaced, dissatisfied; the surplus object that partially represents the function that produces it; an object that symbolizes that which is lacing in the subject.

Notice that I read "lacing" in the subject. Surely the word that is meant is "lacking", as in lacking in the subject, but "lacing" is what appears in the text. Surely there is a typographical deity marking the fallen state of academic prose.'

Although Harry really liked that last sentence, it seemed to strike no particular chord in the audience. He wondered if anything had. 'I feel I must make full disclosure,' Harry went on, 'My wife Jamie owns 127 pairs of shoes, last count. She likes to buy beautiful shoes. And something else: she does not inform me when she wants to buy a pair of shoes. And then there's this: they satisfy all sorts of desires, for her and for me, and they are pleasing to the eye – a lovely ending punctuation to the statement of her body's sentence.' What Harry didn't say was that he liked making love to Jamie in shoes. Not his shoes, hers. He had a not-so-hidden agenda; he wanted to have her in 127 shoes. This was something he didn't tell anybody, including Jamie. He thought maybe he had a minor shoe fetish. He didn't think it was a problem, not really, he didn't think it was anything he needed to see a professional about. It wasn't like he was into feet. It was the shoes that touched him. But none of this left the chamber of his dulled skull that day.

He went on, and when he finished, the usual splattering of conference applause flared and died, and then the q & a began. The Canadian poet asked him how his views were received by his colleagues. Harry said, 'Actually, they haven't read it. This stuff is unpublished.' There it was again, Harry admitting publicly the difficulty of finding anything of his in print. Everywhere in Australia the question came up: 'Where are your books? I'd like to buy a copy.' 'There aren't any books,' he said, 'they're all out of print.' He'd been interviewed numerous times on the radio, in

Brisbane, Sydney, and Melbourne, and everytime the interviewer, wanting to be helpful, asked where people could get his books, Harry was forced to admit, 'Just at the moment, there are no books. That can be purchased, I mean.' He had even been interviewed on Turkish radio, under a tree on the grounds of the Writing Centre. What his work might have to say to Turks living in Australia, he had no idea, but the young woman was pleasant and a good interviewer, and they passed a leisurely hour talking about Texas and cowboys and the TV show *Dallas*. After the radio interviews, when he took taxis anywhere, he felt he had to state right up front, 'Listen, I just thought I should tell you at the outset that none of my books are in print.' After all, he didn't want anybody in Australia who perhaps hadn't listened to the radio or attended the festivals to miss the news. He felt like a drummer with empty suitcases; he had nothing to sell. Self-published authors with their wares in hand swarmed the grounds of the former insane asylum and Harry bought their thin little paperbacks. He wouldn't have been surprised to see a small aircraft swim by in the bright blue air, trailing a banner that read: *All of Harry's Books Are Out of Print.*

Harry was in one of those sloughs where he sent stuff around and it came back – or didn't. Some of his pieces were piling up frequent flier miles, and some were becalmed in distant waters. A Harry-and-Jamie story about Dominica, an obscure island in the Caribbean, was lying to with sails set in far-distant Singapore, where it had been sent a full two years ago, to a magazine that Marvell had recommended but believed was now slowly dying. The list of defunct periodicals to which Harry had submitted stories, return postage enclosed, continued to grow.

The Thai novelist snagged a question, the Canadian poet another, and then a woman, addressing Harry, didn't ask a question so much as make a statement. She said that Harry's voice bore the markings of a privileged white male hegemony. That Harry's voice was meant to silence women, who had been silenced throughout history. That Harry's voice sounded the unmistakable note of patriarchy. Oh Christ, thought Harry, why hadn't he read something else, something benign? Before he launched into an answer, he glanced more closely at the woman. She had red hair and a fierce demeanour, and it appeared as if she could use a new pair of high heels herself.

But Harry was nice. He always was. He'd been brought up that way. And he'd never tried to silence a woman, not ever. As far as he knew, women were always putting in their two cents worth. The women he knew, anyway. The strong ones. He knew a lot of strong women. Jamie was one. Mimi was another. Bridgett. Try silencing them. So Harry said to the woman, 'That is an interesting point you bring up. Personally, I find the male hegemony argument somewhat dated if not irrelevant to my own situation.'

He continued on with a rambling, semi-coherent answer, trying to keep the floor and dilute the questioner's anger. Harry was willing to concede that being born an American was an advantage, though not, in his opinion, superior to being born Australian, which was to be granted the chance to inhabit a fair and pleasant, peaceful land compared to crazy, shot-up America. And if he was so privileged, what was he doing here? Why wasn't he at a posh hotel with an entourage? Harry had always wanted an entourage. He thought he'd be good with them, avuncular, generous, and in turn the entouragees would love him. In their memoirs they'd dwell on his largeness of vision, his fundamental modesty in the face of great accomplishment.

But of course Harry had no entourage, and his supposed hegemony had shrunk to cab fare and a modest honorarium. No, that wasn't right. Nothing had shrunk. This was as grand as it got for Harry. Often at readings in Texas there weren't any honoraria at all, and he had to buy his own beer. Sometimes there wasn't even an audience, and sometimes there was only wine of the kind purchased by secretaries for Department of Anguish gatherings. The non-attendance at book signings had become a regular feature of Harry's life. The last time he had had anything to sell, several years ago now, he mustn't pause to count, too depressing, he had sat at tables in those big chain bookstores where perfectly innocent people, upon seeing an author with a stack of books in front of him, suddenly remembered that their youngest child was likely suffocating to death in the car or their favourite dog was missing, as they rushed pellmell from out of his sight, anything to avoid eye contact with the author.

The woman remained unconvinced. In her book Harry was a familiar type, the plantation owner; he embodied the rich iconography of imperialism. He gave off the old, familiar scent of late capitalism, his territory marked like a feral cat's. In the personals it would read: Hegemonic White Male Patriarch Seeking Submissive Third-World Companion for Travel And Etc. He was convicted out of his own mouth, apparently, and there didn't seem to be a bloody thing he could do about it. His was the voice on the verandah, the old colonial authority re-enacted every time he spoke – for this kind of listener, anyway, who heard what she wanted to hear.

And it was true: Harry did enjoy a rambling chat on a verandah. He hadn't a verandah himself, of course, as he owned nothing, but Marvell had a marvellous verandah overlooking a body of inland water somewhere north of Sydney. Marvell lived on an island, and his verandah was attached to the house in proper verandah fashion. It gave upon the sylvan scene. It was there that they spun their conspiracy theories. Both believed the CIA was behind most disasters that appeared to be accidents or the work of 'lone assailants', and in the early stages of their friendship Marvell even believed that Harry was CIA. Harry actually wished he were CIA; he would have enjoyed the steady, secret income, the travel, the elation of a double life well lived. Graham Greene came to mind. But Harry had only the one life, and in the struggle to lead it well he was falling behind. Everybody had, it seemed, a verandah or a version of a verandah; only Harry hadn't. At his age, that is, of his class, that is.

They liked to sit there in the failing light, as the day cooled to a final chill, as the day dog, a neighbour, went off duty and the night dog, a neighbour, came on, and as the cockatoos ceased screaming onto the verandah to cadge crumbs and crackers. It was quiet then, and with the wine and the night you could hatch conspiracies that whispered in the dark of the oldest continent there was. The Kennedy assassination was too easy, and Harry had long since imparted the little nuggets of nuance and fact that he had access to in America and for which Marvell hungered. Marvell was the better theorist, and throwing him a fact was like watching a marlin take the bait and head to deep water, only to surface suddenly, exploding above the sea with the hook planted firmly, theory in hand. The one they liked the best, the forgotten one, was Jonestown. All those bodies lined up in such orderly rows. Impossible to believe the official story. Marvell had worked out the time frame required to poison that many people. It didn't add up. It would have taken hours. You've been in queues, he said. You've seen how long it takes to process people. The Jonestown scene was a mob. What was it? Nine hundred people or something? Absurd. The whole story was preposterous. But it had worked, hadn't it. Nobody talked about Jonestown anymore: the greatest forgotten story in recent American history.

This trip they had a fresh narrative to construct. It changed daily, it was beautifully open-ended, it assumed the parameters of myth with every new detail. Di's death and burial. On an island, Harry reminded Marvell, who was quick to see all the Arthurian parallels. Harry had watched the funeral service, gorgeous and unforgettable, from his comfortable bed in the Hilton in Brisbane, drinking, luxuriating in the spectacle and pathos of it all. Now on Marvell's island the death preoccupied them for a number of evenings, and one morning on the bus into the city Harry, who never wrote poems, found himself writing one. He called it 'Princess Di'.

> Coded, it was –
> All there in the names:
> Princess, die – the imperial mode
> Princess die – a sentence uttered
> By a colonial subject
> Imperfectly tutored in
> The Queen's tongue;
> *Viz.* Conrad's Congolese
> Regarding Kurtz's corpse.
> Finally, the scale of death:
> Do Di, which inference, speculation,
> And the playboy's ethic suggest Dodi did.
> Do, Di – another command.
> In Egypt they understand.

Harry didn't see himself at all the way the woman in the bad shoes saw him. He didn't feel powerful; he felt a little shabby, dishevelled, his clothes a mess from living out of bags. He had a cold, he could use a shave, he wouldn't mind another beer, a movie deal on his last book (out of print) would be nice. If asked, and he hadn't been, he could put together a list of desires as long as your arm.

He wished, for example, that he could recall what had happened the evening before. There had been an author's lunch at one of the better Italian restaurants in Leichhardt. They had all sat at a long table and consumed great quantities of retsina, a yellow-looking Greek wine that had a slightly gasoline taste – 'It's the resin,' Marvell pronounced, who was quite fond of retsina – and in point of fact Harry found that he rather liked it himself. (What alcohol did he not like?)

One prominent writer, an old friend of Marvell's, had not come because he refused to dine at a restaurant that did not serve martinis. But the restaurant was fine, perfect for the rainy afternoon. They could sit there hours on end with the waiter's blessing, a youth from Spain who lurked in the back and rarely came round to their table. Across the street at the nail/massage salon uncommonly good-looking girls sauntered about, on one errand or another. Their lithe movements provoked much discussion among the authors at the table.

After two or three bottles of retsina, it was time to order. Harry was seated next to a locally famous critic, an academic who had built his entire career out of criticism. Harry admired such concentrated devotion and wished he had a similar capacity. The critic critiqued the menu – it must be a burden, Harry thought, having to produce a judicious, measured opinion about everything. The critic recommended the gar fish. Harry, compliant as usual, ordered the fish that he suspected would have many bones, but perhaps he was getting it confused with carp, which had a very poor reputation in the U.S. When the gar fish came, it was long and lean and easy to eat; the meat flaked off nicely. Next to him the critic ate his with the precision and symmetry of a cat in an animated cartoon. When the critic was done, there the skeletal gar fish lay, its spinal cord a thing of beauty. Harry's looked mangled rather than artfully dissected.

The good cheer and the gossip continued until late in the afternoon, and then muddled good-byes were expressed, and after that Harry had only the vaguest recollection of the evening. Marvell and a party of writers, including Harry, an Englishman, a Korean, and a poet from New Zealand, had gone to a raucous pub in Balmain, a storied literary suburb where in the sixties and seventies the best and brightest of Sydney's writers lived and wrote, Michael Wilding and Frank Moorhouse and the lost Vikki Vidikkas and scores of poets now vanished or gone into sales. At the raucous pub Harry had consumed along with the others vast quantities of dark draught beer that kept appearing before him as though by magic. Then, and this was the part that Harry had no recollection of at all when, the next day, Marvell filled him in, they had all decamped for dinner at a cheap Indian store-front take-away place.

'Did I eat?' asked Harry.

'I don't remember what, mate,' said Marvell, 'but you did eat, I'm sure of that.'

'And then?'

'Then everybody went home.'

It must be true, because when Harry awoke that morning he was in his bed in the house in Gladesville, a boring, distant suburb where he was house-sitting for the duration of the month. He felt like a sewer, but it wasn't anything he couldn't bear. He limped down to the local pub across from the bus stop and ordered a VD. It was becoming a verbal tic. This time the bar-maid, who was fully clothed, said, 'What's that you said?' And he had to explain that he'd misspoken. It would be that kind of day.

Finally the session ended, and Harry, feeling by now that whatever vaporous support he might have built up among the crowd with his reading, had been dissipated due to his ineffectual, dazed answers (the woman certainly seemed unsatisfied by anything Harry was able to dredge up) – and so Harry felt he needed nothing so much as that third VB to begin to bring the day into some kind of control.

A bar had been set up in the room next door, and as Marvell had told Harry that drinks were on the house, Harry had made himself a familiar figure to Harold, the barman, a wonderful old bloke in a dark suit and tie who looked like one of the innkeepers in *The Shining*. Harry had been as charming as he could be to Harold, but the old boy was on to Harry now and rebuked him, saying, 'Look, sir, you're going to have to start paying for the beer.' Chastened, Harry forked over $4 in coins.

Beer in hand, he went outside to join Marvell and Jared, another close friend, and Marvell's publisher, whom Harry didn't know. They sat in chairs on the lawn in the sun that even so early in the day bore down potently. Overhead, planes from distant lands trundled through the crystal-clear sky, vibrating into Sydney International, the swoosh of sound drowning out the valvéd readings going on in the tents on the grounds of the old asylum.

Through the deafening upheaval of air, the Canadian poet came up to them. She possessed amazing teeth, the kind of teeth that cost a great deal of money.

She chided them for being men sitting around drinking beer. Would it make a difference if we were Greek peasants? Marvell asked. She ignored the question. Then she said it was sad that none of them knew an Asian language, and Barry, the publisher, rattled off some impressive Japanese. Bored, she walked away, Harry noting her departing back – she had good legs, too. He thought better of Canada than he had in some time.

Left to their own devices Harry and his friends sat in the sun drinking their beer and talking of the days, not so distant, when a pretty young woman with good teeth was a legitimate object of desire, like shoes, like anything beautiful.

'I say,' said Jared, 'didn't she have a lovely gum line?'

They all agreed she had a lovely gum line.

Harry felt himself one with his mates in the bush, only they weren't in the bloody bush, they were in a Sydney suburb. He felt the tyranny of distance; Jamie was so far away he could hardly imagine what she might be doing. He felt himself in a lucky country, a workingman's paradise. He was fairly certain that no one in the former asylum or anywhere near it carried a concealed weapon. He felt bronzed and golden, an ANZAC lad he almost felt. That was the way Australia took him, and he had another sip of the warming beer and felt a continental contentment that was almost like the afterglow of sex, but not quite. He wondered what shoes Jamie was wearing today, which was yesterday Australian time.

Pursuing Wild Dreams

Adrian Caesar

Tony Young woke up and immediately felt sick. This was usually the signal that he had a creative writing class to teach that day. The fear of his own fraudulence, the fear of having nothing to say, the fear of what dreadful revelations might be encoded in a student's writing and be read aloud to the rest of the class produced in Tony an advanced state of nausea. But today, that was not the problem. He remembered that teaching was over for the year. Perhaps it was the hangover and the boringly predictable mid-life crisis that seemed to be causing stomach-churning procrastination at every level of his existence. There are things that he has to do today, this week, that necessitate getting out of bed, But how to achieve the impetus is the question. A hot shower, cups of tea, pain-killers. That's the way to go. Tony has a large nostalgia for the days when cigarettes also eased his passage into the day.

A large part of the problem is work. Tony has done fourteen years hard labour for the College of Knowledge, teaching what used to be called English Lit. to all manner of coves destined for careers in everything from car mechanics to the law. Teaching poetry to butchers is his favourite description of what he does. This is often met with derisive hoots or jibes about teaching 'killers'. Tony finds such self-righteousness a source of acute hyper-acidity. But it's also true, alas, that there's precious little poetry taught anymore. The Department has become one of 'Language, Literature and Communication'; it teaches Indonesian, Communications, Cultural Studies, with Eng. or even Aust. Lit. steadily being reduced to a sideshow. Furthermore, any residual idealism about challenging the students with radical views has long since dissipated. There's not much difference between teaching at the College and any other University; some of the students evince enthusiasm, interest, intelligence in the critical analysis of text and society, but leave to get married and join the bastions of conservatism. Whether that is a multinational, a government department, the military or the law hardly seems to matter. Heartburn continues.

When he first got the job, Tony was told that no one would or could interfere with what was taught in the class room. But now Tony is told that the students are our clients; they could buy their courses elsewhere, we'd better toe the line. So the standard of intellectual living is gradually falling. Tony is soon to see the introduction of compulsory courses in 'Strategic Studies' and 'Leadership' for all students at the College. The Department of Lang. Lit. and Com. is to participate in the 'delivery' of 'Leadership Studies'. No one has yet worked out what strategies are going into 'Strategic Studies' but we're told its for everyone's benefit. People who have the temerity to oppose these 'developments' are dis missed as living in the past.

Another indignity Tony recently suffered was being asked to teach English language skills to overseas postgraduate students. They come here to gain a Masters degree in Cultural Competency. Or at least that's the ostensible reason. It's all part of cooperation in the region. Tony had rarely experienced anything as awful as trying to teach four students from an Asian country together with two Australians the rudiments of English Grammar and essay writing. One of the overseas students copied his assignments off the web. Consulting with the programme co-ordinator from another school, the problems were readily admitted. 'But listen, mate,' Dr Willing advised, 'You just can't fail him. He's got sensitive connections and there'll be a diplomatic incident.' (Dr Willing, of course, does not exist; he is a composite character, a figment of Tony's imagination.)

Tony didn't know whether to believe Dr Willing or not. But took the line of least resistance. It was clear if he protested, things would get tricky. Dr Willing produced the clinching argument. 'You see, these fellows have different cultural expectations and standards. What might be plagiarism to you and me is their way of paying homage to the master. If somebody can say it better than they can, the attitude is, why not?' Why not, indeed. Who was Tony to argue with that. Obviously some kind of conservative cultural imperialist. No thanks.

The bright news is that a research programme has been funded to work out the cultural differences operative in such cases. Tony has not answered the questionnaire.

In the past, Tony has used poetry and the romance of writing poetry as an antidote to the various frustrations of working at the university. But this no longer works. He does not quite know why. Being told by an earnest research postgraduate that of course poetry was dead didn't help. The demise of the little magazines, the withdrawal of major publishing companies (not that he'd ever had his poetry published by any such), the retreat of the art into a coterie community event – 'Get on the web, mate, set up your own page. You can put your photo up and publicise yourself' – all this has flattened Tony's passion.

Then there are the other poets. You have to be part of a club in order to have an audience at all. Tony hates clubs. He is a deeply unsociable socialist. Which brings him to a different and more immediate problem altogether.

In the shower, Tony considers his dilemma. Months and months ago he agreed to contribute to Graham's Festschrift and it is now only three weeks to the deadline. He desperately wants to write something but has no idea what. Graham is a distinguished writer of fiction and criticism who holds a personal chair at one of the country's oldest universities. Graham has written an enormous amount of high quality work, so the task of celebrating this achievement is not a little daunting. Tony does not quite know where to start. He cannot, he thinks to himself, bear writing literary criticism. The flesh is willing (although his penis does not resemble the ultimate phallic signifier of power) but the spirit is very weak indeed. No, there has to be another way. He thinks of talking to Graham and explaining his failure to produce, and then an idea occurs that maybe the best thing to do would be to write a letter to Graham's fictional alter ego, Michael, in appreciation of one particular book. At least this would avoid the 'academic' tone and the composition of footnotes, which, in his present state of mind, are quite beyond Tony's capability.

He brewed a cup of tea, booted up the laptop, took two Panadol for the hangover, and began:

Dear Michael,
I was very pleased to be asked to contribute to your Festschrift not only because I admire your work so much, but also in remembrance of the good times we've shared in Singapore, Canberra and Sydney. My problem, however, is that I don't know what to write. I am not adept at short fiction. I offered a poem but the editors weren't impressed. That leaves Lit. Crit. which seems somehow too formal, and anyway, most of my Lit.Crit. is about poetry whereas most of yours (with the exception of your wonderful book on Milton) is about prose, and I'm supposed to be writing something that coincides with your interests. As an aside, it may astonish you to learn that I'm still managing to teach Milton. It astonishes me. I don't suppose I'll be able to get away with it much longer in an 'environment' which is 'delivering client-oriented services in a flexible manner'.

Perhaps I will be able to sneak Milton on to the 'Leadership Studies' course next year.

But as you know, I'm not a scholar of the Seventeenth Century. So instead of writing about Milton's *Paradise Lost,* I thought I might write about yours; for this is how I think of *Wildest Dreams* – a book that spoke loudly to me when I first read it, and, on re-reading convinces me that it deserves to be thought of as a contemporary classic. I think of it in terms of *Paradise Lost* because it charts Graham's journey from his first intoxicating (and intoxicated) experiences of Sydney and his writerly ambitions there, through several stages of hope only to be plunged into a world wherein literary-political or political-literary dreams have become nightmares and Graham sees himself surrounded by the forces of coercion, control and constraint which separate him from any meaningful co-operative venture. His only recourse at the end of the book is the determination to keep writing. I'm doing my best to follow Graham's implied advice.

But to summarise your book in this way is to immediately lose the source of its richness and to make it sound like some conventional semi-autobiographical memoir. What I love about the book is the way the darkly-comic tone and the form complicate the narrative. Neither the protagonist nor the reader is left in despair and thus the reactionary trap of modernism is avoided. Graham reminds himself, and I am reminded 'to live in hope and not to get so fascinated by the system's own self-image of eternal indestructibility as to believe in it. False hopes, no, he knew enough not to believe in them. But irrevocable pessimism, that was the real danger, the destructive danger, that was what had to be refused'. I gain vicarious comfort from this and direct comfort from the achievement of the book; its brilliantly self-conscious analysis of Graham's relationship with and resistances to 'the system' constitute both its literary and political triumph. Socialist realism *and* modernist influences are brought together to achieve a self-reflexive narrative which never loses its commitment to the portrayal and critique of social reality, but always avoids the easy gesture or utopian fantasy.

I enjoy the early chapters of the book for their evocation of the aspirant writer's life in the bohemian and libertarian worlds of Sydney's 1960s. There is a good deal of fucking, though often the women figure as mediators in the relationships between men ('tokens of exchange', as the theorists would have it) and this is eventually used to provide a subtle critique of the Australian shibboleth of mateship. Similarly, the whole anarchistic ethos of the libertarians is nicely dissected as Graham caustically observes that 'There was a marked pecking order in this anarchistic society. There were top people and not top people. . . . It seemed to be possible to fuck your way into being a top person.' Graham, needless to say, avoids this path, remaining true to his romantic socialist and aesthetic idealism. Nevertheless, he is rightfully grateful that Australia is less stitched up than his English birthplace: 'Well people no doubt fucked in England, but never, it seemed to Graham with the same gusto, the same ease and readiness.' Quite so.

It is not until the escalation of the Vietnam War and Graham's involvement with the anti-war movement that the world and the book begin to plunge away from this atmosphere of youthful engagement and experiment towards a darker and more disturbing vision. For it is during this period that Graham begins to suspect that public demonstrations and petitions are merely a means of government agencies tracking, infiltrating and monitoring potentially subversive movements and therefore neutralising them. It is at this time too, that there are revelations that the CIA had funded the Congress for Cultural Freedom and the magazines *Encounter, Partisan Review, Preuves,* and *Quadrant,* This is the heaviest blow; it signifies to Graham the 'global suborning of intellectual life. The conscription of literature to covert political ends'. It is also the beginning of paranoia: 'Now everyone would suspect everything of having been suborned. Revealing the secret guidelines was the ultimate stage in the operation, the clinching manoeuvre; now there could never be trust again'.

Although Graham admirably still seeks change and challenge by engaging in small-press publishing and the life of writing, the dominant issue of the book is the increasing pervasion of a paranoid vision which sees the infiltration of the state and its agents into every sphere of life. Graham unfolds the idea of the capitalist state as covert totalitarianism. University teaching, the book industry, literary festivals, and the supply of dope are all seen as part of the same racket, and are all arenas where secret agendas are pursued by cohorts of the state. The web of connectedness, the illusion of community that Graham has dreamt of joining through his literary endeavours is transformed into a web of political entanglement and entrapment for which the only antidote is vigilance and retreat into privacy. The book ends with a story within a story wherein the protagonist swims to 'an island' and escapes.

All this is confronting. And still the tone is teasing. Does Graham believe what he is saying? Does Michael? The matter is inexorably complicated by the literary play with the idea of 'plot' and the protagonist's admission that 'dope helped' in the construction of the paranoid vision. 'Plot' gives Graham access to an 'overview' like that of Dickens or Balzac, otherwise difficult to attain in a world 'of atomised, isolated existence, each individual locked in a specialised role, social relationships fragmented and reduced. . .' And, of course, it has given the 'plot' or at least a good part of it, to the book we are reading. 'Where did conspiracy end and personal psychology begin?' Graham, typically, asks himself, just as he has asked difficult questions about the relationship between personal psychology and political beliefs throughout the book. But this is of course the point. In order to avoid what Auden calls 'the preacher's loose immodest tone' we are given instead not only Graham's vision but also Graham's hesitations and uncertainties about his vision.

However, writing as I am after the events of September 11 2001 and only a few days away from a General Election, (it's no wonder I woke up depressed) the paranoid vision has never seemed more apposite to the political realities we are living through. Graham's perspicacious analysis of the role of the CIA in supporting the Mujaheddin is suddenly the stuff of ABC reports; chemical and biological warfare threatens to become a domestic reality; the destruction of the twin towers in New York produces paranoia on every side of politics and justifies governments in casting ever greater veils of secrecy over their actions and motives.

The whole of the operation in Afghanistan is covert. We know that there are bombs dropping and people dying. But that's about it. The absurd pretense that this is all about catching Osama Bin Laden must surely crumble. What new invention will take its place? Why is it a good idea to replace one set of thugs in Afghanistan with another? What is the relationship between the 'war on terrorism' and 'the war on drugs'? Clearly, the USA always needs a 'war' of some sort. There has to be an 'enemy' in order to keep the social fabric from imploding.

Meanwhile in Australia, even articles in the Murdoch press are protesting about the lack of information flowing from the Department of Defence and pointing out how this is an assault on democracy.

Yesterday, I received an e-mail from an American source asking me to put my name to a petition defending academic freedom in the United States. Inevitably I thought of the 'lists' that Graham writes about with respect to protests during the Vietnam War. Sign an e-mail petition and be monitored? The e-mail complains of the American government trying to stifle freedom of speech and applying pressure on the universities to provide confidential information about enrolled students. It will inevitably be argued that all this surveillance is for our own good. Suddenly, I'm living in the world of Graham's book.

I could go on. The point I am trying to make is that *Wildest Dreams*, seems in so many ways to foreshadow all this; it is a text for now and for the future, and one that demonstrates the possibility of political fiction even in these most depressing and decadent of times.

I shouldn't conclude without a word about poets and poetry. In your book, the mordant evocation of the atmosphere created by a gaggle of poets desperate for publication is all too recognisable: 'the poets besiege you day and night, read you poems for breakfast, drop manuscripts off for you to read, come back to get a poem back, change their mind, cross out dedications, get stoned, get you stoned, waste the day, waste another day, no, no poets, poets are the pits'. Given this less than inspiring experience, I'd like to acknowledge your generous interest in and response to me and to other poets and their poetry. Perhaps this is another small signal of the relationship between Graham and Michael?

Well that's enough from me. Here's to you and your writing past, present and future.

With very best wishes,
Tony

Writing the letter made Tony feel better. When he'd finished it, he felt ready for a drink. Sitting on the deck with a glass of chardonnay, he watched the honey-eaters busy in the eucalypts, and stroked the cat with an indolent hand. He thought again of Graham's vision (and Michael's). At least there was still the writing. Even though there were so many social and economic forces which seemed designed to discourage or stop serious work, it was important to find ways of keeping going. To find an island, and write a book. That is the way forward. Easier said than done, but still the way forward. Tony poured himself another glass and raised it – he drank a toast, to Graham and to Michael.

Paranoia, Surveillance and Literary Politics

Ian Syson

At the end of 2000 one of the Australian left's Cold War remnants, *overland* (the magazine I edited until 2002), conducted a survey of its one thousand subscribers. We obtained a response rate of one-in-five which, we were assured by marketing people, is a terrific response from which can be made reasonably accurate assessments of our readership. Most responded positively to what they saw as recent changes to the magazine, some referring to a 'new direction', others believing we were 'returning' to an older spirit.

The responses were in the main very positive about almost all aspects of the magazine and the direction it has taken of late. The great majority said either that we have returned the magazine to its proper political role or that the magazine has maintained that role all along. This suggests that we are doing something right for a number of our readership, and it would be easy for us to be relaxed and comfortable about this state of affairs, especially when both circulation and critical notice are growing. However I am nothing if not perverse and I am troubled by a couple of marginal responses: one younger reader was worried about our continued focus on the Cold War as an issue for discussion and an older ex-communist historian – while enjoying our Cold War coverage and renewed and heightened engagement with left politics – expressed some doubts about our ability to maintain the magazine if we weren't going to cater for younger readers. Both respondents felt that our further focusing on the Cold War would cost us readers in the long term.

Their assumptions are threefold: the Cold War is in fact over; the Cold War as a theme and the kind of politics associated with it will not attract young readers; getting the history right is not an interesting subject for potential readers. While there's something tempting in all of that, part of me just doesn't want to let the Cold War go. I'm just not sure it's over. In any event, it seems too important a moment in Australia's history for the lid to be put on the dustbin just yet, especially when the left wing has just had too much of its own way in the arguments of late for the historical record to be left as it stands. I'm thinking here of the way in which two figures like Ron Brunton and Robert Manne are seen as representing wide polarities in the debate over the stolen generations – and the way in which a whole leftist history of pro-Aboriginal politics gets written out of the debate.

Anyone who reads *Wildest Dreams* will see that these are issues that get to the heart of Michael Wilding's literary activities. His entire literary career (as publisher, critic, academic and writer) in Australia is a process of battling against the influence of the Cold War right – among other forces. As I suggested in 'Michael Wilding's Three Centres of Values' (*Australian Literary Studies* 18, 3, 1998), Wilding has had many successes and the odd failure in these battles. But I also asked if Wilding the writer was

> 'right' to continue his seemingly endless fictional repetition of the process of paranoia, surveillance, oppression, resistance, escape and failed utopia? Is this an adequate fictional strategy for a critic whose work is optimistic and celebratory and a publisher whose work is hands-on and activist?

What follows provides some answers to these questions. Moreover it is a story that has implications for *overland*'s role in contemporary Australian culture as well as holding some worrying implications for our culture in general.

The story begins with the campaign (coordinated or not) over the previous decade to denigrate the name and works of Manning Clark. It came to my awareness in 1993 through the attacks on him in the Robert Manne-edited *Quadrant* by Peter Ryan, Clark's publisher at MUP. Ryan called into question Clark's intellectual and, to some extent, his moral worth. A number of responses were made in the broadsheet and other media and Ryan was given extensive space in *Quadrant* to reply to the voices raised in protest.

The debate obtained a kind of left–right character that left me a little baffled. My education by the Marxist activists at the University of Queensland had led me to see Clark as a vaguely right wing historian who had help to supplant the materialist and economic historians of the 1950s and 1960s. That might well be bad history but it is nonetheless the position I and a number of others held. In mid-1994 I came down from Queensland to work on *Meanjin*, from which I moved to *overland* in late 1995. I took over the editorship in early 1997, when it became *overland*. In this period the Manning Clark issue had percolated away.

Almost the first thing I did as editor was commission an essay by Queensland historian Lynette Finch on the *Courier Mail*'s infamous 'Order of Lenin' revelations in 1996 – this was our first assault on the *Courier*. Finch accused the *Courier* and the media in general of duplicity in having constructed Clark-the-influential-historian in the first place and then claiming the credit for trying to drag down their own construct. She also made the point that Clark was not a particularly influential academic historian, especially in Queensland, and was much more important as a popular historian.

This essay got us into an argument with David Williamson who objected to Finch's use of Foucault. But the seeds of a more interesting argument were sown in another article in the same issue by Phil Deery who appeared to prove that Australian communist Ian Milner was indeed an Eastern bloc spy. Phil used an anonymously faxed work of translation (by Peter Hruby) as his clinching evidence.

Shortly afterwards I was contacted by the editor of the *Courier Mail*, Chris Mitchell, not over the Finch piece but the Deery piece. He accused Deery and us of stealing his research and failing to acknowledge a piece that the *Courier* had run earlier in 1997. He intimated all sorts of legal threats and demanded the space to reply, which was granted. And then we heard nothing.

A year later in August 1998, the *Courier Mail* changed tack away from Manning Clark. Having sent Peter Coleman to Moscow to look at the literary archives, the *Courier* published a series of articles by him exposing the supposed treachery of communist and fellow travelling novelists of the 1950s and 1960s. Coleman and the *Courier* then made a call for the Moscow Archives to be fully researched by Australian academics; a call for archival glasnost.

It was at this point that I thought I'd try to turn the tables. Having researched Cold War Australian literature for my Ph.D. (though I hadn't thought of it in that way, my particular area being Australian working class literature), I felt I had some knowledge of the area and a stake in the argument. I'd also had the ironic chuckle that most new researchers to the area have when they realise that the Congress for Cultural Freedom archives in the NLA are closed – archivally *un*free.

First I commissioned another Queenslander, David Carter, to write a rebuttal of Coleman and second I decided to check out just who had control over the Cultural Freedom archives. Funnily enough (and I genuinely hadn't known) it was Peter Coleman – and David Armstrong.

I wrote to Coleman asking for access. He seemed to ignore my letter.

So I phoned him. He said he hadn't made up his mind but was sneeringly rude about me and *overland* (post Stephen Murray-Smith). I asked him just what was the problem, just what was he afraid of me seeing in the archives? He said he didn't want people like me throwing mud at his friends. Just before hanging up he told me to 'Fuck off!'

I think I understood at this point the thrill of the chase that investigative journalists get when their quarry starts to buckle. This conversation became the basis for my editorial in the December 1998 issue of *overland* (no. 153). This issue also included Carter's article in which he suggested there were two agendas: (1) Coleman's old cold war, and (2) a newer assault against 'political correctness' which was using Coleman et al. as ciphers.

Carter argues:

> The real question is why Coleman thought he had anything to say or why the *Courier-Mail*'s editor thought he did. Perhaps their reasons are different. For Coleman, I suspect, nothing has changed since the 1960s. The struggles of three decades ago are still the struggles of today. He criticizes other researchers (by implication left wing researchers who don't want to know the truth) for not looking into the Soviet archive as if there were fellow-travelling troops out there somewhere still with everything invested in defending Soviet or any kind of communism. The irony of *Quadrant*'s Washington gold is so obvious it doesn't need elaboration – although I happen to think there's nothing deeply scandalous about that either except for its covertness.
>
> For the *Courier-Mail* I suspect the issue is a different one, the same contemporary issue that drove along the anti-Manning Clark campaign. Coleman might be no more than a cipher. The clearest hint comes in the sub-editor's introduction to the first article: 'Many of the Australian writers most revered in arts and history faculties in our leading universities were paid in either cash or kind by the Russian Government'. Prichard is probably quite widely taught but for reasons that have nothing to do with her communism. Hewett too. But Waten? Hardy? Cusack? Like the notion that arts and history faculties revere the work of Manning Clark, this is so way off the beam it's breathtaking.
>
> But there we have it: the arts and history faculties dominated by left wingers, apologists for the communists of an earlier generation, and now, no doubt, in favour of feminism, multiculturalism, post-modernism, post-colonialism, socialism, environmentalism, Aboriginalism, Paul Keatingism, Manning Clarkism . . . in a phrase, advocates of the black armband view of history. Cold-war communism and the Soviet Union have almost nothing to do with it. Make no mistake about it. However vapid Coleman's articles are, there is a serious struggle for hearts and minds going on.

morning in 1999 on the train to St. Albans I opened my *Australian* to read Devine's Monday morning heart starter. Anyone who has read Devine at eight on a Monday morning will know what I mean.

In it he reported on my then *four-month-old* editorial and gave Coleman's side of things. Coleman refused me access because he 'dislikes Syson intensely'. This of course is no reason at all, but it does suggest something of an interesting confusion of morals with ethics. Coleman himself on radio national came up with a more valid complaint – my letter was too brief. However, I remain convinced his reason is fear of what I will find and the ends to which I will read it.

Devine called for full and open access to the Moscow Archives. I wrote a letter in reply in which I agreed with Devine but called for full and open access of all archives including Cultural Freedom and ASIO archives. From this point came a real flurry of letters in the *Australian*. I (twice), Chris Mitchell, Philip Deery, Peter Hruby, Carole Ferrier, David Carter all wrote letters generated by Devine's piece.

What emerged from this exchange was utter and unabashed hypocrisy. The old Cold Warriors of the right wanted the archives of the defeated left open for all to see while keeping their side's acts of treachery and weakness hidden.

But the story gets more involved from this point. And Peter Ryan re-enters the story. Around this time it was brought to my attention by Les Louis via Stuart Macintyre that Peter Ryan's name was accidentally left in a released ASIO document indicating that he had supplied ASIO with information on University of Melbourne academic, Max Crawford.

So we planned an issue of *overland* called *paranoid* which looked at several cases of dobbing or spying by Ryan, J.K. Moir and James McAuley.

Remarkably, during the production of the issue the *overland* office was broken into and all of our computer equipment was stolen. On the computers was the nearly complete issue and all of our financial and database information. I milked this for all it was worth in order to gain publicity – all the while keeping secret Ryan's identity as a way of keeping the media interested.

Eventually I let Tony Stephens, *Sydney Morning Herald* journalist in on the Ryan information. When Ryan was confronted with the accusation his initial response was 'I'll sue the cunt' – meaning Macintyre. Later he calmed down and admitted he had talked to ASIO but only once and it was nothing to do with Max Crawford in any case. The question begged is: in that case what's his name doing in the archive?

Stephens reported the story in the *Age* and *Sydney Morning Herald* and it promptly disappeared. It seems that *overland* can find and publish concrete archival evidence of collegial treachery and nothing happens; whereas the *Courier Mail* finds a mad, half-pissed poet who thinks he might have remembered seeing a badge on Clark's lapel and a full-blown agent of influence story emerges.

Enter PP McGuinness: On 29 April 1999 McGuinness complained in the *Sydney Morning Herald* that contemporary left wing commentators were being too hard on the anti-communists:

> One does not expect the former communists to go around apologizing for all their sins and errors of the past, and will judge them on their present behaviour. Why not extend the same charity to the anti-communists?

Apart from the obscene lack of truth in that statement about former communists being called to account for themselves, just what are their past sins of the right that McGuinness mentions? He certainly seems to know more about these sins than those without access to the *Quadrant*, ASIO and Cultural Freedom archives. However, this whole issue is not about blame, it is about archival freedom and openness.

McGuinness laments the passing of a culture of decency where people on both sides could treat each other with respect:

> Stephen Murray-Smith, the first editor of *overland*, was a good and large-spirited man who was well-liked by many who did not agree with him politically. The same was true of James McAuley, the first editor of *Quadrant*.

From all accounts this is a fairly accurate assessment. But in McGuinness's curiously evenhanded and temperate article – possibly the only one of that description he's ever written – one vital difference remains archivally buried. Murray-Smith was kept under ASIO surveillance for most of his adult life. McAuley was part of the team doing the surveillance. If this is McGuinness's idea of mutual respect then I certainly don't want to live in his moral world – or any of his worlds for that matter.

Since the *paranoid* issue, *overland* published further evidence of Ryan's dobbing on fellow academics. In 2000, ASIO archives revealed that six years after informing on Crawford, Ryan participated in the vetting of another academic at Melbourne. There is no reason to think that Ryan was not a serial ASIO dobber. I announced this fact triumphally in the editorial of issue 158, naively believing that we had nailed Ryan once and for all.

Since then the silence has been deafening.

A bit more recent digging in the Archives in Canberra has built an interesting profile on Peter Ryan. Four Ryan informees have been identified and a picture of a developing relationship between Ryan and ASIO is emerging.

Interestingly, Ryan himself was under ASIO surveillance in the early 1950s. As late as 10 April 1953 an ASIO operative was 'not able to give a clearance' to Ryan because of his left wing associations. By the following year things had changed dramatically. On 10 September 1954 it was recorded that 'In view of the information now held . . . it is considered that he should now be re-assessed, and it is considered that he no longer presents a security risk.' Ryan was interviewed by ASIO on 28 July 1954 during which he gave information about a number of academics including Max Crawford.

The records also reveal that in 1956 Ryan participated in the ASIO vetting of Kelson Arnold (already admitted by Ryan to Tony Stephens in the *Sydney Morning Herald*) and Harry Hyamson. It appears that Ryan's assistance to ASIO was such that 'he was cleared to records level by Headquarters' on 30 August 1957. While it's not clear what this means there is a definite sense in the relevant memo that Ryan's status within ASIO was raised at this point.

Recently released material has also helped to fill in a blank space about the revelation (in *overland* 158) that Ryan had participated in a 'vetting action' on 6 October 1960. He gave information on a Gerard Ottmar Gutman (a Dunera Boy). Ryan discussed Gutman's employment history, his political development and his character. It remains to be seen what else can be uncovered and what the press that so harrassed Manning Clark on skimpier evidence will make of the story.

This story reveals some consistent patterns. First, the hypocrisy of the right in their calling for standards from others that they are unwilling to apply to themselves. This also pertains to the frequent calls for evidence we see in *Quadrant*, and more recently the Chris Mitchell-edited *Australian*, in criticisms of thinkers like Henry Reynolds. As has been shown in 'The Massacre of Australian History' (*overland* 163), *Quadrant*'s performance in empirical research is very poor if Keith Windschuttle's work on Aboriginal massacres is anything to go by.

Second, there is a network of figures each on the lookout for each other. Like a stealthy tag team they pop up to continue arguments started by each other or to forestall oppositional arguments in advance.

Third, a small team of figures manages to obtain important strategic positioning within debates that seem to matter. This becomes clear when we see who gets to review what kinds of books: Stuart Macintyre's history of the Communist Party, *The Reds*; Cassandra Pybus's *The Devil in James McAuley*; Pauline Armstrong's biography of Frank Hardy were all reviewed by Cold Warriors of the right in the broadsheet media.

Fourth, this is a group of people, fuelled by their moral certainty and sense that they are defending freedom and justice. Carter suggests a profound ongoing struggle for hearts and minds, especially of students.

Fifth, there is a refusal of the capitalist press and broadcast media to give credence and space to a particular kind of left wing argument.

What this story means is open to question. It is, in part, a story of my obsession with some old, arguably powerless and damaged men. While it *has* become an obsession for me I hope it is not *only* that. The fact that *Quadrant*, for all its silliness and poison, remains the Prime Minister's favourite magazine and one read by many of the country's conservative politicians, suggests to me its central relevance in debates over political policy and conflict. Moreover, if the right wing Cold Warriors are still influencing policy, then it makes sense to believe that at least some of the structures of power and communication from the 1950s and 1960s might be still in place. Perhaps the end of the Cold War is still being fought. More appealing to me is Carter's idea that a new Cold War is being fought using the weapons and foot-soldiers of the old one; where the enemy is not some foreign ideology but a domiciled enemy with no foreign base.

Whichever of these meanings is taken, and there's some truth in all of them, the case for *overland*'s continued focus on the Cold War has been made. I have also made the case for Wilding's repeated focus on paranoia, surveillance and politics in an age when they seem, unfortunately, to be more significant than ever.

Carrying Yves Tanguy up the Stairs

Vivian Smith

Tasmania's French connections survive in maps, monuments and books. All those explorers who nearly made the island French rather than British have left their names from the D'Entrecasteaux Channel to Freycinet Peninsular, and monographs and articles record their impact and influence. In the 1950s these connections took on a new lease of life when the French Polar Exploration ships used to moor at Hobart on their way to and from Adelie Land in the Antarctic, and for a week or more the streets of Hobart would be dotted with red pompoms as matelots made their way around the shops or queued up in the post-office. It was probably because of these visits that Hobart was chosen to be the first port of call for the most important exhibition of paintings to come to Australia since the end of the Second World War.

In 1952 I had been studying French language and literature for several years and was discovering French painting. Although I was always intensely interested in Tasmanian and Australian history and culture, my intellectual appetite was larger than my surroundings could satisfy and I was turning more and more to the European rather than the local for added sustenance. Just before Christmas I was told that a large collection of modern French paintings was going to visit Hobart on its way to Sydney, an exhibition that might well be the forerunner of many other important events. No one had any idea what it would contain, apart from a Picasso or a Matisse or two, but there was a sense of excitement and anticipation. One Tasmanian art student told me she thought this might well change her whole life. The exhibition, which was coming by ship from Melbourne, was due to open in mid January 1953. I was asked to stay around in case help was needed and told that there might be interesting people to meet. One of the features of life in a place like Hobart, which had all the advantages of being a capital city as well as all the qualities of a small town, was that you could get to see and meet nearly everyone who came there, especially in the world of the arts. It was certainly a civilised place.

On Boxing Day the *Mercury* announced that the freighter which was bringing the paintings to Hobart had run aground on a sandbar near Wineglass Bay on the East Coast and that no one saw any way of freeing it.

You can imagine the shock. The Christmas/New Year season can be a particularly difficult one in Tasmanian waters, which are unpredictable at any time. One year a huge school of whales had been washed ashore and left stranded at Marion Bay. Another year two yachtsmen were washed overboard and drowned. A family friend had recently lost his life fishing off Betsy Island near the Iron Pot. The poetry of Baudelaire, Mallarmé and Rimbaud in particular had made me aware of how, in the nineteenth century, maritime disasters could image the uncertain and the unforeseeable. Literature and life! And here was a coastal freighter in the 1950s, on what should have been a routine voyage between two states, caught on a sandbar with an irreplaceable collection of paintings as part of its cargo.

Today of course TV stations would carry the news; helicopters would be hovering over the scene with on the spot reports. In those days there were only brief radio announcements, and you had to wait for the one and only morning paper with its monopoly on the news to bring the latest information.

Le Tout-Hobart was aghast and agog with the news. Nobody knew what exactly had happened. Had there been too much Christmas celebration aboard? Had the captain been drunk? These were questions that no one asked aloud, but in the rolling of an eye or the lift of an eyebrow. So far as I know no investigation was held into the cause of the mishap. There were one hundred and nineteen paintings aboard, many by famous artists, and there was widespread fear that they could be damaged, or destroyed. Their fate became international news. Lloyds of London had to finance the salvaging operation. When it was at last ascertained that the paintings were at least safe, there was the further fear that Hobart might miss out on the exhibition altogether, as it was travelling to a tight schedule. Finally, after nearly two weeks' delay, it was decided to off-load the whole collection. The paintings were safely landed and brought to Hobart by road.

The exhibition was held upstairs in the Tasmanian Museum and Art Gallery, which one entered in those days from the steps near the corner of Argyle Street. The afternoon the paintings arrived in Hobart I was asked with a couple of student friends to help with the installation. The official opening by the French consul from Melbourne was to take place the next day. Everything was running late and as much assistance as possible was needed. It too was a case of all hands on deck.

Many of the items were heavy and bulky, including four remarkable tapestries: Dufy's *The Beautiful Summer*, Gromaire's *The Earth*, Jean Lurcat's *Tapestry of the Great Fear* and Henri Matisse's wonderful Beauvais tapestry of 1947–8, *Polynesia*. These powerful works must have been carried in and installed by the contractors who had transported all the material from St. Helens on the East Coast under the watchful eye of a descendant of the Pissarro family who was in charge of the whole enterprise. But much of the exhibition consisted of medium-sized paintings, some small enough to be carried by one person, others, for the safety and protection of the work, best carried by two.

I have recently consulted the catalogue again and been reminded of the titles of some of the smaller items displayed. There were pieces by Georges Braque, Marc Chagall, André Derain and three buoyant Dufys. Bernard Buffet, who was probably the youngest painter in the exhibition, was represented by a very recent work of 1949 entitled *The Painter*. Max Ernst had a visionary, futuristic piece *The Year 1955*; and there were lively pieces by Dunoyer de Segonzac, Fernand Léger, André Lhote, Miro, Picabia and Picasso. These paintings were not the major achievements of these artists – and indeed the exhibition included artists heard of neither before nor since – but the fact that it was a survey introducing representative names was part of its great value and success.

There were some extraordinary works. Matisse's tapestry *Polynesia* is unforgettable, with its starfish and stars and shells and its lapping underwater blue and tropical white, and Jean Lurcat's Aubusson *Tapestry of the Great Fear* with its leaf and night sky pattern seemed from one angle to dominate the whole room. It was an introduction to an aspect of art that I at nineteen had never encountered. Georges Rouault, with his stained-glass religious figures and social outcasts remained one of my main personal discoveries from the collection. I had recently been absorbed in the poetry of David Gascoyne and his translations of Pierre Jean Jouve had led me on to the originals (a few years later I saw the poet himself in Paris) and at one stage I planned an article on the affinity between the poems of Jouve and the paintings of Rouault – a project that did not exactly evaporate, but which still remains in note form in a folder full of other unrealised schemes. There was a Nicolas de Stael composition in thick squares of colour, a typical Utrillo scene, a Vlaminck of haystacks which could have been painted near Richmond or Pontville, Jacques Villon orange trees and a view of mountains by Zao Wou Ki.

It amazes me to recall that I carried or helped to carry these paintings up the stairs with my bare hands. When I see all the elaborate and necessary safeguards and precautions that are now part of hanging an exhibition, I am astonished at the simple unprofessionalism with which we helped set up this show. But it opened on time and, apart from its inauspicious prelude, without any mishaps. There was a moment of hilarity when it was discovered that some of the workmen had arranged one of the pictures sideways, and someone laughed about artists who had merely framed their palettes. 'Take your foot out of that Matisse', a voice shouted as I stepped back to see if the painting I had hung was at the right angle. Of course it was only a joke, but a fair bit of nervous tension built up in the room during the few hours we were there, and again and again the position of certain pictures had to be altered. It is hard to believe now that I was allowed to carry a Buffet, a Miro and a Vlaminck up the stairs – actually holding them in my hands and helping to hang them on a special hessian frame set up in the room. It was an experience never to be repeated and, in one sense, the closest I have ever been to such famous works. The last painting I helped to carry up the stairs was the one that came to haunt me most.

I have never really much cared for the paintings of Yves Tanguy. His sandscapes full of speckled pebbles and other lunar lolly shapes have always struck me as curiously inert and lifeless. His 'Dark Garden' (*Le Jardin Sombre*) of 1927 is an oddly arid work but it seems to have fed into a strange series of dreams that I experienced at the time. In one my hands became a huge volcanic landscape full of extinct craters and leprous pits, and as I peered down to look closer over a cliff edge, I seemed to plunge and float into a cloudscaped night sky full of sand and ashes. It was a dream that oppressed me for days in what I used to think of as my surrealist phase, and while it was quite probably caused by my excessive smoking – I was practically a chain-smoker at the time – that dream landscape was clearly informed by some of the images in the paintings in the exhibition, particularly the Tanguy.

The exhibition by the painters of the Ecole de Paris came at the beginning of a lifelong passion that has continued undiminished. My self-education in art up to that time owed nearly everything to picture postcards, Penguin Prints, Penguin Modern Painters, King Penguins and the Faber Gallery, as well as to *Art in Australia*. Like places and monuments I had never visited but knew only from photographs, I had already acquired a wide knowledge of numerous works of art and I could recognise them from reproductions. I found it extraordinarily moving to be seeing in the flesh paintings I had only seen in prints, and I remember thinking that it was like looking at the manuscript of a Dostoevsky novel. I had not yet read Walter Benjamin's essay on 'The Work of Art in the Age of Mechanical Reproduction' or André Malraux's *Les Voix du Silence*, both of which emphasise the uniqueness of the presence of the original work of art itself. The notion of the aura that surrounds or even the radiance that emanates from the original object has its problems, but I have certainly experienced what Keats calls the 'pure serene' that fills one in the presence of an artistic masterpiece and I think that I felt something of that in front of Dufy's beguiling *Still Life with Bananas* and Joan Miro's shapely *Penguin* and his other painting, *Forty Eight*, which, like so many of the pieces in the exhibition was a glimpse into the future, focused on the perfectly drawn number 48.

Of course the exhibition contained work that was puzzling; some of it haunting and troubling. I was an inexperienced viewer. Among the many landscapes, still lives, factory and farm scenes, flower pieces, homages to predecessors, abstract compositions, portraits and nudes, there were paintings that I looked at not knowing what to do with what I saw. I had only a few reference points, and no way of knowing whether some of the things I saw were good or bad of their kind. But even the unformulated doubts and uncertainties that I must have felt eventually proved fruitful in unexpected ways.

The show met with various reactions in Hobart, but my general impression was one of excitement, curiosity and a sense of pleasure at the chance to see work which would otherwise have not been available to us in those years. Everybody I knew went to see it, some several times, and people seemed to go on talking about it for months. Then, soon after the exhibition moved from Hobart to Sydney, well-known members of the old guard like Howard Ashton and Norman Lindsay started attacking it and all that they claimed it stood for. 'An Emetic in Oil Paint', Norman Lindsay was reported as saying.

I did not then know enough about Norman Lindsay to realise how predictable his reaction was, or how the *Bulletin* with which he had such close connections would use his outburst for its own publicity purposes.

In time I would learn more about the various strands that go to make up the web of Australian culture. In those years Hobart seemed to be full of post-war migrants (collectively referred to as 'the Balts') who were to have such an impact over the following decades. I was getting to know some of them as I had got to know some of the refugees who had first arrived in the late 1930s. Slowly I discovered that there is a current in

Australian culture which always reacts and warns against foreigners and outside and overseas influences, fearing corruption. It is represented at both ends of the political spectrum: on the one hand by the reactionary attitudes of Norman Lindsay and his circle; on the other by the Utopian poetic visions of Bernard O'Dowd. I discovered it again in Kenneth MacKenzie's novel *The Refuge* which appeared a year after the French Exhibition, and which I read at the time as an allegory of 'young Australia' being seduced by impure old-world Europe. I certainly did not think that Australian artists should uncritically imitate whatever was the latest international fashion, but that they should learn from and make what use they could of what was brought to them from overseas; that there should be constant fruitful interaction to combat entropy and stagnation.

The 1953 exhibition of French paintings was ultimately as important for Australian painting as the pre-war Melbourne *Herald* exhibition had been. Recently published artists' diaries, like those of Judy Cassab and John Olsen, confirm the sense of excitement, innovation and discovery that the exhibition brought with it; and it is a fact that the Tasmanian painters Jack Carrington Smith and Rosamond McCulloch, to mention only two, became much more experimental in their work after the 1953 exhibition. Bernard Smith in his history of Australian painting singles out its importance for Australian painting as a whole. And there is a fine record of the show in the series of photographs that Max Dupain made of it in Sydney.

Much later in the year the French/Australian newspaper *Le Courier Australien* featured half a dozen poems by Ray Mathew, all based on various paintings in the exhibition. Mathew was one of the most widely published young writers in Australia at the time and the verse he was producing showed the ease and fluency with which he could take up a subject and develop it lightly and loosely. Much of his writing was a kind of lyrical journalism and the best of it had an attractive freshness and warmth. When I read his poems in the *Courier Australien* I remember wondering why I had not been moved to write something similar. After all, I had personally held some of those paintings in my arms. Images from one or two seemed to have entered into my dreams. But I had not felt impelled to write poems about them.

When I met Mathew for the first time in Sydney a little later, he asked me if I had started to write poems about Sydney, full of my first impressions. I said I didn't usually write poems while I was travelling about and that I was probably like those cheeses that can only develop in the place where their germs are. He seemed astonished and said he got so worried if he didn't write something every day and hated going a week without having a complete poem to show. This impressed me no end but I somehow realised that whatever happened that would not, could not, be my way. I would bide my time. I would have to find my own way of writing, but it would be mine, and it would be different.

The O in Bondi

Van Ikin

Joe was the best in the business. Which was why he got kind of angry when neighbours said he was working for the Council now. It was true, of course, and they only said it jokingly, but it hurt his professional pride to have it phrased that way.

Sure, he was working for the Council. But how many councils had a sky-writer on their payroll? Especially one with his expertise?

He levelled off for a dive after finishing a 'P'. That was the word 'SHOP' finished. Just write 'AT BONDI' and then he could go home – $3,000 richer.

But Joe did not really want to go home. After all, what was home but Laura? Laura – the mistake of his life. Well, she wouldn't live forever – except that the same applied to him.

It was the same with everything. It all passed away. Even his letters. They were his art, for he was a professional, and his were the finest letters in Sydney. But already the edges of 'SHOP' were growing blurry.

Just like the meaning of Laura had grown blurry those many years ago. It had been fun, at the time, to have a mistress. But then he had been young, and a mistress meant intrigue and excitement. Now the little technical problems had kind of covered over the fun.

Laura was a nuisance. You couldn't even claim on her for tax. Definitely, the fun had gone out of Laura.

Just like his letters faded. Just like everything faded. Everything – including, damn it all, the bright fluorescent paint on his aircraft. The flashy colours had lost their glow, were flaking. So he would have to paint again. Nothing was ever permanent.

Not even Laura.

Well, that was a bit of consolation.

He finished doing 'AT'. 'SHOP' was getting blurrier by the minute. Those strong air currents were doing it.

Which would he prefer, Laura or the war? God, was that all the choice you had? To snap your life into two pieces like that, then decide which bit you liked best. Like a child comparing pieces of candy.

Besides, was there any difference? Laura had faded, and so had any sense of duty. And you couldn't really call a conscript a patriot. But the war had given him his flying skills, whereas Laura gave only an empty pocket.

Joe wriggled deeper into the seat of his plane – and decided that this was where he wanted to stay. Damn Laura *and* the war! Just give him his plane and the long trailing plume of coiling vapour.

There. A white, vaporous 'B' hung in the air, grey-white against the smoky red rooftops far below.

His plane and his letters, that was all he wanted.

Often, when he daydreamed, he imagined doing something really momentous – like being commissioned to sky-write (in colour!) the national coat-of-arms for some important gathering of world leaders. And all the world would be impressed by the blazing cloud created by Joe the skywriter.

Trouble was, the colours would fade, the air currents would distort the lines. And by the time you had finished, the first half would have faded right away.

So Joe sighed, and dipped his wings to finish the 'O'.

'O' was always his best letter, because when he finished he would fly through the middle of it, creating a great vortex that sucked the circle of vapour down into compact clarity. Joe's 'O's took hours to fade.

So Joe flew his plane through the 'O' in Bondi.

And vanished.

Down below quite a crowd gathered – including some irate Councillors, who decided then and there that if Joe did not finish the job he would be paid nothing. Which would make Laura very angry.

But Joe – who had, of course, created and passed through a space-warp – didn't mind a bit. He had found a whole new universe.

And new things take longest to fade.

Among Thieves

Terry Dowling

> O yet happiest if ye seek
> No happier state, and know to know no more.
>
> MILTON, *Paradise Lost*, Book IV

It was the fifth of Ahriman, that day, that Demon month, when word came of a Camelot forming in the East, or so it seemed, for all morning a merlin wind had been blowing, and phantom knights could be seen riding the high road in that direction, some local townspeople following, folk from Teslar and Bakatamin, their eyes bright with hope and wonder.

We new Knights, the Carnevalle Knights, the Trickster Knights, were worried. Many of our troupe, twenty or more, read the early signs and gathered at the long white building of the Clinic, ostensibly so Syko Sans could tarot our shields and personal mysteries for us, though it soon became urgent general discussion. We hated these manifestations. They turned us out of the hearts of those who otherwise loved us. They made us doubt.

Syko was astonished at the turnout. One moment he was alone, listening to Jackie Paris singing 'Skylark' on the antique Victrola, apparently not even aware that the wind had turned and the high road ran with spectres, the next we were at the door in our ones and twos, like shiftless hayseed farmers trying to find words.

'What?' Syko said, standing in the doorway, puzzled, as if he was worried he'd called a meeting and forgotten about it. Then he looked beyond us at the lines of high cirrus, at the shimmering pennons and glistening flanks of the phantaguerres behind us on the road.

'Inside!' he said, and we filed in beneath the faded sign, below the words we no longer bothered to read: LOST WORLD HERALDRY, took our places on the long benches at the sides of the waiting room, looking out the windows or down at our feet or around us at the distinctive, unchanging fixtures of Syko Sans's world: the longshields on the walls (of Knights who had failed or were yet to arrive – Syko never would say), at the mobiles of bone and copper and old wood swerving through the warm air, at the single painting on the wall opposite the door: a brown evening scene – a horse charging down a railway line towards an oncoming locomotive. Alex Colville's 1954 painting, *Horse and Train*. Part of Syko's world. Like the mobiles. The radio. Jackie Paris singing. The words over the door. His world and ours.

Syko recovered quickly, gave the usual reassurances. Most of us weren't convinced for a moment, but were glad to have the words, and to be indoors at least.

'Stay easy on this,' he said, as he always did when we'd been out of it for a while and phantoms came ahead of a merlin wind. 'The signs could be wrong.'

And Beau Galantine, young, often irritating, impressionable Beau, the other Beau in our troupe, tried to help. 'The signs are wrong,' he said.

Candletrain, Twentyman and Properjohn laughed and shook their heads, not at Syko but at Beau. The others looked back out at the high road, at the shimmering *desues* moving on their way.

Beau Galantine glanced once at me and continued. 'We've been out of it too long. Our judgement's impaired.'

Not the best thing to say to veterans, yet the sort of thing an enthusiastic novice like Beau would say. My long-suffering lieutenants smiled at one another, might have scorned him had I given the cue by smiling first.

'The wind, the resolutions,' Twentyman bothered to say, and foolish Beau actually interrupted.

'Like at Landis. Residues from last month's display. Or someone's doing rogues to ruin morale. Look at us!'

'Beau could be right,' Syko said and stopped four of us – me included – answering then and there, from delivering our fond reprimands. 'They're not good resolutions. More like at the end of their cycle.'

Normally we wouldn't have believed it, Syko crossing us like this, making Lars Twentyman, John Properjohn and big Boss Candletrain lose face before the troupe. At least I hadn't spoken. Everyone watched the Clinic psychologist turn back from the window, remove the optics he wore to verify these things. We wore circuited tech armour as always; Syko had his usual dun-coloured fatigues and the white coat with the Caduceus as DNA Helix as Gordian Knot as Tree of Life on the breast pocket. It always trapped the eye, somehow led you away from the elaborate pattern back to the Colville painting — to the horse plunging ahead towards the train, completing that eternally sought, eternally denied rendezvous.

'It's a kind of encounter that's needed right now,' Syko said. 'I think what you do is go out and clear the road, accept local missions, let yourselves be seen. Business as usual. You power up, burn awhile. If these spooks are real, they'll firm up and you'll be dancing for your lives. If they're *desues*, you tilt them, scrap their signals, wraith them out. Either way, the marks see it, tell stories we can use. It's bread and circuses, gentlemen.'

'It's overreaction,' Properjohn said, clearly annoyed. 'Just what we can't afford, Sy. No real strikes, so we coyote at windmills. Bad precedent. Exactly what you said not to do last month.'

Syko looked exasperated for a moment, though fleetingly so. 'Don't quote me back to me, John. I'm like you. I do this a day at a time. Each wind. Each manifestation, you hear me? Whatever comes along that road. Read 'em fresh. That's my skill. My gift. Yours is working the grid. So this time, John Properjohn, you go out and toss these phantaguerres. Next time will be next time.'

Properjohn looked abashed, and Syko saw he needed to make amends, to let my Number One save face on this. 'But you're right to challenge me on it, John. All of you. Don't stop. It's a month since Landis. We're talking public relations here. We'll all feel better for it.'

'Do us good,' I agreed, taking the initiative as well, knowing Syko would never let us go out to humiliation. To ruin, yes, bloody death, suffering and soulcatch, but never humiliation. We Knights were replaceable; the troupe's reputation was not. For our part, the pride of victory, our dignity, was pretty well all we had, working at the legend what we had to do. What the Heraldry was all about.

Which made me suspicious and worried. Syko could have planned this whole thing, foreseen the merlin, the hint of a Camelot, the turn-out of downgraded phantaguerres we would never have bothered with. Syko could be downplaying it, expecting something more. Fearing something more. Either way he was handling us as usual.

'Tarot your shields,' the pyschologist said, as if it were genuine mission, as if a major quest were indeed underway, and some of our troupe – Engelin, Graysmark and Salmerdine – began passing out virgin longshields from the flipcase against the far wall.

'Check and display!' Syko called, activating his own tech, holding the wand forward as we moved to obey. 'John, what do you have?'

'Watershield,' John Properjohn said, turning his elongate Norman/Sapphire towards the older man. Where there had been template neutral was now a roiling blue field marked with a distinctive white spindle.

Syko consulted the bookplate on his left forearm, read off the heraldry. 'Toan. Fourteen hours. Nine of Pentacles. Middle field.'

'Copy,' John said and left the Clinic.

So it proceeded: Candletrain and Twentyman, Engelin and Graysmark, Sacradown and Salmerdine and young Beau Galantine, Briarforth and Reevers and the others getting their heraldries and encodements, filing back out into the horseyard, powering up their aermounts so their suits sweated mandelbrots and they rode on twisted light.

It was exciting to watch an encodement, how each handled the empowering, took on aspect, stood aer-fashion in their individual ways, helped make the grid. Soon the full company was assembled in the yard but for me, mounts roiling, shields fixed and gleaming. Many of the townspeople left off watching the phantaguerres; here were the Carnevalle Knights after all, the Trickster Knights primed and ready. It confirmed the phantoms, the likelihood of a Camelot, the clear message of the freshening merlin.

They only awaited my joining them, to lead them astride our wondrous mounts into the turgid afternoon.

'Thanks for that, Beau Gentry,' Syko said. 'I didn't handle that too well.'

'John's okay. And, look, they're happier already. It's a good move, Sy.'

'We need to try different approaches,' he said, but then saw I was studying the Colville painting on the far wall again – *Horse and Train* – the horse charging down the track towards the Old World locomotive, never to turn aside, determined to win. To matter. That image had become the mysterious unstated icon of the Trickster Knights.

'Trouble rationalising again?' he asked me.

'Right.'

Syko glanced out into the yard, then down at what I had, saw Fireshield, the spread razorlines bifurcate silver on red, knew it wasn't a reading being sought. 'Let's have it.'

'You still allow I could be dreaming this? We could?'

'I do. But like I said, we're in the system. How can we know?'

'I worry about it.'

'You do, yes. More than most. But it's what we have, Beau. Since you've had these feelings, I've run simulations. Hypotheticals. Comp confirms what we already allow. It can't do much more.'

'It's in the system too.'

'Right. You, me, all of us. But I give it what you give me, okay? We're dreaming this. You're dreaming this. Virtual Reality. We're in a closed tech environment, collective trance with moments of truth breaking in, dreaming Shiva waking up, the lot.'

'Sy – ?'

'Like I said, I won't hold back on you, Beau. I promise. It's too important. I'm here to see you do your job well. You give me your hypotheticals, I'll run them. But so far, nothing.'

'Is it – ?' Beau hesitated. 'Is it a new thing?'

'What, questioning the binding reality? I told you before. No. It's entirely appropriate, dealing with these modal shifts. It's the name, isn't it? Lost World. Lost World Heraldry. Presupposes something to be lost from.'

'Nothing unusual then? How many have you logged? How many troupe leaders, how many Knights, have asked?'

Syko Sans frowned. 'Beau – '

'Please. Quality of life, remember?'

'Right. Quality of life.' He scanned the bookplate. 'In my fourteen years here, thirty-two. That's before Lensdraco, before Taltergast and Periard. They were good leaders like you. They asked my predecessors the same questions all the time. It's correct procedure.'

'They really did?'

'It's on record. I can show you transcripts.'

'Your remedy has always been quest, I suppose.'

Syko gave his winning smile. 'Getting out there, yes. If that merlin's wired, if that Camelot turns and those rigged-up *desues* go full-form, we've got major trouble. It hasn't been like this since – 'Again he scanned his bookplate, where references paced whatever he said. ' – Lensdraco's day. That's ten years, Beau. It does rogue like this. Just a police action, a ride-and-show, a clean-the-table, then the wind turns mordred, and we lose life, whole towns, a few more map-edges curled and gone. You get me, Beau? Some troupes never recover.'

'And that's why.'

'That's why. I would have told you, but – ' He smiled. ' – I expected you to bring it up. Every mission now Beau Gentry has to ask. You're a good commander, Beau. Keep questioning it. All of it. Everything. Keep me hopping with these hypotheticals. Now get out there. There are phantoms on the high roads is what we're sure of, and possibly a full Camelot polarising. But if that wind goes mordred, those phantaguerres could prime in an instant. Keep our lads keen. But, for heaven's sake, don't tell them too much about this. It's 'need to know'. Just a morale mission till you're sure. Right?'

'Understood.'

'On with it then. I've got simulations to run.'

I glanced once more at the horse locked into its fateful instant in the sepia light, its refining, defining, vital moment of individuation, endured Syko's patient smile while I did so, then joined the others in the yard.

The *desues* folded in curdled light – blistered, blinked and fell away. The folk from Bakatamin and Teslar waved and cheered us on towards Saru, our longshields like holy tongues, like bright pins joining us to the land. They wanted Camelots, these humble townsfolk, true demon knights to test our mettle, to smash us and teach us humility, but when their erstwhile champions proved false, they sent us on our way with blessings and high praise and added new chapters to our legends.

We flowed upon the land. Graysmark had point, bore the flag of the Trickster Knights, had Lars Twentyman and Boss Candletrain for company. Still in aspect but not sparking, they had their helmets back. The road was clear ahead, the rolling countryside clear and empty, brilliant greens and golds, soft browns and ochres sweeping off to the rich blue at the horizon. Engelin and Sacradown were next, shields at rest, lances aslant: Engelin's to the right, Sac's to the left, making their St Andrew's brother-cross which John Properjohn and I looked through as if through a gunsight. The others came behind, shouting and singing in the clear bright air.

'We are the antic Trickster Knights,
We are the ones who dare.
The Carnevalle, Carnevalle
Bold chevaliers.
We are the biting light of sun,
The dancer's favoured step,
We're all *étrangers*! *Inconnus*!
We're noble-born, (*Messieurs* to you!)
From Dare-You Bridge to Lost World's Edge,
Such bold chevaliers.'

'You worrying 'bout this, Beau?' Properjohn said, bringing me out of the song, keeping it small, easy, so I missed the edge of what he meant. He knew why I'd stayed behind with Sy.

I remembered Sy's words and smiled. 'I'm doomed to be the philosophical type, John. You know that.'

'We could die at this.'

'What?' The unexpected vehemence of his words surprised me. 'Hey, listen. My worries . . .'

'You're our Captain, Beau. You worry, we worry. That's how I see it. That's how Tailke and Lensdraco handled bad winds. Shared up front.'

'Look, nothing before its time, okay?'

'We swiped some *desues*. Why are we really out here?'

'Sy has tech. You saw. He reads the winds sometimes. The merlin felt wrong, John. We do a precaution run like we do valid mission.'

'But he didn't call us in.'

'What? He would've.'

'Wake up, Beau! He didn't call us in. We came ourselves. Not even full muster, now here we are going through the numbers. A suspect merlin. You want to talk about that?'

'John, can we just wait on this?'

'Your judgement's out, Beau. You should've questioned it.'

It happened so quickly; none of us could have foreseen it. Boiling up from behind a low hedge – a too low hedge, nothing could've been behind it! – were thirty, forty phantaguerres of the terrifying Salis Rosa subset. They were onto the road before anyone could raise a coherent shout, chitinous blacks and deoxygenated reds, moired burgundy and old rose, hot and spinning.

Engelin was cut down and flensed almost at once; while Graysmark skewed his mount and kept the flag, but barely, forming a triad with Twentyman and Candletrain. At the rear of the column, Reevers, Magralayne and Briarforth were gone, Bracken and Browncastle as well, their mounts grounded and overturned, their armour split open by the phantoms' filaments and hooks.

Properjohn and I did duo to reach Titramere and Jeevejack, lost Jeeve before we could four our energies and make a grid. But we broke the filaments that sprang from guerre to guerre and meant to hold us, pushed out onto the meadow and rounded on the mêlée, charged in to help Sacradown, Bother Bors Lee and Salmerdine. The road was a surging flux of energies and hard strikes, rupturing filaments, battle cries.

But we were turning them. The glistening tide of phantaguerres had lost resolution, were retreating ahead of us towards Saru. While Properjohn and I swung back to aid Twentyman and Candletrain and their winning duo-grid, Titramere, Bother and Salmerdine continued ahead. Graysmark reached the duo first, added flag, made trio, then as five we followed the others.

Only to see the trap close: phantaguerres piling up along the road, fifty, sixty or more – Lock Blackhedron leading them, incredibly so, the very devil himself. I saw Titramere, Bother and Salmerdine reel back and go under, raced forward to bring our grid and hard strike where it could save the others.

I couldn't remember battle like it, could scarcely believe it was happening. Lock Blackhedron seemed to be everywhere, coursing among his fiercest guerres, calling his mad-word, 'Antry, antry, antry' over and over, whatever direction that gave.

I would not have it. My men going under. I would not. I swept forward, let the others see me, drew them after.

'Me, Black Lock!' I cried, amplifying to shake the road.

The big head snapped round, lacquered and glistening.

'Antry!' he cried in turn, recognizing me from a dozen previous mordreds, and opened up part of himself to reveal his 'maiden's bed', deep, wet and razor sharp, my final resting place if the grid was drawn too thin and failed.

But Graysmark kept the shape, kept close and gave me flag, and John Properjohn, Lars Twentyman and Boss Candletrain spun trio hard after so we hit Lock Blackhedron as a spike, lucky accident that, impossible to plan at aer speeds, but it toppled him, sent his attendant guerres tumbling in sync scatter. They recovered at once, but energy had bled wild from Black Lock's fall, killing grass and companions but, best of all, breaking formation.

Graysmark got his flag to the fore, and Properjohn managed a hard strike with his sword that split Blackhedron wide. His 'maiden' snapped shut – no time for such extravagances now – and though his wound sealed itself soon enough, there was further diminution. Black Lock powered back, brought his remaining guerres in to make a usable channel.

'We have 'em!' Twentyman cried, and he was right. The phantoms were vorticing around Blackhedron, hiding him while he powered down into whatever niche the spoiling merlin gave.

'This is it, Beau!' Candletrain roared. 'What it's all about! This!'

And counterpoint to his words, Twentyman was there, wielding his sword, Reducio, shouting: 'I love this! I love this!'

Properjohn was grinning now, happier with every strike, crying 'Yes! Yes!' and young Beau Galantine had an idiot grin of his own, though he was breathing too hard to speak, thank goodness.

I crowed with it too, giving in to the euphoria, the elation which came with doing the task: striking, reining back, plunging ahead, the sublimity of the grid, the flagging and rallying. Boss was right. Lars was.

The purpose of the horse – to rush forth, to feel the wind in its mane, to be itself. The train too, yes, fulfilling function, being train, rushing on, defining what it was.

That's what drove the Trickster Knights – the task, the doing, the dealing with, delight in that. It was sublime.

So even as I swung and struck, unformed the demon wraiths, I cherished the Colville painting that brought this to me now, this moment of joy.

'Take it with you!' I cried. 'Keep it with you!' Whatever those words meant. But something to do with the machine. The charging animal. Things irreconcilable – that did not belong. The mystery of that.

Yet the thinnest dagger blade of recollection pushed in as well. What Properjohn had been saying when the phantaguerres first appeared. What Sy had said: It's a kind of encounter that's needed right now.

And I knew – in that transcendant moment as the last of them went *desue* and was wraithed out: I am deep in my function, as far now from questioning as I can be. When I challenge it – see the whole and not the elements – then I'm troubled, disquieted.

Which, strangely, perversely, made this whole thrilling fulfilment suspect.

I was being handled again, dealt with still.

'John!' I cried. 'What you were saying before?'

'What was I saying, Beau?' Properjohn cried, grinning, powering down, exhilarated.

The dagger point of recollection became sharper doubt.

'Listen! All of you! We're biased into this. Whenever we question it.

We're self-adjusting. Most fulfilled when we're doing our designed jobs.' I hated saying it. 'Designed.'

'What?' Candletrain roared in his triumph.

'What's that?' Sac called out, his mount jostling in.

'We did it!' Beau Galantine cried. He had Karsanjic, Magganis and Tottry with him, all smiling too, the bravest fools.

'We turned Black Lock!' Twentyman said. 'We did! Turned 'em all!'

'Celebration, Beau!' Graysmark cried, waving the flag. 'Wait till Sy hears this!'

The dagger pushed harder, became panic. If it was Virtual Reality, self-maintaining, something had to regulate the variables, protect it from – what I brought to it by asking. Just what I was doing discommoding these men.

I reined about, needing to tell Syko. Such a simple thing. That there had to be control systems. Regulators. Homeostasis.

The wind was blowing harder.

'Hold this place, John. Lars, Boss, all of you, keep this place while I check with Sy. Black Lock may return.'

And I gave them no time to respond to my patent lie, but rode, fled, boiled across the land, desperately holding the truth before me, making it my flag, my opposing force, as I rode into the wind, into that wind, closed my helmet against the stinging sand.

Reined into the empty yard, rushed into the Clinic at last. Found Syko at his console, pushing back, standing, a look of surprise and concern on his dear face.

'What?' he cried. 'Beau, what?'

And I almost had it. Something about truth. An only order.

Sand hissed against the Clinic outside. The longshields stirred on the walls, the mobiles moved along coarse and clashing arcs, brash ruin in the hot dry air. The Colville painting shifted, beating, lightly beating on the wall.

Horse and Train. Horse and Train. Horse and Train.

The restless shields, the stinging sand, a steady wind now, gallop percussion in the changing afternoon – all real, ultimate truth, of course, the only sharp irresistible truth there was. Due cause to celebrate, yes – victory over Blackhedron and this. What more could we ask? What more?

'We won, Sy! It was a trap; it was Black Lock and we won!'

'Bless you, Beau,' Syko said. 'You did it! Bless all of you.'

Outside, stronger now, the mordred wind blew.

THE LOST WORLD HERALDRY FOR 'AMONG THIEVES' IS:

Name	Sign	Key	Reading
Beau Gentry	Fireshield	Gridoc	Ten of Swords
John Properjohn	Watershield	Toan	Nine of Pentacles
Lars Twentyman	Earthheart	Okrum	Page of Cups
Boss Candletrain	Skyswift	Dedda	Queen of Pentacles
Grace Graysmark	Riverdoor	Chjee	Six of Swords
True Engelin	Sunderwind	Tippett	Seven of Cups
Martyn Salmerdine	Seadrift	Hinder	King of Pentacles
Bother Bors Lee	Treewind	Ebel	Three of Wands
Thomas Briarforth	Starshield	Ash	Eight of Wands
Stefan Jeevejack	Sandshield	Bula	Six of Pentacles
Sente Bracken	Firetree	Terrot	Two of Cups
Bright Magralayne	Goldfire	Sotheri	Five of Swords
Beau Galantine	Sunwind	Alca	Page of Swords
Jovis Titramere	Greenshield	Wing	King of Wands
James Sacradown	Firesong	Karda	Nine of Cups
Anthony Reevers	Oceanshield	Vace	Nine of Swords
Nat Browncastle	Riverwall	Creon	Four of Wands
Ned Magganis	Mountainfield	Ajje	Page of Pentacles
Strider Karsanjic	Firehand	Slee	Five of Wands
Almont Tottry	Windsong	Nji	Six of Cups
Syko Sans (honorary)			The Magus

Michael Wilding: A Select Bibliography

(This does not separately list the publication in journals and anthologies, or in translation, of some 160 stories and fictional episodes and 30 essays that are collected in the books listed below. It also excludes reviews and occasional journalism.)

FICTION

Novels and Short Story Collections

Aspects of the Dying Process. University of Queensland Press, St Lucia, 1972.

Living Together. University of Queensland Press, St Lucia, 1974. Serbo-Croatian translation by David Albahari, Decje Novine, Beograd, 1985.

The West Midland Underground. University of Queensland Press, St Lucia, 1975.

The Short Story Embassy. Wild & Woolley, Sydney, 1975.

Scenic Drive. Wild & Woolley, Sydney, 1976.

The Phallic Forest. Wild & Woolley, Sydney; John McIndoe, Dunedin, 1978.

Noc Na Orgiji [Night at the Orgy]. Stories selected and translated into Serbo-Croatian by David Albahari, Kultura, Beograd, 1982.

Pacific Highway. Hale & Iremonger, Sydney, 1982.

Reading the Signs. Hale & Iremonger, Sydney, 1984.

The Paraguayan Experiment. Penguin, Melbourne and Harmondsworth, 1985. Bengali translation by Geeta Sen, Papyrus, Calcutta, 1995.

The Man of Slow Feeling: Selected Short Stories. Penguin, Melbourne, 1986.

Under Saturn. Black Swan, Sydney, 1988.

Great Climate. Faber and Faber, London, 1990. Published in USA as *Her Most Bizarre Sexual Experience*, W.W. Norton, New York, 1991.

This is for You. Angus and Robertson, Sydney, 1994.

Book of the Reading. Paper Bark Press, Sydney, 1994.

Somewhere New: New & Selected Stories. Central Queensland University Press, Rockhampton; McBride's Books, Colwall, UK 1996. Punjabi translation by Tejpal Singh, *Kiteon Navan*, Sahitya Academy, New Delhi, 2001.

Wildest Dreams. University of Queensland Press, St Lucia, 1998.

Raising Spirits, Making Gold, and Swapping Wives: The True Adventures of Dr John Dee and Sir Edward Kelly. Shoestring Press, Nottingham; Abbott Bentley, Sydney, 1999.

A Whisper from the Forest. Selected stories in Japanese translation by Sokushin Ezawa, Seizansha, Tokyo, 1999.

Academia Nuts. Wild & Woolley, Sydney, 2002.

Uncollected Stories

'Frrried Potatoes'. BBC Radio, Morning Story, August 1960.

'Stevie Agonistes', *Isis*, 18 January 1961, 22 and 25.

'Hnut'. *Isis*, 7 November 1962, 12–14.

'A Little Fire in a Wide Field'. *Granta* 64 (28 January 1963), 23–4. *Squire* April 1966, 44–6.

'They Might Have Been Brother & Sister'. *Squire* November 1966, 8–21, 31, 34.

'Yes, We Unzip Bananas'. *Westerly* 1968 no. 2, 5–7; *Westerly 21; an Anniversary Selection*, ed. Bruce Bennett and Peter Cowan, Fremantle Arts Centre Press, Fremantle, 1978, pp. 66–9.

'The Glass Bridge'. *Westerly*, 1970, no. 2, 5–11.

'Letter from the Library'. *Eighth Assembling*, ed. Richard Kostelanetz and Henry James Korn, Assembling Press, Brooklyn, U.S.A., 1978, unpaginated.

'I Sit on My Swivel Chair'. *9.2.5.*, 2 (1979), 10; *9.2.5: Workers' Poetry from Australia 1978–1983*, ed. Jeltje, Collective Effort Press, Melbourne, 1999.

'Report of a statement from the editorial & publishing manager'. *Neos* 9–10 (1985), 37.

'Tales from 1001 Publishers' Lunches'. *Assembling 13*, ed. Charles Doria, Assembling Press, Brooklyn, U.S.A. 1987; *Rrat* 3 (November 1997), unpaginated.

'The Black Rocks'. *Westerly* 42, i (Autumn 1997), 13–16; *Oasis* [UK] 98 (September 1999), 5–7.

'The Last of the Long Hot Summers'. *Social Alternatives* 17, ii (April 1998), 43.

'The Great Refusal'. *Social Alternatives* 17, ii (April 1998), 44.

'Market Forces'. *Gargoyle* [USA] 42 (1999), 334–339; *Overland* 155 (Winter 1999), 5–8.
'Asia Hand'. *Ariels—Departures and Returns: Essays for Edwin Thumboo*, ed. Robbie Goh. Oxford University Press, Singapore, 2001, pp. 118–24.
'Symposium'. *'Gladly Wolde She Lerne and Gladly Teche': Felicitation Volume for Professor Yasmine Gooneratne*, Argus Publications, London, 1999, pp. 133–8.
'Space Circles'. *Mosman 2088* (September 2000), 26–9; *Descant* [Canada] vol. 32, no. 2 (Summer 2001), 230–8.
'His Echoing Song'. *Rrat* 4 (December 2000), unpaginated.

Autobiographical Essays

'Nephew's Story'. *Westerly* 42, iv (Summer 1997), 34–8.
'The Badfather'. In *Daughters and Fathers*, ed. Carmel Bird, University of Queensland Press, 1997, pp. 98–117.
'Adventurous Spirits'. In Craig Munro, ed., *The Writer's Press: UQP's First Fifty Years*, University of Queensland Press, St Lucia, 1998, pp. 43–59.
'Among Leavisites'. *Southerly*, vol. 59, nos. 3–4 (1999), 67–93.
'War and Pacifism'. *Text*, vol. 4, no. i (April 2000) [electronic].

Related Films and Videos

Or Forever Hold Your Peace. With Richard Brennan, Kit Guyatt et al., 1971.
The Phallic Forest. Director Kit Guyatt, producer Michael Wilding. Australian Film Institute, 1972.
Reading the Signs. Director David Dunn, producer Jim Berrow. Central Independent Television, Birmingham, 1988.
Buying Jeans in Balmain. Belgrade Film School, 1988.
Michael Wilding interviewed by Don Graham. University of Sydney Television Service, 1993.

NON-FICTION

Books and Monographs

Milton's Paradise Lost. Sydney University Press, Sydney, 1969.
Cultural Policy in Great Britain (with Michael Green). UNESCO, Paris, 1970.

Marcus Clarke. Oxford University Press, Melbourne, 1977.
Political Fictions. Routledge & Kegan Paul, London, 1980; Hale & Iremonger, Sydney, 1984.
Dragons Teeth: Literature in the English Revolution. Clarendon Press, Oxford, 1987.
The Radical Tradition: Lawson, Furphy, Stead (The Colin Roderick Lectures 1992). Foundation for Australian Literary Studies, Townsville, 1993.
Social Visions. Sydney Studies in Society and Culture, Sydney, 1993.
Studies in Classic Australian Fiction. Sydney Studies in Society and Culture, Sydney; Shoestring Press, Nottingham UK, 1997.
Among Leavisites. Privately printed, Sydney, 1999.

Edited Books

Three Tales by Henry James. Hicks Smith, Sydney, 1967.
Australians Abroad (with Charles Higham). F.W. Cheshire, Melbourne, 1967.
Marvell: Modern Judgements. Macmillan, London, 1969; Aurora, Nashville, 1970.
Julius Caesar and *Marcus Brutus* by John Sheffield. Cornmarket, London, 1970.
We Took Their Orders And Are Dead (with David Malouf, Shirley Cass and Ros Cheney). Ure Smith, Sydney, 1971.
The Radical Reader (with Stephen Knight). Wild & Woolley, Sydney, 1977.
The Tabloid Story Pocket Book. Wild & Woolley, Sydney, 1978.
The Workingman's Paradise by William Lane. Sydney University Press, 1980.
Marcus Clark: Stories. Hale and Iremonger, Sydney, 1983.
Marcus Clarke. University of Queensland Press, St Lucia, 1976; 2nd edn, 1988.
Air Mail from Down Under [Australian Short Stories in German translation] (with Rudi Krausmann). Gangan, Vienna, 1990.
The Oxford Book of Australian Short Stories. Oxford University Press, Melbourne, Oxford and New York, 1994, paperback, 1995.
History, Literature and Society [Festschrift for S.N. Mukherjee] (with Mabel Lee). Sydney Studies in Society and Culture, Sydney; Manohar, New Delhi, 1997.

UNCOLLECTED ESSAYS AND CHAPTERS IN BOOKS

On Australian Literature

'Adam Lindsay Gordon in England: The Legend of the Steeplechase'. *Southerly* XXV (1965), 99–107.

'Christina Stead's Australian Novels'. *Southerly* XXVII (1967), 20–33.

Reprinted in Jean C. Stine and Daniel G. Marowski, eds, *Contemporary Literary Criticism*, vol. 32, Gale Research, Detroit, 1986.

'Two Cheers for Keneally'. *Southerly* XXX (1970), 20–40.

'Short Story Chronicle'. *Meanjin* XXX (1971), 255–67.

'Write Australian'. *Journal of Commonwealth Literature* VI (1971). 19–30.

'Marcus Clarke's *Old Tales of a Young Country*'. *Southerly* XXXIII (1973), 394–408.

'Marcus Clarke in the Colonial City'. *Southerly* XXXIII (1973), 441–50.

'Marcus Clarke's *Chidiock Tichbourne*'. *Australian Literary Studies* VI (1974), 381–93.

'Marcus Clarke's *His Natural Life*'. In W.S. Ramson, ed., *The Australian Experience: Critical Essays on Australian Novels*. Australian National University Press, Canberra, 1974, pp. 19–37.

'A Random House: the state of Australian publishing'. *Meanjin* XXXIV (1975), 106–11.

Introduction to New Australian Writing Issue. *Stand* XVI (1975), 106–11.

'The Short Stories of Marcus Clarke'. In Leon Cantrell, ed., *Bards, Bohemians and Bookmen: Essays in Australian Literature* [Essays presented to Cecil Hadgraft]. University of Queensland Press, St Lucia, 1976, pp. 72–97. Reprinted in Janet Mullane, ed., *Nineteenth-Century Literary Criticism*. Gale Research, Detroit, 1989.

'A Survey', New Writing Issue. *Australian Literary Studies* VIII (1977), 115–26.

'D.H. Lawrence in Australia: Some Recently Published Letters'. *Australian Literary Studies* IX (1980), 333–7.

'Small Presses and Little Magazines in the 1970s'. *Australian Literary Studies* IX (1980), 501–7.

'Jack Lindsay'. *Overland* 83 (1981), 40–3.

'William Lane and the *Worker* Book Fund: Progressive Books at Cost'. *Southerly* XLI (1981), 329–34.

Introduction to Jack Lindsay, *Life Rarely Tells*. Penguin Books, Ringwood and Harmondsworth, 1982, pp. vii–xvi.

'"My Name is Rickeybockey": The Poetry of Robert Adamson and the Spirit of Henry Kendall'. [The 15th Herbert Blaiklock lecture, University of Sydney, 1985.] *Southerly* XLVI (1986), 25–43. Reprinted, revised, as 'The Poetry of Robert Adamson' in *Australian Literature Today*, ed. R.K. Dhawan and David Kerr, Indian Society for Commonwealth Studies, New Delhi, and Advent Press, New York, 1993, pp. 179–91.

'Recent Australian Fiction: Janette Turner Hospital and Don O'Kim'. *Working Papers* 29 (1988), Australian Studies Centre, London, 17 pp.

'Australian Short Fiction in Context'. In Edwin Thumboo, ed., *Perceiving Other Worlds*, Academic Press, Singapore, 1991, pp. 297–304.

'Australian Fiction'. In Bruce King, ed., *The Commonwealth Novel Since 1960*. Macmillan Press, London, 1991, pp. 19–32.

'Henry Lawson, Ethnic Writer'. *Outrider* 9 (1992), 104–9.

'The Modern Australian Story'. In Margaret Harris and Elizabeth Webby, eds, *Reconnoitres* [Festschrift for Professor G.A. Wilkes]. Sydney University Press in association with Oxford University Press, Melbourne, 1992, pp. 168–75. Reprinted in *Critical Survey* 6 (1994), 112–17.

'Australian Images: Sydney and Melbourne'. In Malcolm Bradbury, ed., *The Atlas of Literature*, DeAgostini Editions, London, 1996, pp. 284–7.

'Australian Literary and Scholarly Publishing in its International Context'. *Australian Literary Studies* 19 (1999), 57–69.

'Realism'. *Overland* 156 (Spring 1999), 43–4.

'Australian Publishing in a Global Environment'. *Antipodes,* vol. 14, no. 2 (December 2000), 152–4.

'Marcus Clarke'. *New Dictionary of National Biography*, Oxford University Press, Oxford (forthcoming).

On Nineteenth and Twentieth Century Literature

'*Portrait of a Lady* and the World and Choice'. *Balcony* I (1965), 28–35.

'Literary Criticism and the Mass Media'. *Dissent* (Melbourne) 18 (1966),

4–7. Reprinted in *The Mass Cultural Debate Part I*, vol. 13 of *Literary Taste, Culture and Mass Communication* ed. Peter Davison, Rolf Meyersohn and Edward Shils, Chadwyck-Healey, Cambridge, 1981.

'James Joyce's "Eveline" and *Portrait of a Lady*'. *English Studies* XLIX (1968), 522–5.

'The Literary Criticism of F.R. Leavis'. *Oxford Review* 7 (1968), 69–75.

'Literature, Politics and the University'. *Ancora* (Winter, 1970), 40–6.

'Fiction as a Political Vehicle'. *Journal of Australian Political Economy* 10 (1981), 65–75.

'Beyond Postmodernism'. *Foreign Literature* [Beijing], 118, iv (28 July 1992), 9–10.

'Jude Revisited'. *The Thomas Hardy Journal*, XI, iii (October 1995), 41–2.

'The Poetry of Robert Yeo'. In Bruce Bennett, Jeff Doyle and Satendra Nandan, eds, *Crossing Cultures: Essays on Literature and Culture of the Asia-Pacific*, Skoob, London, 1996, pp. 141–8. Reprinted as introduction to Robert Yeo, *Leaving Home, Mother: Selected Poems*, Angsana, Singapore, 1999.

'Afterword: "Studying Britain"'. In John Milfull, ed., *Britain in Europe: Prospects for Change*, Ashgate, Aldershot, 1999, pp. 248–51.

On Seventeenth and Early Eighteenth Century Literature

'The Date of Samuel Butler's Baptism'. *Review of English Studies* XVII (1966), 174–7.

'Samuel Butler at Barbourne'. *Notes and Queries* XIII (1966), 15–19.

'*Paradise Lost* and Linguistic Precision'. *Balcony* 5 (1966), 25–31.

'Two Missing Shakespeare Documents'. *Notes and Queries* XIV (1967), 134.

'The Epitaph to Gray's *Elegy*: Two Early Printings and a Parody'. *Notes and Queries* XV (1968), 213–14.

'Oxford Aphrodisiacal Licences by "Peter Marvell"'. *Oxford Magazine* (18 October 1968), 6–7.

'Allusion and Innuendo in *MacFlecknoe*'. *Essays in Criticism* XIX (1969), 355–70.

'Michael Johnson: an Auction Sale'. *Notes and Queries* XVI (1969), 18.

'Apples in Marvell's "Bermudas"'. *English Language Notes* VI (1969), 254–9.

'Marvell's Reputation for Probity and Patriotism'. *Notes and Queries* XVII (1970), 252–4.

'Jonson, Sin and Milton'. *Notes and Queries* XVII (1970), 415.
'*Paradise Lost* and *Fanny Hill*'. *Milton Quarterly* 5 (1971).
'Butler and Gray's Inn'. *Notes and Queries* XVIII (1971), 293–5.
'Dryden and Satire'. In Earl Miner, ed., *Dryden: Writers and their Background*, Bell, London, 1972; Ohio State University Press, Columbus, 1972, pp. 191–233.
Biographical and bibliographical entries and revisions for seventeenth and eighteenth century English literature in J. Buchanan-Brown, ed., *Cassell's Encyclopaedia of World Literature*, Cassell, London, 1973.
'Flecknoe's "Diarium": A Source for *Hudibras*'. *Notes and Queries* XXII (1975), 310–12.
'Milton's *Areopagitica*: Liberty for the Sects'. *Prose Studies* IX (1986), 7–38. Reprinted in Thomas N. Corns, ed., *The Literature of Controversy: Polemical Strategy from Milton to Junius*, Frank Cass, London, 1987, pp. 7–38.
'Milton in the English Revolution'. In S.N. Mukherjee and J.O. Ward, eds, *Revolution as History*, Sydney Studies in Society and Culture 5 (1989), pp. 38–46.
'John Milton: The Early Works'. In Thomas N. Corns, ed., *The Cambridge Companion to English Poetry, Donne to Marvell*, Cambridge University Press, Cambridge, 1993, pp. 221–41.
'"Their Sex Not Equal Seem'd": Equality in *Paradise Lost*'. In P.G. Stanwood, ed., *Of Poetry and Politics: New Essays on Milton and His World*, MRTS, Binghamton, New York, 1995, pp. 173–89; and L. Sharon Davidson, S.N. Mukherjee and Z. Zlatar, eds, *The Epic in History*, Sydney Studies in Society and Culture 11, Sydney, 1995, pp. 176–92.
'Milton's Radical Epic'. In John Lucas, ed., *Writing and Radicalism*, Longman, London, 1996, pp. 19–38.
'The Alchemical Republic: a Reading of "An Horatian Ode"' (with Lyndy Abraham). In *Marvell and Liberty*, ed. Warren Chernaik and Martin Dzelzainis, Macmillan Press, London, 1999, pp. 94–122.
'Edward Kelly: A Life'. *Cauda Pavonis*, n.s. 18, nos. 1 and 2 (Spring and Fall 1999), 1–26.0
'The Great Transmuter' [Edward Kelly]. *Around the Globe* 16 (Winter 2000–1), 22–4.

Notes on Contributors

DON ANDERSON is an honorary Senior Lecturer in English at the University of Sydney.

CHRISTOPHER BENTLEY was a Senior Lecturer in English at the University of Sydney before he retired.

DAVID BROOKS lectures in English at the University of Sydney.

ADRIAN CAESAR is an Associate Professor in the School of Language, Literature and Communication at the Australian Defence Forces Academy.

BRUCE CLUNIES ROSS is Associate Professor of English at the University of Copenhagen.

THOMAS N. CORNS is Professor of English and Head of the School of Arts and Humanities at the University of Wales, Bangor.

ROBERT CUMMINGS is a Senior Lecturer in English at the University of Glasgow.

TERRY DOWLING (M.A. Hons, Sydney), once a student in Michael Wilding's Creative Writing course, has established an international reputation as a writer of science fiction.

DON GRAHAM is Frank J. Dolby Regents Professor of English and American Literature at the University of Texas, Austin.

JENNIFER GRIBBLE is an honorary Associate Professor of English at the University of Sydney.

LAURIE HERGENHAN, Professor Emeritus of English at the University of Queensland, was founding editor of *Australian Literary Studies*.

VAN IKIN (Ph.D., Sydney) is Associate Professor of English at the University of Western Australia.

BRIAN KIERNAN is an honorary Associate Professor of English at the University of Sydney.

STEPHEN KNIGHT, a founding member of SASSC and member of the English Department at the University of Sydney for many years, is Professor of English at Cardiff University.

MABEL LEE is an honorary Associate Professor in Asian Studies at the University of Sydney.

JOHN LUCAS is Emeritus Research Professor in English Studies at Nottingham Trent University.

ANDREW MCRAE, formerly of the English Department, University of Sydney, is Senior Lecturer in English at the University of Exeter.

S.N. MUKHERJEE, a founding member of SASSC, is a Visiting Professor in Indian Studies, Department of Indian Studies at the University of Sydney.

MARIA SHEVTSOVA, formerly of the Departments of English and French Studies at the University of Sydney, is Professor of Drama and Theatre Arts at Goldsmiths College, University of London.

VIVIAN SMITH, formerly a Reader in English at the University of Sydney, is a highly regarded poet.

BARRY SPURR is Senior Lecturer in English at the University of Sydney.

KEN STEWART is an Associate Professor of English at the University of Western Sydney.

IAN SYSON lectures in Literature and Professional Writing at Victoria University (Melbourne) and retired as editor of *overland* at the end of 2002.

ROBERT YEO, formerly Associate Professor in English at Nanyang University, Singapore, is a poet, dramatist and novelist.

Publications of the Sydney Association for Studies in Society and Culture

No. 1 *Words and Worlds. Studies in the Social Role of Verbal Culture*, eds Stephen Knight and S.N. Mukherjee, 1983.

No. 2 *Feudalism: Comparative Studies*, eds Edmund Leach, S.N. Mukherjee and J.O. Ward, 1985.

No. 3 *Semiotics, Ideology, Language*, eds Terry Threadgold, E.A. Grosz, Gunther Kress and M.A.K. Halliday, 1986.

No. 4 *The Cultural Construction of Race*, eds Marie de Lepervanche and Gillian Bottomley, 1988.

No. 5 *Revolution as History*, eds S.N. Mukherjee and J.O. Ward, 1989.

No. 6 *Words and Wordsmiths, a volume for H.L. Rogers*, eds Geraldine Barnes, John Gunn, Sonya Jensen and Lee Jobling, 1989.

No. 7 *Disasters: Image and Context*, ed. Peter Hinton, 1992.

No. 8 *Social Visions*, by Michael Wilding, 1993.

No. 9 *Theatre and Cultural Interaction*, by Maria Shevtsova, 1993.

No. 10 *The Epic Circle*, by Zdenko Zlatar, 1993.

No. 11 *The Epic in History*, eds Lola Sharon Davidson, S.N. Mukherjee and Z. Zlatar, 1995.

No. 12 *Religious Change, Conversion and Culture*, ed. Lynette Olson, 1996.

No. 13 *The Citizen Historian: Explorations in Historiography*, by S.N. Mukherjee, 1996.

No. 14 *If the Rain Doesn't Come*, by Bob Fisher, 1996.

No. 15 *History, Literature and Society: Essays in Honour of S.N. Mukherjee*, eds Mabel Lee and Michael Wilding, 1997.

No. 16 *Studies in Classic Australian Fiction*, by Michael Wilding, 1997.

No. 17 *Studies in Australian Literary History*, by Brian Kiernan, 1998.

No. 18 *Contemporary Australian Literature Between Europe and Australia*, by Igor Maver, 1999.

No. 19 *Ritual, Power and Gender: Ethnographical Explorations in Vanuatu, Nepal and Ireland*, by Michael Allen, 2000.

No. 20 *Investigations in Australian Literature*, by Ken Stewart, 2000.

No. 21 *The Citizen Historian: Explorations in Historiography*, an enlarged 2nd edition, by S.N. Mukherjee, 2002.